2

The
HERBERT HUNCKE
reader

FOR HUNCKE

Know no other god than this:
the man who places on your mouth
a kiss. Keep no mystery
but his who whispers memory.

Though he lead you to the desert
or over hills where famine
flowers, like the locust
he devours what he loves most.

Saving none for tomorrow, or dawn
comes with empty arms, and he knows no way
to feed himself, feeding off others,
he has many, who find him, help him

you be one and dedicate your life
and misery to the upkeep of this cheapskate
you love so much no one else
seems to bridge the gap

with their common habits and rude manners,
his never were, a perfect gentleman
who leaves no trace, but lingers through the room
after he has gone, so I would follow

anywhere, over desert or mountain,
it's all the same if he's by my side.
The guide and wizard I would worship and obey,
my guardian teacher, who knows how to stay

alive on practically nothing in the city
until help comes, usually from a stranger or youth.
Such I am or was who knew no better
but all that I better forget now since I met you

and fell into that pit of the past with no escape.
You knock on the door, and off I go with you
into the night with not even a cent in my pockets,
without caring where or when I get back

But if once you put your hand on my shoulders
as David Rattray did last evening
that would be enough, on the seventh night
of the seventh moon, when Herd Boy

meets the Weaving Lady in heaven
and wanders forever lost in arms
until dawn when you come no more.

—JOHN WIENERS
1966

The
HERBERT HUNCKE
reader

Edited by
Benjamin G. Schafer

Foreword by
William S. Burroughs

Introduction by
Raymond Foye

Biographical Sketch by
Jerome Poynton

BLOOMSBURY

First published in Great Britain in 1998 by Bloomsbury Publishing Plc, 38 Soho Square, London W1V 5DF

First published in the USA in 1997 by William Morrow and Company, Inc., 1350 Avenue of the Americas, New York, NY10019

ISBN 0-7475-4007-1

Printed by Clays Limited, St Ives plc

1 2 3 4 5 6 7 8 9 10

BOOK DESIGN BY LEAH S. CARLSON

IN MEMORY OF LOUIS CARTWRIGHT (1947–1994)

FOREWORD

BOB BRANDENBERG SAID I COULD GET RID OF THE MORPHINE RIGHT away. I had some morphine Syrettes, and I went down to Henry Street, and there was Huncke. Huncke thought I was FBI and said, "I don't want to be bothered really."

The elements were so mixed in him. He was a character, a rarity, a real picaresque antihero in the classical tradition. Huncke was a great storyteller, usually about his misfortunes. I remember once he had a terrible black eye, folded over, and I came down to Henry Street and said, "Well, Huncke, I'm going to get a leech to put on that." He said, "Oh, no, you're not going to put any leech on me." Back then they still kept big jars of leeches in barber shops.

He said to me at one point, "If it wasn't for your money, I wouldn't have this habit." He had all habits you could possibly get.

In *The Thief's Journal*, Genet says there are very few people who have earned the right to think. Huncke had adventures and misadventures that were not available to middle-class, comparatively wealthy college people like Kerouac and me: "Some write home to the old folks for coin. That's their ace in the hole." Huncke had extraordinary experiences that were quite genuine. He isn't a type you find anymore.

—WILLIAM S. BURROUGHS
Lawrence, Kansas

CONTENTS

INTRODUCTION

THERE REMAINS AN INDELIBLE IMAGE OF HERBERT HUNCKE THE WRITER, forever frozen in time: homeless and alone, crouched in a Times Square pay toilet with notebook on his knees, furtively composing his latest tale from the underground. It was before he had met Kerouac, Burroughs, and Ginsberg, long before any notion of literary recognition. Toiling in obscurity, he transcribed his travels and adventures as a hobo, drug user, and petty criminal, since leaving his upper-middle-class Chicago home in the late 1920s. "To live outside the law you must be honest," sang Bob Dylan, and Huncke's code of honor speaks to this higher order. It also speaks of a lost America, of boxcars and all-night cafeterias, pool halls and rooming houses, and always the open road.

The discovery of Herbert Huncke by the Beats in the late 1940s was something akin to novice explorers' stumbling upon a great archaeological find. He was the *Ur*-Beat: Kerouac's lonesome traveler, Burroughs's junky, Ginsberg's angel-headed hipster. Primitive and incipient, Huncke's life and writings became the Rosetta Stone of Beat sensibility, not only for the experience imparted therein but for the prose itself. Spontaneous prose and cutups were mature elaborations in Beat literature. The earliest writings of Kerouac and Burroughs were marvels of clarity. This clarity is best embodied and preserved in Huncke's deceptively simple and plainspoken style. To write as one speaks is one ideal of literature, and Huncke's prose accomplishes just that, to such a degree that the experience of reading him is akin to sitting across from him in one of those famous all-night sessions, where tales were unraveled and the human condition examined into the early hours of the morn.

I first met Herbert Huncke in 1978 in a bar on New York's Upper West Side, at a book party for his old friend William Burroughs. I was standing at the bar with a friend when Herbert passed by, and we called to him. He was elegantly dressed (as always) in suit and tie, olive-green in color, set off by a russet wool knit sweater. He drank brandy from a snifter, and smoked Players cigarettes, likewise William's current brand. Of course I knew who he was. If ever someone's reputation preceded him, it was Herbert Huncke. Yet I was unprepared for the refined gracefulness of his speech and deportment. He was loquacious, but his choice of words was exacting. His manner was elevated and noble. He was aware of his charm, and wielded it deftly. All in all, he bore the air of one from another era, which indeed he was. Whatever one might say of him, he was unmistakably a *writer*.

And yet there was another level operative in this encounter, and I would call it aversion. There was a sense of danger to this character. A confidence game was being played. I sensed that not only would he cheat, con, or deceive, but moreover he would probably do so on general principles. Little did I realize how true that would be. Over the next eighteen years I, like all those who knew Herbert, was given my share of instruction from the master: engage me at your own risk, accept me for who I am, and complain not of the consequences. To befriend Herbert was to enter into a consensual agreement in which nearly all rules of conduct were challenged, save those of acceptance and style. He was the Duke of Deception and bore the office with the haughty air of ruined nobility. He was one of nature's aristocrats, and more often than not what he rankled in me was my own hypocrisy or pride. In the end I came to feel that Herbert embodied a higher morality than the common one he so cavalierly betrayed. Call it Huncke's Paradox. If there was one notion that Herbert returned to in his conversation, time and again, it was the relativeness of all experience: everything is determined by its relation to something else. "It's all in the way you see it," Herbert would often reiterate. "I see it one way, you see it another. Both are valid." Or, in an even more familiar and succinct phrase of his: "So be it."

There is no shortage of war stories on the part of anyone who knew Herbert. Trading these stories was (and still is) a common activity of his friends. Why then, one might ask, did one continue to associate with the man? The reasons for this are less remarked upon. To engage Herbert Huncke was to enter into a world in which life was examined with a broad, knowing eye. Herbert was a philosopher of the streets. Human nature was his subject, and he approached it with sympathy and penetration. In this regard his range was truly Shakespearean: life as the Human Comedy. Not that all of it is funny, but that it is all so various and improbable. And what he loved most was to sit late into the night, in a bar, a cafeteria, or later in his Chelsea Hotel room, and discuss the peculiarities of human behavior that so delighted him. He was a student of the human condition and he sketched his ideas and observations with a writer's eye. To be in his presence was to participate in this great act of creation: the bringing into existence of a world so vivid that one felt more alive and connected to the very cosmos than one did at any other point in one's life. It was also to experience the lost art of conversation, for he listened as carefully as he spoke.

Until Herbert entered his eighties, he was remarkably fit and healthy, maintaining a busy daily routine that began with a visit to his methadone clinic, usually followed by lunch with friends, visits to local booksellers, and various small errands around town. On occasion he would give readings or attend book signings. I recall an appearance before an eager freshman English class at New York University, where his honesty and charm won him a crowd of new admirers. Although his range of friends was all-inclusive, he valued the company of young people above all. Often he would impart sage advice, not without an ironic chuckle, that he should be counseling others on how to live. He loved to wander the streets of Manhattan, and to accompany him on such walks was to see the city as an open book. Every block held stories of crash pads, speakeasies, all-night jam sessions with Charlie Parker or Dexter Gordon.

In his eightieth year his health began to fail. His small furnished room, number 828 in the Chelsea Hotel, now became the center of his activities. The Grateful Dead, in a fitting homage, paid his rent in the final years. Here he continued to write and to receive friends. Photographers, rock journalists, and literary historians increasingly sought him out, and he was unfailingly generous with his time. "Talk is my stock in trade," he told one visitor.

Almost daily medical attention, and frequent hospitalizations, became the norm in his final year. Dr. Gabe Zatlin and his colleagues at Beth Israel Hospital attended to him with great professionalism and kindness, often making house calls in the summer heat. Without a penny to his name, recompense was out of the question. But like everyone who knew him, they were repaid with an uncommon mixture of old-world wisdom and charm. I can still see Herbert in those final weeks, sitting on the edge of his bed, wrapped in a favorite Guatemalan shawl, taking in the marvelous view of lower Manhattan and the Hudson. "I wish I could say I'd hit upon the answers to the great mysteries of life," he mused, as if to sum up his life. "But it doesn't make any more sense to me than it did on day one."

—RAYMOND FOYE
Woodstock, New York

BIOGRAPHICAL SKETCH

*"More harm is done under guise of goodness than ever realized
by foul deed or evildoer. Nevertheless, I wish I was good."*
—HERBERT E. HUNCKE

HERBERT EDWIN HUNCKE WAS BORN IN GREENFIELD, MASSACHUSETTS,
in 1915. His family moved to Detroit and soon settled in Chicago.
Huncke's father, Herbert Spencer Huncke, spent two years in an Illinois
reform school before graduating from a technical high school on Chicago's South Side. He was fascinated with automotive mechanics and was
a self-described member of the "nuts-and-bolts crowd." His company,
H. S. Huncke & Company, sold precision tools.

Huncke's mother, Marguerite Bell Huncke, was the daughter of Col-
onel Edwin Bell, a colorful rancher in Laramie, Wyoming. Marguerite
Bell was raised on a ranch but sent to finishing school for her education.
She learned French and was proficient in horseback riding and shooting
a gun. High tea was a common social event for women in Laramie, and
Marguerite would have been expected to know how to host one.

Her grandfather, from Herefordshire, England, was a world-
renowned cattle breeder. Her father, Colonel Bell, was of an adventurous
disposition, legendary in temper and skill with a lariat and gun. He cap-
tured and sold wild horses in Texas.

When the colonel got mad, "the air around him fairly crackled. He
inveighed against everything and everybody, all creatures great and small,
in language that jolted the ears of sensitive listeners and was outstanding
only from the standpoint of pure invention. . . . There were any number
of men who could have thrashed him in one minute but for some reason
no one wanted to. Possibly when he got through telling them his opinion
of them they were too stunned to act."*

---

*James F. Wilson, "E. J. Bell: A Personality of the Old West" (unpublished memoir, pre-
sented to the American Heritage Center, University of Wyoming, June 1974), page 4.

A pretty good description of Huncke too.

Huncke's father met Marguerite Bell when she was sixteen. He delivered an automobile to Colonel Bell and was hired as a chauffeur and mechanic. They married after Colonel Bell's death.

The Hunckes settled in Chicago, where Huncke's uncle, Oswald Huncke, was an insider in Chicago's notorious political machine. He sold insurance to the Chicago Board of Education, was an Illinois state boxing commissioner, and served on the Board of Elections for Mayor Big Bill Thompson. There was tension between him and Huncke's father.

What should have been a seamless marriage between the Bells of Laramie and the Hunckes of Chicago wasn't. Money caused friction between Huncke's mother and father. They were always fighting.

Herbert Huncke was not a "nuts-and-bolts" kind of kid. His father tried to teach him about electricity and how to handle tools, but each lesson ended in disaster and frustration. Huncke was more interested in wandering the streets at night, walking along the lakefront, through the park designed by Frederick Law Olmsted, and meeting people who wanted to meet him. He also liked cruising the expensive shops on Michigan Avenue. Grandma Bell had expensive tastes and she encouraged the same in her grandson. As a boy, Huncke always felt closer to his grandmother than his parents or siblings.

Huncke was willful, and at age twelve he ran away from Chicago, heading for New York City. He got as far as Geneva, New York, where a motorcycle cop picked him up on the side of the road. What Huncke would never forget was how free it felt to be away from Chicago. The smell of the onion fields. The freedom of the road.

His parents divorced in 1927.

Huncke took to staying out all night, visiting speakeasies with his grade-school sweetheart, Donna, and her brother, Johnny. A cab driver gave Huncke his first stick of pot, and Huncke and Johnny tried to turn on. They didn't get high at first, but they soon learned to smoke marijuana and they had many laughing fits along the shores of Lake Michigan, in and around the lakefront property where men cruised each other.

Huncke read about Shanghai opium dens and smugglers in a book called *The Little White Hag* and it made a lifetime impression. His aunt Olga spoke Chinese and had taught kindergarten in Chicago's Chinatown since 1915. Huncke learned he could buy top-quality heroin for twenty-five cents a bag from a Chinese dealer in the neighborhood.

Meanwhile, Huncke's mother took him to art exhibits. Pablo Picasso had an early solo exhibition at a modest Chicago art society in 1928. Marguerite took Huncke to see the show, and he talked of the exhibition in 1996, remembering the last painting mounted in his line of vision as he left the gallery.

Huncke dropped out of high school during his sophomore year but continued to read and write throughout his entire life.

When Huncke was fourteen, he met Elsie John, the hermaphrodite who wore his henna-red hair long on one side and short with an exposed sideburn on the other. Elsie John worked at a circus on West Madison Street and sold heroin on the side. He and Huncke took a bust together but Huncke was let go as he was a minor. He never saw Elsie John again.

Huncke began having experiences with men along Chicago's lakefront. He was molested (see Huncke's story "In the Park") and learned about his own capacity for treachery, having trysts with lonely men ("Youth").

After the start of the Great Depression, Huncke left Chicago again, heading west, traveling with Steinbeck's Okies to California. On his return he rode the rails to Chicago, picking up his first freight out of Reno.

"I tried to pass myself off as a schoolboy," he said. "I carried a cigar box. In it I kept a clean set of shorts, socks—a toothbrush, toothpaste. A comb. A bar of soap."

Arriving back in Chicago circa 1930, Huncke learned his father had remarried. His new stepmother had a baby grand piano and was expecting. Huncke's mother had an upright and was living with Grandma Bell.

Huncke went back on the road, heading west ("Ponderosa Pine"). He also traveled south to Nashville, Memphis, and New Orleans ("New Orleans 1938"). He hitchhiked to Detroit to hear a jazz singer, only to be asked to leave as white people were not allowed in that bar.

"Just let me stay for one song," he asked. The bouncer complied.

In 1939, Huncke arrived in New York City. He was twenty-four years old. The man he hitched a ride with dropped him off at 103rd Street and Broadway.

"Where do you want to go?" the driver asked.

"I've always heard about Forty-second Street," Huncke answered. "I'd like to go there."

"Walk straight down Broadway," the driver said. "You'll find Forty-second Street."

Huncke bought a carnation for the lapel of his jacket and started walking down Broadway. He found Forty-second Street and became quite familiar with it over the next eleven years.

Throughout the 1940s, Huncke lived on or near Forty-second Street. He had started hustling sex while living in Chicago, but he honed his skills on Forty-second Street. "Spencer's Pad," "Russian Blackie," "Detroit Redhead 1943–1967," and "Whitey" all document his life at the time. Lunch hour would find Huncke at Bickford's Cafeteria or in Bryant Park behind the library, where closeted businessmen met him and took him out to lunch.

"It wasn't until I reached my late thirties," Huncke explained regarding his own sexual preference, "I succeeded in combining the two in a manner of being heterosexual today and homosexual the next—allowing neither to influence me more than the other."

Years later, another Beat icon, Neal Cassady, confided that he had (despite his legendary libido) never been a hustler.

"I was afraid I might enjoy it," Cassady explained.

"That's what you hope for," Huncke responded.

Huncke had always been close to music and New York was no different. He frequented the jazz clubs on Fifty-second Street and socialized with both Charlie Parker and Billie Holiday. He was close enough to the scene to pull several small burglaries with jazz great Dexter Gordon. Together they broke into cars, stole fur coats, and sold them to prostitutes they knew in Harlem.

During World War II, Huncke shipped out with the merchant marine. Going to sea was a relief from the rigors of Forty-second Street. His ship was shelled off the coast of England, and he scored morphine on the beach at Normandy three days after the invasion.

He always returned to New York.

In 1946, Huncke was approached by Dr. Alfred Kinsey of Indiana University, who was conducting research for his groundbreaking study of American sexual behavior. Dr. Kinsey was interested in the sex industry of Forty-second Street, and he asked Huncke to be his liaison. Huncke agreed, with one important proviso: "It'll cost you."

Huncke "confessed" his sexual history to Dr. Kinsey and developed a friendship with the man. Soon he was recruiting local hustlers who'd agree to talk with a stranger about their sex lives. Kinsey paid him two dollars per recruit.

During this time, Huncke met many Barnard and Columbia University students and their associates exploring Forty-second Street, learning about life outside of the academic world and American mainstream. They liked Huncke's ability to tell a story, and thought he must possess some kind of secret knowledge.

It cost them as well.

They paid Huncke back by making him into characters in their books and poems. See Jack Kerouac's *On the Road*, William S. Burroughs's *Junky*, Allen Ginsberg's *Howl*, and John Clellon Holmes's *Go*. Pretty soon, they too were telling their sexual histories to Dr. Kinsey.

In the 1950s, Huncke lived almost exclusively in New York State prisons: Sing Sing, Dannemora, Rikers Island. When a junky runs out of luck, the legal system starts eating away with "prime-time" jail sentences. One wrong move—one clerical error—can take ten years out of a person's life, and those ten years for Huncke were the 1950s.

Huncke didn't have a drug habit in prison, but he could not write there either. Until then, Huncke had always written in small notebooks he carried in his pocket. As he moved from one semilegal apartment to the next, most of his writings were lost, left behind with roommates and landlords.

He didn't hear from his Columbia student friends when he was inside—he read about them in the newspaper. He read about Joan Burroughs, one of his favorites, shot and killed in Mexico. When she lived with Edie Parker (who later was briefly married to Jack Kerouac) he had helped decorate her apartment with presents from heists he performed on Staten Island. It was also in prison that Huncke saw a letter from his father to the warden in regard to parole recommendations.

"He's always been a weak sister," H. S. Huncke wrote. Parole denied.

By the time Huncke was released from prison he was relatively clean, no habit. His old friends were published writers and political activists. He moved in with poets Janine Pommy Vega, Elise Cowen, and John

Wieners, and also the musician, artist, and magician Bill Heine. One of Huncke's masterpieces of descriptive drug consciousness, "Easter," describes these times.

In the 1960s Huncke went corporate. Fewer burglaries. He switched to more calculated, and sometimes possibly legal, scams. Relying on his reputation as a thief, Huncke would sell pawnshop claim tickets for fictitious tape recorders. It wasn't necessary for him to steal one; he could just tell someone he'd stolen a tape recorder and then sell the customer a bogus pawnshop ticket to claim it. He was always in the midst of life's con—busy pulling innocent listeners in—holding their ears—sounding for the depths of their souls—and their wallets, if necessary. And often it was necessary.

For the most part, Huncke lived on his ability to tell stories. Everyone was good for a touch. Ten dollars here and ten dollars there. Occasionally he would hit the jackpot and have a place to stay for a couple of years. He would move from one friend to the next, holding his host's attention sometimes as briefly as a night and other times for decades. His ability to know people, almost immediately, was legendary. He was a keen judge of people and remarkably apt at contributing to the intellectual growth of his friends. He kept good company.

Huncke's Journal was published in 1965 by The Poets Press. Irving Rosenthal, former editor of the *Chicago Review*, founder of *Big Table*, and star of Huncke's story "Irving, in Part," spent a great deal of time helping Huncke organize his work for publication. Eila Kokkinen, also from the University of Chicago, typed Huncke's manuscripts after finishing her day job at the Museum of Modern Art. Huncke would come by her apartment at night and retrieve the handwritten originals to sell to book sellers and collectors. Rosenthal tried to interest an editor at Grove Press in Huncke's writings, but the editor thought the stories too sad. Harvey Brown (poet Charles Olson's patron) was interested in publishing Huncke with his Frontier Press, but changed his mind, deciding the prose was too childlike.

In 1968, long before the mass emergence of tabloid TV, Huncke gained considerable notoriety through his appearance on *The David Susskind Show* as an authentic, self-proclaimed heroin addict. Susskind liked Huncke and helped him place a story, "Alvarez," with *Playboy*, his first mainstream publishing credit. R'lene Dahlberg, another University of Chicago alum, became one of Huncke's closest friends throughout the seventies. In 1978, she published an exquisite letterpress edition of two of Huncke's best stories, "Elsie John" and "Joseph Martinez," through her Pequod Press. It wasn't until 1980 that a full collection of Huncke's stories, *The Evening Sun Turned Crimson*, was published by Cherry Valley Editions.

Huncke went on the methadone program in the late sixties. His legal dose was 100 milligrams a day. Enough to kill. Huncke had a very high tolerance for drugs and was constantly re-investigating his drug use. When Huncke had extra money he purchased drugs on the street for himself or for others. He shared his money and he shared his drugs, particularly if someone had just given him a twenty. He didn't understand the accumulation of wealth for a rainy day. The rainy day was yesterday; today was sunny—particularly if he could score.

Just shy of his eighty-first birthday, Huncke's urine turned up "dirty" at the methadone clinic. He tested positive for heroin, cocaine, methadone, marijuana, and Valium. His doctor looked at him and seemed about to cry.

"Why do you do it?" she asked.

"I've been doing it my whole life," he replied. "Why can't you just let me be me?"

Huncke could talk the wings off an angel. Rules were made to be talked around. Before entering the hospital for the last time, he decided to move into a nursing home.

"I do very well in institutions," he explained.

—JEROME POYNTON
New York City

PART ONE | HUNCKE'S JOURNAL

EDITOR'S NOTE

THE FIRST COLLECTION OF HERBERT HUNCKE'S WRITING WAS PUBLISHED in 1965 by the poet Diane di Prima. With the help of friends, di Prima invested twelve hundred dollars in a secondhand press that came with a week of free printing lessons, and The Poets Press was born. Operating out of a storefront on New York's Lower East Side, The Poets Press published *Huncke's Journal* on its first list, along with such writers as A. B. Spellman, Kirby Doyle, and Zen poet Philip Whalen. The Poets Press continued for three years, publishing roughly thirty books, tracts, and texts, including titles by Jean Genet and Clive Matson.

Huncke's Journal contains writings dating roughly from 1948 to 1964 (known dates are supplied throughout) and demonstrates Huncke's remarkable range within the memoir form. In it are prose poems, solitary musings, teenage memories, sketches of various New York City scenes, and magical flights of imagination describing the crush of activity, personalities, and energy surrounding the amphetamine scene of the early 1960s.

Some of the stories from *Huncke's Journal* reappeared in the 1980 collection *The Evening Sun Turned Crimson*. "Youth" was retitled "First Love," while "A Story—New York" became "The Savior." "Cuba," "Frisky," "Beware of Fallen Angles," "Ponderosa Pine," "In the Park," and "Cat & His Girl" were also published in *Evening Sun* but, like the others, with degrees of revision. Elements of both versions of these stories have been combined in the present collection.

Di Prima recalls the original manuscript as handwritten, "just scrawled pieces of paper in that big rounded handwriting. Huncke said he wanted it to look like one of those school notebooks with a blue cover." Thus *Huncke's Journal* came to resemble a journal not only in its candor but in appearance as well. Di Prima usually paid authors in copies of their books, but "Huncke asked for a ticket to the west coast instead. He came by to pick it up and stole a statue of an Indonesian sea goddess on the way out.

When I asked him about it years later, he said he had to have a present to give to the people he was to be staying with."

In his autobiography, *Guilty of Everything*, Huncke recalled, "*Huncke's Journal* came to be published in a funny way. One day in the year prior to its publication (1965), I ran into Diane di Prima on the street. I'd known her from the scene and have always liked her. She had just begun The Poets Press with her old man of the time, Alan Marlowe. She asked me if I had anything she could publish. I said I'd look around for some things. I finally grabbed a whole lot of stuff at random I'd had in various places and gave them to her saying, 'If you can do anything with these, fine.'

"She published one or two things in her *Floating Bear* journal, and then she put together my first book. *Huncke's Journal* was the second of the Poets Press publications. The title came, I believe, from Diane herself. At the time there were rumors to the effect that I was working on something called the 'Confessions.' Actually, Ginsberg thought of that, not me. I wouldn't have used the term, but it came to be known as such. Of course, more people were apt to believe Ginsberg than myself."

The first thousand copies of *Huncke's Journal* sold relatively quickly. Di Prima published a second edition, adding a short introduction by Allen Ginsberg praising Huncke's writing as "equal in delicacy of expression to Sherwood Anderson's Merciful Ones." Di Prima moved to San Francisco in 1968, taking most copies of the second edition with her. Eventually she left them in boxes on Haight Street to distribute for free, most of them ending up, as she puts it, "in the hands of the hippies and street people."

SONG OF SELF

HERBERT E. HUNCKE

My name; although I'm known generally as Huncke and by a few as Herbert and in the past as Herbie. It is seldom I'm referred to as Mr. Huncke, and when formal introduction is required it is usually—Herbert Huncke.

I mention all this concerning my name simply because recently I've grown to dislike my name—not because my name is Herbert Huncke but rather because I've reached a point where my name (any name I might have had) by its mere utterance creates an almost weary and loathsome feeling in me. When I say it to myself—and frequently I say it to myself—I am immediately aware of a sense of disgust as though the sounds I make are significant of not only me but of a new and strange disease and I am sure, for at least the instant, I am at last slipping into an insanity from which there is no escape.

For several years I've been confident I will become insane, in fact I've felt thusly almost as far back as I am able to recall.

Once, when I thought I would become a writer (I was quite young— fourteen at the time), I made periodic attempts to write poetry, and on this particular occasion I became aware fully of the sense of pending insanity. It was shortly after dawn and a huge glistening sun was ascending a delicate blue sky. It was early summer and people were beginning to enjoy the bright colors of summer attire. I was living on Superior Street just east of North State Street in Chicago in an old wood-frame house that had been converted into what is called studio apartments. The house was well constructed and the rooms were large with high ceilings and windows reaching the full height of each room.

I had spent the few hours just preceding daybreak bathed in moonlight, watching the sky thru one of my windows (there were two in this room—huge windows which could be flung up quite high, letting in all the outside sound and scent and air, on either side of a fireplace with a white mantel with two large brass candlesticks with tall green candles), allowing my thoughts to dwell as they would and pondering over my problems and the magnificence of a daybreak.

I had sent my minute energy quota into the central urge aiding each rent in the block of darkness, tugging at each fold of light to make way for the one great power: the sun.

And now, as I descended the front steps to the street level—the sun was hurling and spiraling across a huge space of blue.

To one side of the steps was a flower bed sparsely filled with yellow jonquils, and I glanced at them and then toward the sidewalk to observe several young women who were rapidly walking past and talking of their work and of something amusing, and when they had almost reached the corner they began laughing. Their costumes were charming and one wore something with large figures of poppy red which I liked.

I was rather frightened and deeply impressed. I stood a long time thinking about it, becoming more convinced each instant, I was doomed.

Several hours later when I had finished my breakfast and returned to my apartment, I tried putting into a poem all which I had felt and I was rather pleased with what I had written, although I can't remember any of it and the actual writing is long misplaced—along with everything of myself at that time.

It wasn't long after I began traveling and ceased considering Chicago as my home.

THIS MORNING MORE SELF-INDULGENCE—GRANTING EVEN GREATER range of complaint—bemoaning my plight—riddled with self—self in all phases—self-loathing—self-pity—self—always self—and no courage wherewith to pulverize and smash—grind down—sift and sift again— oh no—I remain and see—and feel—and sense the putrid promise— know in essence—full force—the tortured presence—aware the tainted meat—luminous decaying—conscious—the pinched nostril—the trou- bled eye—the tensed—slow—withdrawing—the separate search for es- cape—the bewildered reason—and deeper still—another set of vocal cords—screaming vituperation and in subtle counterpoint—steady and measured—the throbbing whispered phonetic assemblage persistently declaring—"I will go—I will no longer inflict my vileness upon you"— knowing it a lie—since—this is it—not only here but everywhere—the knowing—the tender muscle crunchy—the purple veiled vein—juicy— rarely sweet—the maggot awaits birth—resting cradled in putrescence and laved with green bile—

Lay out the binding gauze—row upon row—mix the jellied fluids. Cleanse the injectors—open sacks of formaldehyde—rubber tubings—red rubber gloves. Hone the scalpels. The first slice is important and should be clean and true. Basins to catch the freshets of red blood—soon to pale and turn pale hue—wads of cotton to stuff the asshole—the nostrils—puff the cheeks—fill out the hollows.

And it is right—they turn away and hope I will go—leave—find an- other place. How long should one have to contend with the burden of my being on the scene? It is certainly not their doing—I can't even function efficiently enough after—lo—these many years to have my own hole to crawl into.

And besides how tiresome my driveling statements of love are to listen to. What is the matter with saying something sexy—for a change at least.

I could yell—fuck—fuck—fuck—aloud—and then speak in raptured tone of slit pink cunts—and hard throbbing rigid cocks—and drops of semen—sucking warm come—bodies adhering to one another—rhythmic plunge and thrusts of red phallus—grinding thighs and muscled bellies—pink teasing tongues—moistening the slick-headed pricks—darting into the anus—licking the asshole—wetting the genitals—deftly manipulating the balls—exciting the stiffened prick and giving way to the wet red lips eager to wrap round the straining shaft—the head hotly pressing forward into the throat—swelling at the final shove—plunging deeper as bursting jets of hot juice stream forth and the whole body writhes with delight—or of melon-like breasts—thickets of pussy hair—of mating and loving—of wildly jerked-off cocks—of fingers in snatches of love and sex—of fucking—sucking—licking—eating—jerking off—and finger fucking. Why not?

Oh, I will try—must try to get away somehow. I could never bear pity—already I believe they pity me—and all is lost.

January 16, 1964

SUICIDE

IN ALL PROBABILITY COMMITTING SUICIDE WOULD BE THE PROPER course, yet I find myself reluctant to take the final step. Periodically all through my life I've contemplated doing away with myself—either by jumping from a tall building or preferably shooting myself through the temple. At moments such as the present I find my existence overwhelmingly futile and know it is pointless to continue on when there can be no change.

It is simply that I haven't the nerve. I lack the drive required to push myself over the brink. It is like all I do—at the crucial moment I fail. I am as negative as one can imagine and have always found it difficult to finish even the simplest task if the opposition becomes even slightly evident. Certainly there can be no wrong in eliminating a nonentity.

What is particularly strange to me is that—although I feel little other than loathing of myself and fully recognize my insignificance—and am weary—miserable—discouraged—and wish for death—way down inside something remains stubbornly alive.

1948

YOUTH

WHEN I WAS A SCHOOLBOY—AGE FIFTEEN—LIVING IN WHAT WAS CON-
ceded to be a respectable middle-class neighborhood in Chicago—I had
my first encounter with love.

In the apartment building in which I lived with my mother, brother
and grandmother (my mother and father had been divorced two years
previously), there were several women who owned Chow dogs and they
would pay me to take their dogs out for walks. This afforded me opportunity to make something of a show of myself—since Chows were quite
fashionable—and as I considered myself at least personable in appearance,
it rather pleased me to imagine that people seeing me walking along the
Drive must surely think me the owner and certainly attractive with my
pet straining at the leash. Frequently I would walk one of the dogs late
in the evening and it was on such an occasion I first met Dick.

I had decided before returning home to stop by the neighborhood
drugstore and as I was leaving someone spoke my name. I looked into
the most piercing brown—almost black brown—eyes I had ever seen.
They belonged to a man who at the time was in his late twenties—fairly
well built—not too tall—with somewhat aquiline features and exceedingly black hair which he wore combed flat to his head. I learned later
he was of Russian Jewish parentage.

I was very much impressed by his appearance and felt a strange sensation upon first seeing him which was to be repeated each time we met
for as long as I knew him. I never quite got over a certain physical
response to his personality and even now in retrospect I find myself conscious of an inner warmth.

As I was leaving the drugstore and after he had spoken my name and
I had smiled and flushed, he commented that I didn't know him but that
a friend of his had spoken with me one evening about my dog and that
I had given him my name, and he in turn had given it to him when they

had seen me walking and he had asked if his friend noticed me. He then asked me if I would object to his accompanying me home so that we might become better acquainted. He gave me to understand that he wanted to know me. I was no end pleased by his attention and became animated and flirtatious.

We had a thoroughly enjoyable walk and from that point on I began seeing him fairly regularly. He was in the recording business and second in charge of a floor of recording studios in one of the large well-known buildings off Lake Shore Drive a short distance north of the Loop. He knew innumerable people in show business and I spent as much time hanging around the studio as could be arranged. Sometimes we would lunch together or stay downtown for dinner or go to a movie or he would take me along while he interviewed some possible recording star, and it was after some such instance at the old Sherman Hotel that he suggested since it was late I call home and ask permission to spend the night downtown. This I was anxious to do as I had long had the desire to sleep with him.

I was still rather green as to what was expected in a homosexual relationship, but I did know I was exceedingly desirous of feeling his body near mine and was sure I could be ingenious enough sexually to make him happy with me.

Actually I had but little experience other than mutual masturbation with others of my own age, and although I knew the word homosexual I wasn't exactly aware of the connotations.

We spent the night together and I discovered that in fact he was nearly as ignorant as I and besides was filled with all sorts of feelings of guilt. We kissed and explored each other's bodies with our hands and after both ejaculating fell asleep in each other's arms.

This began a long period in which he professed deep love for me and on one occasion threatened to throw acid in my face should he ever discover me with someone else.

The affair followed the usual pattern such affairs follow and after the novelty wore off I became somewhat bored, although it appeased my vanity to feel I had someone so completely in my control. Had anyone threatened my supremacy I would have gone to great lengths to eliminate them from the situation.

About this time it was necessary for him to make a business trip to New York, and when he returned he was wearing a Persian sapphire ring which he explained he would give to me if I would promise to stay away from some of the people and places I had lately been visiting. I promised to do this and considered the ring mine.

One evening we had dinner in a little French restaurant we frequented, and, while eating, a very handsome young man joined us whom Dick introduced as Richard, who was attending classes at the University of Chicago and was someone he had met recently thru some mutual acquaintance. We sat talking and suddenly I was startled to see the ring on Richard's finger.

Richard was considerably younger than Dick and really very beautiful. He was blond, with icy blue eyes—innocent and clear. He was very interested in life and people and kept bombarding us with questions—about our interests, the theater, music, art, or whatever happened to pop into his head. He laughed a good deal and one could feel a sense of goodness about him. He was obviously attracted to me and asked permission to call me on the phone so that we might make arrangements to see each other. I complied and began making plans about how to get the ring away from him—after all I felt the ring was mine—and I wanted it.

And so it happened that I succeeded in twisting one of the few really wonderful things that occurred when I was young into a sordid, almost tragic experience which even now fills me with shame.

As I have already said—Richard was good. There was no guile in his makeup and he offered his love and friendship unstintingly. It was he who first introduced me to poetry—to great music—to the beauty of the world—and who was concerned with my wants and happiness. Who spent hours making love to me, caressing and kissing me on every part of my body until I would collapse in a great explosion of beauty and sensation which I have never attained in exactly the same way with anyone since. He truly loved me and asked nothing in return but that I accept him—instead of which I delighted in hurting him and making him suffer in all manner of petty ways. I would tease him or refuse him sex or call him a fool or say that I didn't want to see him. Sometimes I would tell him we were finished, thru, and not to call me or try and see me, and it was after one such episode on a beautiful warm summer night—when I had agreed to see him again if he would grant me a favor—I asked for the ring and he gave it to me.

The next day I visited Dick at the studios and—with many gestures and words of denunciation—flung the ring at him, telling him that we were finished and that anyway he wasn't nearly as amusing as Richard—

and that maybe or maybe not I'd continue seeing Richard—and that in fact he bored me and I only felt sorry for him—and that I would never be as big a fool over anyone as he was over me—and besides my only reason for knowing him at all was so that I could get the ring.

Dick became enraged and began calling me foul names which he sort of spit at me and pulled from his desk drawer a pistol. He was waving it in front of my face and at the same time telling me how cruel and heartless I was and that he could forgive the stupidity of my actions in regard to himself but that the harm I was inflicting on Richard was more than he could stomach and that I would be better dead. Suddenly he started shouting—"Get out—get out—I never want to see you again." By this time I was shaking and almost unable to stand and stumbled out of his presence.

The following day in the mail I received a letter from Richard containing a poem—that read almost like this—

> A perfect fool you called me.
> Perchance not as happy in my
> outlook on life and people
> as you—
> Yet in like manner—playing the
> role of a perfect fool—
> Gave me a sort of bliss—
> You in all your wisdom—will
> never know.

Shortly after receiving the letter I called Richard and asked to see him. He refused to see me and at that time I would not plead. A strange thing had happened to me—I had become aware—almost overnight—of the enormity of my cruelty—and I was filled with a sudden sense of loneliness—which I have never lost—and I wanted Richard's forgiveness.

Richard never forgave me and I have only seen him once since the time he gave me the ring—and that was only long enough for him to tell me—he was trying to forget he had known me.

It was a cold winter day.

Nor did I ever speak with Dick again. Not so many years ago—I read in the paper—he is dead.

1959

CUBA

CUBA IS WHAT IS KNOWN IN PRISON JARGON AS A PEDDLER. HE IS A REAL hustler in the sense that if there is anything in the way of contraband to be obtained within the prison—such as eggs, meat, grease, winter overcoats, shoes, shirts, tailor-made pants, special hair preparations, aftershave lotion, etc.—he is the man to see. When any new young boys or fags or potential broads appear on the scene, Cuba is the first to know and loses no time making contact.

When I met him he was serving out the last year of a ten-year sentence. He was paroled on one occasion and deported back to Cuba. He refused to remain and, through some manner or other, succeeded in returning to New York where he immediately became a dope pusher. He operated fairly effectively until he was caught and returned to prison.

I don't recall a great deal of his past history although I became friendly with him and he spent much of his time telling me about himself.

The first time I saw him he was coming across the prison yard. It was summer and he was without a shirt. The entire upper part of his body was a mass of scars—from the shoulder to the waist—and once seeing him in the shower I noticed a continuation of these scars on his legs. He obtained those scars—which are like shrimp-pink-colored welts—by lacerating himself on numerous occasions with razor blades. Whenever he becomes enraged or has a fight or does something of which he is deeply ashamed, he slashes himself afterward. Just a short while before I left, he went into his cell after an episode in which he had beaten a man severely in a fight and had been punished with sixty days' keep-lock—sixty days of almost solitary confinement—and cut himself so much that something like 172 stitches were required to stanch the flow of blood.

He is short of stature with a well-proportioned body. He is of light tan color with—other than the scars—a smooth, almost delicate-appearing skin quite free of chest hair and nearly beardless. He has pleasantly symmetrical facial features with a large brown mole on his left cheek. His eyes are a deep innocent brown. He wears, at all times, a thin gold chain with a large—nearly the size of a quarter—medallion given to him by his mother, and a thin red silk cord with a tiny rose shaped knot on it—of which he is quite secretive, refusing to explain and resenting having anyone touch it—around his neck.

He considers himself a great lover and is always in the midst of a passionate affair with one of his fellow inmates. He constantly speaks of the size and shape of everyone's ass and will exclaim in positive terms, "Man, I got to cop!" each time he sees an ass which especially appeals to him. He goes to great lengths arranging meetings in the yard with his most recent desire and will entice them up to his court where he surreptitiously feels them all the time, trying to convince them that they should try and get a job in the mess hall where he is working and that all he wants to do is kiss them on the ass. He will say, "Man, I no want— fuck you—just love you. Man—I like your ass. Come in the mess hall. We have our own shower there. We turn steam on in the shower— nobody see—I cop lots that way. You let me love your ass—I jerk off." Sometimes he is successful and goes around beaming at everybody and tells his friends all about how this time he has a lover that really loves him—and that this time he is not only going to kiss ass, but he's going to get in. He keeps himself well supplied with cigarettes from peddling activities and sees to it that his current interest is never without smokes.

He is a very kind person and is always doing unexpected favors for people he likes. He gambles a great deal and, if he wins, sometimes gives his winnings away to people he knows haven't anything of their own.

About a week before I left the prison, someone turned a note to the Principal Keeper about him. Just what it was supposed to have contained, no one was quite sure, but whatever it said apparently caused the P.K. to refer Cuba's name to the prison psychiatrist, who promptly called Cuba up for an interview, the result being—Cuba was sent over the wall to the State Hospital for the Insane.

When prisoners are transferred from the main prison to the State Hospital they are, if violent, placed in strait-jackets (restraining jackets they call them), and, if not violent, are handcuffed and ankle-shackled.

When we last saw Cuba he was being literally dragged into the waiting station wagon wearing a restraining jacket.

DANCING IN PRISON

I have been in prison—they don't dance in prison—nobody dances unless perhaps, in the cell alone—snapping fingers and wearing ear-
phones—and of course in dreams.

And there are good sounds in the prison I was in because it is close
to Canada—Montreal—and they like fine sound and many of their
programs are dedicated to young jazz musicians and it is not always
commercial and some of these cats come on. And then there is some
crazy stuff too—right here—that occasionally reaches there. Also, in
the yard, groups with horns, guitars, and anything to drum let go and
clap hands and beat and I've heard it great—in fact there was one
wayout man on a sax who blew all the time alone or with others—
in the cell alone and sometimes with a guy two cells away who would
pick on a guitar and listen to jazz and these guys would really let go
till seven o'clock, when the bell would ring for no more talking.

They sometimes talk about dancing, remembering past experiences with
social chicks—"who could dance their ass off, man"—or going to the
Palladium and even sometimes the old Savoy and innumerable other
spots, specially when name bands were on the scene—Basie—Elling-
ton—Kenton—all of them. Of course names are mentioned like Miles
Davis—Yardbird Parker—and Shearing—and Sarah Vaughan—Anita
O'Day—Keely Smith—Dakota Staton—and I could go on naming a
while yet—but most of these are for hearing only—I don't suppose
that is actually true because one can dance to any sound.

Anyway, I danced last night and it made me very happy. I am not a
clever dancer—that is, I don't ever know what I am doing—particularly
with my feet—but I always sort of let go—and wow I get some great
kicks. And I did last night.

A STORY—NEW YORK

I HAVE ALWAYS THOUGHT OF MYSELF AS A GOOD TALKER, AND ONCE I talked a man out of shooting another man, although I didn't succeed in talking him out of his violence. He was a man filled with frustration and constant anxiety which would erupt into great outbursts of denunciation toward anyone he felt at the particular time had treated him—as he understood it—unjustly, and was apt at such times to resort to physical assault. He wasn't of large stature, but possessed an abundance of energy, and could, if not checked immediately, inflict much pain. Fortunately these outbursts occurred seldom, and although verbally he was constantly attacking his supposed enemies it was only on rare occasions he gave vent to his more violent impulses.

At the time I am speaking of he was in between steady women and had been shacking up with a girl who was attracted by young boys. She was something of a whore, though she would go to great lengths to deny it and preferred having people think she was being kept by some old man that went to sea who sent her an allotment. She had been making the Forty-second Street scene for quite some time, and I had gotten to know her through one of the boys she had picked up.

Just how they met is rather vague, but it seems the main attraction was a certain satisfaction each derived from comparing notes concerning their prior loves. He was just getting over being jilted and she had just gotten rid of her most recent boy because she had decided he was queer since he didn't wish to go down on her, which was what she liked best.

They were living in a small pad on West Fifteenth Street and we all three would sit around smoking pot while they did most of the talking. Both sort of considered me a harmless friend each could confide in and frequently called upon me to settle disputes.

He was very possessive and had threatened to beat her if he caught her making it with anyone else. She was always reassuring and called him—her man.

One evening he came in unexpectedly and caught her balling a young kid. I was with him and knew the kid from the square and managed to get the kid out of the pad before too much trouble developed.

She was contrite and begged forgiveness, explaining that he hadn't laid her the previous night or given her head, and of course he knew how hot-natured she was and besides the kid had practically forced her. He admitted to being indirectly responsible—yet no goddamned punk was going to lay his old lady and get away with it. He rushed over and grabbed his gun—which was a gift from his brother, who had brought it back from overseas—and, with me in pursuit, rushed out into the night to find the no-good-son-of-a-bitch and blow his brains out.

We headed more or less toward Forty-second Street, stopping at various bars en route. He kept up a steady tirade against the poor kid until I could only hope that by this time the kid was somewhere at the other end of Brooklyn.

At three in the morning on the corner of Forty-third Street and Eighth Avenue just off the corner heading toward Ninth Avenue, we ran into him.

It was a slightly cool morning and the few people on the streets were rushing either toward the subway or bars or just to keep warm. The three of us standing in the reflection of the streetlamp must have made a strange and frightening picture. The one pale and shaking—pleading not to be hurt. Another livid with rage—filled with confusion—tense and ready to kill. And the other keenly aware of the drama and horrified—talking, talking, talking against events over which there seemed to be no control, and telling first one and then the other to keep cool. Beseeching the very atmosphere to help prevent the pulling of the trigger. It was a very tense and explosive moment and all I could do was talk. Asking, explaining, reasoning, constantly pointing out the stupidity of the situation and the sheer horror of the whole scene. It seemed that gradually things began to relax, and then suddenly it was over.

We spoke of the incident many times and later he was glad—sincerely glad—he had calmed down—and has frequently thanked me for my talking.

I no longer know where he is for sure, though I hear via the so-called grapevine he is now in Cleveland, still angry and lonely.

October 1959

I LEFT BOB ABOUT TWO O'CLOCK THIS MORNING. HE HAD DECIDED TO visit Irma and I felt it wiser of me to remain away from the encounter. We had walked down from the pad through Central Park. Prior to our departure we drank over half a fifth of a Spanish brandy which Bob is particularly fond of and we felt very good. The park is exceedingly delightful at night and we indulged in a very interesting conversation involving sense of honesty, consciousness of mental telepathy, our own responsiveness to each other's worth, and many intriguing bits of honest revelations. I made some effort to explain my present frame of mind about Vernon and, although nothing lastingly great was achieved, there were several instances of intense purity of feeling. We had both, earlier in the evening, been weary and by now felt exhilarated. We had smoked a stick of pot and it is doubtful as to whether any two cats could have managed any greater high than the one we were on. Bob became very eloquent and gave me several verbal scores vibrating with good thought and sending warm waves of telepathic impulses. Bob's sensitivity serves him well and frequently his speech is startlingly keen. We both thoroughly expounded our opinions about the true reality which we both feel is seldom sensed because of the crassness of the overall pattern of daily life and the false values which are foisted on us as real.

In my usual clumsy manner I blundered in with the first bite of depression. I do this unfailingly and it is one of my anxieties. From then on a pall fell over us, and although the joy of freedom continued, it began its departure. We were once again taking up the shackles and would soon be wearing them. It is as though I eject a poison.

1959

STRANGERS

I

EARLY MORNING AND THE SOUND OF TRUCKS AND VOICES TINGED WITH sleep and occasional alarms ringing and the sky fleeced with clouds and pale blue. The air not yet warm but already greeting the new day with fresh river breezes. Light spots here and there on brick walls—light, from the faintly glimmering sun.

A stranger cold and tired and lost and afraid and filled with sorrow. Whose father shed tears at his departure from home and bade him not return until he has a job and is dependable and to be relied upon to follow in the footsteps of his three quite dependable brothers. A stranger insecure and haunted by his unhappiness when not working but unable to work because he is unable to adjust to the routine demanded of him when he does work.

Seeking merely to be free of anxiety which verges—so he fears—on the insane. Young but willing to accept his defeat—to place himself among the others who are lost and bewildered and frighteningly insecure. Who rhapsodizes over filling a little black lunch pail and setting out for his labor with the great majority but who cannot because he is a revolutionist and does not know it. Who loathes himself and believes he is a fool. But who breathes from a heart that is kind and good—but hurt. Who fears jail but has been there because of a fondness for automobiles. Whose legs ache from having been so long on his feet and feels sure paralysis is setting in or perhaps rheumatic fever. Who is frightened of sex but curious and rather in awe.

A pitiable fellow indeed. I like him and I hope I can do something for him and help him to become a bit more complete.

II

I watched them talking and looking at each other—occasionally one or the other glancing around—sometimes commenting to each other about what they had observed—then returning to their original conversation—each engrossed in the other—a certain aura of comradeship emanating from them—obvious to anyone observing them.

They were young—one of medium-light complexion—flat—semi-harsh masculine features—inclined toward stockiness—the other dark—with sharp pointed features—thin and tall so that he draped a chair rather than sat in it.

When I had first noticed them another fellow was sitting with them, and the lighter-complected of the pair directed many of his remarks in his direction. Although he pretended an interest in what was being said, he was far more interested in what was happening around him. Watching the passing flow of people going by the window—every now and then looking back over his shoulder to see what was taking place in the rest of the room. Finally he saw someone he knew passing along the street and—with a quick good-bye to his companions—darted out onto the street.

The two remaining apparently discussed him for a few moments—talking and making gestures obviously referring to the recently departed acquaintance.

I had no way of being sure—but from watching, I decided they were part of the usual Forty-second Street crowd of hustlers—with a special interest in each other. Of course—the possibility I am romanticizing exists—but there was something in the way they looked at each other—plus an off-handed manner of accepting one another—that made me feel I was not mistaken in believing a feeling of love was exchanged between the two.

Much later—after they too had gone on their way—and I had grown weary of sitting still—deciding to walk along the street—I chanced upon the darker of the two standing talking to a much older man—passing by overhearing a snatch of conversation between the two—the younger fellow saying, "I need ten dollars—I have to pay"—not hearing the finish because by then I had already passed.

III

"Oh," she said, "I hate to go home. Don't you hate to go home? Why, I paid a whole dollar to go and see that picture with all the colored people—you know the one—they pray—oh, they pray a lot and sing."

The other one said, "*Porgy and Bess?*"

"Yes—that's the one—I didn't like it—just wasted the dollar—but I hate to go home. I always come here and sit—I would rather sit here than go home. The place I live is nice—real clean—the room good size—real big—new furniture. Pretty—kind of like that modern stuff you see in them movie pictures. Still it's only a room—and I gotta stay someplace—but I hate to go home."

The two women were old. The one who hated going home—was alone—had nobody—not even a cat. The other one had a cat and Joe. Joe was her boyfriend—she saw him once a week. It was nice. Made her fell less alone than her friend. She guessed she could understand. She would sure miss Joe.

Both were short in stature—faces heavily plastered with cosmetics— wrinkled. Both were bright-eyed—peering around watching everyone. Both smoked constantly—one holding her cigarette between thumb and forefinger—brandishing it in the air—emphasizing her frequent remarks with jerky bird-like movements. Both wore gaudy bright-colored dresses.

Finally Joe's woman got up to go. She walked over to the cashier, paid her check, went out thru the revolving doors. As she passed by the huge plate-glass windows, she turned—looking in the window—and with a little-girl-like gesture wig-wagged her fingers in farewell to her friend.

The woman who had remained took out her lipstick—carefully made up her mouth—lit another cigarette—looked over at me—and said, "You know—this ain't a bad joint. They got pretty good coffee—and they let you sit here as long as you like. I guess it don't look right for a lady to sit so long in a place—but you know something—mister—I hate to go home."

IV

I just saw a sad humorous scene. Two men—shabby and dirty—in front of a liquor store. One man was standing perfectly still—looking like a huge mechanical doll that had just run down—one arm slightly lifted— the other hanging stiffly at the side—the head turned a bit to the side—

eyes staring straight ahead—unblinking—the face expressionless. The mechanical doll with perhaps a defect in the mechanism—so after each jerky movement there was a pause before the next motion. First he would take a step—stop—cock his head to one side—blink his eyes once or twice—look downward—lift his hand—spread his fingers—peer at the change he had been clutching—close his fingers—let his hand fall to one side—stand motionless, his face blank of expression—then take another step or two—pause—and go thru a repetition of the same gestures as before.

I stopped and watched him cross the sidewalk to his friend—extend the hand holding the change—open it—dropping the money into his friend's coat pocket—assume almost the same position as that of the man standing.

They stood next to each other without speaking—the only sign of life in either one the occasional blinking of the eyelids.

I watched them for a full ten minutes and neither changed position or gave any indication of being aware of one another.

They may still be standing.

HALLOWE'EN

HALLOWE'EN TWO YEARS AGO—THE FIRST FOLLOWING A FOUR-YEAR IN-carceration in a N.Y. State prison and shortly after release—represented in a sense the beginning of a whole new scope of awareness for me. Prior to the aforementioned period except when very young—my early teen years—I made a point of remaining removed from the obviously Bohemian world of open rebellion—pointed non-conformity—studio gatherings—fireplaces—all-night discussions—political and religious—psychology—stupidity—parental and commercial—unique out-of-the-way eating spots and complete sexual freedom—the intelligentsia and knowing about art—visually—auditorially—poetically—who was saying great and ponderous things—in novels—plays—and any form of the written word—the theater—the dance—and music. Instead I lived in middle-class environments as indifferent to middle class standards as though they failed to exist. I lived aimlessly surrounded in the beginning with all the smart sets—callow—empty—glittering nothingness—eventually becoming the typical leech. My main desire to be supported lavishly—expensive clothes—an automobile—long and sleek—preferably a convertible—a Doberman pinscher sitting next to me—the top down—a beautiful woman—fashionably gowned—travel and debauchery on an international scale—my commodity in exchange—my body. Unfortunately there were few buyers and those were far from able to supply any of the extremely choice luxuries I wanted. Also I soon learned I was unable to restrain myself sufficiently to give the impression that I was rare enough to merit high price—and could be had as easily for nothing—as long as the stimulants were many and in plenty and there was much laughter and I was free of even the slightest degree of responsibility. There were of course innumerable causes for my attitude all outside consideration, and it was only me alone and again faced with the constant problem of having a need of the basic require-ments—food—shelter—and ordinarily presentable clothing—who became aware of my self-loathing—gradually becoming obsessed with the desire for death and an escape from the rest of my fellow creatures—aware intensely again and again—of how beautiful the world is—and of my maladjustment and despicability—knowing how completely unworthy I was of even a glimpse of the sheer marvel of a delicately hued flower—the glow of the sunrise—the white beauty of the moon—the wonder of the sea—a tree—a rock—a blade of grass.

Soon I became a thief—no longer desirous of prostituting my body and discovering it was far simpler to sneak around here and there taking things I could convert into money—or money—and, except for perhaps working with a partner, no need to deal in a so-called personal way with other people. I was free to become more obscure—sinking closer to what I soon believed was basic reality awakened originally with the aid of magic opium. Always there had been the opiates—heroin—morphine—Dilaudid—Pantopon—and it was thru their mysterious chemical magic I became truly conscious of God—the world—and the great wonder of life, and—when all else failed to stir my inner being—the quick fix again revealed the splendor—giving me reason to live until death. Nor has there been a change. It is still from the exquisite beauty of the poppy I seek solace.

As I became a thief and less concerned with surface evaluations—the opinions of the majority—recognizing only a few friends—and not always sure of them—learning at the same time of the world of the spirit—linking me—all of us—together—it not mattering our outer hulk—only in this world—this life—beginning to sense the oneness of the inner force—observing the drive and what became to me the direction of the individual entity toward the "is" of life—feeling instinctively—and with assurance—all becomes the one God—the one indestructible force—power—energy—drive—call it what you choose—or by any word—I became more fully aware of a sense of peace. It is true I did not like being a thief—but then neither did I like the idea of being respectably a slave—a wage earner—an eight-in-the-morning-to-five-in-the-evening drudge—and somehow didn't see myself as more objectionable—in the final analysis—than the corrupt politician—the money-hungry lawyer—doctor—boss—or company man. The task master who says, "Do it this way—or lose your job. What do I care if your children are without necessities—or you can't pay your bills—the rent—buy food? The job has to be done." Or the cop who accepts a bribe today and arrests tomorrow. Or the man of the church who leches after young boys—or girls—

and blesses with one hand, holding out the other for silver. Or the man who sells the slogan of lies about bad breath—body odor—the decided advantages of one brand of the same bread over another of identical mixture. Or the man who sells the twenty-five-cent bottle of chemical distillation called wine to the alcoholic who needs a drink of good whiskey—not synthetic beverage—or the man who lauds whiskey and votes to send the narcotics addict to jail.

And finally as a thief I became a prisoner and served my time and came out of prison and—two years ago—once again saw a few of the very few people I had learned respect of before my being sentenced.

They—those of them—creative and basically honest—at least as they understood honesty—had moved forward and had started speaking aloud—and had written great poems and books—and the world had made a place for them—because of their beauty and fineness, and because they are beautiful and good they were kind in their knowledge of me and welcomed me back and—now part of Bohemia—asked me to join them attending several Hallowe'en parties and I accepted.

It was good to be back with people interested and actively engaged in creative work—believing in a new sense of inner value—inner value in this instance referring to God and love and openness and a search for peace—both individually and collectively.

Everyone—or almost everyone—I met that occasion seemed fine and good, and it was with a sense of pride and humility I learned many of them knew of me thru some of my writing, and references and stories told by one or two knowing me and having spoken of me.

This as I mentioned earlier began a new period in my life—and I have become a bit of a figure in the New York Bohemian scene. A great deal has occurred not only to me but in the world in general during the last two years. I have grown wearier of my life and am anxious to make the big transition. I want to die—not because I especially dislike life—but mostly because I have grown rather old and am tired.

As for the world—there is even more talk of bombs—bigger bombs—better bombs—larger stockpiles of bombs—newer concepts of bombs—and more decided challenges. Threats—and open defiance.

There is also some talk of peace—but it is mostly submerged beneath references to dust fallout—atomic destruction machine—and possible active war.

Yesterday's headlines—our great American president states, "We now have sufficient bomb power to blow Russia off the face of the earth."

Enough of hate—breeding hate—resenting each other—we need more love.

There is of course the possibility—in order for us to truly evolve into something worthwhile—beyond our meager little niche in the inconceivable vastness of the universe—we have—like the Phoenix—to end in fire—and be reborn of the ashes.

October 31, 1961

PETER

I JUST FINISHED EATING PETER AND WASHED HIM DOWN WITH BEER—
lager beer. He was tender and juicy—succulent—sugar cured and lean.

I swallowed his heart whole. Sucked his bones clean—leaving them
in a pile—neatly stacked—marrowless.

Of his hair I'll weave a silken jerkin—a scarf—to wrap around my
throat and a sash.

Of his bones I'll build a bed—spend hours lying upon it—dreaming—
his skull a pillow for my head—the birds will come there and find me
dead.

They will peck me tearing tiny morsels of flesh. Some will fly away—
dropping me into the sea—for fish. The sun will dry me out and the
wind scatter flakes of dust over the earth.

Slowly our bones will pulverize as we gradually become powdery—
the rain blending us together—washed across the earth in tiny rivulets—
seeping down to the roots of the trees—grass—flowers.

They will find our skulls—the last to go—clasped jaw to jaw—in
caricature of a kiss.

PHILL

PHILL SMILED BEGUILINGLY TONIGHT—ASKING ME WHEN I WOULD WRITE about him. At the time I didn't know. Giving the idea a little thought I decided—without doubt—Phill would be written about. It is not my stick—or long suit—habit to attempt a definition or description of a new acquaintance—but I would at least in this instance say his name and maybe exert a little effort to describe him.

He is a rather straight cat who has found or finds drugs a kick to him. He is young and married and a father.

There is difficulty with his home arrangements primarily because his wife becomes afraid there will be no home—and becomes annoyed when he does things he is interested in—sure that he is up to no good. I have only surmised these are the details—and am sure—if these aren't it—there is something else about the same level—causing irritation. He has spoken of his wife and child several times and is deeply concerned with their situation now and what it might become. He relaxes—spends money—picks up on any of several stimulants—so to speak—he likes—digs a little sex and is filled with remorse and talks of giving the scene up altogether. I rather wish he would although I am not at all convinced he will.

He has a beautiful face and I am aware of good things when he smiles. His face is sad sometimes or has a slightly impish quality. He is certainly physical and sex is a major point with him. Much of this is retained in his face—especially the eyes. His body appears to be free and graceful. There is of course his conscious masculinity and the degree of masculinity he is unaware of possessing. He is an attractive young man.

I like hearing him talk although I am never exactly sure of the direction it will take. He has a fairly positive code of ethics—which is bad enough but accompanied with doubt—misgivings—and being unsure—it is absolutely nothing. He has made it on the scene a couple of times. I like him.

He has been kind to me and several times been uncomfortable but determined to remain and accept or believe in what is happening. Like Noah—there is the sanitary—or simply ordinary caution—and the quality perhaps of a Jewish tie difficult to break away from. Both Noah and Phill in some ways are alike—in a sense—or in most of the other ways glaringly different.

Phill would like and does like sharp clothes. He should have an extensive wardrobe—big cars and a lot of money. Oh! for the proverbial playboy existence—all good—but there is always the sad cat on the outside.

Phill could without doubt issue orders and all would be smooth. Follow the leader and you could be sure of making it—deviate a fraction from the powerful hand of the infringed-upon and there is no money—what can he do? Anyway vocation becomes a hang-up—some were going and some remain. Except for those he had chosen—perhaps it would be fine if he had some hound's-tooth slacks. One day he is least in anticipation—and of course that is the day everything falls upon the scene. Perhaps he will get with it next time.

He talks very hip and is hip, but stupidly I had thought on the strength of what he said something could happen—and now somehow I know there will be frustration for him—for his wife—and the family bit in general.

Yet his family—a good home—car—landscape in Brooklyn or wherever—would pacify him. If he wants home life and children—otherwise what is he doing—and no responsibility is attached—fist fight—or cock fight. He always gets back to the way—he invariably has what he needs and wants.

He is a quiet cat who silently dreams the future home—and all necessary his wife and child be happy. He talks of takes and hustles and sometimes an easy buck—and he also collects exceptionally good money when he is employed as a plumber. I prefer believing there are only a few—if any—takes, nor has he any particular pet plan or scheme—this has absolutely no mud slinging. He can smoke his pot—make his gig—and be thru for all night. Harold Goldfinger knows how weary I've become—always been.

(new entry)

It seems I lost track again and automatic writing took over. This is very strange. I can only ask to be believed. I am not sure I will be believed although unquestionably there are those who will try and believe me and will. As close as I am capable of understanding what takes place is—I am in a semi-high state—between half-awareness and half-unconscious behavior—perhaps half-fallen asleep. Yet I can remember back in each instance thus far—a concern with what was written—a sort of perplexity. My habit of not reading or rather of ignoring of the manner of speech or wording—my writing—and letting it alone until later—or seldom changing it even then—has proven good to me. It is a rather frightening experience—realizing there is a period when you have only vague awareness of your consciousness of the time knowledge—or the moments you were writing something you believed to be an ordinary continuation of your story—theme—or subject—discovering upon reading—if it is a continuation it is not in the usual sense and in all probability is an outcropping of strange thought patterns developed without restriction or conscious effort—simply an effect, a result of cause you knew nothing of or understand now it has occurred. I am satisfied in a sense with what is written. It seems impressive. I desire having the experience as frequently as possible. I do not know how to bring it about and can only hope it will be a steady occurrence. Apparently it is a combination of everything within the moment—the atmosphere—the light—the shade—the temperature—each emotional registration—the nuances and connotation of tone—of sound—all, to the least stirring of the air. I cannot explain.

(new entry)

Phill called yesterday and said he might fall over—maybe cop some boo. I didn't encourage him and he didn't arrive. Again today about noon he called and said he'd like to get some schmeck. I suggested he call me a little later at Margo's—I told him I had spoken with her and she had mentioned a cat's name who was visiting her I knew to be using a little schmeck and maybe I could do him some good. He asked how much it would cost. I told him six dollars. He then said something about a chick asking him to get her some pot—a ten-dollar bag—and she told him he was to take a good cut. It sounded good and I rather liked the idea of money entering the scene.

It failed to work out as I had hoped. He called later and everything seemed practical—the cat said he would cop for Phill—and Phill came on over. He sat around most of the afternoon—listening to conversation of no interest to him—but had promised to get in touch and then failed to do so. I saw him much later and he apologized for not calling, saying something about loss of time hanging him up—he was sorry but he knew I could understand. Phill had finally grown weary of the whole scene and cut into a chick he knows who straightened him. I returned to Erin's and he came by. He was zonked and wanted to nod off in the apartment. I reasoned with him explaining it simply could not be done—also I wanted to make sure Margo would get rest—and the only way I could be sure was for me to take her home. I told him to go to Noah's and wait for me. He did go to Noah's—I did take Margo home—but he did not wait for me and when I went to Noah's there was no one there. I met both of them later on the street. Phill was still high. He was annoyed—and suddenly said, "I am going home." He walked away—his back very straight—stepping along very carefully—never looking back.

FRISKY

THE LAST FEW WEEKS—ON OCCASION—I'VE HAD REASON TO VISIT DON Neald and Jimmy's pad on Bleecker Street. Tom Sato—an Oriental cat about forty or forty-five years of age—actually set the place up originally and still lives there with Don and Jimmy. It is a strange place—consisting of three rooms—opening up from the front—intended as a store—above street level one flight up and running to the back room, where at some point someone decided to make a sort of built-in wall seat to run the full width of the back wall, setting it back under a pair of arches that extended in front of it about three feet. To one side is a plain brick wall with a huge iron pikestaff caught on it at an angle. Opposite is a window looking out at the courtyard, with heavy red plush drapes. Between these and the next window is a table, a mirror hanging above it and a lamp with a Japanese shade. Along the wall next to the bare brick area is a large double studio couch with end tables; next a chest of drawers and a closet. The colors in the room are somber browns and dark greens and reds. There is an air of the old and decayed in the atmosphere—and one would hardly be surprised to discover at least one haunted sister—pale-faced—communing with the dead, or perchance a stuffed owl burning—and a coffin.

The front room with its storefront packed with frames and stretchers—an old bench—the windows dirt laden—never any daylight—is long and oblong in shape—the walls holding several wall plaques—and a number of very dull-toned paintings in wide oak frames or, in one or two instances, tarnished gold. There is a divan and an overstuffed chair—a shaded light hanging from a cord just above. Between the front room and the back room is a small section containing shelves and a small wash-basin—one step down from each of the rooms. Everything is old and worn—dusty and threadbare.

Apparently two or three weeks ago several young unusually beautiful girls began staying there along with Don, Jim, and Tom Sato. From what little I was able to learn of their backgrounds, they grew up together—all about the same age: the oldest twenty-one or twenty-two, and the youngest eighteen. Terry, Penny, Barbara, Dexie, and Frisky. There is one other beautiful child, fourteen, who occasionally falls in, stays a while, maybe turns on a shot of amphets, and then disappears into the city outside.

The night El Flower and I put Deborah on the bus to California, we returned downtown to the location of the Catholic Worker's headquarters, where we spent a short time speaking with a friend of El's. As we left, El suggested we try and cop a bag of horse—asking me if I knew where we might accomplish same. I immediately thought of Sato's. We walked over to the Bowery at Delancey and headed up toward Bleecker. En route, we ran into Nick and a friend of his. I spoke briefly with Nick, who said he was headed to Sato's and to pick him up there. But we followed closely behind and entered at almost the same time. I said hello to everyone, and El acknowledged introductions, his eyes lighting up the scene, darting around the rooms, observing the girls. Frisky was half reclining on a divan talking to a young cat—Jerry—I had only seen once before. Everyone else was located in the back room. As we entered, Don raised up and asked if either of us had any amphets. When we said no, he fell back down, grumbling about not having turned on all day. He said, "Wow—all these people cutting and out—this ain't no shooting gallery." Nickie and his friend proceeded to get straight, cooking up their shit. Barbara was in the process of getting dressed, and at the moment was applying some kind of eye makeup. Penny had moved over to watch Nickie. I sat down in a chair facing the couch. Terry was curled up alongside Don. Looking toward the back, I saw Tom Sato apparently sleeping on the long wall seat. A spread of some kind, partially obscuring him from view, hung in one of the arches. Don was still muttering unintelligible sounds, every other one a grunt or snort, taking on form as "Amphets—tired—chaos—confusion—too many people."

Suddenly, looking directly at him, I said, "Hey, man, are you complaining because I fell in? If you don't want me cutting in, all that is necessary is that you say so." He answered by saying, "Well, you know, Huncke, it isn't you exactly, but strangers." I answered immediately, saying, "Are you referring to Flower? Wow—he's good people. Not only that—I am usually careful who I introduce, and to whom I introduce. Also—there are few people on this point any cooler than me." Don said, "I know, man." Just then Penny spoke up saying, "It's just—

Don doesn't want so many people falling in at once." I didn't say anything—looking the scene over—thinking fuck these people—or how
hung up can they get. If I'd had any amphets, nothing at all would have
been mentioned other than "Great—can we turn on? Have you enough
so we can all get a shot?"

Meanwhile, El spoke to Nickie, asking him if as soon as he had finished, would he cop a bag of schmeck for us? Nickie said yes. Just then
Jimmy walked by and, looking at me, said, "You look annoyed, Huncke."
I didn't answer. El turned to me and began questioning me about
whether or not I trusted Nickie. I started to say, "Yes, of course"—and
then it occurred to me that the whole routine was pretty fucking stupid.
"Shit, no—I don't trust anybody. There ain't no motherfucker alive I
believe in. Everybody stinks." Jimmy interrupted to say, "What's the
matter, man?" I replied, "Nothing, except people. Fuck people. The
more I know of them, the less I want to be around them." At the moment, I was irritated with Don and his whole stupid attitude. It annoyed
me he should dare have opinions of me, especially since he knew me
not at all personally and was only mouthing things he had heard said.

Nickie finished shooting up, picked up the money from El, and cut
out, saying he'd be back as soon as possible. After he left, his friend came
over and joined us, saying, "My name is Johnny Walsh." He began telling us of himself and how he had just beaten a federal rap. It had taken
two years and a lot of money. The talk became general, everyone speaking of one thing or another—mostly of drugs. Someone mentioned having turned on with synthetic cocaine the night before, also making a
comment about wishing some were available at the moment. A couple
of hours before, El had thrown me a large bag containing just what they
were talking about. El looked at me and said, "You got it with you,
man?" I nodded yes and he spoke aloud, saying, "Look, I don't know
what the stuff is, but Huncke and I have something that is supposed to
be artificial or synthetic coke. If you want to use some, you're welcome."
Don jumped up and said, "Yes, man, I sure would appreciate shooting
some up." Johnny Walsh asked to see the stuff, saying he'd like to try a
little, asking me if I was going to shoot some also. I really don't like the
idea of synthetic anything—much less cocaine—but I was feeling nervous and it occurred to me that possibly I'd get a lift. I said, "Yes. In
fact, let me go first." I'd had some experience with it once or twice
before and I know just about what to put in the spoon. I cooked up,
drew the stuff into the dropper, and shot up. For a moment, nothing—

and then a strange freezing sensation in my mouth—and on the tip of my tongue and around the gums—and a momentary rush to the pit of my stomach. I felt a bit ill for a moment—and then all was well. Everyone was watching me. They began asking questions about whether or not I felt it—if I liked it—if it was good. I shrugged my shoulders, saying, "Yes—no—it's OK—not really great—just a slight rush—over with now—nothing is happening." Barbara said, "You look happy, I'm going to try some."

Meanwhile Johnny Walsh had taken over and was in the process of preparing himself a fix. He proceeded to take off, saying—after he had removed the needle—"Man, I don't feel anything." Don was next, then Barbara. Penny and Jimmy went out for soda and cigarettes. El was getting restless. He had an appointment at the Metro coffeehouse he didn't want to miss. He said for me to wait for Nickie and we would meet later at Noah and Paul's. As he was walking toward the front, Frisky passed him, asking him if it would be all right for her to take a little shot, too. El answered, "Of course," and she came on through into the back room.

As she passed me she smiled, then stopped a moment, extending her hands to me. "Let's see how strong you are. Here, put up your hand." I took both of her hands in mine and we exerted strength and pressure to see which could force the other to bend their arms. She was quite strong. We both began laughing. "You're stronger than I thought," I said. She looked pleased. Suddenly she withdrew her hands and went over to the table with the works and the stuff. She paused a moment before the mirror—pulling her dress into position—fluffing her long black hair a little around her ears—twisting one way and another in order to see herself at different angles. She was half smiling, looking pleased. Johnny Walsh was sitting at the table and she asked him to please fix her a shot. She continued standing—fussing with her appearance—putting lipstick on—smoothing it down on her mouth with her little finger—brushing a light coating of mascara onto her eyelashes. She was wearing a bright turquoise-blue dress—trimmed with orange and black bands around the neck and bottom of the skirt. She had low-cut dark blue sneakers on her feet and bent down to loosen the laces of one which she kicked off, grimacing and remarking about a blister on the back of her heel. Johnny had prepared her a shot and she sat down to tie up. Seeing her, for the moment the thought flashed through my mind—perhaps she shouldn't take very much, if any—and then it was gone. I was still very annoyed with Don—and besides, apparently they had all been shooting together for quite some time and she probably knew what she was doing. Also Nickie was overdue and I was becoming bugged waiting. Barbara was sitting opposite me and Penny and Jimmy had just returned with bottles of Coca-Cola and packages of cigarettes.

I saw Barbara, who was looking in the direction of Frisky and John, suddenly stiffen—a look of fright on her face. As I turned to look I heard her gasp and let out a little scream. I saw Frisky rise up halfway out of the chair she had been sitting in—fling her arms out stiffly—throw her head back—spin to one side—and fall to the floor in a state of convulsive spasms—her whole body rigid and quivering. Johnny leaped from his seat and Jimmy rushed across to her side, calling her name—bending down—they began trying to lift her—turning her first to one side and then the other. The girls all started talking at once, making suggestions. Everyone started moving around. The two fellows succeeded in lifting her off the floor and moving her into a half-reclining position on the couch or bed where, one on either side, they tried holding her down. She was breathing in gasps from deep in her throat through gargling saliva. She was choking on the bile accumulated in her throat. Every now and then she would partially come to and strain to rise up—her eyes wide open staring straight ahead. They continued to hold her in position until she would pass out again.

Meanwhile Tom Sato had leaped from his bed, thrown on his hat and coat and rushed out, presumably to try and find out what the antidote for the stuff might be. Barbara and I had collected the works together. I arranged mine and placed them in my pocket. I had tried to make several suggestions about how to handle the girl and was either not heard or simply ignored—and besides, I was not at all sure about what should be done. Jimmy had called me a couple of times asking me if I knew exactly how to handle the situation and all I could reply was—no.

I decided to leave. I spoke quietly to Barbara, asking her to please let me out and to close and lock the door after I left. Barbara was shaken and her eyes were filled with tears. "They should try and let her cough up the bile and saliva," she said. "She is choking this way, and no one will listen to me." There was nothing I could say except "Don't worry, baby—she'll be all right." As Barbara let me out, she repeated her statement and said, "I know I'm right." I told her to take care and stepped out onto the street. I walked straight home to the apartment to find El already there and waiting. I explained what had happened and he became upset, exclaiming, "Oh, man—what a drag—wow—that poor chick."

In a short time the three girls—Terry, Penny, and Barbara—arrived across the hall at Margot and Nickie's, saying as they came in, "She is dead." I was shocked and asked them to explain about what had happened after I left. They told me that finally Tom Sato and Nickie, who had returned, helped get her into a taxi. Her pulse had stopped beating, and she had turned blue. Someone had called a policeman explaining that she had committed suicide. I don't know any further details except she was reported a suicide and dead on arrival.

THE MAGICIAN

WINDS ARE STILL. HEAT HANGS HEAVY AND OPPRESSIVE. LOW GRAY clouds illuminated by the lights of the city seemingly glow in the night sky. A dog howls somewhere the next block over. The night is haunted. September demons chitter and chatter. Stair steps creak and moan with weight of evil forces ascending six flights up to gain entrance to the three rooms of my dwelling. Each room contains individual shadows teeming with the spawn of black magic. A purple taper burns a flickering flame casting unsteady light.

My nerve ends are exposed and raw. Each minute sends waves of sticky warmth through my being. I am sure the magician approaches. He has planned the instant of unleashing his power be drenched in blood. He has selected me to release the flow. I did reject and received vitriol. He placed symbols required to fill my heart with sharp pain. He cried fool—accusing me of benevolence—then whispered the pitch-black words rich with magic force—appointing me his executioner. I did not understand his interest in me when first he began giving me freely of the crystal-clear elixir and I was as one reborn. I listened to his flute voice rise in early dawn light—he alone—and I allowed to walk by his side. This in early spring—the morning stirring with gentle, faintly warm wind—while the city around us began discarding the drab soot-polluted winter colors—replacing them with bright blue—red—yellow—and all gay pastels of spring promise. I but realized his magical capabilities. He began revealing himself in the role of a lover—selecting a fine beautiful woman I also loved—to create beautiful magic truths for and asking her to share his search for truth—at the start gentle—patient—kind—carefully explaining the complexities—demanding only truth from her but not always believing. Still, in the beginning he would listen and understand and approve and smile and speak in detail at great length, about beauty—purity—white magic. Then as he watched her belief strengthen—grow—accept—learned her strength—observed the completeness of her

innocence—he sensed the depth of his evilness and became frightened—
feeling confident much of evil within himself must be matched in others
and she surely must contain her share. And besides, all honey and no
spice—who in hell did she think she could kid?

So gradually he began releasing his black power—finally calling her
ugly—a liar—a dirty selfish bitch—resorting in his frustration to absorb
entirely her true essence of beauty—to slapping—pinching—kicking—
stealing her food—very nearly chaining her to his side—never permitting
her to leave his presence—screaming foul names—hating her because
she revealed her greatenss—and more so because he began losing his as
he revealed his insecurity—his smallness and inability to exist indepen-
dently of her or anyone else he might fortunately have drawn into his
orbit. His potential as a magician—a creator—became less until even his
most loyal followers began turning their backs—shutting their doors—
hardly interested in his continued existence. He decided on extinction—
annihilation—suicide. His plan was to have himself killed—cause as
much dissension—confusion—and general discomfort as possible.

I had followed closely his relationship with our mutual love—seldom
making even a vague effort to interfere. She kept me informed of her
feelings at all times and I felt quite certain she deserved the respect of
being allowed to decide for herself when or if she desired leaving him.
He had woven magnificent and intricately created magic worlds for her
private observation. She had witnessed complete opposites of the same
truth and knew it to retain the same truth. New and greater depths of
reality became hers and she learned the world filled with magic.

His beauty and creative ability had been so fine—when he began
changing, she was unable to accept the change as coming from him—
believing instead herself to be at fault. It was when he became increasingly violent her first doubts about his greatness took root.

Up to the point where it was impossible to be in their presence when
they weren't bickering—he making accusations—she on the defensive—
he threatening—screaming names at her—nymphomaniac—whore—
cunt—sex freak—striking out at her—she flinching anytime he moved
toward her—I had stayed clear except to try and reason—and a few
occasions hold on to him in an effort to keep him from hitting her again.

I am something of a coward and short of stark tragedy I couldn't
see any way of breaking up their relationship. Also a number of other
considerations were—at the time—not to be ignored. Nevertheless I did
decide—at the first chance I'd get her away long enough to break the

chain of thought—giving her an opportunity to obtain an accelerated, varied change process. In order to accomplish so radical a break in the pattern, considerable functioning on principle of being on the alert was required, the moment propitious to leave—depart—scram—split—take off. It arrived two o'clock one morning.

Returning from a walk on moon drenched—ruby-red stoplights lined intermittently—Avenue C—the city almost livid in crystal brightness. Opening the door of the apartment my glance became arrested on her beauty—she sitting crosslegged on a huge square four-peopled mattress—a low, flat-appearing, somewhat functional table—made of three drawers, one top to a desk—the several other units used satisfactorily elsewhere. Gray—beige—black—shades of black—demon-shaped— African-figure-shaped patterns seeming at first glance devoid of any consistency or relationship, an early magical creation from the organic inks— iodines—violets—one of his early possessions was used as a spread. She was stretching forward a tiny Japanese brush stained black-purple toward a small crock or jug. She looked at me intently a moment slightly bent forward—her long gold-brown hair hanging over the sides of her face. She suddenly laughed—rocked gently over to the side—dipped the brush—and straightened up making calligraphic symbols on a large piece of oatmeal paper. Again—stopping abruptly—she looked directly into my face—asking, "Are you happy? Is everything all right? Have I spoken harshly—or in anger—to you? You must never worry—or brood— about my appearing angry. It can't happen with you," and she started her painstaking calligraphy again. Vivaldi's *The Four Seasons* was on the phonograph—tuned to a fine rich medium. My big black cat came in thru the fire escape balcony window, stirring with his sweep of tail the Chinese wind glass.

A wave of alert perception filled each of us with smiles—the whole thing was funny—ringing tingling—the waves of activity—opening doors—walking across the room—rustling papers—no sound from the magician—he had had a busy day—everyone wanting curses.

There were these—and now there is none.

And it came about I arranged the first rift between them. He slept while I abducted her—encouraging her to see as I saw. Still she remained reluctant to leave him without explaining why she was leaving. This would have created additional confusion and at that point was to be avoided.

She was finally persuaded against her will to attempt a short trip out— into the country.

I felt considerably relieved about the danger threatening her but was somewhat skeptical of how he could make the adjustment. His rages of anger and perplexity were intermingled so completely I began immediately feeling confident of his basic goodness. Almost sure the evidences of evil I had observed were my own projections. He was extremely humble and began declaring his love for her to everyone. His promises of how he would work only for the future happiness of us all were many and profuse. Life was unthinkable without her—he had done great things in the beginning and would be even greater in the future. He had to have her by his side.

And she returned quickly—more radiant and beautiful than I had ever known her—anxious to forget past behavior and begin working toward a world of miracles—a world filled with magic.

Her eyes had been opened—and as he began slipping back into his demonic habits she was aware and began rebuffing him—until he became desperate and again raised his hands—stamping his feet—snarling and glaring—screaming and threatening. Their lives filled with dissension—and although he called on all his powers, they failed him. He could not submerge her beauty nor detract from her basic innocence.

Soon she began observing new people more intently taking in the scene. He could use all his tricks—he would never again be able to convince her of anything—unless she wanted to believe. Still he retained one powerful hold. She was learning magic and there were still many symbols he could teach her.

He became amazingly ugly in appearance. His smile false—his voice hollow and empty. He was always moving around—never still. He had always been a thief—nothing big—small things—preferably with sentimental value to the owner. One couldn't take him visiting—he was sure to take things. At this point not only was he stealing—but he became possessive about things he wanted, personally accusing everyone of what he himself was guilty. He became a living embodiment of contradictions. He was desperate.

It was much too late. He lost completely what influence he had built up and there was no possibility of establishing anything worthwhile.

It was about this time he hit upon the idea of having me kill him. He wanted death—and what better way to bring it about than to have me cause it?

I had never tangled with him physically other than in brief skirmishes and he knew it would require a great deal of agitation to cause me to become violent but—and this is important—he also knew, brought to the point of violence, I would have practically no control. All I would need would be a knife.

She has been away the last few days and he has been wandering the streets. He is rather to be pitied.

Now he slowly climbs the stairs seeking the end. I have half decided to do it. He'll knock—I'll ask who it is—he'll reply at the same time demanding I open the door—I can open the door—stick him—and it will be done, but this is really too final. I think I have something better—something he will live with the rest of his life. He'll have to find someone else for his dirty work. I have in my hand an eyedropper filled with a slow-acting poison and a hypodermic needle specially dipped in a germ-infested solution containing the hepatitis bug.

Meanwhile the girl and I have recently planned to sail on the Scandinavian ships together. She can become a stewardess and I can take anything. Sounds great.

I'll open the door—I am calm and ready. He isn't sure of what to expect. I can see him as he turns on the last step. His eyes are dull and glazed. His hair stands on end—his clothes are filthy—he is tired. He tries to appear sinister. In one hand he caries a flute and in the other his book of symbols. As he comes closer he begins pleading with his eyes for anything—it doesn't matter what—death—an hour's rest—a change of clothing—I open the door wide—the candle flame dances wildly for a moment—caught in the draft—he enters—and as he turns to look around I plunge the needle into his flesh. His eyes fill with horror—he tries to struggle but I have already thrown a head lock on him—also the dropper is almost empty.

It is over and he sits staring into space. He has cursed me with any curses and all curses.

We are laughing because neither of us, she and I, exist in a reality. We are figments of his imagination. And anyway his imagination has had it and we are moving on to a new environment.

There will be no more black magic from him—he is finished. Already he turns saffron.

I can hear the boat whistles from where I live. On a foggy morning they seemingly call to each other ceaselessly. Some are near and loud and strident. Others pick up the call until finally off in the distance there is only a faint tone barely heard. Sometimes they sound simultaneously. One can pick out the riverboat, the tug—the ocean-going steamers— little boats all talking to each other helping create the opening music of a New York morning.

The whistles are silent tonight.

BEWARE OF FALLEN ANGELS

I REMEMBER THE SCENE FULLY, AM ABLE THIS INSTANT TO SEE BOTH ELISE and Bill vividly—their clothing, their faces, their posture, the particular area wherein the whole distance between them was almost split dead center—the essence of their individual selves meeting at that point and neither would give way. I remember the way of Elise's sitting and the way of Bill's half-crouch, his left buttock resting on the heel of his left foot, the right leg bent downward at the knee, the foot flat on the floor, acting balance to myself to one side in a straight-back chair—watching and listening.

The setting was strangely beautiful. There was a quality of the unreal about it as if perhaps of a new dimension. Color alive and glowing everywhere—reds deep-hued and warm, to faintest pink and flame—blues almost black and shaded thru pale to peacock—yellow—orange—green—violet—umber—mud tones—and clear pure light. Huge squares of heavy drawing paper worked on with blue and red ink—applied by brush in a seemingly casual manner rapidly by Bill—who held chunks of a red and blue jungle from another world which filled the recesses of the front windows. Streamers a foot wide, and of varying lengths from two feet to six feet of a parchment-like material—containing one area after another of every conceivable color, shade, and tone within which faces took shape before the eye—hung like Chinese banners here and there through the two rooms. A huge square of cloth stained in shades of violet and red, spots of palest green, and larger sections of black—the center a large mandala—the rest moving out from it—animal shapes or Tibetan monks standing alone and in groups at prayer or worship—was stretched taut over one wall filling it nearly to capacity. Beneath it on the floor were two mattresses, one on top of the other—spread with an Indian-patterned blanket of light and dark green, and an Afghan shawl of all colors. A set of shelves holding books sat between the two windows at the foot of the bed, while along the wall opposite the hanging, all remained bare but for a small handcarved wooden chest—probably Italian workmanship—holding two or three brass bowls and trays and a photograph of Marcel Marceau in greasepaint and dressed as a sort of harlequin. At the head of the bed beneath one end of the hanging, a large square-shaped portable phonograph (capable of deep tonal and volume control) sat—a record of Middle Eastern teahouse songs on the turntable—the strange notes and increasing tempo electrifying the air with rhythmic vibrations. A brass Buddha sat on a black wood block at one side of the opening between the two rooms. A thin veil of lavender-gray smoke from a clay pot holding incense eddying upward wreathed the head. Next to the pot of incense were two bowls (one wooden, the other copper) holding rocks and colored stones, beads in all colors, several odd-shaped gold-plated figurines, chunks of wood, two or three strips of fur and several phial-shaped bottles with frosted glass stoppers. A book on witchcraft and the Tibetan Book of the Dead had been placed alongside the bowls, and the whole group of objects appeared like offerings upon an altar to a pagan god. It was here that Bill had stationed himself and, half crouching—his hands moving about constantly—reaching toward a bottle of ink the color he wanted at the moment—holding it for a moment before unstoppering it and setting it back on the floor—picking up his flute and placing it to his lips—blowing several sharp notes that cut into the sounds coming from the phonograph—lowering it from his mouth and twisting it in his fingers—touching lightly with his hand the bands of silver wire bound round the body of the flute just above the mouthpiece of a silver ring screwed or forced into the end—replacing it finally where it became another item among his work materials scattered in front of him. Brushes—pens—knives—scraps of wire—bottles bound in colored cloth with seals of sealing wax holding it in place, or silk thread wound around the necks—needles—scraps of paper and cloth—several squares of pastel-hued suede, folded and stacked—a few pieces of rice paper in the process of receiving visual creation—all spread out so he could touch first one, then the other—or splash color on them—or carefully execute a magic symbol in silver or gold paint or heavy black ink on the surface. He was never still—always changing things. He lit a black wax candle and—selecting a fair-sized gray rock—dropped hot wax on the top, and then set the candle in it until it cooled—then moved it next to the Buddha almost behind him. The light from behind gave an effect of seemingly emanating from him, creating an aura of shimmering light around his head. Directly opposite him on the other side of the room stood a huge refrigerator with a large bowl of fruit on top. Periodically some one of the three of us would open the door of this monster in search of food or more often to open the freezer section to take out one of the three bottles of amphetamine solution Bill had placed there after mixing and dissolving it carefully in accordance with his almost ritualistic formula. He had always believed in order for amphetamine to be at its best there was a prescribed way of preparing it—it should be allowed to freeze before it is used. I am inclined to accept his theory as I have never used amphetamine that gave me as much of a lift or was as much pleasure to take. Next to the refrigerator was a straight-back chair with a profusion of clothing draped over the back and piled on the seat—coats, sweaters, scarves, shirts, gloves, and a hat. A table—square in shape—with an India print of a red background which was spread across the top and hanging down on all four sides almost to the floor—occupied the space next to the chair—the surface a conglomerate collection of cups, spoons, ashtrays, saucers, salt and pepper shakers, matches, cigarettes, burning candles—one was in a tall thin brass holder, and another was stuck in the top of a wine bottle, the sides thick with melted wax drippings. A book of poetry was opened and placed face down, here and there were spools of brightly colored silk thread, a small pair of scissors, innumerable small containers of pins, needles, and small objects of all kinds. At an angle facing the table yet able to observe the entire scene without changing position sat Elise—her long black hair loose and falling down her back to her waist—a faded blue shirt, open at the throat, pulled tight over her full breasts and blue jeans—without shoes—one leg stretched straight in front of her, the foot just reaching the edge of the table cover, which she was playing with by idly moving her toes—the other leg was raised and the foot rested on the edge of the round basket-like chair. Occasionally she would bend her body forward and rest her chin on her knee. She was smoking chain fashion, lighting each new cigarette in the corner of her mouth and letting it stay while she stroked her leg with her hand or perhaps searched through the stuff on the table for something she wanted at the moment. She was in a highly tense state and was angry with Bill. Now and then she would feel around beneath an orange-colored cushion covering the seat of the chair in which we sat until she located a small envelope containing pot which she would bring out and pass it to me in order to roll a stick or joint. Immediately above her head on the wall hung a large Japanese print of some god of children—the composition done in delicate strokes of the artist's brush. On the same wall were two very delightful drawings done in watercolor by Lafcadio Orlovsky—one depicting a carnival scene and the other a sort of cubistic pattern of triangular color forms. Across from her I sat with my back to the door—separated from Bill by a desk stacked with books, papers, portfolios, pencils, pens, a letter opener, paper clips, Scotch tape, paste and glue, notebooks, letters opened and unopened, and a red clay flower pot in which grew a tall avocado plant rather gracefully—the stem bare of leaves except near the top where there existed only a few but in sufficient number to cause a bending of the stem in such a way it appeared to resemble the pose of a dancer.

We all three had been together without interruption for at least five hours and it was now well into the early hours of morning. A strange sense of the mystical lay like a patina over our efforts to communicate. We were aware of each other separately yet always collectively in a manner of telepathic consciousness. The very air seemed vibrant with electrical particles. Two related and at the same time divergent viewpoints had become focal centers for energetic discharges of thought. In some instances, they were assembled with minute attention to detail and balance of rationalization and frequency unleashed at the instant of conception. Bill believed in the power of magic and of the Phoenix Bird always arising from the holocaust of flaming destruction—thusly did God accept all things, including the dark forces, and saint or sinner, devil or angel were the same. Buddha could lead one closer to the God force than anything known by Western concept. Sweetness, delicacy, innocence, girl and boy, poetry, home, and personal possessions were abhorrent and had to be sacrificed to action and creativeness, and if all crumbled around one—leaving one exposed, torn, hungry, homeless—then this was a cleansing and a setting-free and it meant nothing. One imagined personal suffering and should be glad of the opportunity to aid creativity. Magic was his tool, and he would use it to help him create no matter who or what was destroyed in the process. Elise held other beliefs to be true and strongly resented the evil she felt was the very life blood of Bill. She refused to see him—to look at his work—to accept the magic to be trusted and did not believe it to be true. At best he was a charlatan and unworthy of respect. Hers was a God of wrath and there were saints and sinners, devils and angels, and they were all around us. She was a Jew and no one other than a Jew could understand her. There was no meeting of the mind, spiritually or physically, being possible between them. His words meant nothing—he used them only to try and cast a spell—he wished only to bring harm and pain—his desires were base, and smacked of the bestial. She loathed him and wanted him to leave. He was only a dabbler, and as for beauty in his work, she could not see it, finding it irritating and vulgar. She did not fear his power and she had no desire to use his amphetamine because it was an evil drug destined to cause a knife between the ribs as a final result of steady use between any two or, for that matter, group of people. He might mix his solutions so they become crystal clear—pour them into bottles of pale blue, lavender, or green—clear glass or frosted—drop as many pebbles and precious stones to rest at the bottom as he chose—it was not a magic elixir. She moved about in the chair; both legs rested on the floor. Her hands were clasped in front of her—her elbows resting on her knees, her face turning full gaze upon Bill—a swift glance toward me and then darting here and there around the scene—then back to Bill and her eyes brown and sad and burning.

Bill returned her look for a moment and then began moving objects within reach from one place to another—his head twisting side to side—and his eyes darting about. Finally, he picked up his flute and began blowing several test notes—his fingers moving and pressing over the openings of the sound or note control locations—suddenly hitting a sharp, angry tone—blasting it out; it was shrill and piercing—full of complaint—almost hate. He stood up and reached for the refrigerator door, opened it, reached in and removed a dark blue bottle, then turned around saying, "I'm going to shoot up. Where are the works? I can't find my works." He put the bottle down on the floor as he started moving around, here and then into the next room, poking behind the books, feeling along the edges of the mattress—rounding suddenly and pawing around the back of the chest. He pushed the bowl aside, lifting the Marceau photograph and muttering under his breath, saying once out loud, "There's something wrong. Somebody is against me—where are my works? I put them down, and they aren't where I put them," and glared toward the wall—shifting to the Buddha, to me, to Elise, to the table top, the desk, the floor. He gradually paced across the full length of the two rooms, stopping in front of the stack of suede pieces, reached down—and there were the works. He removed the stopper of the blue bottle, squeezed the pacifier on the end of his dropper sending air and drawing it back through the needle, and—satisfied all was in working order—he squeezed once again—and holding it compressed set the end with the needle down into the bottle—and let go. Slowly, the crystal-clear amphetamine solution filled the dropper until, when it was a little more than three-quarters full, Bill removed it—and after holding it a minute looked at me and said, "You want it first?" I had been waiting to take off again—not because I was down—but because I wanted to try and get higher and wanted to shoot up as soon as possible. I reached for the fix, dug out a square red bandanna from a pocket, twisted it into a sort of rolled length and wrapped it around my arm as a sort of tie or tourniquet. I tucked the end in so it would hold and, holding my arm up, looked for a spot to hit. My veins have never collapsed permanently, and although there is scar tissue over the area of my tracks, I still have all kinds of spots I can hit without difficulty. I closed my fist, opened it, closed it several times and the veins of my arms stood out plainly. I picked one in the center of my forearm, rested and adjusted my elbow until I obtained a balance, and then, hovering the point over the spot, began pressing and tapping it into the skin and toward the vein—touching it—and (with good luck) the vein had been penetrated. Blood seeped up into the needle—into the dropper—forcing the solution to slowly rise. I was satisfied I had made a hit and, again squeezing the top, sent the blood back and the amphets into the vein. I felt it almost instantly— the rush to the head like a short circuit. My body began to pulsate or grow tiny antennae all quivering in anticipation—and my aliveness took on new substance and was alerted to the waves of energetic forces sweeping around me. My personal force developed an awareness and it was as though I would receive communication at telepathic level. The surroundings—already capable of absorbing force—drive, spirit, and the flow of magic—sensed—almost felt—never seen—only the results of utilization had been conducive to all the nuances—or many. I was thoroughly elated. Finishing, briefly washing the works, I handed them to Bill. He went thru much the same procedure of drawing up the stuff— the tie-up—and the actual shooting. He could absorb a large amount at one time—mainline—and turn on in a flash. He started doing his work.

Elise had sat through the scene without comment. I asked her to turn on, but she refused. She was playing with a handful of small items—two gold-plated lead figures of Indian or Tibetan gods, a neatly patterned brass wire ornament found in the street, several rings of silver and turquoise and lapis lazuli shaped or cut like an Indian scarab. Her eyes had become dream filled, and when she emptied her hands into a lacquer tea box, the many small trinkets (stones, unset jewels, and strange objects) sort of clattered into the box. The box was hers, and she didn't want Bill to touch it. He offered her a shot of amphetamine and she refused. She turned on once in a while; preferred Dilaudid, Nembutal, seccies, any of the barbiturates and, most of all, heroin. She was stimulated by amphets but didn't like the agitation and storm within oneself she had to contend with and it was only seldom she would take amphets.

Elise and Janine were sharing the expenses of rent, etc., on the apartment. Janine came and went as she desired. She spent most of her time with Peter and Allen but mostly with Peter. Peter and Allen were almost ready to sail for India—there were three nights remaining; and then they would be gone. Janine had met Bill and was fascinated. She has seen him once or twice previously—once taking off with him. This was three nights before Peter was to leave, and supposedly they were together when, unexpectedly, the door swung open and in she walked. She smiled at everyone and said hello. She said, "I'm going to see Peter later—he and Allen are visiting friends. I want a little amphetamine, Bill, please." Bill fixed a dropper and gave it to her. She turned to me, asking me if I would perform the task for her. I said yes.

Both Elise and myself were pleased with Janine's presence. Once I looked up to observe what seemed to me to be a rather speculative smile and glance on Bill's face as he allowed his eyes to rove over the scene and rest a while on Janine. Perhaps in that moment he felt or knew they were doomed but had to come on—had to make a disgusting display of himself at complete cost of the night's opportunity—had to eventually make it an experience great and one to remember. Janine smiled toward Bill—sounding him in some way they rather had between them. Janine was genuinely touched by the genius of Bill. Yet she felt a deep sympathy toward him and a sadness because he was so at the mercy of people's whims, as much as he held in contempt those not his supposed followers, refusing to concede even the slightest degree of his supposed freedom. His was a force both powerful and consuming, and when it surged through his being, his face, his body, and all physical aspects of himself became twisted and tortured, visible to the observer yet denied vehemently and in foulest language. His true beauty lay within—perhaps only his eyes betraying what that might be—until he began creating, when his movements became fascinating to watch—his verbal outbursts, partially incantations that were melodious to the ear with an air of the mystic and magical—and one could easily be caught in the spell until at the last either one of his exquisite hangings lay open before you—rich in color and design—or his paintings—or carvings—or whatever—and you knew—because you had seen with your own eyes—these were not the results of contrived effort but instead had sprung from the inner being leaping out through his finger tips. Janine wanted to know him—to see him, to listen to him, to learn at least some of his magic. She opened to him and he responded—both naturally and with speculative forethought. He could certainly dig her—if she was at all sensitive—and he was inclined to consider her a somewhat spoiled child hardly aware of anything but beauty to see; and then, she just might be able to set him up fairly permanently financially. He was aware enough of her circumstances to feel confident she was due to be completely free in a short time when Peter and Allen sailed for India. He had been attracted first by Elise— not only because of her strange beauty but also because she was a challenge. Still, Janine was fantastically beautiful in many ways and he was sure she lacked strength and that he could swallow her whole. He had failed to accept one very important feature of her personality—she simply could not lie. It was impossible for her to try. Nor was she in any way a conniver unless (as it happened occasionally) she had to try and keep things going—that is—keep a place where he and his followers could work and ball. But in the beginning she still believed it possible to talk straight and be answered accordingly.

Sitting to one side, always stoned, my whole self was imbued with all that was happening around—the scene, the people, and many many layers of consciousness just awakened. I watched Bill and Elise, Bill and Janine, Elise, Janine, Bill—and I was unable to understand the overwhelming goodness and the almost devastating evidence of possible evil. Ethically speaking, it was my responsibility to remove or at least try to remove Bill from the premises. Elise did not want him there. Elise and Janine had been sharing the apartment and Bill was obviously a threat to so neat an arrangement. Elise surely loved Janine and, regardless of the circumstances, did not want to see her harmed. Of course some of the statements about a sorry end, etc., were (even were they to happen) hardly worth the mentioning. And also (which is of utmost importance) she had absolutely no right to interfere—at least till such time as Janine called for help. And even then, there is the problem of who has any right to try and alter deliberately what there is with any two people. True, it is unpleasant to see a woman knocked down—her eyes blackened and so forth—but in most cases, I've discovered that the woman is as guilty as the man. Elise—beautiful Elise—knew it was pointless speaking directly to Janine. Janine would continue to do exactly according to her dictates.

And I did not fear for her. Still, I did not want to run the risk of being alone—not because my loneliness bothers me, but mostly because I respected Janine's decisions—knowing full well that she had a clear picture of what she was searching for. And were I to come on as though I failed to believe in her, she surely would have withdrawn—and, in all probability, entirely.

Elise spoke to Janine, inquiring of Allen (whom she truly loves) and Peter, and suggesting Janine not take any amphets. Janine answered her question concerning Allen and Peter—but told her it was none of her fucking business if she, Janine, shot up all the amphets in the world. She had taken most of her clothing off and tossed it in a heap—left the room for a small bathroom to one side of the room we were all in—and began filling the tub with water.

Things seemingly became a bit tenser. Elise shifted positions—spoke with Janine several times, and maybe Bill. I'd rather drawn attention to myself, attempting to reach everyone at some point or another. Janine at some moment turned to me and half inquired, "Amphetamine is good—isn't it, Huncke?" I am sure I didn't give her an honest answer—maybe not dishonest—the truth being that statements and questions declaring me as the authority—the undisputed one of knowledge so "he" must be accepted as having the final say—always leaves me in a quandary. Fuck it. I did mouth some kind of an answer. And besides, Janine liked amphets. Also (and of some importance) she didn't want too much push from the outside. She preferred her own means of obtaining her answers. She possessed curiosity concerning living and wanted to search on her own—I was honored she trusted me.

At any rate—one goes back—in a sense—to the original plan of trying to tell a story and finishing it in a concise ending.

I know Elise did not like Bill. This is not true—she was ambivalently attracted, yet at the time of making a statement, it was of the evil lurking around. She was annoyed by Bill's interest in Janine and warned Janine that he would bring only harm. Janine did not concern her behavior with the result of what she was doing. Bill had claimed an awareness of magic—a familiarity with witchcraft—he could teach and prove his point.

Elise got up, walked over to the bed and flopped down. Charlie Parker was blowing. Bill had started another hanging. I had moved over to the table while Janine sat opposite in the chair Elise had vacated. She was waiting for the tub to fill. Bill joined us for a few minutes as we all three picked up on a jolt of amphets. We all enjoyed the action and Janine was interested in all that was happening around. Bill spoke with her and she seemed pleased and asked questions of her own. He answered by discussion and his creativeness—incantations (permitting observation) not recognizable as incantations—thinking perhaps there might be association of the idea of magic—but certainly his only words were of his belief in magic. Janine watched and listened. The tub was full and she stepped behind the door, disrobed and sat in the tub, her movements and splashing audible. Bill put down his work and picked up his flute, walked over and stepped inside near Janine. I know little of their talk, their attitude toward each other, or how they looked at one another— but Bill taught Janine breathing exercises for long periods of submersion in water—breath control. Toward the last, they called me in to join them. I heard Bill say to Janine, "He has paranoia—he thinks I have hurt you." I was confused, and at the same time it was of almost no significance. Any importance credited was a waste. It was debased of me to have feared for Janine or wondered about her actions. I went in and Janine was radiant—freshly bathed and still in the tub sitting modestly— her long blond hair let down. She looked at me a moment, her eyes huge and straining to see all she could—half-smiling, momentarily drawing one hand thru the water and then back again—then speaking, said, "Sit down. Bill has been showing me breathing. You are not worried, are you? How is Elise?"

Bill was squatting by the tub fingering his flute—a sort of half grin was on his face—filling his eye with Janine and making friendly acknowledgments of my being there.

There were two candles burning—one on top of a set of drawers that reached above the tub and the other stuck on the edge of the tub.

I sat for a moment or two feeling all is well—it won't matter if I leave for a while. I spoke of probably going out—a walk maybe—or simply to snoop about—maybe, if lucky, cop a bag of pot. At any rate, I'd cut by Jerry's and if I'd see him, all would be well—we could turn on. We had all been smoking off and on through the day and night—it would be great if we continued. We all three jived for a few seconds—and I departed.

PONDEROSA PINE

YOU SPEAK OF PONDEROSA PINE AND I AM CATAPULTED BACK—OH, WAY back—and it is late summer outside Potlatch, Idaho. It is sunset—the sky riven with saffron—ice green—lavender—and changing pinks from flamingo to palest hue, overlaid with haunting black cloud shapes. The road is yellow dirt and sand packed down and spread with rough-cut white stone and gravel. It twists through the cluster of gray clapboard houses—past a railroad track—a train of flatcars loaded with massive tree trunks fresh cut from the vast forests covering the hills for miles and miles around—too huge for the sawmill—a painted red frame building on the edge of the community—where many of the town's people work—the others employed mostly in the forests—axing—cutting—felling—hauling the great majestic trees—the countryside reverberating all day with the agonizing thuds of their crashing death—and we are in an open Model T Ford and we pass the sawmill—the general store—a beer parlor—where on several occasions just before the time I am speaking of I have gotten drunk downing the frothy pitchers of ice-cold beer brought to the table by a dark-haired bar maid—wise in the ways of a beer parlor in a lumber town—able to laugh and toss joke for joke with the red-faced heavy-bodied lumberjacks—still wearing their caulked boots—I once saw two of them in a fight—and when one had fallen—the other stomped on his face in a fury until the face looked like a hunk of raw beef when he was finally rescued—and red and black—green and black—orange and black—blue and black checked shirts—and all of this in a flash in my mind as the road rounds the last of the houses—the evening darkening blue-black in the distance, bedizened with the lights of thousands upon thousands of cosmic worlds, the stars and planets. The road now heads into the forests—only the tops of the great trees still visible individually—seemingly brushing the sky—all below a great mass of blackness, the headlights penetrating the mass—revealing brown tree trunks on either side and green foliage—the limbs of the trees begin too high up for us to see them. My companion is a young Norwegian boy—seventeen—the son of one of the foresters at the ranger station near Potlatch. It is his father's job along with two or three others to keep up on the maintenance of the fire towers—to patrol the area and keep weather reports. The father has made this his life work and is a good but stern man who has raised his son—he hopes—to follow in his footsteps. The son is extremely proud of his father and in all probability will do as his father desires. When he returns from this little excursion or trip he has invited me to accompany him on—I had wandered up into that part of the country several weeks prior and had asked if they had some work I could do around the ranger station and they said yes—and I stayed until leaving on this trip which was to take us over into Montana to visit relatives—a cousin or uncle—if I remember correctly of my traveling companion—he will be ready to enter agriculture college at Moscow, Idaho. He is not very talkative and I sit back drinking in the heady aroma of the pine forest almost intoxicated by the richness of the beauty of the night.

We drive steadily through the night—stopping once in a small town at a lunch room for great steaming mugs of coffee and thick sandwiches of ham and cheese and homemade blackberry pie—then on—spelling each other at the wheel—the road always winding and twisting—alongside rushing streams for several miles up into the hills—past ravines and valleys—once up the side of a mountain—the road zigzagging all the way up and then all the way down the opposite side. Once in a while we hit stretches of pavement but for the most part the road remained dirt and gravel.

Dawn found us not far from the town of Kellogg, Idaho—a good-sized town where we stopped and freshened up in cold spring water—checked the condition of our car—drank coffee—discussed our further route. It was decided we drive through the Coeur d'Alene country and around the Coeur d'Alene lake, after which we would pick up a highway leading over and through mountain ranges into Montana.

The topography had changed and we now hit stretches of flat open country with mountains way off in the distance. Huge rocks and boulders lay profusely in all directions. The soil was full of rocks and there were only a few gnarled and twisted live oak trees to be seen instead of the lush green forests. We arrived in Coeur d'Alene—drove thru and picked up a road following the shore of the lake—brilliant blue and clear—the shoreline ragged and stony—short windblown and twisted trees leaning toward their reflections in the water. A wind had sprung up and massive cloud formations plowed across the blue sky. The water of the lake became choppy—the surface agitated with small rolling white caps. The scene was magnificent and awe inspiring—beautiful and cold and real. I filled myself with it and can at this instant not only see it all vividly but smell the freshness of air—and hear the whistling of the wind.

We eventually reached the end of this wonderful stretch of earth and water—coming down off the lake road on to a paved highway leading directly into the mountains to be crossed into Montana. We began climbing—higher and higher—until our engine was heated and we were carrying a banner of white steam smoke from the radiator cap at the front of the car. Halfway up we came upon a small place at the side of the road where we pulled in to rest awhile. Near was a fresh mountain stream rushing downward where we filled cans and poured them into our hot and thirsty car.

The weather had begun to change and to one side of us and, back over the jutting angry-looking peaks of the seemingly endless chain of mountains, we could see rolling gray and black clouds constantly illuminated by flashes of lightning and accompanied by reverberating rumbles of thunder relentlessly bearing down on us.

Once again we began the ascent—slowly crawling toward the top. We had no means of protection against the storm—there was no top for the car—and when it hit there would be nothing to do but let it drive down on us.

Gradually we reached the top and looking back could see the black rain curtain—feel the oncoming rush of rain-laden wind. At the top of the mountain was a short distance of straight road bound on either side with fairly dense growth of tall and at this time writhing trees. As we started to drive this respite of straight terrain—high up above the world—near the lowering, furiously rolling clouds, the full force of the storm struck and we could go no further. We pulled over a little onto the shoulder of the road and stopped.

The wind a mass of heavy raindrops relentlessly tore at us as though infuriated at not being able to lift us from our spot and fling us crashing into the heavy gray boulders just ahead—abating an instant and then with renewed vigor attacking our flimsy little car—shaking and rocking it with the fury and force of its anger. Long jagged sulfurous bolts of lightning drove with full force into the ground around us filling our nostrils with the smell of burning ozone. Thunder crashed deafeningly down and around our heads and all the earth trembled. The roadway became a rushing flow of water—a tree was struck—and split in a great screech, the top half falling toward the ground pulling the wound open further, the life of the tree no longer protesting. With this sacrifice to the greed of the storm, it began to slacken, passing on over—only occasional flashes of lightning, and instead of crashing thunder there were only low rumblings becoming fainter in the distance. The rain had ceased altogether—the clouds began clearing away and soon the sun—bright and warming—appeared.

We of course were thoroughly drenched and, what was worse, unable to start the car. We worked with it—checking the motor—cranking—but all to no avail. It was utterly impossible to get it moving. Finally we hailed a passing car and asked for a tow to the first filling station. The people—a man and his wife—were accommodating and towed us down to a station on the other side of the mountain in Montana. There we discovered all was lost—not only were things flooded but completely burned out—the Model T had had it—it would carry us no further.

My friend was very disappointed but decided it best to call his father. He called and his father said we were to stay near our present location—the boy's mother would pick us up in the family car the following day.

We stayed in a motel not far from where we had made the call. He was very disappointed with the entire experience and failed to share my enthusiastic impression of the storm—nor was he impressed by what I considered the wild, almost breathtaking beauty of the lake and the forests we had driven thru—saying at one point he supposed they did have beauty but in his opinion they were just a lake and a forest—and a forest was a forest no matter what one said about it—and yes the storm was sort of exciting but he would rather have his Model T working—after all he'd earned the money to pay for it and now it was just a loss.

His mother arrived the next afternoon and we drove straight back to the ranger station near Potlatch.

I guess he had decided I wasn't a very stable kind of person because—although I remained several days at the station before leaving to go head back home—he never came around to say hello, and once or twice his father—who had always in our short acquaintance been friendly and considerate—was somewhat sharp in his replies to questions I asked him.

Anyhow—you spoke of Ponderosa Pine—and this was Ponderosa Pine country—and I remember it all clearly. Of course there was Tamarack and yellow pine and white pine—but Ponderosa is a beautiful name—and maybe—just maybe—there really wasn't any Ponderosa there at all—but please let it suffice—of the other three—white and yellow and Tamarack I am sure—and somewhere in the past I've been around Ponderosa country—of that you may be confident. It is only that I am a little forgetful these days just where all the things I've been around or near are located.

I wouldn't have bothered with further explanations except—I dislike being caught in an outright lie—and it is just possible Ponderosa Pine is strictly native of California and it would be most embarrassing to hear this—after having given it root—in a manner of speaking—in wild rugged Idaho. And at this point—that is right this moment that will already be of the past—when you hear of it—or read of it—I sincerely believe that by now Ponderosa Pine must thrive in Idaho—and if it wasn't there when I was there—someone planted it there, and in no time it began to flourish.

The forests of Idaho are or at least were truly wild and beautiful. The great tall trees reaching to the sky and on the stillest days—with hardly a breeze stirring near the earth—one hears the whishing of the tree tops way up high enough to always feel the wind. And at their feet—wild flowers—ferns—flowing streams—berry bushes and morning glory vines. Sometimes—of course—they have grown very close together in groves like clusters on the side of the mountains—and no sun has penetrated down through to the earth—there are only blankets of dark brown needles sere and dry.

There is wildlife—deer and bear—pheasant and grouse—rabbit and squirrels—there are only non-poisonous snakes—and many kinds of birds.

As I said before it is surely Ponderosa Pine country—and if anyone asks you to visit Idaho, please make sure you don't refuse—and if I am around still, please, please see if you can swing an invitation for me as well. Every now and then it all comes back to me in a rush and—strange as it may sound coming from an old drug-soaked city character like myself—I long to see all I have spoken and much I've left unsaid again. Perhaps my most carefree hours were spent there—and maybe it is impossible to recapture any of it—but I sure as hell occasionally long to give it a try.

IN THE PARK

MORNING—EARLY—BREAK OF DAWN—THE SKY CLEAR AND BLUE—THE sun's rays reaching downward through the leaves and boughs of the trees outside our windows and bird calls prominent above the occasional voices of the early risers and the sounds from the stirring around of those just awakening. I have just returned from a long morning walk through the streets of the city. I have always enjoyed walking and much of my life has been spent roving city streets through the hours of darkness. Some of my more welcome memories and recollections have to do with my youth in Chicago and many—many—nights spent wandering through the city streets and parks and along the lakefront, finally resting atop a stone piling perhaps or on a bench watching the sunrise. I had adventures and strange experiences—frequently meeting and becoming involved with other night people. I learned much about sex and about the vast number of people who make up the so-called less desirable element in our American way of life. Haunted people—lonely people— misfits—outcasts—wanderers—those on the skids—drunkards—deviates of all kinds—hustlers of every description—male and female—old people and young people—and they come from every section of the country.

Were I requested to select the strangest—the most unusual—the most vicious—the most dangerous—generally the most outstanding—the saddest—the most frightening—the kindest—the one most in need of love—or the one most apt to give love—I would be completely stymied—and at this point—there are many I have forgotten. There is one who stands out from the rest slightly—perhaps because he was my first encounter with someone who was—according to even extreme comparison with what I had been taught was sane—beyond the limit and undoubtedly very sick and well along toward maniacal. He was unquestionably an excellent example of just what can happen to a human being in a society geared to greed and power where the human element is almost entirely ignored except in lip service to man as an individual—and which remains actively indifferent while spewing forth a constant mounting percentage of the population into the group known as—human waste—which is accounted for by recognizing the tragedy as a sociological hazard to be expected in the best of organized societies.

I was about fourteen when I met him, and although I was conscious of his aloneness it wasn't until considerably many years more were added to my age I realized—with any degree of compassion—the stark horror he himself must have sensed almost constantly regarding his existence.

It was toward dusk of a warm late summer day—walking through a somewhat remote section of the park—thickly wooded and little used by people out near the lakefront—that I first became aware of him. I had left the path that wound around and through the area and was intending to make a shortcut through the trees and bushes to the edge of the lake. I had just pushed through a heavy clump of bushes into a clearer area when I suddenly saw him standing a bit to one side of the trunk of a large tree. He was partially facing toward me and I was rather abruptly halted—mostly because of being surprised by seeing him—he smiled—and said, "Hi." I answered—saying, "Hello—you kind of took me by surprise." While answering I looked at him more carefully—taking in his appearance in detail. He was thin and not much taller than me—with sharp pointed facial features—and though his thin, rather long mouth carried a smile, his eyes—light blue in color—remained cold and hard. His hair was dark blond—almost brown—straight and long—and part of it fell to one side of his face—covering his ear—and as I watched he raised his hand and pushed it back—only to have it again fall down as before. His hands were large—with exceedingly long fingers—and somehow didn't seem to go with the rest of his appearance. He was wearing a white shirt—somewhat soiled and haphazardly tucked into his black trousers. He wore an old pair of badly scuffed brown shoes.

As I began moving—intending to continue on my way—he stepped almost directly in front of me and reached out and took hold of my arm—up near the shoulder—and partly over the muscle. His long hard fingers dug deep into my flesh and as he applied pressure I winced with pain. He had taken me almost unaware and—for a moment—I was as intensely frightened as I have ever been—my entire body seemed suffused with panic. I started to struggle—trying to break away. He exerted more force and for an instant I thought—he is going to kill me. He began speaking to me in an imploring tone—begging me not to get scared—he wasn't going to hurt me—although he could. "See," he said, and he raised one of his hands up toward my face—to show me the gleaming blade of a knife. "I won't hurt you—come on—over this way," he said as he began pulling me along with him toward some tall bushes.

By then my fear and panic had subsided. Somehow seeing him up close had helped dispel some of the fear. He was younger than he had first appeared—probably somewhere in his late twenties—and also he had stirred my curiosity in some fashion.

I can't remember all that transpired in the short distance we covered, but I had started talking and had succeeded in establishing a sort of friendly note into the situation, so that as we reached the bushes he removed his hand from my arm and—although he still carried his knife—he seemed less menacing.

It was still quite light and, although the whole area was filled with shadows, one could see plainly.

We pushed into the bushes—stooping over a bit to avoid being scratched on the face—with me in the lead. There was a clear space in the center and we stopped. It became obvious to me immediately that he had been there before. Lying on the ground was a black jacket folded—and a leather briefcase. He told me to sit down and as I did he squatted down in front of me for a moment, then sank down to a sitting position on the ground—his legs stretched out in front of him. He was in a position where—although he was in front of me—I was facing his side. He fumbled in his pocket and found a couple of cigarettes—one of which he gave me. Putting his knife down somewhere along his side away from me, he located matches and lighted our cigarettes. He allowed himself to lean back a little and drew deeply on his smoke. We had both been quiet while this had taken place and I was a bit startled when he threw his cigarette down suddenly and said, "Look at that—ever see anything like it?"—and he reached down to the fly of his pants—pulled it open—and drew out his cock. It was enormous. "Bet you never saw one that big before," he said as he began slowly masturbating. He was quite right—I had never seen anything—even remotely comparable in size or length—and my thought was that he was some kind of freak of nature and that this was some kind of malformation.

"You're a nice kid," he said. "I think you wouldn't laugh at someone who is different—just because they are different. Here—put your hand on my cock. Just hold it—don't move it—but squeeze—not too hard—just squeeze. I want you to see some pictures."

I reached over and held his cock in my hand—complying with his request. He picked up his briefcase—opened it—and began removing stacks of photographs. He put them down by his side and then—putting the briefcase out of the way—he picked up one of the photographs and showed it to me. It was the picture of a little girl maybe seven or eight years old completely nude. Looking at it more closely, I could see where pencil marks had been drawn around the small mound of her pussy to look like hair. "Ain't she a little doll?" he said. "Do you think I could stick this into her?" And pushing my hand away he grabbed his cock in his hand and furiously jerked it for a minute or two, all the time muttering out statements—about how good it would feel and about it being best and a favor to a girl to get fucked young and especially with a big cock because then—later—no other cock unless bigger could ever hurt her. He threw down the first picture and began picking up one after another—showing them to me. Most were of children and many were of children without clothing. In one there was a little boy and a little girl, and apparently he disliked the idea of the little boy having a penis because he had blotted it out with black ink. There were several of naked women and he described in detail how thrilled they would be if he were to fuck them. Finally he returned to the first picture. This apparently was his favorite and he gazed at it almost tenderly. All the time he had continued playing with himself and now he reached over and began fumbling with me. The whole experience had been unnerving and I hadn't had an erection, but as he opened my trousers and began playing with me I grew excited. He looked at my cock closely—making little comments about my never comparing to him—and that I would never save some little girl from being hurt. He stopped playing with me—telling me to begin jerking myself so he could watch. As I began he applied himself more vigorously to his own masturbation—all the time talking about fucking the little girl. "I got it in her now—oh, it feels good—it's way up in her belly—I've got my big prick in her little tight cunt—it's in up to the balls—oh, it's good—I'm going to come in her—I'm getting ready—oh, I feel it coming—all my hot juice is for her—oh, watch." With that he ejaculated—over and over again— his whole body shaking and quivering—and as he slackened up—he started weeping.

CAT & HIS GIRL

SEVERAL YEARS AGO—WHEN I WAS COMPARATIVELY NEW ON THE SCENE involving most of the people I've come to know since then (and their activities) and when I was still unable to recognize or distinguish who comprised the hardcore group from those similar to myself who had just fallen on the scene, or had been part of it only a short while—I met a very beautiful young girl who, at the time, was one of the people I saw regularly. She was pretty obviously coupled with a cat whose reputation was of a questionable nature insofar as his relationship with women was concerned, and I recall distinctly wondering how it was that anyone as apparently hardened as himself could find the patience to spend time with anyone as completely unskilled in the ways of living in this particular type of environment as the girl. I observed and watched both of them closely. It was soon evident that his interest was at best superficial and—instead of possessing any deep regard for her—he held her in contempt and was merely using her as a means of keeping himself in pocket money—since she always had money that she supposedly obtained from her parents which she promptly turned over to him. They lived in my apartment for a while and I got to know both of them.

Frequently he would disappear for a day or two at a time and she would sit around waiting for him to return—watching and listening to the innumerable other people who were either permanent residents of the place or who came and went constantly. Most of these people were engaged in some creative endeavor or another and possessed, in most instances, a full-scale temperamental nature usually associated with the idea of the typical artist which they seldom made an effort to curb or control, and I remember thinking she was amazingly calm and seemingly undisturbed by the constant flare-ups of temper and erratic behavior of her acquaintances—especially if (as I suspected) she came from the ordinary middle-class background of present-day society. Much of what was happening was certainly unconventional and extreme and I couldn't help but wonder at her not being obviously shocked. But if she was surprised ever, she succeeded in effectively keeping it to herself, never in my presence revealing the slightest degree of anything being other than what she had been accustomed to most of her life. Her personal conduct remained shy and unassuming—retaining always evidence of nothing more than what one might expect from any ordinary, conventionally raised young girl.

Her appearance was striking mostly because of her very vivid coloring. Her facial features were very finely molded and impressed one with their delicacy of line. Her eyes were a deep rich brown—a trifle sad in expression. Her hair was a rich chestnut brown—slightly unruly and falling to her shoulders in length and accentuating the cameo quality of her face. Her skin was very pale except for her cheeks which were always slightly flushed and tinged with pink. Her mouth was full-shaped and red. She seldom smiled but when she did—her whole face lit up and one felt one's self gladdened just seeing her. She was not very tall and although at first glance seemed thin, was in fact full-figured with rather large breasts and well-rounded hips. She had long legs—beautifully shaped— and was perhaps a bit vain about them, because one of the few times I saw her lose her composure was when she discovered a run in her stocking and refused to leave until someone got her a new pair.

Occasionally we would find ourselves alone in the apartment and it was then I got to know her a little better and began taking a personal interest in her. Prior to the first time we talked together I had accepted her along with the rest of the scene as charming to look at but hardly anyone I might become more intimately involved with. There were any number of beautiful girls around, and besides, I didn't much care for the cat she was making it with and therefore, other than observing her, I had made no effort to get to know her.

The first time we spoke, we had been alone in the apartment about an hour and I was busy straightening and sorting a stack of drawings that someone had done and left in a pile and scattered about my room. She approached me hesitantly and asked me for a cigarette. I gave her one— extracting one from the package for myself—and as I was lighting it she leaned over and took a light also, then drew back and said, "I think I like you. You don't seem mean and selfish like most of the others around here. Tell me, do you like Gore, the fellow I'm with?" I was a bit startled

by her directness and since I didn't care much for Gore, hesitated a moment before replying. She noticed my hesitancy and spoke again saying,
"I don't think you do like him. I've noticed you seldom speak to him."

"No, I don't," I said. "Frankly, I don't think I trust him—not that
he has done anything to me personally—but somehow there is something about the manner in which he speaks to people that makes me feel
he is false."

She sort of bobbed her head up and down in agreement as I was
speaking, and when I had finished she said, "That is how I feel, also. I
don't know exactly how I became involved with him and I want to get
away from him—but I like all these people and this place. It is a new
experience for me. You see, my mother and father think I am insane.
They have had me locked up twice. The last time, I ran away and they
caught me and I had to go back and now I am out on probation. My
parents hate me and I hate them and I am willing to do almost anything
to get away from them. When I was twelve—I'm almost seventeen
now—they caught me having sex with a neighbor boy and they raised
a lot of hell. My mother said I was depraved and my father called me
whore and beat me and I fought him with a knife and he was cut. Now
they don't leave me alone one minute and I have to sneak out of the
house, and when I do I stay away for days and they look for me. They
have reported me to the probation officer and—when they catch me—
I'll have to go back into the hospital again. They give me money and
sometimes I steal it from my mother's cash box or my father's pockets.
Gore wants money and I can't get him any right now. He said I should
try turning tricks and maybe I will." She had said all this in a rush and
sat looking at me as though she expected me to immediately solve all
her problems. I was startled by her sudden outburst and her story had
made me sad. There was nothing I could say or do to reassure her and
perhaps help her. I did suggest she think about tricking a little longer
before trying it—telling her she should wait and—if she was going to do
anything of that nature—she would be wiser to wait until she found
someone else to make it with and I was sure Gore would only cause her
pain and unhappiness.

After that, she remained around the place a few more days and then
disappeared. I asked Gore about her and he said she was a dumb broad
and had probably been sent back to the hospital and he hoped to fuck
he'd never see her again.

Several months passed and one day, walking on Avenue C, I ran into her. She was looking very well and seemed glad to see me. We sat in a little restaurant and drank coffee and talked. She said she had gone back but was out again and had met some other cat whom she liked and who she guessed liked her although there wasn't love between them. She was happier than she had been. She said she had turned on junk several times and liked it. She had apparently managed to come to some agreement with her parents and she was now allowed more freedom of action. From then on we would occasionally meet and she kept me posted concerning events in her life. Once or twice she had obviously been straight on schmeck and once she asked me to cop for her. And then one day she met me and told me she had fallen in love. He was a spade cat and beautiful, she said. I wished her well and said I'd like to meet the cat.

I didn't see her again for almost six months, and when I did, I was unprepared for the extreme change in her whole personality. She had grown sharp and somewhat hard. She had changed her hairstyle and was wearing more makeup. She said she was tricking regularly and doing very well. She had a habit and wanted me to cop for herself and her old man. I copped for her and we made a meet for later when she would have some more bread and I could cop for her again.

From then on, I saw her steadily, and although I heard of her lover from others and from her, I never met him. Then again she disappeared—and that was the last I saw of her until about six months ago. Again she was taking junk but this time alone. She and her old man had parted. She had grown visibly older and was seemingly reconciled to her loneliness.

Meanwhile, I had met her ex-lover. I had heard that he was a mean cat and had treated her badly, so I was a bit reluctant about developing his acquaintance. But gradually, after we had become better acquainted, I liked him. He is quite handsome and has never given me cause to mistrust him. We have never become close friends but I have learned to respect him over many others.

We had never spoken for any length of time until the other night—when he began speaking about how they had first met and how deeply in love he had fallen with her.

"You know, man," he said, "I really wanted to make a go of it with her. I guess it was mostly her family that messed us up. In the beginning, we both had jobs and were getting along really great until her father discovered I am a Negro. Man—he really came on—at one point saying, 'I know how to handle niggers.' He took her home, and as soon as she could, she ran away and came back. From then on we stayed more or less in hiding. She had become disgusted and started going out on dates some girl she knew would arrange for her. She began making money and would come home sometimes with two and three hundred dollars. Whether you can believe this or not, I have always disliked the idea of a chick hustling or of my living off the bread she'd bring in. But at the time, there seemed to me nothing else to do. Anyway, our lives became hectic—we were using junk, and twice she ODed and I thought I'd lost her. We had managed to avoid her parents for a while but they had hired detectives, and one Sunday afternoon, they came in on us and she was dragged home. Again, the same routine took place—she came back, we hid, she hustled, and we shot junk. By this time, we were beginning to get on each other's nerves and our little affair was strictly on the skids. At one point, we thought maybe if we could get married, we still could make it. I called her mother and father and made an appointment to see them. I kept the appointment and talked to them, asked them to let us get married. Her father almost had a stroke and swore he would see her dead before he'd allow her to marry any black-assed son of a bitch. There was nothing to do but accept the situation as it stood, but we both knew it was almost over. Finally one day, during one of the panics, about two hours after she had left on her dates, I got a call from Harlem Hospital— she had been rushed to the emergency ward after being severely beaten and found unconscious, but was doing all right and wanted me to come and pick her up. She had been worked over badly and her face was almost frightening to see. I took her home with me, and during the four or five days of her recovery we decided to call it quits. And that was that. Once in a while we run into each other, and she is doing OK but somehow she has changed. She stays high most of the time and makes it first with one, then another. All she really wanted was love but I guess it is the one thing she is least apt to ever get."

I had listened to him quietly, and when he was finished I could only think of how tragic the story was and of the vast amount of stupidity and cruelty inflicted on the two of them and how little chance she ever had of discovering any kind of happiness.

January 19, 1965

AM COMPLETELY EXHAUSTED FOLLOWING LAST NIGHT—THE FINAL HOURS of the early morning spent alone—Freddie Herko's pad—now almost entirely denuded not even a candle stub for light—only the glow from the lights outside—all in shadowy darkness—haunted with Freddie's spirit—benevolent and kind—but restless—faint rustlings in the other room—strange dark shapes—huge one instant—smaller the next—some smooth and silky to the touch—others furry and slightly coarse.

Mirror shards and scraps of cloth—old pieces of wood—a lovely knee-high table—black lacquered—an old couch spring—bits of writing on the walls—one in particular—referring to the brightness of the sun—can't recall the full quote—names—strange designs—symbols triangular and circular—wooden boxes—pots and pans and weather sticks—an old chair and a full-length door frame—and strange kitchen utensils.

Gone the bits of gold mesh and jeweled trinkets—the box of photographs of male body builders—partially finished collages—the lengths of draped black net—white lace—and the drapes of blue and wine red—the pots of growing plants—the strange bells and bright-colored squares of oddly patterned cloth—the cinder blocks—brass pots and pitchers and the magic and beautiful profusion of feathers and stones and sticks and jewels—beads and chains.

No touch of Freddie or Debbie left—only their restless spirits. And the floor is white and—if one closes one's eyes—Freddie bounds across the full length of the room—waves his bejeweled scepter and in stately grace—her hair falling free around her shoulders—swath of black crepe wrapped about her lovely form—falling to the floor in gathered folds—a goddess to kneel before in loveworship—Debbie steps forward—her arms flung wide—and for the instant the palest blue flame illuminates the room—and one's being receives unencumbered the power and love—known alone in purity and life—not as we know it but in the fullness of the infinite—enters our very souls and the flame flickers out—

as we absorb the infinitesimal change—our spirits—never again to be the same—closer the great surging burning force of joy—beauty and reality—and we have known magic—only alas—to have our tongues trip over the word—our eyes look downward—and all but a few of those we tell remain skeptical.

November 1964

FAERY TALE

ONCE UPON A TIME THERE WERE THREE GIRLS SITTING IN A ROOM WITH three men. There was something one sensed as enchanted about the girls—one was very young and she wore a beautiful headdress made of soft silk—rich with delicately patterned outlines in rich brilliant shades of blue—and she wore a gown of simple lines made of linen—and tiny kid slippers with mosaic-like cutouts near the tips of the toes and they may have been of Moroccan origin. Her eyes were dark brown and sparkled with hidden light. Her laughter was gay and musical. And one of the girls was tall and thin with long blue-black hair which fell down around her shoulders and she wore black ballet tights and a white silk shirt and leather sandals upon her feet. Her eyes were dark brown and brooding and her laughter was hesitant and sometimes sad. She was not as beautiful as the very young girl—but she was beautiful.

The last girl was the strangest of the three and the oldest. Her hair was brown and in curls all around her face. She was a small girl and plain. Sometimes her laughter was shrill and sometimes low and indistinct. Her eyes were brown and very sad. She was very quiet and lay upon a couch curled up in a small ball and watched everyone.

Two of the men were young. The third man was old—very old.

One of the young men was tall and thin and when he walked he swayed slightly from side to side as though caught in a cross current of gently blowing wind. He had many colored sticks in his hand and he would select one with his other hand, and swinging his arm and hand downward he would touch the stick to the surface of a large square of blinding white paper, and moving his hand first in a sweeping arc—and then in a slow straight stroke or in tiny spasmodic jerks—he drew with his colored stick upon the white paper and soon a picture appeared. And the girls were delighted when they saw it and exclaimed at the strange design and the bright color. And he smiled saying, "This is a magic picture."

Thereupon the other young man spoke and said, "Magic picture indeed. Nothing great about that—all pictures are magic pictures—if one knows what to look for." He plunged his hand in his pocket—fumbled inside the pocket a moment or two—and withdrew his hand. Holding his hand forward for all to see—he opened his fingers slowly—and lying in the palm of his hand was a little pile of green herb of some kind. "I will show you some magic," he said. He removed a small pipe from his other pocket and carefully poured the little pile of green herbs into the bowl of the pipe. First he tamped it down and then he struck a match and—holding the flame close to the green herbs—he drew a deep breath through the pipe and ignited the green herbs and the air was suddenly filled with a pungent odor—like leaves burning in the fall of the year. "This is magic," he said. "Draw deeply several times through the pipe—and soon you will become aware of a new consciousness."

Everyone did as he bid them do—and soon the atmosphere in the room was of another dimension—and everybody said they saw the world in a new way—and they were impressed with this great wonder.

And then the old man brought forth a silver tipped wand and a small package he opened—revealing an amount of glittering crystalline powder he melted and dissolved in water. Dipping the tiny wand into the resultant solution he then pressed the point of the wand into his skin near one of his veins—waited an instant—and then withdrew the point. His eyes became brighter and more alert—he seemed suddenly to be younger and he laughed and looked around the room at each person and said, "Now you have truly witnessed a magical feat. By injecting a little of that clean glittering crystal into myself, I now see the world more clearly and recognize the harmony and peace of living. Will each of you try a little? Oh please do—for I love each of you and want you to be happy." And he fixed a little of his magic powder for everyone—and everyone tried it—and all were pleased.

The room in which the three girls and the three men were sitting—talking—laughing—sometimes painting pictures—occasionally playing with and petting a small dog—gray and woolly and curly-haired—impish and merry and mischievous—who is the constant companion of the oldest of the three girls.

Everyone in the room is imprisoned in this room in a house painted white and located between two thoroughfares to the old city marked A & B. From the windows they can look into a beautiful garden of trees and flowering bushes. Early each morning bird song greets the first light of breaking day. No one other than those who have entered this realm of enchantment knows the garden is there.

The room casts a strange spell that can be broken by the old man—or by the little dog—but there are three musical notes that must break into the point of awareness before these six people may return to their separate identities. Now they form a whole in the beyond world of magic—and neither is one recognizable individually from the other nor can they voluntarily depart from the other.

There were colored hangings—rich in tone—pictures—alive with forms and shadings and vivid lines and rainbow-hued—cushions and candle flames—brushes and bottles of dye—bowls and saucers—silver spoons—and lantern-like lamps—and a Tarot deck of cards.

All want out—none are satisfied—and, like all people, are anxious to return to the familiar world of those things they—but shortly—were praying to escape from. "Please—old man," they cried "gain us our release—please—please." They looked at the old man and each offered him a token—one a small ruby—one a silver clip—one a scrap of silver-threaded purple silk—one a small copper cup and one a scarab-carved lapis lazuli. They set their offerings before the old man and he smiled and said, "First one of you must give me something I can make a flute of."

And then the little dog picked up a small stick and trotted over to the old man and dropped it at his feet. He picked it up and—lo and behold—it was a straight shaft of bamboo. The little dog gazed up at the old man—and the tip of a little pink tongue showed—and the long fluffy ears were cocked slightly—and there was a bright twinkle in the eyes. The old man patted the little dog and said "This will do just fine." He removed a small knife from his pocket—and quickly made three notches in the bamboo stick. Then—placing the end of the stick to his lips and his fingers over the notches, making them beat a short tattoo—he suddenly blew through the stick and three beautiful notes ascended into the air.

And alas—all the magic beauty fell away—and pictures became pictures—and hangings became dyed cloth—bowls and saucers became ashtrays—and candle flame a burning candle—and the room returned to being just a room and the garden became a few trees and bushes in a back yard—and the bird song became a cacophony of twittering and chirping—noisy and a bit irritating.

The girls lost their enchanted look—and became just girls—the men just men. Only the little dog remained impish and cute—sly and cunning.

The old man sighed and putting down his impoverished flute—he walked to the now visible door—it had been hidden by a long hanging— opened it and without saying a word closed the door behind him and walked away. Once—just once—the little dog barked.

The five people left behind became busy donning their identities.

"I must meet my lover—at one o'clock," said the young girl as she fussed with her hair putting it in place. "And I have an important meeting with a freedom group," said the black-haired girl as she slung her handbag over her shoulder. The plain girl said, "Oh, I'm tired—and now all this magical nonsense is over—I can go back to sleep. This is my room really—you know—and although I like each of you—I prefer my solitude." The two men sighed and said, "Well, it had been interesting but frankly—this magic business is pretty wishy-washy stuff—and it doesn't put food in the old stomach." And all but the plain girl and the little dog departed.

And as she fell off to sleep—she missed the little dog picking up the stick and carrying it back into the far corner of the room.

PART TWO | THE EVENING SUN TURNED CRIMSON

EDITOR'S NOTE

PAM AND CHARLES PLYMELL FIRST MET HERBERT HUNCKE IN SAN FRAN-
cisco in the late 1960s . By 1974 they had started up their own publishing
company, Cherry Valley Editions, named for the town in upstate New
York where it was located. Beginning with chapbooks produced on copy
machines, Cherry Valley Editions grew to publish some of the finest
contemporary fiction and poetry decades before the larger houses picked
up the scent.

  The Evening Sun Turned Crimson was published in 1980 in a paperback
edition of a thousand copies. Huncke expressed dissatisfaction with the
original cover, which featured a screaming man plunging a hypodermic
into his arm atop the New York skyline. A second edition of a thousand
paperbacks and two hundred hardcovers was issued, this time with a
cover photo of Huncke by his close companion of over twenty-five
years, Louis Cartwright. For a time, the Plymells kept Huncke supplied
with copies, which he would sell himself. Both editions are eagerly
sought by rare-book collectors, as is Huncke's first book, *Huncke's Journal. The Columbia Review* compared *The Evening Sun Turned Crimson* to
"*The Autobiography of Malcolm X,* that combination of poignant memory
grafted to historical pathos."

  The Evening Sun Turned Crimson forms the bedrock of Huncke's writing, and most of it was written in the early to mid-1960s. Beginning
with the title piece, one of his earliest childhood memories, *Evening Sun*
chronicles Huncke's Chicago youth and travels from 1920 to 1939,
Times Square denizens circa 1940s, early friendships which would later
form the nucleus of the Beat Generation, William S. Burroughs's Texas
cotton/marijuana farm in the late 1940s, and New York scenes of the
late fifties to mid-sixties.

THE EVENING SUN TURNED CRIMSON

I REMEMBER SO MANY STRANGE HAPPENINGS FROM THE PAST. SOME-times I can sit after having taken a shot of heroin for several hours com-pletely absorbed by visions of places and people and the odd twists which make one person or place or experience a bit outstanding from every ordinary routine.

Once when I was a young child I had been invited by friends of my parents to spend several weeks in the country living in a summer cabin as it was called—where there was a large flower garden and an even larger vegetable garden and great huge trees and hills and a beautiful winding river where I swam and went canoeing. There were narrow gravel roads twisting and climbing up and down hills—shaded on either side by old and gnarled trees where occasionally simply out of pure joy I would see one I could climb up into—sometimes reaching almost the very top branches which I would cling to swaying slightly from my own weight, and while gazing out over the landscape I believed I could see for many miles and my whole body would delight at the softly blow-ing wind.

The people I lived with owned a big brown and white collie dog named Tamer and he was my constant companion. It was my first en-counter with a dog as a friend and I talked to Tamer as though he could understand everything I said—revealing secrets to him I had never shared with anyone.

The cabin or house was built at the top of a hill and from the screened front porch one could see clear over to the opposite side of the river. Immediately in front of the house the hill began descending and it was rather a long distance down to the riverbanks. In the evening the view of the setting sun was beautiful.

The one very unusual happening of that summer for me had to do with a sunset, and all these years I've remembered every so often that particular sunset.

I was a fairly intelligent child and usually could be depended upon to obey instructions and behave in a self-reliant manner. Therefore when one afternoon I was left alone there was very little worry on the part of the people who had left me. I fail to recall why they had to leave me behind when they drove away, but they had praised me and explained there was no need for me to have someone with me on this occasion since Tamer was to be left behind also, and surely I was big enough to help myself to the food which had been prepared and set aside for me and going to bed would be no problem. They assured me they would return before the next morning and of course I was too sensible a boy to be afraid of anything like the dark.

Actually I was thrilled at the prospect of having the house all to myself and reassured everyone that I was quite capable of taking care of myself. I think I was five years old at the time or perhaps six and extremely precocious.

And so suddenly I was all alone and master of the house. It was getting late in the afternoon and for the first time since I had come to this place I became aware of the sounds around me.

I had heard them before but not quite as I was hearing them now. Everything took on a new dimension for me and—although everything was familiar—still there was seemingly something new about everything. I realized for the first time I was alone and I became a bit uneasy. It is rather difficult to explain now and was then, but I had to admit to myself perhaps I wasn't very brave after all, and this business of being alone was a good bit different than simply being indifferently aware of others being around or near.

I spoke to Tamer and kept him as nearby as possible; even though I was still a long way from real fright it still felt good having him close. He and I moved through the several rooms of the cabin, and although it wasn't dinnertime I decided to have something to eat. There were only two neighbors and they had their places a good distance from our place and—although I could look through the kitchen window and see another house through the trees—it seemed rather far away and again I was aware of being alone. I ate half-heartedly and shared some of my food with Tamer, and then decided to go and sit on the front porch and watch the people below either rowing or paddling their boats and canoes, with every so often a small motorboat spreading a wake which would cause the other river craft to rock rather roughly, and the people in the boats would break into smiles and the women invariably reached for the sides and their laughter sometimes carried up the side of the hill and could be heard by those of us watching from the security of our front porch.

On the evening of this story as I walked from the interior of the house out onto the porch, I became aware of the sky which had turned a wild furious crimson from the huge glowing red disk of the sun radiating shafts of gold light and or at rushing speed plunged below the horizon. I stood—nearly riveted to the spot bathed in pinkish tint and surrounded by an almost red world—everything reflecting the sunset—and filled with awe and an inward fright I felt the intenseness of my being alone, and although I've suffered acute awareness of loneliness many many times throughout my life, I've never sensed it quite as thoroughly or traumatically as on that evening when all the world turned into burning flame and it was as though I was already in the process of being consumed. I was not brave at all any longer and was out-and-out afraid—plain scared—as I've ever been in my life.

Very slowly and carefully I looked all around me, speaking in whispers to Tamer, and finally, along with Tamer, withdrew into the room which had been mine since coming there to visit. I climbed into my bed and tried to coax Tamer up beside me. He simply refused and stalked in a somewhat haughty manner out of the room, disappearing from my view—and eventually I suppose settling down for the night in his own spot.

There isn't much more except to say the sun setting on that warm summer evening was one of the most frightening experiences in my life. Today a sunset can fill me with an awareness of beauty that nothing else can.

BRIEF AUTOBIOGRAPHY

I WAS BORN IN A SMALL TOWN IN MASSACHUSETTS. ODD IN A WAY BE-
cause my father was born in Chicago and my mother in Laramie, Wyoming, and neither of them did any traveling until shortly before my birth.
My father obtained work in a factory manufacturing precision tools used
around motor and machinery constructions. This was his chosen field
and one he was respected in—later becoming something of an authority
whose opinion was a decisive factor on several occasions among his associates concerning a point requiring the knowledge of an expert. At any
rate going back to Greenfield, Massachusetts, in 1915, my parents and
grandmother—my mother's mother—were living there and I was on the
way. My mother was quite young—fifteen and in ignorance of sex. My
father was very nearly as bad although a few years older. At any rate he
violated my mother in a rather crude fashion, so the whole idea of sex
became repellent (to her) and remained so until I was in my early teens
and began opening her mind to a more honest approach—later having
the satisfaction of knowing she accepted lovers and became better adjusted as per result. This followed nearly twelve years of marriage with
my father, then two years of living separately and finally divorce.

I know my birth caused pain and fear and perhaps my mother never
quite forgave me. We were friends but she always betrayed me, and this
became her way of balancing the score. She was truly a spoiled child
who had wanted to sing and become part of the theater world and wasn't
quite clear how she had become a wife and pregnant. I gathered later
my grandmother was mostly responsible. She was a young wealthy
widow and wanted to see a little of the world. My mother presented a
bit of a problem and she presumably decided since my father was there—
presentable and showed promise in his line—it was a good match.

My mother had also received generously from her father and when
the estate was settled she had enough to help my father establish himself
in Chicago as an independent businessman. My mother was having her

first contact with the opposite sex. They made a good-looking couple and marriage was logical. All of it has never been quite clear in my mind—and I speak of it from what I have heard from my mother, my father, and my grandmother.

My father was apparently going thru some kind of training period which lasted four years. I therefore spent my first four years in the New England town of my birth. We supposedly lived well and I have a very faint memory of a sled—some kind of fur coat and mittens—and being drawn along thru a world of snow and ice, finally reaching a little bridge festooned with icicles over a solidly frozen stream, the banks piled high with snow, and becoming afraid my father would let go of the rope and along with the sled I would slip off the bridge into the ice and snow below. This lack of trust in my father never changed.

There is another vague memory of Greenfield—having something to do with a wire basket I had climbed inside and tried rolling down a hill in. My mother came on the scene, and whether or not I was punished I can't recall, but I do remember her annoyance and her screaming at me.

The next positive memory occurred in Detroit where we lived for approximately a year and where my brother was born. I was playing on a porch—slipped and cut my head in such a way that it was necessary to put stitches in the wound to close it. Also, it must have been about then I developed a fear of fire engines and would run and hide under the bed whenever I would hear one roaring thru the streets.

Next there was Chicago and my real troubles began. Everything I did was wrong and what was supposed to be a substantial American middle-class home was really a household of screaming hysterical women and an angry, confused and frustrated man. There was very little peace. My mother began unleashing her resentment of the injustices she felt were being perpetrated against her. There was no love, and among the adults only nagging and arguing. There was at least one scene in which I recall my grandmother removing a pair of scissors from my mother's hands by force because she was threatening to cut her throat. There was much mystery about my father's activities away from home. Other women—that type of thing. My mother was always complaining—arguing first with my father and then with my grandmother. My father became about this point openly hostile toward my grandmother, allowing this attitude to grow over the years into intense hate.

Most of the love I was at all aware of came from my grandmother and I strongly resented anything which might lead to being separated from her. She indulged most of my whims and it was in her presence I could be myself. She was a very beautiful woman—selfish and indifferent to anything not affecting her directly. She had conditioned herself to believe she was entitled to and could get along with only what she considered the best. She spent fantastic amounts of money on clothes—going only to the places money was the important factor. Elegant and expensive hotels—restaurants—and living quarters. Much of this spilled over onto me and I have never quite lost my taste for the things money can buy. All in all she was never far away from us.

BRIEF AUTOBIOGRAPHY II

YET IN A SENSE UP 'TIL THEN THE WORLD HAD BEEN MY OYSTER AND IF I can recall any happiness in my childhood it will in all probability have to do with other persons than my parents—or with some adventure of my own.

Maybe with my grandmother who loved me with a love I believed in—even at this date—aware it was the only honest love I knew as a child. Grams accepted me. I could dance in front of her—twisting—turning—trying to spin all in an effort to become like the music filling the room from the Victrola I never grew tired of listening to—and she would know and I could throw my arms around her when the music stopped and she would gather me laughing and exclaiming about my loss of breath—sometimes she would tell me stories about the West when she was a young girl—and speak of Indians or Billy the Kid—and of camping trips up into the Rocky Mountains, describing mountain streams cold and clear, rushing downward—of wildflowers—of hunting mountain lions and bears—of ranch life—or of my grandfather I've never known who died before I was born—who when alive rode horse-back—and owned thousands of head of cattle—and made money specu-lating in the cattle-buying markets—selling out at great profit—and how he had given my mother a pony when she was about my age. She had loved her years in the West and there was a feeling of pride concerning the good and the bad she had seen or lived thru. She and I knew I could secretly be a great cowboy—ride a horse—toss a lariat—live out West—but I'd probably spend most of my life stuck in Chicago. She enjoyed taking me along with her when she had shopping to do or simply wanted to have lunch in some good restaurant—and I enjoyed going along. I didn't mind wearing my good clothes and using good table manners—I always knew there would be some new kind of food to try or maybe I could have what was called a club sandwich and—without fail—ice cream or some pastry I'd never tried. We got on well together—she would perhaps comment on the place and speak frequently of the people around us—or most often of the plans for my future and some of the things she would sometime want to do for me. I was perfectly comfortable and stimulated by the people and maybe simply by the idea of eating in a restaurant. I would really be thrilled if we had gone somewhere they used luncheon music as an added attraction. We loved each other and were happy together but my father resented the idea—telling her she was making a goddamned sissy out of me—to leave me alone. She would draw up very proudly and bend forward to kiss me—telling me to run along and play elsewhere—my father was tired and didn't mean what he had said. So with my grandmother there was some happiness other than that I stumbled on in the world away from home.

Much of what I have spoken of was during the twenties. My mother cut her waist-length golden hair one day in exchange for a style called a bob and a shingle. The change startled the older members of the family far more than me, although to this day I remember her sitting in front of her dresser brushing so many strokes of her brush through her gold-colored hair. Skirts were short—frequently above the knee. My mother loved them because they displayed well-shaped legs. My parents were examples of the young smart set. They drank gin and smuggled whiskey. My father paid his bootlegger once a month and referred to the transaction as an account. They were entertained frequently and did much entertaining of their own. The people they knew as friends were usually in the age group of middle to late twenties for the men. The women were apt to be younger—in their early twenties. The men were mostly in business for themselves and making money rapidly. They belonged to a country club and played golf on weekends. The women joined bridge clubs and played bridge at least two afternoons a week for money. They drank all afternoon when they were playing and I could hear the chatter amid the laughing I would walk in upon after school when it was my mother's turn to have the club at her home. Women were driving cars of their own—my mother's best friend had just received a new car as a gift from her husband and she and my mother made use of that car. My parents prided themselves in being modern. They all had the whole world in their pockets and it lasted about nine years for some and for many only a few years longer—and for the remaining it never changed although the pace certainly slowed down to a near stop but not quite. All of a sudden everything was in turmoil—stock market crash—well-known names linked to suicide—swindles—underhanded deals. Talk about lost fortunes overnight—the millionaires being hit. Small business-men were hurt also—but the majority—like my father—had good solid backing and only had to hold on until the financial world made some adjustments. All would be well. Unfortunately for thousands upon thousands of people everywhere—the only changes were progressively worse—until at last there was hunger and extreme deprivation. People couldn't work because there was no work. Bank savings had been lost—many banks went under and closed. There was talk about depression. Finally Roosevelt was elected and the government began projects to help revive conditions—Works Projects—Conservation Camps—etc. The country slowly began coming alive with a whole set of new rules.

My father had borrowed heavily from my grandmother to keep his business going—signed notes he later stole back and destroyed, refusing to repay any of the loan. A short while following the market crash, my parents decided they would be wiser to split—the first move to be a period of separation. Our large apartment was given up and my mother, my brother, my grandmother, and myself moved into a smaller so-called efficiency apartment in a first-class middle-class neighborhood. It was not a great distance from where we had been living and I was to continue attending the same school. On the way home—my first day—I met a brother and sister who lived on the same street I did in a lakefront build-ing and why didn't I come to their place after checking in at home—we could fool around on the beach. The boy's name was John or Johnnie and he was twelve—a year older than his sister whose name was Donna—who became my first love—the first girl I kissed. I was the same age as Donna and we sort of permitted John to take over the responsibil-ity of finding things for us to do. Their parents were divorced and they were living with their mother also and this gave us a common bond. We three became inseparable for the next seven or eight years.

The three of us were rather wild. We began smoking almost immedi-ately and I did it openly before my mother—offering her a choice of that or not seeing, but knowing I was sneaking round and doing it any-way. She became reconciled to the idea, accepting it as part of the new values she had just started to acquire. As a disciplinarian my mother was completely ineffectual, and from that point on I was almost entirely on my own and came and went as I chose. There were certain rules in the beginning I had to accept, but it was only about a year or two later when there were no rules and I did exactly as I pleased. I had, along with John and Donna, turned on to a little gin we had stolen from a bottle belonging to his mother. We had felt rather exhilarated and considered ourselves pretty wise. We spent much time going to movies and talking about sex and resenting school and telling each other we would avoid all the stupidities of parents. Johnnie had always been deeply attached to his mother and it was mostly because of this I tried reaching my mother a little more honestly and met with luck. I was startled to realize how much more about sex and the world I was aware of than she. She was lonely and—upon discovering I was no little boy but someone she could talk to—she began talking. She was a romantic and up to this point refused to accept the fact that the world was real and that there was such a thing as sex and it was not necessarily bad or evil. She had never once in her life acknowledged the truth. There had never been any warmth in her relationship with her mother, nor for that matter could either of them be honest with the other.

My grandmother was way beyond my mother in worldly knowledge—but peculiarly enough simply would not tell her own daughter a few basic facts. I decided I would try and help my mother to become a woman. It wound up I succeeded fairly well—by then I had been abused by her—my trust never once kept—betrayed systematically—screamed and cursed at—my most vulnerable spots deliberately revealed—lied about and to—yet there were times we actually communicated, and today I can look back on our relationship and recall only the pleasant and funny aspects. She was as much a victim as anyone could be and, until my concern, defenseless. She would have in all probability ended up in a mental institution.

We remained in our new surroundings a little over a year when my parents decided to live together again—this time selecting an entirely new part of the city to set up their home in. Same type of neighborhood as always but a little sharper location closer to the heart of the city. I liked it considerably better. They selected a comfortable apartment and started a routine which finally ended a year later in the divorce court. My mother was to keep the apartment and have custody of her children—my brother and myself—and to receive $250 every month from my father for the upkeep of the home and our maintenance. A beautiful deal until my father began feeling the pressure and started seeking a way to get out from under. My grandmother's money had started running out and she requested payment on one of the notes—a sum of $3,000 or $4,000. He hit the ceiling—he couldn't do it at the moment—she would have to wait.

Johnnie and Donna had talked their mother into moving into a place less than two blocks away. Again we were constant companions—older and wiser—less innocently amused than before. Donna dated an outside acquaintance—occasionally preferred being with Johnnie and me.

I was passably good-looking with an abundance of sex appeal. I started ejaculating about eleven and since had been having sex of all kinds steadily. I had played around with and laid a young girl I met at school—not once, but many times. I had run across a strange character with a canoe he would carry down to the lake shore and then paddle out to one of the breakwaters offshore—there he would take his clothes off, lying naked in the sun for hours. He took me along when I first met him, and as soon as our clothes were off he began sucking me off—it was one of the wildest sensations I had ever known. Sometimes I would wait for him. I liked head and let him give it to me as frequently as could be arranged. I introduced Johnnie to him and as often as not Johnnie would go along with me.

About this time Donna was sent to a Catholic school where she withdrew to some extent from Johnnie and me. While in school she became friends with a beautiful young girl from Kansas. When vacation time arrived Donna was invited to spend several weeks in Kansas. She accepted the invitation. When she returned she was hopelessly in love with the girl and believed herself definitely a lesbian. I had but recently discovered the whole homosexual scene and was entirely sympathetic to her feelings. We spent many hours—just the two of us—shutting her brother out for the first time—talking and discussing the possibilities of the future. This was in fact the beginning of a period filled with happenings and experiences I can't possibly hope to recall in chronological order. The three of us became well known and moved thru and in and out of many scenes taking place. Donna changed lovers rapidly and started drinking heavily. There were parties lasting many days. People drinking themselves drunk and sober again. Occasionally someone would suddenly fall out flat and would be picked up—placed somewhere and left to sleep it off while the party ground out to the end. There was an air of desperation about the people involved in these routines as if they were deliberately seeking self-destruction. They were on the whole beautiful people in appearance but filled with anger and hate. Love was spoken of and declared but seldom meant more than the sex involved. The large gatherings of lesbians invariably revealed the women in their most obnoxious displays. Screaming, kicking and biting—threatening each other—stealing lovers—engendering huge seething scenes aflame with jealousy and ugliness. Frequently Johnnie and myself would be the only males present. Johnnie was accepted with liking and far more respect than I was, and most of the time had it not been for him and his sister I wouldn't have been around at all. It was shortly prior to the repeal of Prohibition and beer flats were popular. These were apartments where beer and whiskey were sold. Frequently poker games would be in progress and some of the games would get hot with several hundred dollars in the pot. Usually it was the more masculine types that played and they were at their best. Many were good players and enjoyed themselves. Many had girls out on the streets hustling. The girls would begin returning around two or three in the morning and were ready to start a little steady drinking. Once or twice a few had fallen in with pot or tea as it was called then, and I picked up for the first time one morning and got so stoned I was unable to move. It was up to then the most unusual and soul-conscious experience of my life. I heard music for the first time—that is, really heard it—saw people I had known in an entirely new perspective, becoming aware of entirely new levels of consciousness. I was entranced and on the spot became a confirmed smoker. It is great, great stuff and should be smoked by everyone. I have had three or four soul-shattering experiences with other things but nothing has delighted me quite as much as my first high on pot. No matter what I have been doing or where I might be at the time, smoking pot is sure to have enriched the moment.

I discovered where pot was easily obtained and copped steadily from then on. It was very cheap and I could pick up a Prince Albert tobacco can packed full for one dollar or at most one dollar and a half. Sometimes I'd buy five or six sticks for twenty-five cents.

NEW ORLEANS, 1938

I RECALL A NIGHT IN NEW ORLEANS ON ST. CHARLES STREET—WALKING. It had been raining—the streets were glistening—pools of rainwater reflected the night. Sounds of drops of water dropping and spattering on the leaves of the magnolia trees. The streets were deserted—only an occasional passing automobile. I was crossing a side street when as I glanced up I saw a man approaching. He was about my own height. He was of stocky build, inclined a bit toward fat—wearing dark trousers and a white shirt open three buttons at the neck—exposing a heavy growth of black hair. His complexion was swarthy—his eyes were small and dark brown. His hair was black and oily which he wore combed straight back from his forehead. His hands were in his pockets—a dangling cigarette hung from the corner of his mouth. Slightly lurching toward me, he asked me for a match.

As I gave him a light for his cigarette he stood in front of me—wavering—sort of off-balance—placing his hands on my shoulders—squinting his eyes—staring into my face—saying, "You look like a nice guy. I bet a person's color doesn't make any difference to you. Want a drink? Come on—I'll buy you a drink."

I was strictly on the bum—any situation had—so to speak—to be taken advantage of—also I was curious about the man.

We turned off St. Charles Street—walking in the direction of—I believe—South Rampart Street near a railway depot. Reaching Rampart Street we entered a saloon—almost the first we encountered. The interior was lighted by a single unshaded lightbulb hanging suspended in the center of the room. A large neon-trimmed jukebox occupied space along one wall. Several tables surrounded by straight-back chairs were placed around the room—at one slouched a dark-skinned Negro—wearing blue denim overalls—his arms and hands hanging limp toward the floor—his head resting on the tabletop. At the bar—which was painted bright orange—two men stood talking. A record with a lot of horns and beating drums was on the jukebox.

We stood at the bar drinking wine. The man was telling me something about cockroaches. He kept saying, "Never kill a cockroach—never kill a cockroach." Several were walking around the spots of spilled wine and beer—waving their antennas. Suddenly he said he wanted to get laid. "Let's go and find a bar where there are some women—come on—I know where one is—it's not far—just around the corner."

We departed along Rampart Street for about two blocks. The street was bare—lined solidly on either side with stores. One streetlight shone dimly—set high up on a pole—two men were walking—hands in their pockets—talking—hurrying—just out of the glow. We turned down a side street a short distance into a store—the glass windows painted black on the bottom halves. Inside—another unshaded light bulb—a few tables—no jukebox but a number of people—some standing at a short bar of unpainted lumber. A few were women—rather bedraggled appearing—none young—clothing rather shapeless—hanging askew. They were speaking, almost shrilly moving around—laughing, watching everything with their eyes. One came slightly stumbling toward us—carrying a wine glass—saying, "Is you going to buy me a drink—honey?" She was thin—not young—her hair sticking out in stiff wisps from beneath a black hat. She was short in stature—light brown in color—with small facial features—her mouth narrow—open showing bad teeth—two or three missing in front.

The man bought her a drink. They began talking—joking lasciviously at one another. He asked her what she charged for a lay. She said, "A dollar—I'se a good lay, mister—I'll show you a good time." He replied, all he had was seventy-five cents—and he wanted me to go along and watch. She agreed. She led us out of the barroom down the street to a small brick building set back a small space from the street—lighted inside the hallway at the top of a flight of stairs by a gas-jet flame—into a room just off the top of the stairs—holding a large brass bed—a dresser and mirror with a kerosene lamp burning, sitting on the surface in front of the mirror—a straight-back chair and a small table—a large white crockery pitcher—a bowl set on top of a bedside stand.

Without removing her hat she flopped backward on the bed—pulling her skirts up around her waist. He approached her clumsily—finally lowering his weight down on her—his pants partway down to his knees.

They began squirming and panting. She began repeating obscenities—supposedly to excite him—interspersing remarks about him being good also, saying, "Come on, daddy—oh, daddy—you'se good—you make baby feel good"—moving more rapidly and frantically. This lasted a long while—until perspiration was rolling down their faces making a squelchy sound as they would come together.

Suddenly he stopped—arose from her—mopping his face with a handkerchief—then fumblingly pulling on his pants—saying, "I ain't going to pay you—nothing happened—you ain't any good." She stood up—her clothing half-falling into place as she sort of tugged at it—saying, "Please, mister, I did the best I could—it's hot—you been drinking—please, white man—I needs the money—a half-dollar—that's half—a quarter so I can buy a drink."

I had been sitting. He motioned for me to leave ahead of him. As I walked through the door he followed close behind. We moved rapidly down the stairs—back out to the street in the general direction of St. Charles Street. Reaching a better-lighted area—we stopped—saying good night. He gave me a dollar just before he stumbled away—disappearing into the night. I never knew whether he gave the woman any money or not.

TATTOOED MAN

MARDI GRAS JUST PASSED IN NEW ORLEANS—THINKING ABOUT IT RE-calls to mind Don Castle, the tattooed man I had met one evening on Oak Street beach in Chicago—later running into him in New Orleans. He was a rather strange man—an ex-junky freak-show worker and poet—tattooed from a line circling his neck, like a collar, to his wrists on both arms and his ankles on both legs. There was a large red rose tattooed on his penis he delighted in telling about—describing in detail the discomfort and pain he had suffered at the time of the actual tat-tooing. He lived alone and claimed kindredship with spirits from another world. He was something of a mystic—talking for hours on end about God—what God is—what God wants for mankind—and how after death God absorbs into his being—representative of central life force—the en-tity we know as ourselves. He said that he had seen God and talked with him.

He was a lonely man and often spoke lovingly of his days as the tat-tooed man in a side show—when he knew the India-rubber man—the fat woman—the bearded lady—the sword swallower—the snake charmer—geeks—midgets—circus people—roustabouts—clowns—ani-mal trainers—tightrope walkers—trapeze artists—all kinds of people con-nected with side shows and big tops. For some reason he had gotten away from all that—no longer in touch with the only element he felt comfortable in. He was vague about what had happened but I gathered, from conversational bits, he had started using junk—finally getting hooked and eventually having a run-in with the police—having served time. At any rate he felt he could no longer go back.

ELSIE JOHN

SOMETIMES I REMEMBER CHICAGO AND MY EXPERIENCES WHILE GROW-
ing up and as a youth. I remember in particular the people I knew and—
as frequently happens—I think, with people, I associate whole periods
of time as indicative of certain changes within myself. But mostly I think
about the people and I recall one person rather vividly, not only because
he was out of the ordinary, but because I recognize now what a truly
beautiful creature he was.

He was a giant—well over six and one half feet tall with a large egg-
shaped head. His eyes were enormous and a very deep sea-blue with a
hidden expression of sadness as though contemplating the tragedy of his
life as irrevocable. Also there were times when they appeared gay and
sparkling and full of great understanding. They were alive eyes always—
and had seen much and were ever questing. His hair was an exquisite
shade of henna red which he wore quite long like a woman's. He gave
it special care and I can see it reflecting the light from an overhead bulb
which hung shadeless in the center of his room while he sat crosslegged
in the center of a big brass bed fondling his three toy pekes who were
his constant companions and received greatly of his love. His body was
huge with long arms which ended with thin hands and long tapering
fingers whose nails were sometimes silver or green or scarlet. His mouth
was large and held at all times a slightly idiot smile and was always painted
bright red. He shaded his eyelids green or blue and beaded the lashes
with mascara until they were a good three quarters of an inch long. He
exhibited himself among freaks in sideshows as the only true hermaphrodite in human life and called himself Elsie John. When I met him he was
in his early thirties.

He came originally from somewhere in Germany and before coming
to this country had traveled—travailed if you prefer—much of Europe
and could talk for hours of strange experiences he'd had. He was a user

of drugs, and although he liked cocaine best he would shoot up huge amounts of heroin, afterward sitting still like a big brooding idol.

When I first knew him he was living in a little theatrical hotel on North State Street. It was an old hotel and in all probability is no longer in existence. Apparently at one time it had been a sort of hangout for vaudeville actors. It was shabby and run down and the rooms were small and in need of fresh paint. He lived in one of these rooms with his three dogs and a big wardrobe trunk. One of the things I remember distinctly was his standing in front of a long thin mirror which hung on the wall opposite his bed—applying makeup—carefully working in the powder bases and various cosmetics creating the mask which he was seldom without.

When I met him he was coming out of a lesbian joint with a couple of friends and upon seeing him for the first time I was sort of struck dumb. He was so big and strange. It happened that one of the girls knew him and he invited us all up to his room to smoke pot—tea as it was called in those days. His voice was rather low and pleasant with a slight accent which gave everything he said a meaning of its own. When we were leaving he suggested I come back, and it was not much time until I became a constant visitor and something of a friend.

He liked being called Elsie and later when I introduced him it was always as Elsie.

We began using junk together and sometimes I would lie around his place for two or three days. A friend of mine called John who was later shot to death by narcotics bulls while making a junk delivery—they grabbed him as he was handing the stuff over and he broke free and ran down the hall and they shot him—joined us and we became a sort of threesome.

Elsie was working an arcade show on West Madison Street, and though junk was much cheaper then than now he wasn't really making enough to support his habit as he wanted to and decided to begin pushing. As a pusher he wasn't much of a success. Everybody soon got wise he wouldn't let you go sick and per result much more was going out than coming in. Eventually one of the cats he'd befriended got caught shooting up and when asked where he scored turned in Elsie's name. I will never forget the shock and the terror of the moment the door was thrust open and a big red-faced cop kind of shouting "Police" shoved into the room followed by two more—one who sort of gasped upon seeing Elsie and then turned to one of the others saying, "Get a load of this degenerate bastard—we sure hit the jackpot this time. This is a queer sonofabitch if I ever saw one. What the hell are these?"—as he became aware of the dogs who had gathered around Elsie and who were barking and yipping. "Goddamned lap dogs—what do they lap on you?" he said as he sort of thrust himself toward Elsie.

Elsie had drawn himself up to his full height and then suddenly began saying, "I'm a hermaphrodite and I've got papers to prove it"—and he tried to shove a couple of pamphlets which he used in his sideshow gimmick toward the cop. Meanwhile one of the others had already found our works and the stash of junk—about half an ounce—and was busy tearing Elsie's trunk apart, pulling out the drawers and dumping their contents in the center of the bed. It was when one of the cops stepped on a dog that Elsie began crying.

They took us all down to the city jail on South State Street and since Johnnie and I were minors they let us go the next morning.

The last time I saw Elsie was in the bullpen—sort of cowering in the corner surrounded by a group of young Westside hoods who had been picked up the same night we were—who were exposing themselves to him and yelling all sorts of obscenities.

SPENCER'S PAD

SPENCER HAD A PAD ON FORTY-SEVENTH STREET. IT WAS ONE OF THE
coziest pads in New York and one which it was an experience to visit
for the first time and also to relax in. It existed in a period when the
world was particularly chaotic—and New York exceptionally so. For me
it represented the one spot at the time where I could seek surcease from
tension and invariably find a sense of peace.

Spencer had gone to some pains to make it attractive. He painted the
walls a persian blue and the woodwork a bone white. He kept the lighting soft and had placed big comfortable chairs around his main room.
Along one wall he placed his Capehart with records stacked to one side.
Long soft rose drapes hung across his windows. A chest sat between the
two windows and opposite a fireplace was a studio couch (the same side
of the drapes) faced with a long coffee table.

Spencer presided over all this with great benevolence and good will,
making each of his guests welcome and concerning himself with their
wants.

Spencer never used drugs—although I have seen him try pot and recently he told me he had sniffed heroin. But anyone was quite free to
use whatever he chose and Spencer always managed to maintain environ-
mental conditions conducive to the fullest realization of whatever one
happened to be using.

The Capehart was exceptionally fine and acted as a sort of focal point
in the pad. Great sounds issued forth from its speaker and filled the whole
place with awe-inspiring visions. I can recall one incident clearly when
the people on Forty-seventh Street stood along the curb listening and
some were dancing and they were laughing and we were in the window
watching while music flowed out on all sides.

At the time the streets of New York teemed with soldiers and sailors—
lonely and bewildered—and many found their way to the pad where for
at least a little while life took on some meaning. Often they gave love

and always found it. Some discovered God and hardly knew of their discovery. There many heard the great Bird and felt sadness as Lady Day cried out her anguished heart.

Others came also—Forty-second Street hustlers—poets—simple dreamers, thieves, prostitutes (both male and female), and pimps and wise guys and junkies and potheads and just people—seeking sanctuary in a Blue Glade away from the merciless neon glare.

There were young boys who came and swaggered and talked wise and then spoke of their dreams and plans and went away refreshed and aware of themselves as having an identity.

Spencer accepted them all and gave of himself freely to each. The pad was his home and in it he could accept any confession and seemingly strange behavior, idea, thought, belief, and mannerism as part of one— without any outward show of censure. Within the confines of his home one could be oneself.

Spencer lost his pad partly because the people in the building in which it was located resented his show of freedom and partly through a situation which developed out of a relationship with a young man.

Vernon was a young man who came to New York in search of a meaning to life. He wanted to write, he wanted to act, he wanted to be loved, he wanted to love, he wanted anything and everything. His background was somewhat more interesting because of having been raised by a father who was a minister of the Baptist church in his home-town but who apparently was too busy preaching the gospel to give his own son other than scant attention. His mother had made an effort to make up the difference but her main interest remained with her husband.

Vernon had been in the war and had accomplished nothing more than the nickname Angel among his friends because he was always talking about God and because he would listen to anyone's problems. Also he learned to smoke pot.

His appearance was rather striking and upon reaching New York he had no trouble making contacts. Just how he eventually met Spencer I don't know, but meet they did and became good friends.

One night they had both been out drinking—Vernon smoking pot and both taking Nembutals—and had returned to the pad to get some sleep. Both stripped naked and fell onto the bed and into a deep sleep. When they awakened they were in Bellevue.

It seems one or the other must have accidentally brushed against the gas plate opening a valve and that the neighbors, smelling gas in the hallway, upon investigating traced it to Spencer's and, being unable to rouse anyone, called the police who broke in and finding them both out cold had them rushed to Bellevue—which, after reviving them, decided they be held for observation. Spencer has since told me it was a harrowing experience.

Meanwhile the people in the building all got together and signed a petition requesting that Spencer be evicted. As one old queen who had the apartment next to Spencer's told me, "My dear—it was really too much. It was a regular black and tan fantasy. Both stark naked—and who knows what they had been doing—Spencer so dark and Vernon pale white. It would have been bad enough if both were the same color. Really, if Spencer wants to end it all he shouldn't try and take one of his lovers with him."

I saw Spencer not long ago and once again he has a charming little place of his own but it isn't quite the Forty-seventh Street pad.

RUSSIAN BLACKIE

FIRST TIME I SAW RUSSIAN BLACKIE, I WAS STANDING AT THE OLD TIMES Square Bar—Forty-second Street and Eighth Avenue—now long gone—and he was rather weaving back and forth—both arms spread wide—clutching the edge of the bar with his hands—moving his head slowly from side to side—glaring straight ahead toward the huge mirror which made up the back bar—obviously very drunk and, as I learned later, loaded to his ears on Seconal and pot—at this point—tossing off double hookers of straight whiskey. Although the place was crowded with many of the regular habitués—most of whom knew Blackie—immediately around him was a cleared space—no one wishing to get too close to him as he was, even when stone cold sober, unpredictable—and drunk—if nothing else—was always full of anger and hostility.

Blackie stood about six feet tall and was broad-shouldered—neither slim nor heavy. His hair was almost blue black and he never allowed it to become long or unkempt. His facial features were regular and well shaped. He was considered a very handsome man. His eyes were deep brown and when one spoke to him—looking directly into his face—it was always difficult to read his expression and one could never be sure whether he was angry or pleased—amused or disgusted—bored or entertained. He was immaculate about his dress—favoring dark-colored suits—well tailored and properly fitted—with white shirts and neat conservative ties. In winter his overcoat invariably was of chesterfield styling and frequently he would go without a hat—but always wore gloves and they fitted his hands like another skin.

This was in the middle of a cold spell—the wind sharp and penetrating—cutting deep into the marrow of one's bones. Although Blackie was very intoxicated he had somehow retained his dapper appearance. I didn't know anyone I wished to spend time with and didn't remain long in the bar—what time I did stay was spent in observing Blackie and in a sense scrutinizing him. At some point—he found something amusing—

a great smile broke across his countenance. His teeth were large and even and very white and—seeing him smile—he stood revealed as a very intriguing and attractive person and the thought flashed through me— he would undoubtedly be a great guy to know.

I departed—and it was several days before I saw Blackie again and this time I was introduced to him. We each acknowledged the introduction and went our respective ways. From then on we would meet every day. Most of these times—we'd say "Hi" and keep going—once or twice we had coffee and killed about fifteen or twenty minutes talking about Forty-second Street—making scores—the whole Times Square scene— and the usual everyday topics such as weather—the approach of spring and how drunk we'd been the night before. Once in a while I'd see him with other Forty-second Street characters. He knew everyone on the street but when not alone he was usually with a couple of fellows—and known to be hardcore Forty-second Street hustlers—who were sharp dressers and reputed to go out occasionally on jobs—maybe a stickup or burglary. I had seen one of them knock a guy flat in one well-aimed blow. This same cat later became a good friend of mine—now married and a father—living in Brooklyn. The Russian and I finally became close friends through a series of events which were in a degree cumulative and seemingly unrelated. As I grew more familiar with the environment of Times Square and particularly Forty-second Street, I learned to at least recognize my neighbors—or the people who lived and participated in the activities of the area. I joined or became part of the crowd that hung around the cafeterias—Bickford's—Chase's—Hector's—the Automat— and many of the places of business and amusement which remained open all night. I got to know the hotels and stayed in them—sometimes alone but often with people I'd meet—mostly men and occasionally women. Now and then sitting at the tables with other cats—like myself, living principally by their wits—I'd speak of my scores and gradually I became known and trusted—I suppose is the term best applied when people speak of their exploits in the underworld and expose their secrets. I became acquainted with the thieves who had become professional in their lines: pickpockets—boosters—muggers—a few stickup men—and automobile hustlers—and many who never revealed their specialties exactly but hinted at knowing everything in the book—as they might have said.

Talking at different times with various people frequently we'd be joined by the Russian. Once he fell in and spoke to me directly about doing him a favor—copping some Seconals for him. He had run out, it seemed, and wouldn't be able to see his druggist until the next day. I had lost no time in locating a drugstore following my arrival in the city that supplied me with bennies first—which had just become illegal without prescription. Later the same store sold me anything except narcotics.

I obliged Blackie and copped for him. Next—when he asked me to do the same—I took him with me and introduced him to the druggist. And then one night zonked out of my mind on schmeck—pot—Benzedrine—and Seconals, I met a cat I had become friendly with who was a kind of john or mark. He would come to Forty-second Street after finishing work at his place of employment. He was lonely and attracted to young men of the knock-around—Times Square hipster—hustler types. He was a good spender and one always ate—and got a flop—and besides he came on fairly straight and one could relax and pretty much be himself with him. We spoke for a few minutes and he commented on how high I appeared and added that although he expected to see a friend from around the Square he'd promised to give money to—and if I understood I couldn't expect to receive any money in the morning—he would like me to meet the cat and come along.

I accepted the invitation and met Blackie for the first time in an environment away from the hardcore Forty-second Street. He proved to be an amazingly congenial and affable companion—obviously well versed in ways of being entertaining and agreeable. Apparently he had known our host many years and from parts of the conversation between them I gathered—although their acquaintance began in the usual fashion for both of them—it soon ripened into a friendship of mutual respect. Blackie seemingly delighted in telling of his exploits and one could sense the amusement he stressed conversationally as being part of his interest in all of his activities involving the manner in which he lived and—at one point—he told of taking advantage of several opportunities to make money and named several people they both knew as victims—while they both gossiped and reminisced. Both were conscientious about keeping me posted—frequently drawing me into communication—asking if I was aware of a particular place or building—or had I seen a particular person hanging around Bickford's—giving quick biographical and descriptive clues as to exactly whom they might be discussing.

We all three got very high on Seconals and ale.

At any rate—from then on Blackie became part of my life with a certain consistency and we remained in close proximity—our relationship with various people overlapped and we shared experiences together.

We were never as close as Blackie was with many people but a sort of bond grew and existed between us. There are innumerable aspects to his personality I wasn't aware of and would be pressed to analyze. We did share a kind of love and mutual regard for each other.

There was a reserve and hardness in him difficult to penetrate—yet there was always a straightness—perhaps—or consciousness of beauty in all his actions.

The Russian—as he was frequently called among his more intimate associates—impressed me and my life became—in a sense—richer or greater for having known him.

I suppose there were women in his life during the time I knew him—important and emotionally involved with him—but oddly it was his closest friend's girl and later wife Blackie showed interest in and spent much time with. His friend Frank trusted him implicitly—nor do I think his trust was ever misused (Blackie had the old-fashioned concept of loyalty—believing one does not covet his neighbor's wife). I am inclined to think perhaps she may have tried testing her womanly charms but the Russian stood firm. They all three remained staunch friends and after the marriage and arrival of the first child it was amusing to see Blackie—red-eyed and angry—appearing—glaring defiantly out toward the shadowed corners of the room—ready to sweep clean the darkness of lurking danger in defense of Frank Junior—proud and pleased with the responsibility of babysitting.

There was a slight change in Blackie's personality and general requirements after Frank married. Where once there had been a partner to rely on at a moment's notice—it now became a matter of operating alone—more often than not. He was and may still be an effective hustler. Still he did become more settled and was less apt to be seen staggering from one side to the other—ready for a slug-fest or to simply belt someone for the hell of it. Two years after the birth of the first baby there was a second baby and by this time Blackie was well trained.

We ran into each other about a year ago. Except for a little more weight—and less ebullience—he is very much as he has always been.

DETROIT REDHEAD, 1943–1967

WHEN I FIRST MET HER SHE WAS ABOUT EIGHTEEN. I WAS SITTING IN THE Forty-second Street Bickford's restaurant drinking coffee and talking with a character known as Johnie Pimples—a young cat—a typical Forty-second Street hustler—open for any suggestion where a dollar was involved but most of the time making it with fags for a place to sleep— a couple of bucks' eating and show money, occasionally scoring a ten spot or twenty—spending it on clothes—a chick—across the bar on his acquaintances—while he gave them a rundown on how smart he had been beating the queer—or how someday he was going to go to Los Angeles—maybe and try and get in the movies—if only he could get rid of all these goddamned pimples. He had heard a lot of actors had had bad skin but what with the latest developments in plastic surgery, there wasn't anything he couldn't do—that is if a guy was photogenic—which incidentally didn't always mean a guy had to be especially good-looking. He knew he was photogenic because some gay photographer—one who always came looking just for him—wouldn't pick up anybody else— good for a sawbuck every time—had told him so.

We had been talking about Pimples' brother—who was some kind of big shot in Brooklyn—something to do with the rackets—who didn't like Johnie—wouldn't let him in the house when he went home. His brother was boss since his mother had died. His old man stayed drunk most of the time and since his brother paid the bills there wasn't anything he could do. We were both sitting facing the street—Pimples had just finished telling me how someday he was going to have a place of his own—make a lot of money—and he'd bet sometime his brother would need a few bucks and that it would sure give him a lot of pleasure to tell him to go to hell—when I watched her walk by—slowly—head held high—carefully looking everyone over—half smiling as she noticed Pimples and continuing on down the street. She was wearing a simple plain skirt of some dark material—a soft pink sweater—loose and fluffy—a single strand of pearl beads around her throat—hardly any makeup—and later I discovered she had on a pair of saddle-type oxfords. At first glance she looked about sixteen and not at all typical of the usual chick found walking alone on Forty-second Street glancing in Bickford's window.

I commented to Pimples about her and he said he knew her. He said she had just busted with Knuckles. Knuckles was one of the local pimps and was known for the rough way he handled his girls—also because most of his girls were fine. According to Pimples this one had hit town from somewhere in the Middle West. Knuckles had spotted her coming out of the Fiftieth Street bus terminal—somehow begun a conversation with her—taken her to his pad—kept her there under lock and key until she began cooperating. He had broken her in with several of the Forty-second Street hustlers—just to get her started—and recently she had cut out with some trick who had eyes for her—didn't care she was a whore—and had set her up on her own—threatening Knuckles with the cops or something like that if he didn't leave her alone.

We continued to sit and talk when shortly she came back and walked into the place and up to our table. She glanced at me and then spoke to Pimples asking him if he had seen someone called Larry. Pimples said he hadn't and asked her to join us for coffee. Pimples got up and walked over to the counter to get her coffee and she sat down at the table and asked me for a cigarette. We talked and she spoke of having come from Detroit, and one or two experiences she had encountered. Then she began talking about Knuckles and how green she had been, but that now she was beginning to learn her way around and there would never be another episode like that one for her to contend with. She opened her purse and took out a pair of brass knucks which she explained she always carried with her and "I've got this also," she said as she removed a switchblade knife from her bag, snapping the blade open. "I can use it— if necessary—although I hope it is never necessary—I hate violence." Meanwhile Pimples had returned with coffee for all of us. We sat drinking the coffee and when we had finished we decided to leave—Pimples had a meet with a fag who—so he said—was good for a double sawbuck—and Vickie suggested if I had nothing better to do I walk her as far as the subway at Seventh Avenue. There was something attractive and enthusiastic, warm and beautiful about her.

I was living on the Lower East Side—Henry Street—with an ex–show queen named Bozo and a fellow I had met on Forty-second Street and had hung around with all that past winter and spring—André—very much the ladies' man—whose real name was Fred Veda. He had lived most of his life in Yonkers, New York. He had left home and was hanging around Forty-second Street—picking up a few bucks here and there—mostly from the colored homosexuals that go down to Forty-second Street to look for lovers and young men. He was well liked by them and had known some for many years. He had lived at one time in the Village with a colored poet. He had met Bozo and Bozo loved him and invited him to share his apartment. André had accepted Bozo, and while I had run into some difficulty in a place I had been living, he and Bozo invited me to stay with them.

While walking with Vickie I suggested perhaps she might like meeting a friend of mine and to come on down to my place for a while. She said she had other plans for the evening but she would like to fall in some other time. We made arrangements for seeing each other again. We became friends.

Vickie wasn't a beautiful girl in the generally accepted sense of the word. She was self-conscious of her height and when we first met she had been in the habit of carrying herself slightly round-shouldered to minimize her tallness. Her hair was an almost mahogany red she wore shoulder length—softly waved and lightly fluffed at the ends. Her skin was pale with a dusting of freckles. Her eyes, green and rather widely spaced, were expressive and always held a sort of bewildered gentle look of innocence. Her mouth was a bit wide with a full underlip and very red. Her body was beautiful with long legs and small well-shaped breasts firm and high she never encased in a brassiere. Her movements were graceful and when she walked she took long free steps. She wasn't beautiful—but decidedly striking in appearance—and later when she became a bit more confident of herself and took to wearing more glamorous-type clothes, she was something to see cutting down the street.

She was a strange mixture of gentleness and extreme violence. She was filled with doubts and confusion. She was lonely and rushed about seeking love and understanding. She felt very much alone. She was unable to make any sort of adjustment—she would try and conform—only to find herself feeling sadly rejected. There was a certain strain of creativeness within her she was unable to release, causing her frustration. She was a dreamer—a lover of the sun and the river. She liked to walk and many was the night we walked all night long, ending up in Chinatown for breakfast.

She became well known and had many people interested in her. Most of the cats from the Times Square area knew her and were in love with her to some extent. There were several chicks she made it with.

Her mother had died when she was a young child and she had been raised by her father. She had a great love for her father and it was when she discovered he was homosexual she had left home. Eventually she became more understanding and learned to accept his deviation—this after she had experienced love for the first time.

Vickie was living up in the seventies in an old brownstone front. She had a large first-floor room with two huge windows that reached from the ceiling to the floor. One could step from either window to stone balustrades on the sides of the steps to the sidewalk. The room was oblong in shape with high ceilings. One entered through two large sliding doors. Opposite the doors was a big mirror built into the wall. Vickie arranged a small lamp with a dim bulb immediately in front, using it as the only light. A street lamp burning outside cast light in thru the windows.

She met André and they fell in love. She had kept her appointment with me and I took her down to my place and they met. He was good-looking and should have lived during the time of buccaneers—flowing capes and hats with plumes. He knew New York from one end to the other and soon he and Vickie were to be seen at any hour in almost any part of the city. They went for long walks and spent hours talking and dreaming of what the future might hold for them. They loved each other unstintingly and planned to get married until his family stepped into the scene and let him know in no uncertain terms they wouldn't tolerate him marrying a whore. Vickie had tricked with his father at a convention and was embarrassed and ashamed when André invited her home to meet his people and they were introduced. It upset her far more that it did André, but his father nearly hit the ceiling when he learned they were planning marriage. The plans for the marriage fell thru.

Vickie continued living an active life—meeting people—settling down to a more practical attitude concerning her prostitution—lining up several johns who were regular weekly customers contributing various sums of money—from one who paid her $50 to one who was giving her $150—moving from a one-room apartment to a three-room apartment—buying furniture—new clothes—occasionally acting as a fence—buying and selling stolen articles of jewelry—learning to play drums—making it with the bop musicians—being seen at Birdland—The Royal Roost—swinging up to Harlem—eventually picking up steady with a cat who was a junky—beginning to take an occasional joy-pop herself. Every now and then I would run into her and we would sit and talk—usually over coffee in some cafeteria—but I wasn't seeing her steady during that time. She had gotten pretty hung up over André and it was a disappointment things hadn't worked out per plan. She said she guessed that was life and that now since she had organized her life—such as it was—perhaps it was well she hadn't married. She was still seeing André off and on and they would spend a day or two together—but the big passion had cooled down. Once I ran into her one morning about five A.M. in Kellogg's Cafeteria on Forty-ninth Street—a hangout for a big group of Times Square pimps—whores—thieves—show people—musicians—potheads—and junkies. She was with two brothers just in from Cleveland, Ohio. I don't know exactly how they had met originally but she apparently had known them for some time and they sat reminiscing about some of their past experiences. She introduced them as Bob and Don Brandenberg and at the same time told me, "They are the greatest. Get to know them." Later—after I did get to know them—Bob told me he had met Vickie about a month prior to when we had met and that they had been introduced by one of the musicians—blowing sax up at the Roost—he had known in Cleveland. He had looked him up when he hit town looking to cop some pot. He and the cat had fallen up to Vickie's and she had turned them on. He and Vickie had eyes for each other so he had made it with her until having to return to Cleveland. He had gone back to Cleveland—taken care of some business—picked up his brother Don—and it was just after they had returned to New York we met.

Don was a merchant seaman and had come to New York to get a ship.

Vickie suggested—since she had a meet with one of her johns later in the morning—I take Bob and Don downtown with me. She said they were nearly broke and were tired. She slipped me a couple of sticks of pot and told me to light up when we got home.

Bozo and André had been in the process of severing their friendship for the past few weeks—and Bozo took an immediate liking to Bob. He suggested Bob and Don stay with us until they could make other arrangements. André took an instant dislike to both Bob and Don and decided to move out immediately. We all managed to settle in comfortably. Don and I spent most of our time looking for a ship. I had decided to go back to sea and we both thought we would enjoy making a trip together. We finally got what we were looking for in the way of a ship—

and we made about an eight-month trip. It was one of the best trips I ever made while going to sea.

When we returned Don decided to go back to Cleveland. Meanwhile Bozo and André split up and Bob and I took over Bozo's apartment and turned it into a tea pad and thieves' den. There were four or five fellows making the place a sort of headquarters. They would spend the night going out and scoring—coming in—in the mornings—with quarts of beer—pot—bennies—and a friend or a chick—and we would sit around and ball—people sometimes falling asleep—so there was some kind of action constantly.

We painted the walls black with yellow panels and a Chinese red ceiling. Long black and yellow drapes hung to the floor over the windows. A crescent-shaped lamp with a red bulb hung from a cord suspended over a black L-shaped couch. There was a distinct Oriental opium den atmosphere.

Meanwhile Vickie had gotten hooked on junk. When I got in touch with her she invited me to come up to her room. She had lost her three-room apartment and all her furniture and was living in one room up on 102nd Street just off Central Park West in a strange building with all sorts of unnecessary staircases—hallways—different levels on each floor—little closets and cupboards in the hallways all painted different colors so the whole effect was almost surrealistic—and most of the people living there even stranger. There were musicians of all kinds—bop—jazz—hillbilly—pop singers—even one old man who used to sit out in front on the stoop—twanging a Jew's harp. There were various types of show people—including a group of out-of-work midgets—who quarreled and screamed at each other all hours of the day and night. There were several young college students from Columbia—three old ladies who were always drunk and sat in a room on the first floor near the entrance every day with the door open—a half gallon of wine on the table—watching everybody who came in and went out—what a bitch she is—or he beats his wife—etc.—loud enough so people could hear. And then there was Vickie and her group of friends, most of whom were using junk.

I began seeing Vickie regularly and using junk with her. In fact—although I didn't give up my interest in the pad downtown completely—I moved in with her.

She had changed considerably from the young innocent girl I had first known. There was still the quality of gentleness and wide-eyed wonder about her but on the surface there was a patina of indifference. Somewhere along the line that certain spark of aliveness distinguishing her from the other girls—that special little flame so completely hers—had been quenched. She now lived entirely in a world of fantasy. We spent hours simply sitting—listening to music. She had managed to keep her phonograph and records—and would place a stack on the changer—then lie back—listening.

Somehow we managed to get by financially even though our habits were costing twenty-five to thirty-five dollars a day. She had kept two of her johns and would see them every week. I still had some money from my trip and was doing some stealing. We lived together in this way for about five months—all through the summer and up until almost Christmas of that year. We had a rather beautiful kind of love—devoid of tension—anxiety—and emotional violence. We were at peace with each other and I look back to that time with a deep feeling of gratitude.

Just about Christmas things began going bad for both of us. We were having trouble keeping our habits going. Money was becoming difficult to obtain and we had gone sick once or twice—making us irritable. We had an argument where we both said miserable things to each other. Things got so bad we couldn't make the rent and Vickie was afraid to go out and leave her things because the landlord might lock the door. Finally we decided to pack everything up and move downtown.

Most of the cats making the scene downtown kind of fell in love with her. She babied them—listened to their troubles—let them tell her about their dreams and plans—played music for them—read them poetry—so they understood it—for the first time. Occasionally when one or two of them had a job they intended pulling—breaking and entering a store— they would take her along and then when they got back they would talk about how cool she had been or how much heart she had.

The bathtub was in the kitchen and it was entertaining to watch Vickie bathe. She was beautiful sitting in the tub with her hair piled on top of her head—the tub overflowing with frothy bubble bath—heavily scented with something called Shanghai.

One morning she had one fellow painting his toenails silver. He was just out of prison—having served almost ten years. He never forgot Vickie and years later when I ran into him, he asked about her and said, "Man—that was some redhead."

She used to go out alone and cut around the city and she took to wearing our clothes. She would put on a suit and a man's shirt or sometimes she would go glamorous in a dress and high heels.

About this time a young Italian cat named Ricci began hanging around the pad. He became friendly with Bob and they formed a partnership. They planned a caper in Washington, D.C., and spent much time running back and forth between the two cities. Finally they made the take in Washington—but at the last minute—when they were making their getaway—one of them dropped a matchpad with a telephone number on it. The cops found it—traced the number—and grabbed them in Washington. We got the news about three-thirty in the morning. One of Ricci's boys from Long Island came by and told us we had better clear out before the police had a chance to locate the pad.

Vickie and I packed up—bag and baggage—called a secondhand furniture man—sold everything in the place to him—and were out and gone by two o'clock the following afternoon.

Vickie had met a young cat who lived in Philly and had pleaded with her to make the scene there with him. She decided to take him up on it—figuring it was a good idea to get out of New York at the time. We said good-bye and it was nearly two years until I saw her again.

Things continued to go along pretty rough for me until I took a fall for possession of a five-dollar bag of heroin and was sentenced to six months on Rikers Island. I served the six months—actually less than six—since I got five days a month off for good behavior. When I came out—I had of course kicked my habit—cold turkey—while in prison— I was very careful—not doing any stealing—getting by bumming off friends and acquaintances until I got a job on a ship and went back to sea. The following winter—shortly after coming back—I went down to Texas and stayed not quite a year with a friend. After returning to New York in the late fall I got hung up again on drugs—acquired a partner who taught me how to burglarize. I worked with him until the middle of the summer—when we split up because he wanted to go back to his hometown. My habit was pretty heavy by this time and again I found the going rough. I was just barely getting by—I was spending everything I'd get my hands on for junk and didn't even have a place to live. When I had about reached the end of my endurance—I was sick half the time— run down physically—without a place to sleep—dirty—worn out—my feet sore and bleeding—ready for suicide—a friend I hadn't seen for some time—and then ran into on the street—took pity on me. He let me sleep in his place. It was days—many days—before I could get up and around. I was exhausted and slept—twenty and twenty-four hours at a stretch. I was more dead than alive and wanted it that way. I didn't want to live. Prayed for death.

Eventually I began coming out of it—although emotionally and mentally I was defeated. I began going out on the streets again and one night at the corner of Fiftieth and Broadway I ran into Vickie. She was looking extremely well—dressed in a black silk coat and gold wool dress. When she saw me she held her coat in both hands spreading it out like wings—and sort of running toward me she reminded me of a big black and gold butterfly. She told me she had been doing quite well—until but recently working as a model—doing a little hustling on the side—living up near Columbia over close to the river—and was half in love with Ricci whom she had been seeing a lot of since returning to New York. She said she had done fairly well in Philly but had gotten homesick for New York. She was vague about what had happened in Philly except to say that she had spent only a short time with the man she had gone there to see. She mentioned having had various jobs none of which suited her very long. She had kept in touch with Bob and Ricci having contacted Don in Cleveland, and although Bob was still serving time Ricci had been home about six months. He had driven down to Philly with a friend about a month ago and they had balled for about a week. He asked her to come on up to New York and here she was. She also told me she was using stuff again—in fact both she and Ricci were—so she explained—half hooked. She had kicked her habit in Philly but when Ricci came on the scene he had some stuff with him and she had picked up. She said she was just on her way to cop and suggested I go along. She said Ricci was waiting for her to come back to her place and after she made her meet we would go up there and get straight.

I joined her and from then on we began seeing each other consistently. Ricci was doing fine but spent much of his time out on the Island with his people. Vickie would stop by where I was living and sometimes we would sit and talk or go out and see a movie. Occasionally Ricci would come along with his car and we would take long drives.

Ricci was anxious to make a big score and he had cased several places out on the Island he thought might be good takes. One afternoon we made one of the spots and—although the take wasn't big—it did get us straight financially for a while. From then on we operated regularly. Things were getting better when one night the three of us got caught.

Ricci had said, "This is a sure thing"—and per result we were overly confident and that was it. We were taken to the Long Island City prison. Ricci and myself were held there for trial and Vickie was taken to the Women's House of Detention in New York City.

I saw very little of Vickie after that. I learned she had finally broken down and written to her father who immediately flew to New York, bailed her out of prison—obtaining permission to take her back to Detroit until the day of the trial and again on the day of sentencing. On the day of sentencing she stood next to me, looking pale and tired. She was wearing something plain. Her hair was neatly combed and she stood with her head bowed. She glanced at me once, and for a moment her eyes lit up and a tiny smile touched her mouth, then once again she looked down and there was little of the Vickie I had first seen and known. The judge gave her a five-year suspended sentence and they whisked her out of the courtroom. That was the last time I saw her.

I went upstate to prison for five years and Ricci was sent to Pilgrim State Hospital.

Almost a month ago I ran into a girl Vickie and I had known and she told me she had made a trip to Detroit last year and had looked Vickie up. She said Vickie had married and has two children. She said she is very much the typical suburban matron and is active in the PTA. We both laughed and agreed we could see her organizing the good mothers of the PTA and that Vickie was surely the one to do it.

I probably knew Vickie better than most of the people she was acquainted with here in New York, and I wonder what she has done about all her dreams and how she has managed to curb her enthusiasm for excitement and adventure. Basically she was one of the most honest women I have ever known.

There are few spots in the city I can go without being reminded that Vickie was once there also.

TATTOOED WOMAN

I HAD WALKED PARTWAY UP THE BLOCK ON TWENTY-NINTH STREET BE-
tween Eighth and Ninth Avenues—thinking how strange—unlike New
York—this whole scene. The feeling of space was what made the difference. The entire area below Twenty-ninth Street, as far down as perhaps
Twenty-seventh Street from Eighth Avenue to Tenth or Eleventh Avenue, is wide open where buildings have been torn down leaving only
rubble. It is as though a great iron claw had reached down from the sky
squeezing, picking, laying flat everything standing above ground, scoop-
ing it up, letting it drop between the pincers back to the earth to lie
forgotten. In the distance toward the river a tall needle-thin steeple sil-
houetted against the color-wracked sky of sunset, the sun a disk of angry
red. Destruction and decay. The houses facing the scene set back from
the street—yards rampant with tall weeds, grass—green stuff crawling up
the sides with tiny purple and red flowers. Windows broken, rotting
wooden banisters and steps with people sitting listless and tired. Half-
naked children playing in the grass. A child on a tricycle, naked to the
waist, a pair of dirty blue jeans exposing half his buttocks, a toy pistol
holstered banging against his hip, scooted alongside me as I returned
toward neon-flushed Eighth Avenue. A young hip-looking Puerto
Rican standing alongside the lamppost called to the boy as we reached
the corner: "Hey—cowboy." The boy laughed racing off down the
street shouting, "Bang-bang-bang."

Eighth Avenue had already taken on evening activities. Several young
chicks came bouncing by, the hipster watching them. Three or four men
came out of the bar talking. A few people shuffling along, heads hanging,
looking at the sidewalk, oblivious to their surroundings. Sound of jukebox, traffic, usual city noises, the rumble of the subway below the street.

The sky had paled into twilight. The reds and greens of the stoplights
standing out more distinctly. Headlights of the automobiles.

I was hungry, deciding to stop in the Riker's for something to eat before returning home. Entering, I was instantaneously aware of a woman standing in front of a large wall mirror, looking at herself adjusting the skirt of her dress. On her upper arm near the shoulder—a tattoo—"Toni." I passed by her glancing casually in her direction—observing in a flash her striking appearance. She was tall with gray-streaked black hair hanging in large loose waves immediately below her shoulders—brushed back behind one ear—one lock fixed flat against her cheek in a spit curl. In her ear an ornate coral and white earring—like flower petals. Her complexion was almost swarthy. She was heavily made up, large mouth painted a vivid scarlet. Her clothing was nondescript, almost shabby. Her dress black, sleeveless, bound in around the waist by a wide black patent-leather belt. She wore extremely high heels and carried a black purse.

Her presence dominated the room. As I sat down at the counter I noticed her speaking with a man who had come in after me. I couldn't hear the conversation but suddenly she raised her voice telling him to go to hell. She began sauntering to the counter swinging her purse with an air of unconcern. Reaching the counter she walked along until sitting next to me. As she seated herself, she said to me, "I hate a phony, baby. I wouldn't attend a dog fight with that prick." She called to the counter man—"Hey, sweetheart—coffee—heavy with the cream." Meanwhile she placed her purse on the counter, leaning it against the sugar container. She then arranged her skirt—afterward patting her hair.

Upon close inspection I realized her age must be well into the thirties, perhaps forty. There were deep lines going downward from the corners of her nose almost reaching the jaw. Beneath her eyes dark, heavily shadowed pockets. Her mouth corners drawn downward as though showing contempt for all she was surrounded by. On one of her hands another tattoo—the sign of the Pachuca. Her arms showed scars from wrist to shoulder. Old needle marks—tracks—where she had tried to hit her veins and missed. Her eyes were glazed, constantly closing, the pupils pinpoints. A junky. Her hands were puffy and dirty, the fingernails painted loud pink, the polish chipped, several nails broken. Occasionally she would look down the counter to where the man she had spoken with was sitting, mumbling—"the bastard, the phony bastard"—then looked straight ahead, slightly nodding.

JOHNNIE I

IT WAS IN 1948—JANUARY—DURING A SIEGE OF SEVERE NEW YORK winter weather. It had snowed for several days—stopped—clearing up—growing milder—the snow melting into dirty slush—then becoming intensely cold—snowing again—covering the streets in white mounds on top of frozen soot-mottled piles of banked snow—burying automobiles in white shrouds—wind-driven tiny ice pellets. Traffic had come almost to a standstill—crawling through the rushes of whistling wind—huddled in coats—earmuffs—scarves—sweaters—gloves—shoulders hunched—from doorway to doorway—to restaurants—subway entrances—seeking shelter along sides of the great graystone buildings. At night the city streets became even more deserted with only a few to be seen on Forty-second Street—probably one of the busiest streets of any city in the world—a few like myself living in cafeterias—sleeping in the all-night movies—staying away from the cops on their beats—who were angry to be out—glad of any excuse to pick a man up—hurry him to the nearest station house in out of the cold—or walking through the underground tunnels down toward Penn Station—through the station into the rest rooms—sitting on the toilets sleeping—sometimes writing—looking to pick up someone who had money and wanted sex—and was willing to pay for it—anxious only for a place to sleep—take a bath—shave—obtain clean clothing—even food. Maybe steal a suitcase—roll a stray drunk—meet a friend—talk—make it until the morning and a cheap movie. I had been living in this manner since shortly after the beginning of the New Year. I was broke—hungry most of the time—poorly clad for contesting the rage of the elements—staying awake using Benzedrine inhalers—occasionally smoking pot—somehow maintaining a junk habit—just managing to keep straight enough not to collapse completely—stealing—ready to make a dollar at anything—always looking for a good take—something big enough to allow me a chance for a bed of my own—a place to live or at least die in out of the cold—not to be found crouched—a corpse in the doorway. I wanted to die and I felt I was dying—could observe death feeding on me—see it in the pallor of my skin—the patches of oozing sores on my chin and face—the tiny red flecks in the whites of my eyes—in the way my skull showed through my skin at the temples—and I could smell it from my dirt-coated bleeding feet—from my crotch—from my clothing.

Sometimes I'd be lucky finding Allen home—who would permit me to sleep for fourteen or fifteen hours—then giving me money enough for food and Benzedrine—suggesting I look for a job—trying to give me incentive—sensing my desolation. His was the only love I knew for a long stretch of time—my only contact with life—and I stole from him—hocking the articles for enough money to get a bag of junk.

It was on a Sunday morning and the snow storm had abated. Exceedingly cold winds swept thru the city. A winter sun hung dimly glistening in a smoke-gray sky. I had seen Frenchy—a Forty-second Street fence—who had a monster-like appearance—large of body with a big round pock-marked face—with small beady piglike eyes—a large, nearly hairless head sitting on a big thick neck—several rolls of fat sticking out over the back of his collar—his skin the color and texture of clay—enter Horn & Hardart's Automat on Forty-second Street—and having stolen a pair of good leather gloves from a guy sitting next to me as I rested in Penn Station—I figured I might be able to talk Frenchy out of a couple of dollars. It was about eleven A.M. and the place was fairly crowded. I had coffee money with me—walked directly toward the coffee spigot—glancing at the crowd—obtained the coffee—walking then over to the table occupied by Frenchy—becoming aware en route Frenchy had been joined by two young men about twenty years of age in appearance—both neat—one quite light in complexion—the other darker—dressed in the uniform sharpie style of the period. They were talking loudly—obviously aware of the people around them—boasting about what an easy job it had been—holding a wristwatch by the band strap—just below the level of the table top—asking Frenchy to buy it—as I sat down. Frenchy greeted me, ignoring an introduction to the two strangers. They had lowered their voices a little but their conversation was still—I am sure—audible to others at nearby tables—and turning to one of them I said, "You guys should soft peddle a little—you don't know who is riding the Erie—maybe you don't care—but please keep it quiet while I'm on the scene—I don't want a bust, nor can I stand a frisk—I got a stick of pot in my pocket." Without being too concerned about the effect this had on them—I turned to Frenchy—showing him the gloves—which he said he didn't want to keep—all he was interested in was jewelry. Finishing my coffee—I nodded to the two cats—said "Be seeing you" to Frenchy—then walked out onto the street—cutting toward Eighth Avenue—and met a cat from the Village who laid a buck on me—asking, "Is there a connection around, man? I have to cop. I'm all right, but my old lady is getting sick. It's too early see my man." I told him, "Nothing happening, man." He was heading toward Seventh Avenue and I joined him until—reaching the subway—he said, "I split here—take it easy—so long."

I continued on until I reached the Bryant movie house where on the spur of the moment I decided to go in and see the picture—meanwhile staying out of the cold—killing a few hours till later in the day when things would in all probability be a little more active. I had just settled comfortably in my seat—glancing to my right—in the row of seats immediately in front of me—I looked directly into the face of the darker-complexioned fellow who had been sitting talking with Frenchy. He smiled—leaned toward me—and sotto voce asked if I would mind him joining me. I replied, "Not at all, man—great." We sat next to each other thru the picture until the end—not speaking much. Once when he said, "My name is Johnnie—Johnnie Terrell—what's yours?" I told him my name—"Herb Huncke—call me Huncke." He looked at me—smiled a little and said, "Man—what a crazy name." At the end of the film he suggested we leave—asking if I would like to get some coffee—and if I still had the stick of pot. I answered yes to both questions. We left walking up Forty-second Street to Sixth Avenue around the corner into the Sixth Avenue Automat.

We sat at one of the front tables—up near a window—watching the people rushing past—glancing at the park—observing the back of the public library—commenting now and then about the passing automobiles. He asked me about New York—what I thought of it—did it really swing—once, apropos of nothing, he said, "I dig the way you comb your hair." Oddly enough—I had been thinking of his hair—which had one wave in the front carefully pushed into place—was long and combed into a precise duck-ass in back—laughing at his remark, said, "As a matter of fact—I dig yours"—and we both laughed.

His general appearance was engaging. He was about 5'8" in height—slim—with well-developed shoulders tapering to a narrow waist. His facial features were sharply shaped—his mouth well formed with warm red lips—his nose small with gently flaring nostrils and his deep brown eyes tending toward almond shape—giving him a rather Oriental look—heightened somewhat by an olive coloring. He was like a mischievous angel might appear.

Unexpectedly he said, "Will you be my partner? I'm lonely and need a friend—I want you for my friend." There was something so discreet and appealing in the manner in which he made the request—I suddenly felt a new stirring of life in me—as though I was being awakened after a long slumber. I felt good—yet at the same time I was filled with a feeling of shame—what right had I to come close to a young angel—what could I bring into a relationship of any kind but death and pollution—I was sick, sick, sick. I began trying to explain—"I'm broke, man—I haven't even got a place to live—the only clothes I own, I'm wearing. I can't even take care of myself—how can I possibly be of any help to you? I'm not even a good has-been. Man, you would be better off to stay away from me." He looked at me—even more intently than when he had been watching earlier—saying, "Forget it, man—just be my friend. I have a little money and you know your way around—between the two of us we'll both get straight. Don't worry—I like you, man—I think you're good people—come on—let's go somewhere and light up the joint."

It was a strange sensation—like suddenly regaining a purpose. After discussing his friend—they both came to New York from Detroit—his buddy was going to continue to Virginia to see relatives—there would be no difficulty.

He had a few dollars and we checked into the William Sloane House YMCA on Thirty-fourth Street—which began a strange friendship. He was a great cat—helped give me back a desire to live. Our knowing each other was a great experience. He taught me how to burglarize—making it a sort of adventure—rather exciting. Eventually we split up. I heard—indirectly—he is serving a big bit in Michigan State Prison.

JOHNNIE II

WE HAD CHECKED INTO THE SLOANE HOUSE YMCA DURING THE AFTER-noon. I was completely broke and Johnnie had taken one of his suits to the pawnshop. The afternoon passed quickly. We had sat talking for several hours. Johnnie had told me of himself and of Detroit—how he had decided to come to New York. He was interested in the theater—liked show business and had met a few celebrities—one of whom he intended looking up at the Capitol Theater where he was blowing with a name band (Glenn Miller's old band)—that perhaps someday he would get into show business—maybe become a singer or even an actor. He spoke of his father whom he loved but who didn't understand him. He wanted him to get a job—any kind of job—busboy—dishwasher—something. His father simply couldn't understand he wasn't cut out to work in a restaurant. He wanted to work but life was still a big adven-ture—after all, who knows, perhaps he would meet a woman he would fall in love with and she would be rich and they would travel all over the world. Maybe go to China—or Tibet—or India—would hunt ti-gers—ride elephants—sail down the Congo—smoke opium—discover a diamond mine—collect rare paintings—have sharp clothes—really live. Then also there was the possibility of becoming a revolutionary—some-where in the Latin American countries—being the leader or at least the leader's right-hand man. Besides, there was deep-sea fishing—voodoo—unexplored jungles—mountains to climb—fortunes to be won at the gambling tables in Cannes. Man—there is just too much happening in the world to get stuck in some two-bit job not paying enough to live on. He asked me if I knew anything about getting seaman's papers—explaining a friend of his had once gone to sea during the war and made a lot of money and liked the sea. He thought it would be great going to sea. I told him I already had my seaman's papers—that we would hit downtown the next day and see what could be done. We made plans for the next few days—discussing all the places we might go if he could get his papers. Suddenly he looked at me and repeated what he had said when we first became acquainted—"I like you, man—you're fine."

We weren't exactly sure what we were going to do concerning the immediate problem of obtaining money but it didn't seem to worry Johnnie and I was still close to death—aware of being alive once again—absorbed by a consciousness of no longer being alone—afraid still to believe in the miracle of being loved—amazed at my laughter—unable to accept—simply—friendship—to think in practical terms of making a daily living—only resolving to make every effort to keep Johnnie near and close to me.

The day had been cold and crisp—the evening was bright and clear—the sky filled with stars. We had stopped by the room—taken showers—dressed in some of Johnnie's clothes—each wearing leather jackets—his black, mine brown—Spanish pegged trousers (my first pair)—sports shirts fastened at the collar—leather gloves—and hats pushed back on our heads, the brims snapped down in front. We hadn't discussed what we would do. I sort of permitted Johnnie to make the decisions and thought it a great idea when he suggested—it being so beautiful a night—that we ride the Staten Island Ferry—get off in Staten Island and take a long walk.

The ride on the subway was fun—Johnnie pretending part of the time he was deaf and dumb, talking with his fingers, smiling at people—laughing at me because I didn't catch on quick enough and became embarrassed when I tried to play his game with him, becoming clumsy with my fingers. Motioning finally for me to join him on the front platform of the subway car where for the rest of the ride he recited make-believe poetry—becoming dramatic—waving his arms around—exclaiming in heavy resonant tones. He was the knight of old—come to save the maiden in distress—to slay the dragon—to fight duels—to ride off into the night on a black stallion. Aboard the ferryboat we stood out in the cold wind pretending to be Vikings—setting sail for distant ports—prepared to discover new lands, new people. Gazing back now and then at the sparkling beauty of New York looming against the night sky—hailing the Statue of Liberty—shouting Ahoy! to the passengers aboard the ferry passing en route to New York—grinning at the disapproving countenances of several of our fellow riders. Johnnie put his arm around my shoulder saying, "This is real fine, man. All New York right here before me. When I feel this good, nothing can go wrong." He began singing—imitating Frank Sinatra.

Upon arrival in Staten Island we disembarked. Johnnie was leading the way—still singing—stopping now and then to comment about some passing stranger—flirting with several young girls rushing toward the ferry who began laughing among themselves—leaning a bit closer together whispering—tossing their heads—pretending to be indifferent.

We walked along one of the streets bordering the waterfront—looking at New York—coming to a standstill once while Johnnie opened his arms wide as though to gather in the whole scene—slowly closing them and asking me if I could imagine what it must have looked like to the first settlers when it was still a wilderness—an island of forests belonging to the Indians—teeming with wildlife—birds—all kinds of wild animals—deer, rabbit, fox, bear. He said he would have liked to have been alive then and have discovered the one particular spot which is Manhattan. He said, "It's great now—but it must have been even greater then. Man—if I had been there I'd have arranged to keep it just as it was—no big buildings—no automobiles—only a few people, carefully selected. Think, man—when you were hungry, there was the river—or you could hunt—and you could have a small garden and grow all kinds of vegetables. You could have had a little house—and a fireplace—and at night you could have sat around talking—telling stories—or strumming a guitar and singing. Wow—man—it sure would have been great."

We continued walking—gradually leaving the waterfront behind—until we reached a somewhat prosperous residential section—located in rather hilly terrain—with houses scattered here and there on the sides of the hills. It was still early in the evening and we could see people eating their dinners. Most of the houses were lit up but occasionally we would pass one that was dark—the owners away—perhaps visiting friends or taking in the theater in New York. At one point we reached the top of a hill with a house situated in a grove of trees about halfway down the side when Johnnie turned to me and said—"Have you ever broken into a house?"

ED LEARY

I HADN'T BEEN IN NEW YORK LONG WHEN I MET EDDIE. WHEN I FIRST arrived I was stone broke—and like every young kid who hits New York I went directly to Forty-second Street. I hadn't known anything about Forty-second Street but the name—nevertheless, there I went—in no time becoming hip to the hustling routine—getting by fairly easily— meeting all kinds of people—having experiences I never suspected possible.

I soon became acquainted with many of the regular habitués—one night getting disgustingly drunk with a kid who was going on his second year as a Forty-second Street hustler—doing a little stealing on the side— taking me along on this particular occasion—showing me how to break into automobiles—stealing such items as suitcases, topcoats, suits or anything of value left in the car—and because we were drunk and hardly recognizing what we were doing, we got caught—each of us ending up serving six months in Rikers Island.

This was my first prison experience and although in many respects unpleasant—at the same time interesting. When we were released we went right back to Forty-second Street.

At the corner of Eighth Avenue and Forty-second Street there used to be a notorious bar where petty crooks—fags—hustlers—and people of every description hung out—known as the Bucket of Blood—although that wasn't the real name. Someone would say, "Man, I've got to cut out now—I'll pick you up later at the Bucket of Blood"—and you knew where he meant. I guess every city has its Bucket of Blood because I have run into several of them all over the country.

The first night following my release I went into the Bucket of Blood and met Eddie. I had been standing at the bar—looking the crowd over and nursing a glass of beer—when from out of nowhere Eddie came over and spoke to me. He said, "Hi—would you like to have a drink with me?" I said, "Sure—why not?" He told me to go ahead and order a shot of whiskey and to forget the beer. He said he had been watching me for some time and figured I was probably broke and could use a couple of drinks. The place was exceptionally crowded with people pushing and milling around the bar—the jukebox blasting some popular record. The whole room was filled with smoke—the overhead fluorescent light filtering through it giving the place an eerie quality. The shouting and talking deafened one—mixed with the blaring sounds of music—the general atmosphere was like a small slice of hell. Eddie said he had seen me before, and asked me to guess where he had seen me. I named a few places around the Square. Each time he shook his head, smiling—at last saying, "It was in jail—over on the Island. I used to watch you in the mess hall at chow time. Your company went in ahead of mine. I noticed how you always kept yourself looking pretty sharp— your hair combed just so—you stood out from the others around you. I tried to meet you but somehow it never worked out. I figured you might hang out around the Square."

Eddie's appearance was good-looking in the sense he bore himself with a quiet dignity—conservatively—with the suggestion of an inner turbulence threatening to come to the surface were he to relax—piquing my curiosity—giving me the impression of depth. His coloring was medium-light. His facial features finely drawn—somewhat sharp and pointed—eyes gray, from within full of light—his mouth thin and well shaped. His hair was wavy—streaked silver gray—of which he was exceedingly self-conscious. He was about twenty-eight at the time I am speaking of—and he was sure his hair made him appear old—then he was sure it was conspicuous or that it made him look effeminate.

We stood talking at the bar a long time—getting a little drunk—telling each other about ourselves—our plans, our experiences, how we had gotten into trouble, into jail—finally one or the other mentioned narcotics. He told me he had first started using heroin or H while in the Army in Panama. At that time he used stuff for a period of about eighteen months until he ran into some difficulty with a girl he was shacking up with who in a fit of jealousy—as I remember the story—reported him to the Army authorities causing him to be dishonorably discharged after being sent to the stockade where he served almost three years. He returned to his beloved Brooklyn—staying off stuff—getting a job as a trolley driver—until one night two years before we met, he pulled into the car barn, stepped down off his car into the path of a car pulling into the barn—was hit—receiving a broken leg. While convalescing he became involved with a male nurse who would occasionally supply him with morphine and he was soon hooked.

I told him of my own experiences with junk in Chicago. Of how along with a friend of mine I had started picking up on heroin—finally getting mildly hooked—having to kick when my only source of supply had been arrested and sent to jail. I explained I was pretty green about the whole routine and that when it became necessary to kick I went to my mother—who had been very upset—but had sensibly taken me to her doctor, who had given me a reduction cure. I told him it had been an unpleasant experience, but I had actually not had too much trouble and that it had happened about three years ago.

During our conversation we both discovered that we were still interested in junk and that we both preferred it to drinking. I mentioned knowing a pot connection who might be around although I hadn't seen him since getting out of jail—that I liked smoking pot—we called it gauge or tea in those days—and perhaps if we looked around we could find him. Eddie said he didn't like smoking it—that he didn't like the kick. He felt if one was going to smoke it should be the pipe—opium. He did suggest maybe the guy would know where to score some H— asking me if I would like to shoot a little stuff.

We had another drink at the bar discussing what we would do if we did score. I told him—as he had guessed—I was broke without even a place to sleep and had come into the joint intending to pick up a queen, score for some loot, and get a place to stay. Eddie said not to worry about that—if I wanted to I could check into a hotel with him—he was planning on staying over in New York for a couple of days anyway— besides he liked me and this would give us an opportunity to get to know each other better—also he was anxious by now to get some stuff and get on. I had taken an immediate liking to Eddie and this plan suited me fine.

Shortly after leaving the Bucket of Blood, along Eighth Avenue between Forty-fifth and Forty-sixth streets, we located Hugh the pot connection and asked him to make a heroin score for us. As it happened he had recently run into some fellow uptown while picking up his supply of pot who had suggested he might run into some of his customers anxious to cop some stuff and get in touch with him—he could get as much as he wanted. Stuff was being pushed in capsules at the time and we asked Hugh to pick up two. Eddie and I had decided to check into a small hotel at Fifty-first Street and Eighth Avenue where I had stayed a few times before being arrested. I was sure we could get a room without difficulty. We arranged to meet Hugh in the coffee shop on the corner in an hour.

Eddie and I continued up the avenue until we reached the hotel where we rented a room for a week, Eddie having decided at the last minute—since he was holding fairly heavy financially—he might as well stake me to a room as it would give him a place to fall into should he return to the city sooner than he expected.

While we were waiting for Hugh to get back we cut down the street to a drugstore where I used to be able to buy anything short of the real McCoy—Benzedrine, Seconal, Nembutal, eye droppers, and hypodermic needles. We bought two droppers and a couple of spikes—needles, No. 26 half-inch, and some wires for cleaning them. Then we stopped at the Automat for coffee and, before leaving, picked up two teaspoons.

We had been doing a lot of talking—feeling each other out about our likes and dislikes—and the more I learned about Eddie the greater my interest in him became. Although I had met thieves and hustlers and knock-around characters of all kinds in the past couple of years, Eddie was the first I met who lived by his wits—impressing me as being competent and capable of carrying out his plans. He was intelligent and carried himself with what is generally termed—in the vernacular of the underworld—class. There was a certain evilness about him which appealed to me, although much later I came to realize the evilness I saw—and this was true in Eddie's case particularly—was mostly projection on my part. Oddly enough Eddie recognized this much sooner than I did—allowing me to relax—and to display what could be called a voraciousness and lack of inhibition with him I have never attained before or since with anyone else.

We met Hugh one time and he asked to come along with us—he said he had never tried stuff and wanted to—he'd heard so much about it he wanted to find out if it was as great as everyone said. The three of us went up to the room and turned on. It didn't take much to get us high—neither Eddie or me had used for quite some time and it was Hugh's first experience. We all three got really stoned and sat around talking or simply going on the nod until the early hours of the morning—finally dropping off to sleep—awakening much later in the day. We all three felt fairly good although somewhat sluggish. Hugh lit up a couple of sticks of pot before cutting out—leaving us feeling good and a bit high. After Hugh left, Eddie and I split what was left of the stuff.

Eddie was an entirely new type of person to me. I had never known anyone like him nor for that matter have I since met anyone his equal in independence and scheming know-how. He wasn't vicious or cruel in any sense—yet at the same time he was completely devoid of sentiment. He spoke in detail of his past life but never once mentioned having any feeling of love for anyone he had known and spoke of his family in an offhand, detached manner. He had lived with several women but seemingly missed none of them and spoke of having left each one in the way one might speak of discarding an old suit or piece of clothing one has become weary of. Yet—and this is what attracted me particularly—there was a certain warmth and immediate concern for—in this instance—my feelings, permeating his conversation and dealings with me not only at the time, but for as long as we were closely associated. There were very pronounced homosexual characteristics in his personality—he permitted himself indulgence in this with me—so that in a sense strong feelings of love existed between us although he carefully avoided its becoming obvious to any of our mutual acquaintances—as well as refusing to acknowledge it even when we were alone in words—only in physical fact. He did say at one time that I was the only male he had ever allowed himself such complete freedom with.

During our discussion prior to going downstairs for breakfast—we decided it would be great to try to score again later in the evening. We had talked about the money situation and Eddie had come up with a plan. Shortly before we had been sent over to the Island there had been a big drive on against the junk pushers. San Juan Hill—a notorious cesspool of crime and corruption of all kinds where—if one was at all known—one could cop anything from ordinary sleeping pills to opium—had finally been cleaned up. For a long time the police had been unable to move in on the district. It was actually a little world—set apart—controlled entirely by the underworld element. Just how they'd accomplished cleaning it up was rather a mystery, but clean it up they did along with the Lower East Side, Broadway, and various other spots. A panic was on among the junkies. There were still a few people able to connect—but on the whole, conditions were bad. A little of this I already knew but Eddie was well informed about the details. He spoke of having run into a Broadway whore he knew who had told him that most of the girls were finding the going rough—unable to score regularly—and were willing to pay almost any amount of money to make a steady connection. Eddie explained that he knew of several doctors in

Brooklyn who—if given the right approach—would write prescriptions for five grains of morphine. He had it figured between the two of us we could score enough from these doctors to keep ourselves supplied—the rest we could sell to the girls along Broadway. He said, "We'll pick up about five customers—steady and dependable—and promise to keep them supplied regularly." The plan struck me as excellent, although I had some doubts about my ability to convince the doctors to write. Eddie told me not to worry—he would tell me exactly what to say—and with my appearance I'd have no trouble at all. This wasn't exactly an original plan with Eddie. He told me he knew a couple of people who were keeping up habits making croakers. In fact, later it became so common that the government men began cracking down on the doctors—taking a number of them to court for writing illicit prescriptions—all of them losing their licences to practice medicine—and many ending up serving time. We got into the racket at the right time and had nearly a two-year run before getting into trouble.

We spent the remainder of the day wandering around Times Square— Eddie introduced me to a couple of the whores he knew who said they were willing to do business with us if we could promise a steady thing. They weren't particularly interested in morphine—since they had heroin habits—but they figured the situation had reached the point where as long as they could depend on at least a daily meet, that in the long run they'd be better off making the switch. We did a lot of window shopping. In those days I was still clothes-conscious—picking out shirts— suits—shoes—and all kinds of haberdashery. Eddie considered himself a sharp dresser and he was. Late in the evening we cut into Hugh and picked up two more caps. He told us his man was hot and didn't like doing business in such small amounts. He told us his man had told him he was trying to get rid of what he had left in one drip—about an ounce—so unless we wanted to take the whole thing we had better look for someone else. We explained we had other plans. Hugh half wanted to come along with us but we said we had business to discuss and we'd pick up some other time. The two of us returned to the room—got straight— Eddie then proceeding to instruct me in how to go about scoring with a doctor.

Actually the routine was fairly simple. My approach consisted of telling the doctor—with lowered eyes, hesitant speech, and seeming humiliation—that I was a drug addict—having picked up the habit while visiting in Florida with my people. We had traveled through the Everglades, and I had picked up a severe colitis condition accompanied by amoebic dysentery—the doctor giving me morphine to ease the pain. This was the general outline of the story, except that I also explained that the doctor who'd treated me since I returned to New York had recently passed on and that I didn't like or feel comfortable with the man who had taken over the practice. It worked, and the next day in Brooklyn the first doctor Eddie recommended wrote for five grains of morphine without giving me any trouble. Eddie had waited down the block for me, and as soon as I came out, he went in. His story was considerably different from mine—having to do mostly with his accident in the car barn and his leg not having healed properly. The same day we each made three doctors. One of them we simply hit on by chance passing his office—deciding to go in and try him. The other two—Eddie said—had been recommended to Eddie by some guy he had met in jail. Getting the prescriptions filled was no problem since they were legitimate—a doctor had written them. We received vials—government sealed—with twenty quarter-grain tablets for each script—giving us a total of thirty grains of morphine at the end of our afternoon's work. The prescriptions had cost around three dollars apiece—and getting them filled averaged one dollar and a half to a dollar seventy-five. Our cash outlay amounted to almost twenty-five dollars, plus personal expenses—which came to roughly five or six dollars. That evening the two girls—along with a friend of theirs—bought all but three grains—at one dollar a quarter grain. Morphine sold or pushed on the street cost four dollars per grain.

We were moderately successful and soon did a steady business—with four, occasionally five, regular customers—Broadway whores—with a net profit of about one hundred dollars a day. Eddie proved an excellent manager of money—although we both steadily increased our own habits, however—cutting down the actual financial gain. One whore alone—a large, wholesome, and good-looking woman named Sal—did forty to forty-five dollars of business with us a day. She was a good money-maker and we could always count on hearing from her—sometimes two or three times an evening. She became a good friend—frequently coming to see us—sitting and talking or shooting up—taking a rest in between her working periods. She was remarkable in that she showed absolutely none of the effects of the usual drug addict. She continued to remain large and healthy-appearing, with bright natural coloring. She was a heavy eater, smoked incessantly, and shot up no less than ten grains of morphine each day. She was amazingly good-natured—seldom indulging in self-pity—never gossiping and always anxious to help anyone. She'd set aside a few dollars a day—for handouts, to the less fortunate sisters or for the innumerable Times Square characters she knew out scuffling and trying to score in one way or another. Sal had a daughter somewhere—with someone—whom she supported. She loved her deeply and never failed—when occasionally the three of us went out for something to eat—often to Chinatown—to pick up some trinket to surprise her with.

Our business venture proved successful and we began laying money aside for a trip the following spring to California. The holidays came and went and one day we realized we had been together almost a year. It seemed incredible. A whole year had passed with things going smoothly—a record for both of us. In the beginning Eddie had been a bit self-conscious about our relationship but even that had ceased to be of importance and he no longer considered it strange. We were unexcitably happy. We had our arguments and sudden flare-ups of temper—but thus far nothing really serious. Eddie had gotten rather melancholy around the holidays but it had passed quickly.

Most of the doctors we had started with were still with us. One suddenly had trouble with the law over an abortion case he was involved in and another had gotten cold feet after some junkies he had been writing scripts for took a fall—mentioning his name to the police—who had promptly paid him a visit. He refused thereafter to write any more for anyone. As for the rest—about six in all—most were not only writing prescriptions for us in our names but would also—for a few extra dollars—write scripts with other names which they'd readily honor when questioned by the pharmacist. There were several druggists as well that we had gotten to know who would always fill our scripts without question.

Most of our doctors were located in Brooklyn. One afternoon I made a trip over to Brooklyn alone in order to pick up an extra script from a doctor who had been with us almost from the first. Eddie planned on seeing someone else—the two of us expecting to see each other back at our place late in the afternoon. It was a beautiful day—all golden and full of sunshine and the first hints of warm weather.

I had seen the doctor—incidentally picking up a quarter-grain fix before leaving his office—returned to New York—stopped by a drugstore—had the prescription filled—stepped out onto the street—and was just getting ready to cross over to the other side—when I was suddenly gripped on the arm by a neatly dressed, unassuming appearing young man who—before I realized what was actually happening—reached into my pocket, removed the box of morphine tablets, and said, "Step over here, I want to speak with you," flashed a badge, and further added, "Federal agent." I was so completely taken by surprise it was several minutes before I became conscious of just why I was being stopped. He was very polite, asking me about the box of morphine—inquiring whether I was an addict or not—and if so how long had I been an addict—but particularly how long this doctor had been taking care of me. He went on further to explain there had been a number of prescriptions written in his name. I answered his questions as honestly as possible without admitting the doctor had long known I was simply a drug addict and was merely doing business with me. He then asked me to step back into the drugstore—while he checked further with the druggist, who assured him that the script was legitimate—having called the doctor to make sure. He and the druggist spoke in undertones for a few minutes. He then turned to me and told me I could go—giving me back the morphine at the same time.

I departed as quickly as possible. I used a somewhat roundabout way of returning home—feeling pretty sure at the same time the man undoubtedly already knew where I lived. When I got in, Eddie still hadn't returned. I called the doctor immediately—describing in detail exactly what had happened—advising him to lay off writing scripts for a while at least. A short time later Eddie returned and I gave him a full account of what had taken place. Eddie was calm about the whole thing—saying only, "Well, man, that's the end of another good doctor." We discussed to some extent whether or not it would be wise to move—finally deciding in favor of staying—figuring if we were due for trouble we'd get it whether we moved or not. Eddie did make other arrangements with our customers about meets, etc. But otherwise we continued along pretty much as we had been. We never did have any further trouble directly as a result of this particular episode, but it did act as a turning point in our general good luck.

Shortly afterward one of our dependable sources of supply began getting nervous and cut us down to one script apiece a week. Almost the same thing happened with a doctor we had only recently contacted. All of them were getting jumpy. Several arrests had been made of doctors in New York and the papers had played the cases up big. We were becoming increasingly worried—having had to cut out one of our customers because we were unable to get hold of enough stuff steadily to take care of our own habits and handle the usual number of customers as well. We began looking round for new doctors, covering neighborhoods we had previously shied clear of. Then one day we solved the situation—we decided instead to write our own scripts. In the same way our first plan wasn't original, this one wasn't either. We were both conscious of the greater risk involved—but we were also aware that we were caught up in a situation we had to contend with no matter what else happened. The whole junk scene—insofar as the user was concerned—was growing worse instead of better. Junkies were becoming desperate—more and more of them turned to crimes of violence in order to keep up their habits. The stuff being pushed on the streets was becoming more expensive and harder to get. There had always been a certain amount of criminal activity involved with junk, but prior to this period it had been kept somewhat to a minimum. Now anything went. Also—and what is probably the strangest aspect of the whole deal—more and more people were taking an interest in junk—becoming curious about it—experimenting with it. The idea was that if you handled junk—you automatically made money.

Eddie and myself were fortunate in that we were pretty well organized and, although our immediate predicament was unpleasant, we felt our new solution would be effective. And it was.

We spent one afternoon going around to doctors' offices—choosing times we were fairly sure they weren't in—picking doctors in most instances whose offices were in their homes—asking permission of whoever answered the door to await the doctor's return—gaining access to their offices—stealing the prescription blanks—usually left somewhere on top of the desk—calling whoever had let us in—saying we had changed our minds and would call later. We worked separately. Eddie picked up three pads and I managed to get hold of two. That evening—choosing a time when we were sure the doctor would be out—usually calling his phone number to be sure—after simply copying a prescription we filled in our stolen blanks—about three of them—went into the drugstore and had them filled with no trouble. The system worked splendidly—although once in a while a druggist would become suspicious and suggest we return later.

We'd worked out a rather cool procedure for filling them out—taking names from the telephone directory listed in the vicinity of the drugstores we had planned on hitting that day. Eddie would write the scripts one day—going along to keep me company—waiting outside until I'd come out—and the next day I'd write the scripts and Eddie would get them filled.

Our life together was still going smoothly, but an almost imperceptible tension underlying our everyday activities had crept in. We were beginning ever so slowly to draw apart. It was noticeable in little things. We had always sort of made a ritual of shooting up together—now sometimes we wouldn't wait for each other. We had always enjoyed going places together—now we started cutting out alone. We began seeing more people—occasionally one of us would leave with one of our visitors—taking in a show alone—splitting from the scene without saying when we'd be back—arguing more frequently and with lesser provocation.

Meanwhile, Phil White came back on the scene. I had found him in the beginning an interesting person—so when he began coming around inviting us out or up to his place to pick up on music and maybe smoke a little pot and keep him and his old lady company, Eddie would decline and I would go along. Phil had just gotten settled with the woman he was living with—whose whole background was a pseudo-respectable setup which she clung to tenaciously—being attracted to Phil primarily because he represented a side of life she secretly felt part of. She was supporting Phil at the time and he felt duty-bound to spend much of his time with her. He liked taking me to their place because he could relax and be himself while at the same time confident I wouldn't do anything to jeopardize his position with Kay.

I don't think Eddie was jealous of my interest in Phil—but he resented him—telling me Phil was unworthy of any sincere friendship and basically a fool and a phony. He admitted having had business dealings with Phil—but assured me Phil was not to be trusted.

Then one afternoon we got the news that Sal had been arrested. We both felt badly and Eddie went down to the women's prison to try and bail her out. She was a multiple offender and they had set bail at fifteen hundred, which we did not have. She had become so much a part of our daily life we felt the loss greatly. It turned out it was the last time I was to see her for many years. I ran into her about five years ago. She was looking much the same—a little heavier, perhaps—of course older—but surprisingly no longer on junk—married—happily getting ready for her daughter's graduation from high school. We talked a while—reminiscing over the past—wondering about Eddie.

New York was exceedingly hot that summer. The heat settled down over the city in a huge blanket. The days were long and humid and nobody was any more active than was absolutely necessary. Somehow we got through the summer—sleeping late in the day—getting up—cashing our scripts—taking care of business—lying around or making Central Park. Eddie had started going back to Brooklyn more often and began talking about moving over there sometime during the autumn. I was a little hesitant about committing myself to such a move mostly because I felt it would only complicate our setup.

September came along with the early fall rains. I purchased an umbrella and frequently carried my extra scripts folded inside. We no longer went out together to cash scripts.

It had been raining all day and was beginning to clear up. We had both slept late and Eddie awakened feeling disagreeable. It was my afternoon to go out, and while Eddie wrote out scripts, I got dressed. I'd bought a new fall suit I liked, and although it still looked like more rain, I decided in favor of wearing it. I affected very conservative attire at the time because—principally—I was working the East Side and felt it wise to be as inconspicuous as possible. I wore a neat white shirt and tie and with my umbrella hanging from my arm—my new suit—and a hat—I looked like the height of respectability.

There was a sudden heavy downpour as I came out of the building. I hailed a cab and was driven to the East Side to the approximate location of one of the stores I had anticipated using. I presented my prescription and was told to wait. The pharmacist returned in a moment saying, "I am sorry but I can't fill your prescription—we are completely out of quarter-grain tablets." Had it been a less unpleasant day, weatherwise, I wouldn't have minded quite as much as I did. I could simply have ignored the entire district and moved on to the next location of my prearranged schedule—later, if necessary I could return home and make out new scripts for a different neighborhood. Since it was so bad—I decided to go to a drugstore a short distance away that I had been to on at least three previous occasions. There were several drugstores most cooperative and I had added this one to the list. My reason being—the druggist had known after my first visit to him that my scripts were phony—surely having checked with the doctor at his first opportunity—and if not after the first time, certainly after the second time I had come in. By this time, the late-afternoon commuters were beginning to pour into Grand Central. Many of them were in the store—located across the street from one of the entrances to the station—making last-minute purchases of toilet articles, etc. Therefore when I presented my script to one of the clerks—one I had spoken with before—he on this occasion greeted me pleasantly—inquiring after my general welfare—apologizing, due to the rush of business, for my having to wait—assuring me I would be taken care of as quickly as possible. There were two entrance ways to this particular store—it is still in the same location and I have been in it many times since—and I was taken by complete surprise when, after having waited only a few minutes, I looked up to see two uniformed policemen rapidly approaching by way of one entrance—at the same time I realized that the two men who were pushing through the crowd of shoppers toward me from the other entrance were plainclothes detectives. Both sets of police reached me simultaneously—grabbing me on both sides— pulling me in both directions—beginning to argue immediately as to who had gotten to me first and should receive credit for making the arrest. It was both tragic and humorous. Finally, while creating a great scene of capturing a dangerous narcotics addict—implying I was danger- ous—pointing a gun at me—telling me to stand still—not to make a move—both pairs towering over me in height—frisking me—grabbing my umbrella—one of them loudly saying, "None of that," as though I had intended using it as a weapon—they pushed me toward the door- way—telling people to step aside—out into the street where a huge crowd had gathered—peering and grimacing at me—some laughing— asking questions—others looking at me as though I were the scum of the earth—some with amazement to see a real live criminal.

They were still arguing about who was to take me to the station— peering down at me—leaning closer to me asking, "Which of us got here first?" I decided in favor of the detectives, thinking in all probability that they would be easier to get along with than a couple of promotion- conscious harness cops. I chose wisely. They turned out to be fairly decent—even arranging to get me a fix when I began getting really sick. I was booked and charged with attempting to obtain narcotics through fraud—a misdemeanor—and was eventually sentenced to another six months on Rikers Island. I kept Eddie's name out of it—not giving them my proper address—telling them that my only possessions were those I had with me—that I had been making it playing cards and shooting craps—that I had not used drugs for long—that I had been living in the Mills Hotel paying by the night. They asked me about the scripts and I told them I had bought them from a guy on the corner of Forty-third Street and Eighth Avenue—one of the kids from Forty-second Street pointed him out to me—I didn't know his name and wasn't sure I could recognize him were we to come face to face. They didn't believe me but there was nothing they could do about it.

While I was away Eddie corresponded with me regularly, sending money for cigarettes and a few of the necessities—such as a toothbrush and toothpaste—soap—and candy. Candy is a must when a junky kicks a habit. He kept me informed to some extent of his activities. Much of what was happening with him I had to guess from the well-known reading between the lines. Sal had finally been sent away for a year—another of the girls had taken a fall—there had been some difficulty at home concerning someone who'd come to visit us drunk and disorderly, and Eddie had been asked to move. He was finding the going rough—and missed me. By the time of my discharge Eddie had gone back to Brooklyn. What he'd failed to mention was that he had—just before moving to Brooklyn—acquired a new partner.

When I got out I went directly to the Brooklyn address. Instead of Eddie opening the door, Georgie, his new partner, opened it saying, "Hello—Ed isn't home just yet. We have been expecting you. I hope you will like me. Eddie thinks we all three can get along real great. He told me what a swell guy you are." Georgie was a nice person but perhaps jealousy caused me to resent him and decide against any plans in which the three of us were to be involved. Georgie had some stuff stashed away and before Eddie got in he gave me a little fix. Eddie arrived all smiles and good will—telling me how much he had missed me—how bad he had felt when he realized—when I didn't come home the night of the pinch—what must have happened. Georgie had something to do and excused himself saying, "You two will have a lot to talk about—I'll see you both later." As soon as Georgie left, Eddie came over, put his arms around me and said, "Man, I've missed you so much—I never thought it could happen that anyone could come to mean as much to me as you do." He explained things had gotten pretty bad financially and that he had originally decided to double up with Georgie to save on expenses, but since living with him had grown to like him. He said he was sure I could understand and that Georgie being there wouldn't make any difference to our friendship. He had it figured the three of us could reorganize our original setup—living in Brooklyn this time but still doing business in New York. He went on to explain he had made some new contacts and we could—with the third party—do even better than when there had been just him and me. I told him it all sounded great but somehow I didn't like it—also I said I wasn't sure I liked Georgie.

The section of Brooklyn Eddie and Georgie had settled in is known as Bay Ridge, and although I stayed there only a short time I liked it. A good number of people living in the district are of Scandinavian descent—many going to sea. The bars in the neighborhood cater to seamen and there is a certain air of the romantic and adventurous. Eddie had discovered several Swedish eating places we frequented often—the three of us creating a strange appearance in our sharp clothes and somewhat obvious disregard of the staid conservative manner of our neighbors. We came and went at all hours of the day and night. It was apparent none of us worked legitimately—still we were never made to feel uncomfortable or treated as outsiders—the principle of live and let live seemingly the opinion of most of the people we came in contact with. The apartment was spacious and comfortably furnished—but I felt a strangeness with Georgie I was unable to overcome and began to think about leaving.

We settled to a routine satisfactory to the three of us—each of us assuming certain responsibilities of our own. It worked well enough and perhaps we could have continued indefinitely. Somehow though—I was uncomfortable with Georgie. I was jealous of the attention Eddie directed toward him—becoming angry on the slightest pretext—finally telling Georgie I didn't like him—considered him weak and ineffectual—stupid and a bore—and that I was going to clear out. Eddie grew angry, accusing me of being unkind and unfair—telling me if I didn't apologize to Georgie I had better make arrangements to live somewhere else. It was true—I had been unfair and I knew it—but it was impossible for me to apologize.

We did spend our last few days together happily, but when I succeeded in locating a room in Manhattan I was relieved to get away. It was fine to once again be alone. We continued seeing each other daily—making the doctors—occasionally falling into a movie—or going to Chinatown for food. It wasn't long before I began meeting new people and frequently when Eddie and Georgie would suggest out going somewhere together I would already have other plans.

And so we gradually drifted apart. I found new sources of supply for junk—beginning to cop uptown in Harlem. Eventually I failed to keep appointments with Ed and Georgie—and it followed that soon thereafter I stopped seeing them altogether.

One day, running into a mutual friend, I learned Georgie had been arrested and Ed had gone to the hospital in Kentucky to kick his habit.

Several years passed and one day I ran into Ed. We were both pleased to see each other but neither of us had any desire to become involved in close association. We talked and reminisced—shot up a couple bags of heroin—spending the night in a Times Square hotel. Next day—Ed had plans of his own and so did I. We parted good friends.

Up until three years ago, periodically we would meet—sit and talk—and once I went back over to Brooklyn with him and stayed over the weekend. Georgie had disappeared completely and I have never run into him.

I never see Ed anymore and I can't pick up any news of him. Every now and then I'll meet someone who remembers us as a team and we'll discuss the good old days. Everyone remembers Ed with good feeling.

It is possible I'll see him again—although in my heart I feel he might be dead.

Looking back over our friendship it occurs to me Ed Leary influenced my life in all probability more than anyone else I've known.

SEA VOYAGE

PHIL AWAKENED ME EARLY IN THE MORNING—APPARENTLY BOZO LET him in—pulling the bedclothes off and exposing me to a cold draft from the open window. Bob and I had shared the studio couch in the front room and we had drawn together during the night to keep warm and I had wrapped my arms around him—something that I secretly wanted to do—and it was with added reluctance that I greeted Phil who stood hovering over the couch sort of clucking with a widespread leer on his face. It was from a pleasant drowsiness and peaceful dream I awakened into the nightmare morning.

A cold chilling wind whined outside the windows and the sky was overladen with gray clouds. Cold city sounds carried up from the streets and there was nothing I wanted quite so much as to remain in bed.

Kay and Phil had recently been quarreling—Kay complaining about Phil's habit and pleading with him to try and kick—and finally suggesting that he and I get a job aboard a ship together so that we both might kick. Phil, in order to restore peace and partly through feelings of guilt and frustration, was won around and had spent the preceding day convincing me the idea was sensible. It wasn't that either of us was anxious to kick but rather that the conditions we were surrounded by had forced us to seek a means of escape.

We both had obtained our seaman's papers at about the same time but had never made a trip together and in some respects the plan was appealing.

At any rate he was now standing over me, insisting I get up so we could go down to the ship companies for jobs.

Bozo was wandering around the kitchen preparing coffee while making little snide remarks about my general indifference to the more practical aspects of life.

Bob had promptly rolled over, pulling the blankets up around his ears and mumbling to the effect he wished we'd get the hell out so he could go back to sleep.

And so I got up.

I had saved a little fix, and after getting straight I dressed while Phil and Bozo sat gossiping about what a dear, fine female Kay was and how understanding. After all, there were really few respectable women willing to put up with a junky and, at least in Bozo's opinion, Phil should be grateful.

Kay was actually a vampire and eventually drained Phil.

We finally got started and went directly down to a company sending out tankers and were assigned to a ship bound for Honolulu. Phil was signed on as a ship's messman and I took utility man in the galley. The man out of the corner of his mouth had told us, "The ship is a hot ship"—meaning that it was scheduled to sail almost immediately—which was good since by this time both of us were anxious to get away as quickly as possible.

We sailed from New Jersey early the following morning. We had rushed around New York all the preceding day, first making a connection—this was to be a slow withdrawal cure—then saying good-bye to acquaintances and friends—making arrangements to have our few possessions taken care of while gone—and a special farewell with Kay. We sailed in a blinding snowstorm.

We had been the last to sign aboard and received what was left of the sleeping quarters. Our fo'c'sle was large enough to accommodate two more—for some reason I never discovered we remained alone—and was situated in the aft end of the ship. It was comfortable and we succeeded in unconsciously turning it into what the captain later suggested looked like an opium den.

Phil immediately climbed into his bunk—staying there for two days, causing the steward to become almost sick with anxiety and to bombard me—though I provided myself with a good supply of Benzedrine and was busy performing my required tasks with what was to the steward amazing vigor—with all sorts of questions. He found it difficult to understand what could possibly be ailing Phil and was somewhat hesitant in accepting my explanation to the effect that he had been drinking—heavily—for the past few weeks. "Don't worry, man, he'll come around. Give him time." To which the steward replied, "I know—but the same can be said for most of the crew—and they're up and working."

The ship was an old ship—having hit the sea about 1915—and in the rough seas creaked and groaned. It had been making the same run for many years and it wasn't until we entered the Caribbean that it settled down. The trip down the Atlantic Coast was uneventful except that en route we gathered several hundred birds. We would awaken in the morning and there they were—roosting all over the ship—and when we began reaching the area off the Florida coast they began departing. By the time we passed through Windward Passage most of them were gone. I don't know what kind of birds they were—although I did recognize an owl which was almost the last to leave—but I was much impressed by them and they were the first of a series of natural phenomena to fill me with awe and wonder during the voyage.

The crew was an interesting group of old-time seamen—the kind that one sees hanging around the bars on South Street along the waterfront in New York, in the Seamen's Institute, or sitting around in groups, passing a bottle of wine among themselves and looking like typical bums. Not one of them had even been to Maritime School and Kings Point was only a name as far as they were concerned. One old deck hand had been around the world eighteen times and could tell stories about every port he had been in. They were a rugged lot—filled with a sense of joy of living I have never encountered in any similar number. They were all friends and many had sailed together for a long period of time.

Phil and I were rather outsiders and it took awhile before they accepted us into their confidence. Phil was more successful than I in making friends with them, and when he finally came out of his two-day sleep it was no time until he knew practically everybody.

The captain was an old Dutchman, burly and gruff, who stayed much to himself in his own quarters. The only time I heard him speak was after he received a report from the steward—this happened outside Aruba as we were leaving on our way toward Panama—that I had refused to sort out some old rotten potatoes—suggesting that if the steward wanted it done he do it himself—and besides it wasn't my job—and that he didn't know what to do about Phil and me—we were good workers but inclined to do as we pleased. The captain had come to our fo'c'sle and after looking around said, "Goddamn—this looks like an opium den. You guys hopheads?" This was said in a heavy guttural accent. We both assured him such was not the case and he left telling us, "Try and get along with the steward—who is a damn fool."

We had an exceptionally fine time in Aruba. As a matter of fact the captain was closer to the truth than he knew—since while in Aruba we had picked up yen-pox and had stayed knocked out the whole time we were there.

Aruba is a small island and very tropical as to climate. We had not been there an hour when out of the clear blue sky a sudden cloud appeared and unleashed a deluge of rain which lasted a short time and then disappeared, leaving once again the blue and gold day. The rain evaporated quickly and everything was left dry.

The people of Aruba are a mixture of light and dark and all very beautiful. There are several nationalities and it was from a Chinese we had obtained the yen-pox.

Phil became involved with a little dark-skinned girl who after they had balled kept trailing him around begging him to stay. We stayed three days.

It was while sailing thru the Caribbean Sea I first became aware of how insignificant I am in comparison to the vastness of the universe.

The sea all day remains a magnificent sparkling surface of blue—deep indigo—undulating in long rolling swells. Schools of spangle-blue flying fish skim the top. Porpoises race and leap in constant play. And at night the sky overhead is either a vast expanse of stars—some of which streak across space in splendid motion which when beheld quickens the heart— or is blanketed with great heavy clouds—black and rolling—lit from above with ceaseless flashing lightning while the sea glitters with balls of tossing phosphorus light. The air is warm and scented with the odor from the distant jungles. One has a sense of concentration of energy and sizzling, crackling electrical force, which seems to be waiting to tear the universe asunder.

It was on such a night we were steaming steadily toward Colón when Phil and myself, along with two others—one a fellow who shortly after we were acquainted had produced a cigar box full of pot, so that we had been smoking pot for the entire trip so far—and the other who had eyes for Phil and had been wooing him by stealing morphine Syrettes from the lifeboats—presenting them to him and beseeching him to have a ball—were sitting and lying on the aft end of the ship, watching the wake and exclaiming about the night and laughing and sometimes singing. The gay boy had been pressing Phil to go below with him and making various remarks full of suggestive sexual connotation—finally capping himself when he suddenly exclaimed, while observing a large, almost perfectly round puff of black smoke which had been emitted from the ship's funnel and was hanging nearly motionless overhead, "Oh look—it's just like a big dinge nut."

We arrived in Colón and were given immediate shore leave. Phil and I lost no time in searching out the native section and were successful in obtaining cocaine and undoubtedly the finest pot I have ever smoked. The man who helped us make the connection was really a cat. He was tall and very dark-skinned, dressed in a delicate pink shirt, light—almost white color—slacks, and a large-brimmed Panama hat with a brilliant red band—and sandals. He moved with truly feline grace and spoke softly thru shiny white teeth. Phil had left me standing in front of a *farmacia*— the whole storefront open to the street—while he was inside with the proprietor wildly searching the shelves looking for anything remotely resembling junk—and I had become interested in two children who were playing some kind of game when he appeared at my side and said, "Hi, man—my name is Victor—you want to get straight?"

He led me down a street—unpaved and with the houses all sitting back from the walk and wide open so that I could see into them—their occupants and what they were doing. It was a still, hot tropical night and pervading the whole street was the aroma of burning pot. Several young girls with high breasts and tight dresses passed us, giggling and swinging their hips and flashing big smiles at Victor, who pretended not to notice. Kerosene lamps and candles shed the only light except that of the night overhead. The scent of lilies blended with and perfumed the pot smoke. Suddenly Victor halted and said, "Wait here, man"—and disappeared. I stood there in wonder and delight. He returned soon and laid a long package—the length of a sheet torn from *The Saturday Evening Post,* and big around as a half dollar—of pot in my hands and then said, "You want cocaine—I get." I said yes and once again I was alone. As before, he returned quickly. I gave him the money—something like ten or twelve dollars—and returned to where Phil, who had settled for a hypodermic needle and a pocketful of Nembutal, Seconal, and Ambutal was waiting. We said good-bye to Victor and started back to the docks to catch the launch to the ship, which lay anchored out in the bay. En route we bought a small white-faced monkey from a boy who had him on a long chain and was teasing him with a stick, causing him to screech and jump.

We kept him in our fo'c'sle where he occupied the section set aside for two other men. I took one of the bunk springs and set it on end facing the bulkhead, and he slept on top and would climb up and down the springs. He was comparatively clean, in that he pissed and shit pretty much in one spot, and most of the time I had newspapers which I spread over his section. He had the run of the fo'c'sle—and took over. When he was pleased or content or after having been fed something he liked—grapes were his favorite dish—he would chitter and show his teeth, but when annoyed or angry—especially if scolded—would set up a din of screeching which could chill one to the bone.

The trip thru the locks was interesting. We stopped in Balboa for a short time but not long enough for shore leave—and then out to the Pacific Ocean.

Life aboard ship had settled down to a more or less even routine. We were making it on Benzedrine—Nembutal—Seconal—Ambutal—a fairly steady supply of morphine Syrettes and pot.

Jocko—the monkey—took to pot like the proverbial duck to water, and as soon as I would light up would jump up on my shoulder and I would exhale the smoke into his little grinning face. He and I would get high and he would balance himself on the rail while I leaned up against it and looked at the sea. He would talk to me in little chittering sounds and I would tell him about how cute and how great I thought he was. One day we saw a huge fish leap out of the sea and plunge back in again. The sea was a molten gray mass with a veil of shimmering vapor hanging just above the surface—reflecting the burning sun—when suddenly it seemed almost to shatter. This huge fish—glistening in the light—exploded in the air for a moment amidst a spray of crystal drops of water—arched—and slid back into the sea. We were both surprised. Jocko actually screeched and I almost yelled to him, "Did you dig that?"

Phil had decided to augment his finances by playing poker—and at this time spent much of his free time practicing how to stack the deck. I don't remember him being very competent at it but at any rate he didn't lose. The games would occasionally last all night and continued until we reached Honolulu.

We didn't spend enough time in Honolulu for me to absorb much of an impression of it. I recall several bars of nondescript nature where we drank rum—a small amusement park—Dole's Pineapple—palm trees—hundreds of soldiers and sailors—the YMCA where I mailed a postcard to somebody—clean streets—high prices—tapa cloth, which I like—and of course the beach and the glass-clear water and its turquoise-blue color. Also, we were completely unsuccessful as to pot or junk, although we did make a drugstore for a fresh supply of Benzedrine. I must admit that what little I saw of the islands from the ship was beautiful—and I might like going back sometime. Unfortunately—everything is too American-ized and concerned with the tourists.

We returned by the same route, and just before getting back to Balboa it was time for the full moon and for several nights I lay up on deck moon-struck. We sailed in a long silver lane. Everything lay revealed in the light of the moon and wore a glowing aura—mysterious to the night—and be-came new—retaining but little relationship to what it was in the brightness of the sun. Everything was bathed in opalescence. The night became a sort of day—strange and weird as if of another world or planet.

Once again we anchored in Balboa. We picked up supplies—bananas, oranges, green stuff, grapes and some staples—and then on back thru the Canal to Colón, where we sailed past while I stood on deck with Jocko sending telepathic messages to Victor—telling him I would never forget him and I would try and make the scene again sometime and to please remember me. We continued on thru the Caribbean, celebrating the New Year with beer and ice cream, and back up past the Florida coast after catching a glimpse of Haiti, and the Atlantic Coast—minus birds—into Chesapeake Bay to Newport News and the end of the voyage.

I left Jocko aboard the ship with one of the crew members who was signing back on and who promised me he would try and set him free—or at least see that he got a good home, maybe in Aruba or even Colón. I would have liked keeping him, but it would have been cruel of me to bring him here to New York. The weather was exceedingly cold as well, and Jocko belonged in the tropics. I could have smuggled him ashore without any trouble.

Phil and I, after we were paid off, took the train for New York and could hardly wait to make our first connection. Junkwise, the trip had been great. Habit-kicking was a complete failure, but neither one of us—as I said before—really wanted to kick.

Bozo was still wandering back and forth between Creedmore—where he had a job as an attendant—and the apartment—bickering and fretting. Bob had gotten himself involved in some big vague scheme and was rushing around in a Benzedrine whirl. Kay could hardly wait to sink her teeth into Phil.

Phil left me in front of the apartment after we had made arrangements for a meet the following day, and I went upstairs—rolled up the last of the fine Panamanian pot, flopped down, and got stoned thinking about Jocko, Victor, the Caribbean Sea and the whole trip.

BILL BURROUGHS

THE FIRST YEAR OF MY ACQUAINTANCE WITH BILL REMAINED ORDINARY in the sense of what is usual in the early stages of any friendship between two people. We gradually began to relax—or at least I did—and a degree of respect for one another evolved. I believe Bill found me interesting and someone he could use as a sort of showpiece to exhibit before his more conservative associates—as an example of an underworld type— and someone he could rely upon to be amusing and colorful. My story-telling ability had always stood me in good stead, and even then my experience had been varied and considerably out of the ordinary as far as Bill's friends were concerned. Frankly, I derived a certain pleasure in being candid and open about myself, and nothing pleased me more than an appreciative group of listeners.

Allen was very young at the time and still rather confused about his future and what he wanted or exactly what he would do once school was over. As usual he was filled with love and deep-felt desire to commu-nicate with his fellow men. Then—as now—he was ready to believe in the best in those he met, and we became very good friends. Allen has never failed me and had always been quick to offer a helping hand. He held Bill in admiration and had seen only goodness and kindness in him. Frequently we haven't seen eye-to-eye regarding Bill. Still, I firmly be-lieve that Allen's awareness of what lies below the surface of Bill's per-sonality has always been closer to the truth than my own. But then Allen sees the world with a less jaundiced eye than I.

And then there was Jack Kerouac—who regarded everyone with sus-picion but looked up to Bill and dreamed of becoming a writer.

We were a strange group, although there were many others, and along with Joan, we were the people who formed the inner circle. As closely as I am able to recall, we were the most constant companions of Bill's life.

Prior to the time I am speaking of, Bill had spent much of his life in various schools. He had traveled and done much that most people live an entire lifetime without experiencing. He was then and is now one of the most erudite men I've ever known.

Time passed and about two years after making his acquaintance, through a series of unexpected happenings—drug addiction, his and Joan's relationship, departure from New York, and a desire to experiment with the possibilities of growing marijuana and Oriental poppies, maybe manufacturing opium—Joan, her daughter Julie (four years of age), Bill and myself lived together in Texas. I look back to it as one of my greatest experiences—and also as the time I finally learned to understand Bill to a great extent—and to at last respect him as I have few people in my life.

Following a general breaking-up of the close group—or better, a spreading-out: with Allen and Kerouac going their respective ways— Allen to sea as a merchant seaman and Jack going into seclusion at home where apparently he continued working at becoming a writer—others drifting homeward to other states and cities—Bill and Joan and Julie began looking for a place somewhere in the Southwest they could settle in a while, and finally located the beautiful little cabin we lived in through the last of the winter of 1946 and up until September or almost October of 1947. It was situated on the edge of a piece of property consisting of some ninety-seven acres in the midst of a pinewoods which began at the top of a gentle incline with the cabin in an enclosed yard or fenced-in area at the top and several sheds and an old collapsing barn— and then rolled downward into a bayou, twisting and turning its way thru the country—a place of tropical vines and Spanish-moss-draped trees—where sunlight filtered through the heavy lush green-growing vegetation and one felt one could get lost—or have strange adventures— and that it had always been there since the beginning of time and had barely felt the intrusion of man. It was wild and beautiful and mysterious, and I always imagined I was entering a great steaming jungle each time I would go down to explore its shadowed depths.

The preceding year had been hectic and discouraging for me and I was extremely anxious to depart New York. All through the month of December and immediately following the first of the year I had spent much time following up the possibility of obtaining a berth aboard a tanker and of going back to sea. I had been given a lead on a tanker company that had sold a number of their ships to the Chinese and were supposedly anxious to sail their ships to Shanghai where the crew was to be discharged, given plane tickets back to the States, and then rehired in order to staff another ship bound for China to once again follow the same procedure of disembarking—flying back to the States—and making the same voyage—or perhaps become a member of another crew sailing elsewhere. It sounded made to order for me, and the afternoon I received word from Bill and Joan—plus fare and expenses for joining them in Texas—I had been given notice to report the following day at one of the piers in Brooklyn, to board a ship ready for sailing to Shanghai. I had been hired as a second cook at a salary of $350 per month with an additional bonus of $500 payable upon my return to New York. I am unable to recall what the bonus was supposedly for or what risk or inconvenience it justified but it sounded attractive—and besides just the mere thought of leaving NYC was stimulating. One can easily see my dilemma when Joan and Bill's message arrived and it became my problem to immediately reach a decision of whether it be Texas with Joan and Bill—or China and a quick return to NYC plus a good supply of money, and that had long been a desperate need. Let it suffice that curiosity and love for Joan tipped the scale in favor of joining Burroughs and helping him with his plans for experimenting with the soilless growth of marijuana and Oriental poppies. The idea was, if successful, I might become his partner in developing an American opium outlet, and perhaps corner a small part of the already thriving and fantastically lucrative junk business. I immediately wired Texas announcing my date and hour of arrival.

In the most recent of Joan's letters she had spoken of the remoteness of their location, and therefore when they sent my ticket it was for as far as Houston where I would be met by Bill and driven in his Jeep by him the last fifty miles to the little town of New Waverly, which was exactly twelve miles from where Bill had settled and was the nearest town or community of any size to his place.

Until then my dealings with Bill had been mostly brief and usually of a business nature. He had been much more closely involved with Phil White. He had met Phil the same night he had met me about two years previously. We met a very short time after my return from a great trip along with Phil down through the Caribbean Sea, the Panama Canal and into the Pacific to Hawaii and back. Phil and myself became crew members of this old tanker just at the end of the war, and although we had not been overly anxious to make any trip at the time, we were nonetheless rather concerned with cutting down our narcotics habits and this trip seemed ready-made for the purpose when we first set sail. It worked out quite the opposite, and although the voyage had been great and exciting it thoroughly failed to fulfill the original purpose. We returned still hooked and perhaps using a shade less junk than at the beginning. Running directly into an old queen and acquaintance who had access to the ship's medical supplies—plus no compunction about stealing the morphine Syrettes from the lifeboat kits—had been the major cause of our continued use of stuff, even while at sea. There was something ludicrous about going to sea ostensibly to stop using junk and completely failing. Just who in hell expects to board a ship out from the mainland and then discover shortly after losing sight of the shore that they have just run into the proverbial one chance in a thousand, the one person—the medical officer excluded—who has a direct line to the medical supplies—and at the same time, immediately becomes enamored with one's partner and friend, and is more than willing to turn over the keys of the ship's stores or do anything at all within his scope to prove his love and willingness to cooperate toward making his loved one happy?

Both Phil and myself had squandered our payoff quickly—it was comparatively small. Both of us had spent a great deal of money in each of the ports we stopped in and had drawn heavily on our salaries. About a week and a half after our return we were sitting talking in the pad we were staying in on Henry Street (Bill describes the place fairly accurately in his first book—*Junky*) and waiting for Bob Brandenberg to get home. Bob was a young cat who worked up near Columbia University as a soda jerk and shared the pad with us. We expected to borrow enough money to pay for the filling of the prescription of morphine we had gotten from one of the Brooklyn doctors we were seeing at the time. We had used the last of our money to pay the doctor and so far we had met nothing but refusal and apologetic explanation from everybody we'd asked to borrow from, and so Bob was our last hope. Neither Phil nor I was sure of what we'd do if Bob failed us, and therefore we were in rather depressed moods when Bob finally arrived bringing Bill Burroughs—Wm. S. Burroughs, and later alias Bull Lee—with him.

Bozo, who owned the apartment, was cleaning and washing after dinner in the kitchen. Phil and I were sitting talking at the kitchen table and gossiping with Bozo.

Bob introduced Bill and we asked him to join us at the table. He looked around as he was taking his coat off and finally, handing both his hat and coat to Bob, sat down. Bob had gone on through the bedroom and was preparing to settle down for the evening, busily moving from one room to another, constantly talking and asking questions. Phil and

Bill were becoming acquainted and Bozo was offering everyone tea or coffee and half-apologizing because of his surroundings and the general slum nature of the neighborhood. I had observed Bill only a moment or two but decided I didn't feel friendly toward him—sizing him up in my mind as dull appearing and a bit smug and self-opinionated and certainly not very hip. Looking at him intently it entered my mind he could conceivably be a policeman or plainclothesman—maybe even FBI—he looks cold-blooded enough to be one. That old chesterfield coat he's wearing went out of style fifteen years ago, and that snap-brim hat: Don't he think he's the rogue. Those glasses—he looks as conservative as they come in them. Glasses without rims must make him feel like he's not wearing glasses at all. I don't like him—and if Bob doesn't ask him to leave, I will. I finally stepped into the other room with Bob—speaking to him of my suspicions and asking him where and how he had met Bill, and most of all why he had brought him home. Bob laughed and reassured me. Bill was trying to pick up a little easy money by selling a sawed-off shotgun. Bob explained he had become acquainted with Bill at the soda fountain of the drugstore where he worked. He said Bill apparently was a steady customer—usually shopping in the store sometime during each afternoon and then stopping at the fountain for a soft drink and a chat. They had become friendly and one afternoon Bill had asked Bob if he had any idea of where he might sell the gun. Bob had been delighted with the question, undoubtedly flattered because of Bill's confidence. Bob wanted nothing quite so much as recognition as an underworld character—preferably in the nature of being thought of in terms of racketeer-gangster and all-around hipster. Bob had spoken of Phil and myself and of the scene in general at the apartment, and had asked Bill to await our return at the apartment and then Bob would escort him downtown and in all probability either Phil or I—or perhaps he himself—would be able to negotiate some kind of deal.

I wasn't completely convinced of Bill's harmlessness and used several arguments in favor of having Bill depart—and had almost reached the point of taking the matter into my own hands when suddenly I heard Phil say, "What's that you just said, Bill? You have morphine? What are they—morphine Syrettes? That sounds very interesting. How many?" Bill and Phil had been hitting it off splendidly and the one thing needed to solidify Phil's interest in his behalf was the mention of having drugs in his possession. Already Bill was telling him how a friend had come into possession of at least a gross of morphine Syrettes and had given them to him to dispose of. He continued, saying, "I am not sure but I think there was a holdup in a drugstore and one of the stick-up men was his friend and had decided after clearing out the cash register to investigate the narcotics cabinet and—seeing this huge package marked morphine—without thinking twice he grabbed it. Later he came to me and asked me if I could get rid of them at a profit. Also he gave me this goddamned shotgun. I don't want the damned thing and want to sell it."

Phil had listened closely, and as Bill finished his little speech Phil called to me, saying, "Hey, Huncke, our friend here has some morphine. He says he wants to sell the stuff and will let it go cheaply." Bill interrupted to say, "Well—as a matter of fact I want to sell all but one or two of these Syrettes. The one or two I keep I'd like to try taking—in order to see what the experience of taking an addictive drug is like. Have either of you any knowledge of this stuff, and if so, do you know how it is taken?"

Phil began laughing and I found myself amused, since we had been using exactly what Bill had to offer, and instinctively I knew Phil was already scheming some way to latch onto the supply and for as little as possible. I knew my desire to lay hold of the stuff was actively developed, and—although I still didn't feel that Bill should be trusted—in thinking about it, I couldn't see where Phil and myself could get into too much trouble since it was Bill who was trying to make some money on the deal—and deciding to sound out Phil in his feelings in the matter, I abruptly departed from Bob and joined Bill and Phil at the kitchen table. Phil needed no prodding and had started to discuss price and the matter of showing Bill how to take off. Bill had brought a few of the Syrettes with him and in no time we three—Bill, Phil, and I—were in the process of shooting up.

Bill was by this time obviously enjoying himself—and I had to admit to myself just possibly he was a nice person trying to experience something a bit more exciting than what he is usually involved with—and he was apparently honest about his interest in drugs.

In attempting to recall the whole scene I find I am unable to do so completely. I can't remember how the gun was finally disposed of—or if it was, for that matter—nor exactly what arrangements were made for the rest of the morphine. Let it suffice Bill took an immediate liking for taking drugs, and soon he and Phil were animatedly discussing the use of stuff—the various forms of drugs—how long Phil had been using—

how long I had used—of our serving time for possession—how miserable it was kicking—and everything else either of them could think of in the way of questions and answers.

Bill and Phil arranged to keep in touch with each other, and shortly after coming to terms regarding Phil and myself buying the Syrettes, Bill departed.

It was the beginning of a whole new life for Bill. At that time I saw very little of either of them and was a bit surprised about one week later to run into the two of them about one-thirty in the morning getting ready to take the subway at Seventy-second and Broadway. Just what it was that caused me to be that far uptown at the time I don't recall, but I can remember wondering a bit what the two of them had in common. They informed me they were making the hole together as partners, with Bill learning to act as a shill and cover-up man for Phil—helping him to pick pockets by standing near, holding a newspaper open, spread wide— Phil standing behind Bill, fingers feeling the inside breast pocket of the mark's suit jacket or perhaps the overcoat pockets searching for the wallet—or poke, as Phil referred to it. Somehow there was something ludicrous about a man of Bill's obvious educational background becoming a business partner with knock-around, knock-down, hard-hustling Phil, who had forgotten more about scuffling for money illegally than most people ever learn. Still, dope or junk has created many a strange relationship, and this was certainly no more unusual than many I'd run across. My feelings were it would undoubtedly be a great experience for Bill— and also I was glad Phil was doing fairly well—and I guessed Bill was at least indirectly responsible for Phil's seeming good luck. The three of us talked together a short while and I learned that they had been in constant touch since the evening of their first meeting, and that already Bill had a habit—not a very big habit, but a habit nonetheless—and that they had been making doctors for scripts. The Syrettes had long been used up and Phil had immediately coached Bill on how to make a doctor. According to Phil, Bill had been a natural. Just before saying good-bye, we all three decided to meet the following day. I would join them on their forage for scripts. Phil had spoken of several doctors he could no longer make but that he felt sure I could. He mentioned their names to Bill and he agreed it was more than likely. Also three people making doctors would, in the end, be able to obtain considerably more stuff than just two people. And so soon we began learning a little about Bill and his life.

My life at the time was in the usual state of chaos with three- or four-

day periods of no sleep—making it in a Benzedrine haze—hallucinat-
ing—walking along the edge of Central Park peering intently into each
clump of bushes, the shadows alive with strange shapes and formations—
or of sitting many hours at a stretch in some cafeteria talking with the
people of my acquaintance who made up the majority of the Times
Square population—a varied and rootless group, frequently homeless and
alone, existing from day to day, lonely and oddly frightened, but invariably alert and full of humor and always ready for the big chance—the
one break sure to earn them security and realization of the ever-
present dream.

Often toward the early dawn hours Bill, Phil and myself would wind
up our night consuming cup after cup of coffee—well into the day, so
late we were rather early morning—ready to visit our various doctors
and pick up as many prescriptions for morphine and Dilaudid as possible.
We all three grumbled and complained, swearing we would prefer almost
any other method of keeping ourselves straight. Yet in retrospect it was
somehow stimulating and cause for amusement—at least conversationally—particularly when Bill would bait Phil about some episode involving one of his doctors' wives who had somehow learned of her husband's
enterprising nature and his illegal manner of increasing his income—and
had decided to take matters into her own hands. She had started by
refusing to allow Phil to see the doctor, using a flimsy excuse and lectur-
ing Phil about vice and corruption and finally backing out of Phil's way
when he had barked some foul oath or other at her—telling her to shut
the fuck up, that he intended seeing her husband whether she allowed
it or not. Bill had found Phil's description of the scene extremely humorous and enjoyed getting Phil wound up.

About then Bill had discovered a small apartment on the same street
Bozo's place was—and as the rent was cheap he rented it—presumably
intending to move in and set up a sort of studio and working quarters
for himself. He was always rather vague about exactly what sort of work
he wished to do, and it was some time later I learned of his wish to write.

At the time Bill rented his apartment downtown I was spending most
of my time on and around Forty-second Street, hustling, stealing, and
simply hanging around—frequenting several of the bars and cafeterias
either on Forty-second Street or somewhere else in the Times Square
area. It was my third or fourth year on the scene, and not only was I
well known, but I had become a figure or character in my own right—
and very little had transpired within the immediate vicinity I wasn't

aware of. It was about then Kinsey began his investigation or survey of the sex habits of Americans. He had come to New York and intended interviewing as many people as possible, starting at the colleges and finally arriving at Times Square. I was one of the first people he made contact with, and after our interview he suggested my recommending him to as many of my acquaintances as possible. This I was more than willing to do, and in no time we had established a sort of business friendship. I spent much of my time hanging out in a bar on Eighth Avenue and Forty-third Street, and quite often he would stop by and invite me to have dinner with him. One evening Bill joined us and thereafter it was not unusual for Bill, Kinsey and many of Bill's friends and myself to sit in a booth talking, so that we formed a kind of group of seemingly good friends—and although I remained somewhat skeptical of Bill, it was during the time of these gatherings I began to feel friendlier toward him and to respect him.

BILL BURROUGHS, PART II

BILL MOVED UPTOWN NEAR COLUMBIA TO AN APARTMENT OWNED BY Joan Adams. She was studying at Columbia. She was in all probability one of the most charming and intelligent women I've ever met. She and Bill were immediately attracted to each other and from then until her death several years later she and Bill were never separated for very long. She loved Bill ardently and I am quite sure worshiped him in a manner most women seldom attain. He shot her accidentally causing her death.

I of course was an outsider to his environment at the time they met, and when one evening after he and I had been talking and drinking coffee in Bickford's Forty-second Street cafeteria he invited me to visit him uptown and meet his friends, it didn't enter my mind for a moment I would soon be one of the members of his immediate crowd or that from then on our lives would become permanently linked. Yet that is exactly what happened and even now—although we have drifted apart— there is still a very positive bond between us. It was through Bill that I met Allen, who, in a very strange way, has had more influence on my life than anyone I've known.

When I began seeing Bill and his friends constantly—that is, every day—practically living with them—learning to know them more intimately in a way than I had known my own family—my feelings concerning almost all of them, with perhaps one exception—Joan—were those of indifference and, to some degree, hostility. They were all so very, very intellectual—I felt as though at best they were patronizing toward me, and that there was no real feeling of warmth or affection from any of them. Still, they were at the very least interesting, and in a sense—against my will—I found myself becoming involved with them to such an extent it became impossible for me to imagine pulling away. Finally when I was arrested and served my time and returned to find them still friendly and concerned, the die was cast. Since then we have all remained closely connected.

At the time of my arrest Bill was indirectly involved and his family felt it would be an excellent time for him to leave New York.

Following his family's wishes, he and Joan set out for Texas—where they remained for a little longer than a year and where I joined them for a good part of that time.

As I have already mentioned, I corresponded with Joan and Bill—and upon receipt of their invitation to join them in Texas I immediately accepted.

I met Bill in Houston and we began our drive out to the cabin. Bill was looking well and seemed enthusiastic about his plans. He told me he had been using a little paregoric and Pantopon which Bill Garver sent him fairly regularly through the mail. He said that Joan was using Benzedrine and that he was running into difficulty keeping up the supply. He said he had made every town within a radius of fifty miles three or four times already, and he was afraid people were beginning to wonder a little about just what was going on. He said things were in pretty bad shape at the house, and a great deal of work had to be done to make the place livable. He explained that he and Joan were staying at a motel and had been going out to the cabin every day trying to shape things up. He said the bad weather would break soon and then the place would be easier to reach.

He had located in east Texas and we drove fifty miles from Houston over paved highways to the town of New Waverly—a small-sized town about five blocks long: a few stores and a filling station—just off the main highway. We drove on through New Waverly and onto a black mac-adam road which began twisting and turning as soon as we left the town and continued the same all the way to where we turned off onto a sand and gravel road into the pinewoods. We had covered twelve miles from New Waverly through countryside sparsely dotted with small farms and occasional houses along the road. It was beautiful country and as we drove Bill commented about the people and on the probably near arrival of spring. We finally reached the beginning of the woods on either side and then the turn-off. The weather was gray and damp and Bill said maybe it would be necessary to park the Jeep and walk the last half mile because he was afraid of getting stuck. We remained on the dirt road which had just made a little dip. We drove down on one side of the dip, and just before driving up the opposite side we crossed an old wooden plank bridge. The pinewoods were thick on either side and I couldn't help but wonder just what they hid from view. Every so often there would be a rural mailbox and a roadway leading off the road, but there was no other evidence of people or their houses. We remained on the gravel and dirt road about two miles, and as we came to a pair of car tracks which led into the woods, Bill slowed down and turned the Jeep onto them. We drove a short distance into the woods and I could have touched the trees alongside without difficulty. Suddenly Bill stopped the Jeep. He said we had better walk the rest of the way.

My first impression of the entire scene was that we had found a sort of paradise—and I never changed my feelings. It was a truly beautiful section. The cabin was weather-worn—silver gray—and it appeared to have grown out of the earth instead of having been constructed. It was sturdy and comfortable, and by the time we were finished repairing and straightening everything out, it was a snug little place.

Time flew and spring burst all around us. Then came summer and the heat. And before any of us really realized it, fall was upon us—our crops were picked and we were ready to split back to New York.

Talking or speaking of all that took place during that period of time would fill many pages. Let it suffice—it was an experience I'll perhaps never forget. Bill's son was born in July—and by the time we were ready to leave, Bill had been a father of almost three months' standing.

Bill had thoroughly enjoyed himself. He had played the role of the country squire. He had guns—he even acquired a small hound pup before we left. One thing worth mentioning I think is the occasion on which I saw him in a completely new way. It happened one weekend in Houston and I realized for the first time that he was a handsome man.

I spent many weekends in Houston. I had discovered a drugstore where I was able to purchase as many Benzedrine inhalers and all the barbiturates I wished—and paregoric in half-gallons, if I so desired—and therefore when I'd hit Houston it would be for the purpose of picking up supplies. I'd usually take the bus from New Waverly and return the following night about eleven-thirty and Bill would meet me, and we'd drive back to the cabin.

On the weekend I referred to I had several other things to do besides pick up drug supplies, and Bill had half-heartedly mentioned the possibility of his falling into Houston sometime Saturday afternoon. I had hit Houston late Friday and wasn't planning on returning until Sunday evening. As soon as I'd arrive in Houston I'd go directly to the Brayos Hotel, which was located alongside Houston's Chinatown. It had been a good hotel at one time, and still gave good service—although it was somewhat removed from the main section of downtown. I had checked in late and all they had left was a two-room suite, which I took. It was late in June and the weather was immensely hot.

I had made friends with several colored cats in the colored section downtown where I'd cop some pot, and one of the cats who owned a record store would let me borrow one of his record players—and I'd hook it up in my room and turn on while listening to some good sounds which my man had either recommended or I had selected.

This weekend had been no different—except when I hit the hotel after picking up the record player I ran into a cat who was a seaman— young, maybe twenty or twenty-one—and after talking with him a while, invited him up to my rooms. He was a beautiful cat and he spent the night with me—smoking and talking and listening to records. He had never actually relaxed and listened to jazz before, and he was very impressed with what he heard. We had enjoyed ourselves and were both a little surprised when there was a knock on the door. And when I asked who was there, Bill replied. I let him in—and after introducing him to my friend, asked him if he was planning on staying overnight and taking me back with him the next day. He replied that he wasn't sure, but that he had come simply to get away from the scene at the cabin and come to Houston. As well as getting reading material and a fresh supply of liquor, he wanted very much to take a bath.

While he had been telling me this the phone rang, and when I answered, it was my pot man and I arranged to meet him. Meanwhile, Bill had seated himself and was busy talking with my friend. I excused myself—explaining I had to keep a meet with the pot man—and after observing the two of them a few minutes to see if they would get along, I split out.

I kept my meet, copped, and sat around talking with the connection and his old lady awhile, and smoked a couple of joints. I was away about two hours, and when I returned, not only had they gotten along, but the two of them were stone-cold drunk.

I had seen Bill slightly intoxicated many times, but this was the first time I'd seen him really drunk. When I came in, Bill was sitting—straddling a straight-back chair—apparently deeply engrossed in what he had been discussing with my friend, who sat facing him in an armchair. Both of them were half-crocked, drunken leers on their faces. They greeted me with real cheery hellos and assured me I should join them in having a drink. Bill reached over toward an almost empty bottle of tequila and said, "Come on, Huncke, have a little snort. It'll make you feel great." He fumbled around looking for his glass and said I could drink from the glass he'd been drinking from. I thanked him and refused, telling him I thought he had had enough also, and wondering what I was going to do about him. It was obvious he could barely sit up, much less stand.

"Bill, come on—no more, please. I think maybe you better stretch out on the bed."

He stood up and rocked back and forth a couple of times and then made straight for the bed and half fell onto it in a big heap. I walked over and helped him stretch out. I removed his glasses, which had fallen askew across his face. He was half laughing and mumbling something I couldn't understand. It was at that moment—as he closed his eyes and then opened them again—looking around, then giving a big sigh—closed them and then fell asleep almost instantly—as I watched him, I began to see his face in a manner I hadn't seen it before—and I was startled as I recognized the beauty of his features—his coloring and his whole being—relaxed and graceful on the bed. His hair had fallen down over one side of his forehead like a cowlick, and he looked like a strange otherworld creature. His eyelids were tinged faintly lavender and belonged with the sharp aquiline nose and the well-shaped mouth now almost closed—the lips red and finely drawn—the corners of his mouth smooth and free of tense lines. He was certainly handsome, and although his entire coloring was delicate and there was nothing harshly masculine about his appearance, there was nothing feminine either. His was a man's face.

I was very touched, and at that instant a certain feeling of love I bear for him to this day sprang into being. I had always known him to be quick with verbal explanation and always logical and practical. He had always seemed complete master of himself, and now—seeing him defenseless and vulnerable—I understood he was lonely and in many ways as bewildered as anyone else.

I have never forgotten those few moments, and recently when I saw him—an older, more self-contained and seemingly satisfied man—every now and then while we talked, the other Bill would come through much the same as then.

We left Texas finally and drove back to New York. We did some business together with the pot, but we began seeing less of each other. Things had changed considerably for everyone. Allen was beginning to take on stature and was doing a lot of writing. Jack had his first book almost completed and Phil had disappeared somewhere with his old lady. New York was different also. The Times Square scene was undergoing rapid change. There was a drive on to clean things up and it was being taken seriously. Most of the old haunts were closed and all-night cafeterias were no longer all-night places. I moved away entirely from the midtown area. Bill and Joan were no longer around Manhattan, having settled in Far Rockaway or some such place. Occasionally we'd meet, but Bill was making plans to return toward the Southwest—New Orleans this time—and then Mexico.

And so it went. That year came to a close and the next few whipped by. Allen began growing up and Jack was ready for the next big break. My life didn't change too radically, but circumstances kept us all more or less separated. I began seeing Allen more often and soon a sort of pattern was established which remains to this day. Allen has always and still does keep me informed concerning Bill.

The first time I ran into him—about five years after our return from Texas—he seemed almost the same. Then, after being in his presence a short while, I recognized an almost imperceptible difference. He seemed more impersonal, with a slight show of interest that was slightly clinical as though one were being observed through a magnifying lens. At first when we met there was an element of snobbishness both intellectually and socially in his dealings with others, and I think, even at this point I am speaking of, it remained, but he had acquired the habit of not showing it openly—covering it beneath a sort of conversational adroitness. He was pleased to renew our friendship, but underneath or inside I don't believe it touched him very deeply.

Joan was dead—and his changes had been many and varied—and I guessed at the time he felt his loneliness intensely, and much of his time was spent attempting to forget at least most of those happenings which might have helped recall her to mind. Their relationship, from what I personally knew, had been of an extremely intimate nature insofar as Joan was concerned, at least. I am quite firmly convinced she barely recognized the existence of others, with—of course—the exception of their children, whom she loved with pride and great tenderness and understanding. She and Bill had something rare—and certainly, from the standpoint of the observer, very fine and beautiful. Unquestionably the adjustments required of Bill to continue seeking meaning and purpose must have placed him under exhausting strain, and I couldn't help but wonder at his self-control.

We saw each other only briefly—about three or four times—and then he departed for South America. From then on until the present time, we have seen very little of each other, and the information I have concerning his private life has reached me by way of Allen.

When he first arrived back in the States after his long sojourn abroad, we met several times for dinner and conversation with the idea of renewing our friendship. I had felt reluctant about meeting him, wondering perhaps if his only reason for seeing me was due to some idea he might have concerning a sense of obligation to someone from the past who was still seeing mutual friends, but had long ago ceased to mean anything in his life. And then of course there was always curiosity as a possible factor. It appeared almost absurd in my mind that he might genuinely be interested in renewing our friendship—and for that matter I am not completely convinced his original association with me was entirely of a friendly nature, although surely there was no enmity involved. At any rate I couldn't help considering myself rather presumptuous—thinking of the famous William Burroughs in the same breath with good old Bill or Bull or even Bill Burroughs. Still, somewhere back along the line he had touched my heart—and besides, my curiosity and desire to make comparison of present and past personality differences—if any—demanded I see him at least once regardless of his reasons for seeing me.

He invited me to have dinner with him and I accepted. It was truly enjoyable and doubly so because I came away believing he was honestly glad to see me.

We spoke briefly of his stay in Tangiers and of his writing and of his son. He was amusing concerning Bill Jr.—sounding very much the typical father—berating the youth of today and their seeming indifference to the more important aspects of everyday living, their lack of a sense of responsibility, and his son Bill in particular, who—according to his father's opinion—is incredibly indifferent. At one point in the conversation he said, "Why, he didn't even show an interest in the language. Seemed to prefer hanging around bars."

IRVING, IN PART

I MET IRVING AFTER GETTING IN TOUCH WITH ALLEN AGAIN AFTER A lapse of about five years. He had been surprised at my reappearance in his life but was seemingly pleased to see me. He and Peter were living on Second Street in the Lower East Side area. Locating him at all presented a problem. I knew he had given readings in several of the coffeehouses in the city, but at the time I was unacquainted with their names and locations—with the exception of the Gaslight on MacDougal Street—and went there seeking information concerning where I might locate him. The people I first spoke to gave me vague answers, but suggested I remain a while on the slim chance he or one of his friends might come in. I had been there only a short time when Ray and Bonnie Bremser came in. I of course had seen neither of them before, but became aware of them while they were speaking with one of the people I had spoken to—and as they frequently glanced my way during the discussion, I was not in the least surprised when they came over and introduced themselves and asked me why I wanted to find Allen. Ray did most of the talking, and when I told him my name he immediately recognized it, telling me he was sure Allen would be glad to see me. He then introduced me to his wife, Bonnie, and suggested we leave. We took a cab directly over to Allen's. Ray had some pot and we all turned on while Allen filled me in with details about what had been happening with himself and Jack and Bill and the scene in general. I was impressed and anxious to get around and meet a few of his friends. Ray and Bonnie had to leave and Allen suggested he, Peter, and myself go out and visit a few spots he was sure I would like, and meet some of the people. We went to a coffeehouse called the Seven Arts and then to a bar called the Cedar. We met friends and acquaintances of Allen's and Peter's everywhere, and when we started back toward Allen's, Allen spoke to Peter and said, "I think Huncke should meet Irving." Peter smiled rather mysteriously and replied, "So do I." Irving lived on Eighth Street near Avenue D, and because I knew nothing about the area it seemed we were a long time getting there—and also I was thoroughly confused about directions—streets—avenues—and the whole district. We climbed five flights of stairs to be admitted by Irving into his apartment.

When I first looked at him, I was struck by his coloring. His hair almost black—his eyes deep, deep brown—his complexion ivory-toned, and his lips very red. He was wearing a beard and his hair was long. From our first meeting on, I never grew tired of observing his appearance. He is of small stature—his body proportionally constructed on the same scale. His eyes—expressive and always searching—can grow cold and hostile one instant and speculative the next. His features are symmetrical and inclined to be a bit sharp. His mouth is framed with thin, rather well-shaped lips—and when he smiles he shows good white teeth. His movements are gentle and graceful and I will always see him as a little Persian prince.

He was very charming and his enthusiasm about the whole scene appeared genuine. We spoke occasionally while Allen and Peter were busy with a discussion about poetry and poets. Irving asked several fairly direct questions about me, but in such a way I was rather flattered by his interest. I answered as honestly as I could. We did not remain long, and as we were leaving, Irving told me to come back soon.

I can't remember how long it was before I went back to see him, but when I did it began a period when I was seeing him frequently—and we became something of a friend to each other. He is an excellent talker and obviously well schooled and erudite. Enjoyable to be with when in good form.

When we first became friends I discovered he stayed in bed for long periods of time. Also he would not eat. He was very poor and forced to live frugally. He was bitter and depressed. His sense of humor is keen, and I would tell him of something I had seen or perhaps an experience, and I think once in a while my presence was good for him because he would laugh saying, "Huncke, you have had—and do have—the most incredible things happen to you."

At first I thought he was defenseless—delicate—and easily taken advantage of—and was rather angry when I heard someone we all knew to be somewhat unscrupulous had been staying with Irving. None of us should have been in the least worried. Irving is strong and has a sense of determination he can call on in a minute, and will act accordingly. Also, he has a code of moral evaluations he will use to intimidate one if possible, and he is quite positive concerning right and wrong. Irving needs little, if any, protection—on the contrary, it is those he moves against who require protection. He is crafty and sly and quick. I have seen him dart his hand out in a flash and, with his fingers extended in claw fashion, pick a live mouse off the table—where he had permitted it to get, having watched it, searching for food, finally reach the table top—and calmly walk to the window and drop the mouse to a smashed death. All this with a smile, the calculated edges of a leer at the corners of his mouth.

I have heard him—when annoyed with someone's behavior—sever connection with that person coldly—and, with malice, betray the weakness revealed for him alone in gay, not quite Oscar Wildean drawing-room wit—but with rather a bit more vitriolic deadly intent. He can be extremely kind and considerate as well, and I was firmly convinced I at least could anticipate his reactions and he would never surprise me. I had never for a moment since we became friends felt it would be wise to watch myself with him, and therefore talked as openly with him as I ever had to anyone. He led me to believe he was somewhat captivated by my stories, and when we were alone together he was adept at asking questions aimed at causing me to start talking. We were comfortable together, and could and did gossip together with great glee. He was constantly meeting new and beautiful people. There were always people knocking on his door—who came in to stay awhile, or, as in several instances, to stay indefinitely—and if they only stayed awhile and I was there when they departed, I was sure I would get a little biographical sketch of the person with the personal embellishments delivered as asides—always very acid, but funny. He has always done this with everyone, and I believe he is almost at his best at these times.

Irving is keenly aware of being alone and is unhappy much of the time. Clouds of depression hang heavy around him and he becomes moody and rejects people. His dignity will not allow him to relax and—because of a very basic personal consciousness or fastidiousness about manners—trust anyone beyond a certain point. He is firmly convinced he is being hustled—taken advantage of—or being used, and, when aroused, feels a need to pass judgment—deciding on the instant to act decisively and in defense of his level of perception. He will—without hesitation—destroy your most precious possession of the moment, blandly announcing his action is motivated by only what he has decided is to be for your own good.

I had never seen him really let go, nor thought I would ever be the one his finger would point toward in accusation.

I had managed—with financial assistance—to breathe a little life into the scene—had an oz. of good amphets, to use and sell enough of to make up the cost and possibly even realize a little profit.

Irving became a little more excited each time we met, because he thought perchance I would walk away from the Sixth Street pad and arrive at his door some early morning in a state near collapse—my mind a sinkpool of corruption and my brain boiled in amphetamine. I had foolishly developed the habit of visiting him at least once a day, and even now and then twice in one day, giving him minutely detailed accounts of the happenings in and around the Sixth Street apartment. I let myself go completely and failed to realize I was shocking him with my lurid accounts of Janine's and Bill Heine's actions toward each other, of the unending activity and continual flow of people in and out of the place. He was sure we were all doomed.

On the day of my good fortune with the purchase of the ounce of amphetamine, I felt it would be more practical to take it to Irving's where I knew it would be safe while I made contact with a few of the people I knew who were anxious to cop. Elise was staying at Irving's, and on that particular day Ed Marshall had chosen to pay him a visit. Elise opened the door when I knocked and there was Ed. I was an admirer of Elise and spent hour after hour talking with and to her. I felt I had at last succeeded in reaching her, and she was able to grasp my points with knowledge of what I had explained being as close to basic truth at least as far as ourselves and the others of the scene we made contact with were concerned. She liked me and allowed herself to be as open as possible under the circumstances—and suddenly caught the meaning of all I had been talking about since before she decided on moving away from the building in which Allen and Peter were living—and we had thoroughly enjoyed exchanging comments about everything in general on our last two encounters.

Ed had a first-hand experience with the interior of our place on Sixth Street several times in a row, and although it had been exciting and maybe frightening—by his own words—there was no evil and he could hardly go back on his word. In fact, it was always the evil outside which caused the trouble—when dire predictions were forecast and hepatitis sure to develop had you so much as smoked a stick of pot in the place—

and if you had been rash enough to use any of the works or amphetamine, you had better rush to a doctor—he might rescue you before it was too late.

These were the conclusions of all the people who had never set foot in the place but had heard the music from down below on the street—and observed the starry-eyed dreamers and creators, thin and haunted looking, coming and going.

Elise asked me if I had any horse and Ed said he would like just a small taste of the amphets. It so happened I could accommodate them both and we all three took off. I told them of my ounce, asking them to watch out for it while I cut down the street to locate a couple of buyers. I hadn't paid close attention to whether or not Irving was home, but was not surprised when, as I was about to leave for downstairs, I looked up and saw him coming out of his bedroom. We greeted one another pleasantly enough and I said I would be back soon. Irving said nothing, and I walked out in good form because I knew I was going to make some money—badly needed—immediately—and would probably set up a fairly steady operation I could rely on to keep me in money and help me retain independence. It would surely be great to be able to iron out a few hang-ups on Sixth Street caused mainly by lack of money. Also having money would help me apply a little pressure when needed.

I rushed around and ran into Macalee—who was anxious to cop and had ten dollars. We walked back together to Irving's building where Macalee decided to wait below while I went up to make a ten-dollar bag or deck I would bring down to him. I climbed the stairs and knocked, saying my name through the door. Elise let me in, and as I passed her going through the doorway I thought she was looking at me strangely. Ed was standing on one side of the room and Irving walked into the front room on through to his bedroom. I could not believe I had anything in the way of a reprimand coming, and was astonished there was anyone who apparently felt the opposite.

Looking at Ed and Elise I asked them for the amphetamine, saying, "Macalee is downstairs and wants a ten-dollar bag." Elise turned away from me and Ed hung his head, not looking at me, saying at the same time, "Huncke, I'm sorry. We don't have it any more. After you left, Irving demanded we give it to him, and when we did, he flushed it down the toilet."

For a moment I was completely stymied. Thoughts began churning around in my mind. It was gone and not even paid for. What was I going to do now? All my hopes for freeing myself of the immediate problem of money—wiped away. It was unbelievable. Why would Irving do such a thing? If he had objected to my having the stuff in his house, why hadn't he said so earlier? I hadn't made a secret of it being in my possession. I simply couldn't think straight.

Irving was standing watching me with an almost malevolent expression on his face. He was smirking and quite obviously enjoying my confusion.

Anger surged through me—and just what kept me from beating him, I'll never know. I did give vent to a verbal onslaught—shouting and yelling at him—which did very little to change the situation. Finally still in a rage, I slammed out of his apartment threatening to never speak to him again. But of course, eventually I did speak to him again.

I am sure it doesn't matter one way or another, but I have never truly liked him since then—and, at this point, hope I will never find it necessary to be in his company again.

THE PARTY

FRIDAY EVENING LAST WEEK BEGAN A STRANGE COURSE OF EVENTS. IT in all probability was a culmination point. The entire day carried an aura of the unusual, and as evening began—late afternoon, about five o'clock—returning from an errand where I work—I walked in on Janine, sitting doing calligraphy—her legs crossed, head bent low, a huge carpetbag by her side. She was wearing heels—silken stockings—a very pale blue and light beige-colored frock designed to fit tightly thru the bodice—a round low neckline—semi-puffed sleeves—short—exposing the leg to about the knees. She owns a delapidated straw hat she wears constantly, perched at a rakish angle dipped slightly over one eye, her hair caught into some simple style—tucked up beneath the crown—her ears partially covered—the tops and the lower section uncovered. Her presence startled me. She looked up at me, smiled, and quickly glanced downward again.

I spoke to her—quickly—telling her we would leave immediately. I finished speaking on the telephone with Roger—the foreman—who suggested I spend the weekend as I pleased and report back for work on Monday.

I was sure Janine was holding a solution of amphetamine and was anxious to turn on. She had some vague idea about cashing checks. The plan was completely obscure and we began walking—Fourteenth Street—Seventh Avenue—Sheridan Square. We stopped in a diner for coffee, ice cream, and a piece of pastry. I went into the men's room first and then she went into the ladies' room. We both turned on shots of amphetamine—leaving—strolling—talking—finally taking a cab to Thirty-fourth Street—continuing to walk and talk over toward the east side—across Park Avenue—over to Third Avenue—down Third—eventually deciding to ride back downtown to see Freude and John Wieners. It was a truly great evening and Janine had been open, talking, explaining much of what had previously only confused me. The running around from spot to spot—observing the night—speaking of each other—of people—love—Bill Heine—Victor—Peter—Fernando. At last reaching the loft where Fernando began making decided announcements about the immediate future. Telling Janine it had become necessary to vacate the loft and that he was turning over a new leaf. No more drugs. He was leaving the scene until he felt he had regained strength to resume painting. The atmosphere was tense and I began feeling my fatigue intensely. Speaking briefly with Janine—suggesting she consider returning home to Jersey for a short while—and feeling it better I depart, I bid good night and began walking over toward the East Side, intending to return to John Wieners' and sleep.

My eyes felt heavy and my skin had become a shroud of exposed nerve ends—quivering and undulating waves of sensitivity. My mouth was extremely dry and I felt it was oozing musk. My walk took me through a short span of Washington Square, up toward University Place, then over to Eighth Street until it becomes St. Mark's at Third Avenue—where I encountered a young man named Joe who had been introduced to me as a connection for practically anything—pot, goofballs, amphetamine pills of various kinds, and heroin. He was sitting at the foot of some steps leading up into a house partly given over to a small theater group, a huge sign in shades of lavender with white lettering partially covering one side of the front. We greeted each other and he asked me if I was interested in copping. I said I was providing there wouldn't be a big hassle. He said there wouldn't be—that as a matter of fact he was waiting to get in touch with his men or one of his boys at that very moment—that he was going into the house, where a party was underway, in order to pick up a couple of his friends, maybe stay a few minutes—and then cut to where his man would undoubtedly be on the scene. He suggested I join him in visiting the party, arguing against my immediate rejection of the idea. I explained I dislike parties, particularly if I am unacquainted with the people. Also I was much too tired—in fact, exhausted—to even think about it, but I didn't mind waiting on the steps while he went in—took care of whatever business he had in mind. We argued for several minutes and finally he decided to go in without me. He pushed the doorbell and was admitted, while I settled down comfortably on the steps to wait.

It was a warm, almost sultry night and people were stirring about the streets listlessly. A couple of spade cats cut by—a woman, rather strangely dressed—wearing several strands of beads around her neck, and several bracelets on her arm she seemed annoyed with as she passed. She shook her arm rather violently and began to adjust her bracelets with her hand—first taking a huge handbag pressing it against her body. As occupied as she was with her jewelry, handbag, and putting herself aright, she did look at me—sharply—quickly glancing away as our eyes met. Several times taxis passed. I was just beginning to feel relaxed and enjoy my freshly lit cigarette when my name was called out and, looking upward, there was my acquaintance leaning out one of the upper windows. He called down for me to come in and join the scene. Several of the cats he wanted to see were milling around, and it was pointless for me to sit outside. "Come on in, man, don't be a drag—fall in. We won't stay long. I want to make a couple of phone calls. Then straight away to the man." Suddenly it did seem pointless, my sitting outside, and I agreed to join him.

I climbed the steps and as I reached the top the door buzzer began sounding and I opened the door and stepped in.

A lovely teardrop-shaped chandelier hung in the center of the entrance hall. The floor was painted a bright venetian red. One wall consisted nearly completely of an inset mirror. A great wide gracious-appearing staircase led upward into the upper regions of the house. I began mounting the stairs and my friend began calling down to me, telling me to "come up, man—keep climbing—it is up here at the top." When I finally reached him, he began telling me we wouldn't stay long—there wasn't any pot—three girls who rented the house were giving the party—some of his best friends were there but there were innumerable people he didn't know—we could have a can of beer—not to worry—we would cut out soon.

I had little opportunity to observe the general plan of the house—getting a quick impression of many rooms and doors, little side staircases leading even further upward and in one instance the impression of a split-level room. There were people everywhere—in groups, standing alone, sitting on floors—chairs—chests; in couples, some making love, some lying back in each other's arms. Several girls were clustered around a phonograph, listening in rapt attention to a Lena Horne rendition of some torch song. Beer cans were scattered in every direction. Upon first encountering the full blast of this gathering of people, I was immediately conscious of the youth of everyone. I didn't at any time before departing see the entire crowd at once, but I am sure there was no one over twenty-five years of age.

As people became aware of my presence I became exceedingly uncomfortable. There were no friendly faces, no smiles of welcome, no pleasant greetings, and—worse—an increasing wariness of me, so that at one point I am quite sure I was being stared at by thirty or forty pairs of eyes all registering open curiosity, hostility, and rejection. All this before anyone has spoken to me—heard my name—knew for sure I was alive, and not an animated dummy somehow being dragged into their midst for their amusement.

The scene was kaleidoscopic, and I was surprised when one of the girls suddenly took form—looking at me with great paranoia-filled eyes, then calling sharply to my friend, "Please, Joe—let me speak to you"— pulling him after her into a small side room.

My whole feeling was of being trapped and of somehow escaping as soon as possible. I had turned over toward the door through which we had entered to discover several young guys standing in a group—obviously discussing me—almost in front of the door. My mind was beginning to whirl, sending out thoughts—reactions, impressions, feelings of fear, confusion—like the sputtering sparks of a pinwheel.

I was standing in a reception hall with rooms opening off in three directions. Several people had gathered in the room—two half-reclining against a large chest of drawers occupying the largest wall. Two young men were standing in between two of the doorways. I had crossed the room around these people and was just about to follow the young woman and Joe. They had gone just beyond the third doorway, and I could hear the girl whispering in excited rushes of heavy breath to Joe, who would make some mumbled reply. Somehow feelings of guilt swept over me, and for the moment I believed it necessary to speak to the girl—explaining my desire to leave, my not wanting to invade the party in the first place. Just as I was about to follow into the room after them, they reappeared—and I immediately began talking to the girl, telling her I wanted to leave and would do so at once. She became intensely embarrassed—blurting out some statement about my being all right—I should stay—I wasn't to feel uncomfortable—etc. Joe kept interrupting her to assure me everything was great—stay a little while—he was going to speak with his buddies. It would only take a few minutes, then we would go. Meanwhile the girl slipped past me, disappearing into the group in the main room.

Suddenly one of the cats near the door we had entered spoke up, looking contemptuously at me, saying, "You are fucked up, man." At first I was surprised at his rudeness and his language and then I was annoyed—annoyed with the whole stinking mess—plus the utter stupidity of this opinionated ape who stood looking so righteous—mouthing words he didn't even understand at me—someone he had never set eyes on before. "What exactly do you mean by fucked up?" I asked him. "Perhaps you will explain." "Oh, you know, man, fucked up." Just then one of the other fellows standing near moved over to me, saying, "What's your name?" I told him my name and he repeated it after me, saying, "Huncke—what kind of name is that?" I spelled it for him, explaining that it is German. "German!" he almost screeched at me. "German, a lousy Nazi. Well, man, I'm a Jew. It was you bastard Germans who sent my grandmother, grandfather, relatives of my friends to the gas chambers. I hate Germans."

My whole being filled with sadness—and the only thought I could formulate in my conscious mind was that it was tragic that he would use anything as crude as racial hatred as a means of attempting to humiliate me and to inflate his ego in the presence of his friends. I was so completely stymied, all I could think to say was "Wow, man—how old are you?"

Gradually during this exchange, several more people were crowding the doorways. Everyone was talking at once and I was really very frightened that I was to be—at the very least—severely beaten.

Yet I wasn't entirely alone. Looking around me, I became aware of four or five young cats gathering around Joe, who looked at me with warmth and understanding. Obviously the friends Joe had come to see. Beautiful young men, who quickly began introducing themselves—Richie—Don—John—Bert—telling me not to pay attention to these other people. Calling for beer—trying to ease the tension a little.

Still—my belligerent acquaintance was not to be stopped. Raising his voice, he began saying, "This party needs more girls. I want more girls." Looking at me, he said, "What do you want more of?"

My response was immediate. "Peace," I said. "Peace."

"Peace?" he replied. "Peace, shit. What you want more is boys with nice long joints. I know what you are—you're a fag. That's what you are—a goddamned fag."

Joe and Richie both spoke up saying, "Man, you're crazy. Huncke's no fag. Wow—how wrong can you get?" I was utterly speechless—unable to say anything—seething with self-loathing because I didn't raise my hands to this man who tried to belittle and degrade me. Yet also aware of pity for this sick, insecure—in all probability—frustrated homosexual.

Meanwhile positions had been shifted and Joe was now at the door holding it open, calling his friends, saying, "Come on, Huncke, let's split."

Perhaps the very act of our making an exit at that particular moment helped avert what might very easily have been a slam-bang free-for-all. I was glad to leave. Glad to be free from what had threatened to be a violent display. I was rather shocked to think my appearance alone could be the cause of so devastating a situation—one filled with hate and paranoia.

On the street with Joe and his friends, listening to their discussion of what had happened and why, I regained my composure.

Joe was full of explanation about how square they all were—just schoolkids trying to come on like men of the world, showing off in front of their girls. Richie was a bit more perceptive, in my opinion—saying that obviously it wasn't me at all—part of it being Joe and some of his unpredictable escapades of the past that some of the fellows and the girls knew of—and the fear that he had planned to louse up their evening in some way by bringing in a complete outsider.

We all went to the Village to MacDougal Street near the Fat Black Pussy Cat, where we hung around until Joe made my connect for me. I left him and his friends still talking about ways and means of evening up the score at the party.

Walking along alone, thinking about all that had happened, I realized I should have been capable in some manner of having spread understanding and trust—a sense of peace. I was filled with shame because it had not been in my power—or, if it had been, I had not recognized the way to use the ability to open their eyes to beauty.

THE LAW OF RETRIBUTION

SOME PEOPLE HOLD GRUDGES FOR A LONG TIME—PERHAPS UNTIL THEY die—and there is never a rest from the moment the grudge takes shape in their mind until they have retaliated in a similar manner to the one who they believe is responsible, or have evened up the score as one might say. They are on the alert to gain revenge—quite frequently working out elaborate plans and schemes to serve their purpose—and more often than not, it doesn't matter to what extent the other person is guilty. The whole idea of retribution, or of gaining revenge, applies not only to a grudge but to any situation wherein one of two people, or groups of people, has gained or—supposedly unfairly—taken advantage of the other.

It is all stupid and a decided waste of energy, and is one of the worst aspects in human relationships. But, regardless, it does occur, and like all ideas resulting from the idea of competition, there are certain rules of rather rigid nature which affect the entire concept—so that, as an example, if one partner steals from the other or in some way deserts the other, or lies, or cheats, in the world of hustlers, and particularly among those of Latin extraction and background, a knife is often used—frequently a gun. And if the two people involved are male, a so-called man usually—at the very least—promises himself he'll knock the shit out of the bastard the next time there is an opportunity.

When I first began hanging around the underworld, I was cautious and careful of fulfilling—or attempting to fulfill—my obligations in any of my dealings where I had a partner. And the first time I held out—the result of an error of calculation on my part, and an honest mistake—I was ashamed and extremely worried that perhaps the discrepancy would be discovered—and in the vernacular, I'd get my head handed to me. Nothing ever came of it, and when finally I was confronted with a situation—this time with a new partner—where I could gain at the other's expense, it took little argument with my conscience to decide to go ahead—and again I had no trouble. Then came the time when I knew beforehand there would be no way of covering up and my act would be considered an out-and-out burn, and in my heart I knew the only way of evening up—eventually—would be through an act of violence on the part of my partner. I took the gamble of our never meeting again—or meeting so much later the sting of the injury would be dissipated, and I could perhaps talk my way out of the worst of the consequences—and I went ahead and in a sense, got away with it. Although we did meet again much later, all that happened was a verbal tongue-lashing. It is all right to burn one's victims as long as they can be referred to as marks, but never—*never*—burn the guy you work with and who is your partner. Where the line of justification for an act of treachery in one instance—which ceases to be justifiable in another instance—exists is a moot question and one, honestly speaking, I've never understood.

Be that as it may, there is a law of retribution—and recently it caught up with me.

At the time when I made the choice—or acted according to the dictates of my desire—I had been the partner of a Spanish-American cat for a period of several months, and had known him about three years. When we became partners we began dealing junk together, and although he was experienced in the business I was quite green and unaware of much of what might be expected of me—as to conduct when unexpectedly I discovered I was working someone else's territory, or when I was held up at knife point and told to give up my junk or get cut, or the various hypes I'd been subjected to. I soon discovered my co-worker was very unscrupulous as to his manner of dealing with me, and although there was never anything I could use to explain—without having to qualify in some involved way why I felt cheated—I did, in a sense, come out on the short end of the deal. Still, in a sense, I was treated—all the same—fairly, and perhaps could have behaved differently in the final analysis and avoided a very unpleasant experience.

We had been together several months. It was winter, and through some thoroughly high-handed manipulation on the part of my partner I was suddenly without a place of my own to live and was living with him and his girl and feeling disgusted and completely trapped. I became somewhat desperate about what the future might hold in store were I to continue as I had been. One cold, cold morning I got up—and when I went to cook up my usual fix, my partner began complaining about the amount of stuff being used, and ordered me to cut down. I felt that since

I was running the risk of being arrested at any time the least I could have out of the deal was as much stuff as I liked, and I was annoyed with his complaint. Therefore it took very little debating the issue when, later that morning, I had eighteen bags of stuff in my possession—all the merchandise we had between us—and I stopped to visit a young woman I knew—and she suggested I kick my habit—she would help me with the money to get to Lexington, Kentucky, where I could enter the hospital. I decided in favor of taking her up on the plan. I simply remained with her all day until it was time to catch the bus—frequently shooting up—and taking the rest with me—shooting the last of it upon my arrival in Lexington. I had shot up the eighteen bags in less than twenty-four hours.

I remained out of the city several months, and by the time I returned I learned he had been arrested and was serving time. He was gone two years.

He was released not long ago.

I have always known there would be a day of reckoning, and have mentioned it to several of our mutual associates. He had told everyone—and although several people thought he'd forget, I was sure he wouldn't. I was convinced he'd have to prove to his friends, if nothing else, that no one gets away with crossing him.

We met walking along the street. I had paused a moment to speak with an acquaintance, and as I turned around—there he was. He walked up to me, grabbed me by my arm, pulling me close to him, and sort of forced me to accompany him down the street, meanwhile daring me to make an explanation. Suddenly, after walking a short distance, he swung his fist up into my face—cracking me on the lip—continuing to walk—again hitting me—finally hitting me again—threatening to cut me. There was nothing I could say. From his point of view he was perfectly justified, and certainly wouldn't have understood any of my abstract reasoning were I to have attempted explaining. In his eyes he had been lenient. I understood and was grateful he hadn't cut me with a knife.

We parted on somewhat agreeable terms, and at the time I thought it wiser of me to continue avoiding him as much as possible.

I was ashamed of my behavior and promised myself to act always in the future in a manner where I would never again knowingly cause someone to feel the need to retaliate or to put in effect the so-called law of retribution.

CRUISER ON AVENUE B

ANOTHER NEW NOTEBOOK, AND AT THE MOMENT I'M NOT AT ALL SURE of what I want to write about and suppose probably the best thing I could start with is an experience that occurred about an hour ago—a brief encounter with two police officers in a police car or cruiser who called me over to ask me questions. I had known almost positively they were interested in me upon my first becoming aware of their presence. Suddenly glancing to the side while walking slowly along Avenue B at the time, my attention somewhat abstractedly drew toward the entranceway to the Charles Theater or movie house, just beneath the marquee, so that there was an element of surprise in my glance. As I watched, still strolling, their obvious interest in me—and there could be no doubt—the officer behind the wheel, the driver, was speaking of me. He half turned his head toward his companion and continued slowly moving alongside of me. And by then, disconcerted by their intrusion, I was inwardly attempting to appear nonchalant and not in the least troubled by any interest the police could have in my most ordinary life and the dull and spotless course of my daily existence. And on another level, swept through with thoughts of my appearance in the pale light of the slightly misty gray early morning—the strange, rather drained color of my skin, and the several red-colored sores on my face (one on the tip of my nose, another over one cheek bone, both almost like rouge spots), my hair combed and windblown and my eyes large, brown, near-sighted pools of dilation. As all of this was accompanied with momentary flashes of doubt, the possibility of very likely having something of an illegal nature on my person suddenly and momentarily frightened me. Then, thinking about my pockets—my wallet and moving rapidly from pocket to pocket and finally, as I relaxed, sure there was nothing—and at the instant they motioned for me to approach, I had ventured another glance in their direction. After all, I've got almost as much right to look at them as they have to observe me. They called, "Hey—come over here a moment." I remember half a stick of pot in one of my jacket pockets. For a moment, fear filled me to capacity. I immediately began to walk toward them, reaching for my back pocket and my wallet, which contained my identification. (I use my passport as a rule, even though it expired last October and isn't the best ID to have as a result.)

When I reached their side of the street and when I could speak to them so they could hear me without my having to raise my voice, I spoke, saying, "Is there something wrong? Would you like to see my identification?" and handed same to them. I was on the side next to the driver. I looked straight at him, taking in his insignia, which I am never really sure about—never having forced myself to recognize their symbols of rank—thusly never knowing if I am speaking with a captain, a lieutenant, or a sergeant, or a man of simple rank. He was a young man in his late twenties or early thirties; I'd guess him about thirty-two years of age. His facial features were inoffensive, although he bore a stern and mean demeanor. His expression was full of surprise and hostility. He looked me up and down, his eyes stopping as they reached mine, and I could feel his search for an indication of my being a drug user. He asked me if I hadn't just handed something over to a man I had spoken with back up the street. At first, I immediately denied any knowledge of what he was talking about, and then I did recall stopping to speak with Victor, to whom I had handed a slip of paper with an address and telephone number written on it.

ARRESTED

THE SUN BLAZED DOWN ON THE ICE-WRAPPED CITY. PEOPLE PUSHED
thru the wind-swept streets, rapidly seeking the warmth of entranceways,
subways, restaurants, buildings and anywhere out of the wind, huddled
in coats, jackets, sweaters, mittens, and gloves. The sputtering of the
radiator finally penetrated my sleep, and after getting out of bed and
looking out the window, I dreaded the thought of having to go out into
the day. It was late in the morning, but somewhat early in the day for
me to be awake. I had taken a fix just before going to sleep, saving part
of what I had in my possession for awakening. I was broke and had to
take a suit, part of the loot taken from a car the previous week and saved
for just an emergency as I now faced: broke—and the cold too severe to
get out and hustle (and my junk almost gone) to the pawnshop. I fixed,
dressed, and, taking the suit from the closet, rushed down the stairs and
across the street to the nearest pawnshop, which was where I had pawned
several items from the same loot of which the suit belonged. I threw the
suit up on the counter and asked for ten dollars. After examining the
suit, the man behind the counter told me to wait a minute; he turned
and walked toward the back of the shop. This wasn't exactly an unusual
procedure, and it was with surprise and a sinking of the heart that I
suddenly became aware of three men standing behind me. The man
behind the counter had returned and was pointing a finger at me, saying,
"This is the one." Two of the men stepped forward on either side of
me and quickly began frisking me and asking me questions about where
I had gotten the suit, where I lived, and if I thought I was a wise-guy,
and telling me this was a pinch and I was sure unlucky since they just
happened to be there checking on the stuff that I had hocked before.

"This man is the owner," they said to me, pointing to the third man,
"and we're going to see to it that he presses charges. You'll probably go
away for a long time. Are you a junky? You look like one."

ALVAREZ

I FIRST SAW HIM WHEN I CLIMBED INTO THE PATROL WAGON. HE WAS sitting well toward the back, all drawn up into a tight knot, his head sunk between his shoulders, arms wrapped around his body, knees pressed together and pulled up toward his chin so that only the tips of his toes supported his weight. He was wearing a trenchcoat several sizes too large, which hung in loose folds around him, the bottom dragging on the floor, and a misshapen black felt hat with a wide brim, pulled down over his forehead. He was thin, almost skeletal, and had skin of a pale jaundice-yellow color. His face was skull-like with enormous eye sockets. The eyes were large and black-brown, glazed and staring straight ahead. He was shivering, and as I settled into my seat, he began shaking and shuddering; his whole body jerked convulsively. Tears glistened at the corners of his eyes. His nose was running; a thin drop of mucus hung from the tip. He was emitting a strange, almost wail-like sound and occasionally groaning, babbling to himself in Spanish interspersed with broken English of which the words "I'm sick . . . I'm sick . . . I'm sick" were all I could understand. Suddenly he vomited, regurgitating globs of green bile, and fell back afterward on the seat, moaning.

We were going down to police headquarters to be fingerprinted, pho-tographed, put thru the show-up, and formally booked and charged with our respective crimes, examined and thoroughly frisked, interviewed, then sent thru a cold shower and finally assigned to a floor and a cell in the city prison to await trial. I couldn't help but speculate about how they expected to get the man thru the entire procedure (which is an ordeal even when one is in good health) without his collapsing completely.

We were the only two prisoners in the wagon. The cop who was sitting guard over us kept making remarks to me about how disgusting it was to see anyone in such a condition. "The poor sonofabitch would be better off dead. I ain't got no sympathy for you guys. Why do you do it? There ain't nothing worse than junk. How come you ain't like him—you're a junky too, ain't you? Oh well, you'll probably get like that later."

The ride downtown seemed interminable and I was glad when we stopped and the cop said, "End of the line. Let's go. Come on—no stalling." I was still feeling fairly good, but he had to be dragged and cuffed alongside the head before he could manage to stagger and half fall out of the wagon and down the stairs past the newspaper reporters and photographers into headquarters, where we were separated. At headquarters things move slowly and it wasn't until much later in the day that I saw him again.

At headquarters, I was assigned to a cell where I waited until they called me out to be printed and photographed, after which I was taken upstairs to the show-up and then down to a courtroom where I appeared before a judge who decided what bail was to be set, then over to the city prison.

Sometimes, if a junky is very sick or if the detective handling the case is afraid the junky is apt to get sick in the courtroom (something the judges frown upon), arrangements are made for the junky to have a shot. Such must have happened with the fellow who had ridden down with me, because he was certainly in much better shape when they led him into the bullpen, where we were to wait until assignment to our regular cells. Finally our names were called and we were led over to the shower room where we stripped off our clothes and left them in a pile. Each piece was closely examined, seams were carefully felt for concealed needles or stashes of junk. The shoes were banged on the floor and inspected for false heels or soles, while we stood in a shower of cold water or waited shivering until the frisk was over. After dressing, we were led before a doctor and given a cursory examination. We were asked how long we had used junk and what kind. The sick man was behind me in line and, while talking to the doctor, asked for a fix. He was told, "There will be no fix for you. This is jail, not a sanatorium. You kick—cold turkey."

We were both sent to the eighth floor. They try and keep the junkies all together and his cell was two down from mine.

The cells in city prison were originally designed to accommodate one, but in the past few years have been used to hold two. Each cell now contains an upper and lower bunk, a toilet, a small washbasin, a stool or seat which lets down from the wall, and a small metal shelf or ledge which serves as a table. Each prisoner is issued three blankets (not always clean), a sheet, a pillow case and a towel. The bunks consist of a set of springs. There are no mattresses or pallets and sometimes no pillows. Therefore it is necessary to use at least one of the blankets as a sort of pad over the springs. Before there were two springs in each cell, and when it became necessary to put two men in a cell, one or the other was forced to sleep on the floor.

Each floor is broken up into four sections and alphabetically designated A section, B section, C section, D section. In each section there is a flats, the main row of cells, and a tier, or the row of cells, immediately above those on the flats. There are approximately forty-eight to fifty in each section. The cells face a sort of well which runs the full length of each row, extending as far over as a catwalk and surrounding the entire floor. Large full-length panels of small frosted-glass windows extend around each floor. Once one is on the inside, one sees daylight but never a glimpse of the outside.

The cells are opened early in the morning, usually shortly after breakfast, which is served on trays, and brought to the cells by trusties. And regardless of how one feels, it is required the prisoners gather out on the flats and remain there until it is time for the midday meal, when they return to their cells for an hour and come out again for what is termed afternoon recreation. This routine never varies and is only an additional discomfort for addicts who are sick and weak, and in most instances unable to stand for long and who must sit with head bowed over along tables flanking the side of the catwalk (if lucky) or end up sitting on the floor. The cells are closed and one can't get back in to lie down until the next lockup.

I had managed to get through my first day without getting sick. I had fixed only a short time before being arrested so that it wasn't until the following day that the real misery began. I had been put into a cell with a fellow who had been there almost two weeks and who was over the worst of his kicking. Probably the worst thing about kicking a habit cold turkey is being unable to sleep. I have talked to men who have gone three or four weeks without sleep. Nothing is quite so agonizing as lying on a set of springs which cut into you no matter how you try and pad them from squeaking with each breath you take and are lopsided and frequently broken.

The first night I slept fitfully, becoming familiar with the night sounds of a prison—the guard passing with flashlight and jingling keys, farts,

Huncke in a Times Square photo booth, circa 1940 *Ginsberg Collection*

On William S. Burroughs's cotton and marijuana farm, Texas, 1947
Ginsberg Collection

In New York City's Hotel Elite, an SRO, in 1953
Allen Ginsberg

New York City, 1953 *Allen Ginsberg*

Huncke in the mid–1960s *Courtesy Janine Pommy Vega*

Huncke in his
San Francisco
apartment, 1966
Ralph Ackerman

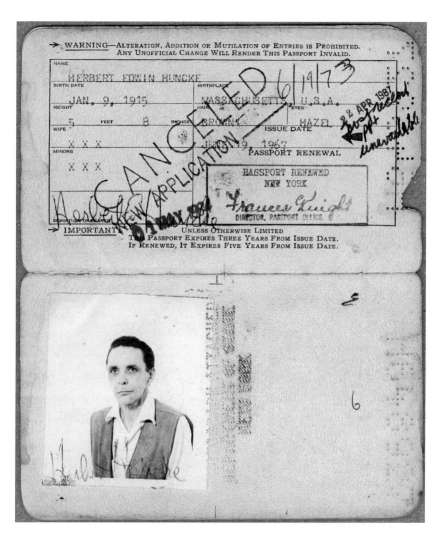

Huncke's 1967 passport photo *Courtesy Roger and Irvyne Richards*

Left to right: Allen Ginsberg, Huncke, and Peter Orlovsky on Ginsberg's upstate New York farm, 1968   *Ginsberg Collection*

With rare-book collector and friend Roger Richards at Greenwich Books, New York City, 1976   *Louis Cartwright*

Left to right: William S. Burroughs, Allen Ginsberg, and Huncke in the
Bunker, Burroughs's New York City headquarters, circa 1978
Louis Cartwright, courtesy David Sands

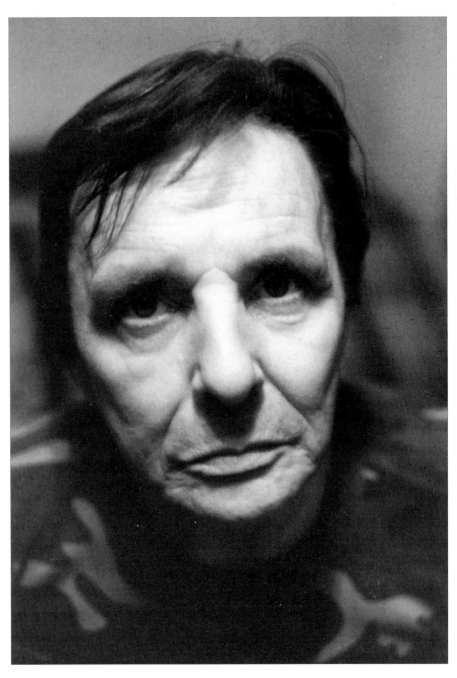

Two portraits of Huncke taken in the late 1970s by Louis Cartwright

Louis Cartwright and Huncke in the
Doubling Cube, a gaming room in the
Chelsea Hotel, New York City, 1990.
Cartwright and Huncke remained close
companions for more than twenty-five
years until Cartwright's death in 1994.
David Sands

Huncke and poet Gregory Corso, 1992 *Allen Ginsberg*

Huncke with poet John Wieners, his roommate
of the early 1960s, in 1992 *Allen Ginsberg*

Huncke and Louis Cartwright in New York's East Village, 1993
Brian Graham

Huncke in New York City, 1994   *Steve Miles*

Huncke in the Chelsea Hotel, 1994   *David Sands*

Still from the documentary *Huncke and Louie,* in
New York City's Chelsea Hotel, 1995 *Laki Vazakas*

Huncke reading at the University of Connecticut, 1995 *Ann Charters*

Huncke in the Chelsea Hotel shortly before his death,
New York, 1996 *Brian Graham*

snoring, groaning, sleep talk, flushing toilets, phones ringing, muffled conversations, closing doors, church chimes, traffic, shouts on the streets below and the constant noise of people sick and unable to sleep, moving and adjusting, seeking the more comfortable position.

My companion of the morning (whose name I had learned was Alvarez) cried, moaned, stopped the guard, begging to see a doctor and asking for something to ease his pain. He called for Maria, Rita, Lola, banged against the bars and was told to "shut up, for Christ's sake. Lay down, you bastard—there are others trying to sleep. Come out swinging in the morning, you punk bastard. You ain't any sicker than I am," by other prisoners. When I saw him the following morning, he looked like a zombie. He staggered out of the cell with a blanket wrapped shawl-fashion around his shoulders—his hair hanging down over his forehead and eyes—shivering and shaking and wracked with dry heaving, unable to vomit anymore because there was no longer even green bile in his stomach. He kind of collapsed into a heap on the floor and remained there the entire morning while prisoners waiting to pass him simply stepped over him. Once, he managed to get up long enough to wander down toward the end of the flats and call to the guard on duty, asking to see a doctor. The guard told him to, "get the fuck back inside—the doctor won't be around until later."

This occurred on a Saturday. He did see a doctor in the afternoon. The doctor gave him a paper cup full of aspirin—about ten—which he swallowed all at once. Afterward, he set fire to the paper cup, holding it straight out in front of him, staring intently at the flame, half smiling, mumbling something in Spanish, until the flame burned his fingers and he dropped the charred remains of the cup on the floor, while the smile left his face and was replaced by a look of sadness. Other prisoners had gathered around him, sort of watching him in awe, talking among themselves, suggesting he was crazy.

On Sunday he remained alone in a corner, once again doubled up in a tight knot, sitting on the floor resting his head on his knees. Several Spanish-speaking prisoners tried talking with him but he wouldn't answer. Or he would look at them out of tear-filled eyes saying, "I'm sick, I'm sick." Once the guard came down and spoke to him. He just looked at him not answering, until the guard walked away. Late in the afternoon, just before lockup, he shit and pissed all over himself. His cellmate refused to go into the cell with him until the guard ordered a couple of prisoners to take him up to the shower and wash the stink off him. They put him under an ice-cold shower. He stood there with his hands hanging at his sides, crying. His flesh hung on his body, exposing each bone. They let him out and he groped his way back to the cell where he fell exhausted on his bunk, his whole being wracked by sobbing. That night he kept everyone awake—calling for God.

Monday to Friday is always busy because the prisoners have to make court appearances. On this particular Monday, Alvarez's cellmate had to appear in court during the afternoon session. He was late returning so that we were all locked in when he got back. He came walking down the line of cells until he reached his own. Suddenly he yelled, "Jesus Christ! The guy is dead!"

Alvarez had died sitting up. When they opened the cell and carried him out to put him on the stretcher, they had to straighten him out. He had died all folded up, his hands and arms wrapped around his legs which were drawn up so that his head could rest on his arms. Once again he had shit and pissed on himself.

He was already dying when I first saw him.

COURTROOM SCENE

THE MORNING FOLLOWING MY MIRACULOUS ESCAPE (IN A MANNER OF speaking) from the shackles of the Law, which was certainly one of my strangest and more interesting experiences with jail and the New York City courts, finds me inwardly glowing because of simply being in the outside world. Also, this follows one of my most intense periods of self-negation and despair. Made of other stuff, I would have managed to hang myself, cut my wrists, end this involvement with life, escape into peace and oblivion. Never have I felt quite as alone or as unbelievably unhappy.

On Thursday afternoon, a hot and humid July day of last week, I cut from the pad intending to try and cop at least one bag of schmeck in order to turn myself and Florence on. Florence had acquired enough bread and we both agreed it would be fine getting straight. I had thrown my clothes on after lying inert and sweaty for many hours in bed at about three o'clock in the afternoon, and made it sluggishly over to Third Avenue and Eighth Street, up Third Avenue to Twelfth Street in front of a barber college where I met a chick of a few years' acquaintance that I hadn't seen for quite some time, sitting on a sort of stone ledge in front of the barber college with a newspaper folded back to the crossword puzzle, and a yellow pencil that she was using to fill in the letters in the puzzle. My eyes had been alert coming up the avenue and I hadn't spotted any possible people to cop from. As I approached, we spotted and greeted one another. The chick's name is Carol and she is a rather sad and beautiful woman of about thirty-five years of age who has had many wild and furious experiences knocking around in and out of the underworld. She's probably a good thief, has been a prostitute, a singer, a general hard type with prevalent lesbian-like qualities, but also likes and makes it with men. She is a trifle on the heavy side in body and looks well in slacks and tailored skirts. There is a small tattoo just above her wrist on the right arm. Her facial features are strong and, to some degree, what is referred to as "coarse." Her nose is inclined to be sharp, and her

sad and cold eyes are set rather close together. She is a mixture of masculine and feminine characteristics. Her hair is straight and is naturally dark,
which she dyes a blond-red and keeps cut short and brushed or combed
not severely but suggestively man-style. She had been using drugs in all
variations for many years.

I sat down beside her and asked, "What's been happening?" I haven't
seen you since last fall. Are you straight?" And then looking directly at
her, it wasn't difficult to see she was obviously on, and I said, "Baby, you
look straight." We spoke generally of a couple of mutual acquaintances,
complained a bit about how hot the streets are these days with bulls
everywhere, talked about a cat we both know serving time over on Rikers Island, who had tried to hang up. I asked if she could help me cop
and she said she had some shit—$3.50 bags—not dynamite, but decent.
As she was speaking, she extended her hand over toward me, palm up
and indicating that she wanted me to give her bread. I laid it in her hand
and she fumbled around the waistband of her slacks for a moment, finally
finding a little black tin box with a sliding top which she slid back and
disclosed about seven bags inside, one of which she handed me. All this
had been manipulated unobtrusively. I continued sitting a moment
longer, holding the bag in my hand, and was just ready to arise and split
when I became aware of a cat standing in front of us who addressed me
saying, "All right, open up your hand." He glared at me and, as I didn't
open my hand as quickly as he desired, he spoke again, in threatening
tones saying, "Don't drop it. If you do, I'll kick the shit out of you." I
opened my hand and he snatched the bag. Meanwhile, he had made
remarks to Carol, asking questions like "You got more? What are you—
a pusher? You got works? Don't lie. I don't want to find anything more
on you. All right, stand up. Hold hands and walk slowly down the street
with me. Make a move to run and I'll shoot your ass off."

We rose as he bid and walked down the block with him to where his
car was parked. I asked him not to make the pinch, explaining I had
only been out a few weeks and that I was clean—to please not make it
so I had to go back. Carol spoke to him also, saying, "Where's your
partner? Give us a break. Wow—I'm going to be sick. I haven't gotten
straight for the day yet. Can we get straight at the station? Where's my
money? It's in the small black purse you took." He bantered with us,
answering some of the questions and telling Carol not to worry, he
wasn't going to steal her money. He was sorry, he wasn't going to let us
go. We had to get smart to ourselves. We had arrived by this time at the

car. He opened the car door, ordered me in back and let Carol sit next to him in front. We drove straight to the East Fifth Street station house and were booked on charges of possession, and at eight-thirty in the evening, I was in the detention cell for the night.

Alone in the cell with the whole night ahead of me, I was ashamed, and sure that many of my friends would at last call it quits. These people had gone to the trouble and expense of getting me out six months earlier from my last bit—and here I was—not on the streets a month, and back in jail. Of course they would be disgusted. I wanted to kill myself. Thoughts of disgust, anger, frustration, confusion, and a complete physical let-down had me exhausted. At one point, I promised myself I'd do this bit and when I'd get out, I'd disappear down at the Bowery— anywhere—never show my face to my friends again, sort of fade into nothingness. What the hell; I'm old anyway. Fuck my writing. Fuck me. Fuck the world. Jail again—motherfucker. Why? Why? Why? Actually, whose business but my own if I use drugs or poison? Is this the way it is going to be every time I move about the streets? Will some bastard cop, hungry to make a pinch and keep his record, show his boss what a great job he is doing and grab me, and it's going to be from here on in jail, jail, jail. Jail in the beginning was an experience, and then gradually, through the years, became a sort of way of living for me which took up long periods of time. I was philosophical about it. I adjusted to it, accepted it as part of my routine. I didn't like it, but then this all went with my way of living, and although I can still make it fairly easy, I'm now ready to stay clear. I don't steal any longer and I am not about to hurt someone, and now, let me alone to shoot my junk and be happy with the people I have learned to love and have faith in. Also, I want to continue writing, and one of the places I can't write is jail. I simply dry up and that is it—no writing until I'm released again. Why in goddamned hell can't they leave me alone? I owe them nothing. I've paid up my scores straight down the line. The scale should balance.

The night finally dragged into the daylight hours of morning. Somehow I had survived without going stark raving mad. I had asked the guard to call Erin for me, and he had, and had said she would see me in the courtroom in the morning. I had relaxed a little upon learning she would be there, and I didn't feel as completely negative.

Saturday morning. Police headquarters is busy with the first of the weekend business. The photo gallery and identification rooms start early, pulling the ID records and seeing that each new prisoner is photographed. All the city's precincts rush their overnight accumulated cases down early and headquarters mills with prisoners and detectives, patrolmen and women police officers lining their cases up and getting through the preliminaries involved with proper procedure before the prisoner can be presented before a court and the case is legally court business. The "yellow sheets," as they are called (I suppose because they are of yellow color), are records of a prisoner's history as an offender, beginning with the first arrest and disposition of the case up to the last arrest and disposition of the case. They are thorough and complete, including every brush with the Law regardless of state, city or town, and, as in my record, date back in many instances to early childhood troubles. I have a yellow sheet four pages long; my record dates back to 1932.

Our bull, a man named Albono, who is a young and mean Italian type, had us through first. My photographs were the first to be taken, Carol's next, and then over to the court building for the initial hearing.

When we were called into the courtroom from the detention pens where we had waited, a court attendant told me Erin was there and had said she would arrange for a lawyer.

When we went before the judge where our cases were read into the court records, we requested an adjournment until the twenty-third of the month in order to have time to arrange getting counsel. The judge set bail at two thousand dollars on Carol, and fifteen hundred on me. We were dismissed from the courtroom, returned inside, and, after a short wait, were sent downstairs to be admitted to the Tombs to await our next court appearance. Carol, of course, was separated and held in the female section, until she was sent to the Women's House of Detention.

I was sent with a group of twenty others to where we were relieved of our personal effects—keys, wallets, watches, papers, or anything we wished held in personal property until we could pick them up at the end of serving our time, if sentenced, or when leaving the court with a dismissal or suspended sentence, or when we could leave the Tombs, no longer in their jurisdiction. Money is also taken, and one receives receipts for the property and money. The money can be spent at the rate of two dollars every weekday for commissary.

Next one is called by name and lined up in a back room facing shower stalls—told to strip down, to turn pockets inside out, and to throw their clothing up on a table in front of them. An officer goes along from man to man, searching through the clothing. Seams are felt, shoes are tapped and shaken out, and after inspection are pushed over toward one. Next, one is told to gather up their stuff, move on along, take a shower, not to put the clothing on until seen by the doctor.

All this follows a line. One is called into the doctor's office and told to stand in front of the doctor's desk. The doctor looks one over for scars, tattoos, needle tracks, and general physical appearance. The doctor (if one is a drug addict) inquires about the period of time one has been using, how heavy the habit is, and how one is feeling. He asks if one has had several diseases such as cancer, tuberculosis, hernia, and several others. He fills out a blue medical card and one is dismissed, told to get dressed, step through the next door, and wait to be given a Tombs ID card, have a forefinger print taken, and to sign their names on cards for prison files.

I made the rounds, received my orange ID card, and saw I had been assigned to the fourth floor. This was considered lucky, since usually drug addicts all go straight to the ninth floor. It is, as a rule, overly crowded and can be one of the most unpleasant places to lie around waiting for trial. There are always sick junkies regurgitating all night long—sometimes screaming—who are thin and drawn—physically debilitated to the extent of having to draw on reserve strength when it is necessary to so much as walk across the length of the cell. When the floor is fully loaded, I have seen as many as four men assigned to a cell overnight. The cells were originally scaled for one man, and are not bad for two. But three and four make it impossible for anyone in the cell to move. There are only two bunks. The others sleep on the floor. All in all, it can be rough and miserable. This sort of thing seldom occurs on other floors, and a man who has once made the route considers himself getting a break if he misses the ninth.

I owe my luck to the doctor. I had explained I was not hooked and was feeling in good shape. He decided to assign me to the fourth floor. When one reaches the floor one is assigned to, one is next assigned a cell, and it becomes his home for as long as he remains, unless he is transferred to another cell later for some reason or other.

There are four sections on each floor, designated alphabetically, A, B, C, D, and two end sections, E and F.

As I have mentioned, the cells were scaled to one man. But with crime on the upsurge and not enough jails, it became necessary to put another bunk in each cell—and there are now two men to each cell.

I settled fairly well into the daily routine. Up early, when breakfast is brought to the cell. Dinner and supper are eaten in the recreation area and one gets one's own tray where it is filled from the chow wagon or carts sent each mealtime to each floor. Next, the men going to court that day are usually allowed to take a shave. Men from the day before who were sentenced are to be transferred to the prison they will serve the sentence in—Rikers Island, Hart's Island, Sing Sing, Elmira—or wherever it happens they were sentenced. The first couple of morning hours are busy getting all the day's business lined up. The men get ready for court or transfer, and work assignments for the men who are serving time and act as helpers mopping, wiping, sweeping, stacking blankets, and passing out toilet paper and soap, washing the trays and pans, and any and all odds and ends that may come up during the day.

There is a good deal of action during the week and the days can slip by rapidly. But on the weekend, nothing happens in the way of action; both Saturday and Sunday seem interminable.

There are periods of lock-out when one must come out of the cell and stay in a sort of recreation area. These periods are the same each day. During the week, first lock-out is about ten o'clock, and lasts until about eleven or eleven-thirty. Then lock-in until one, and back out 'til four, in again until six-thirty, out 'til eight. This schedule varies slightly on the weekend.

Somehow, one can establish a pattern for daily existence.

All the week prior to the twenty-third, most of my time was spent in a state of introspection and trying to find an answer for myself and what was happening to me. Nothing seemed very real and much of the so-called reality I was aware of appeared to me to be made up of a dream-like quality. I was in a state of torpor, surrounded entirely by a fantastic nightmare. I kept searching for some kind of basic reasoning to perhaps at the very least assure me I wouldn't be sent away for longer than six months. I had heard of a multiple-offender ruling where a judge can sentence a man to a penitentiary for an indefinite term—which means from one day to three years—and I am, if nothing else, a multiple offender.

I developed a prayer system wherein I kept asking for God's help and, at one point, requested a miracle—something which would extricate me from my situation in such a way that I would walk out of the courtroom and back into my environment of friends and beloved city streets.

It happened. Before explaining, it must be understood that there was simply no way to avoid pleading guilty, and the least any judge could give me would be six months.

The twenty-third I was in court, having just stepped in, looking around and half-expecting to see a familiar face. There was no one. Apparently no one cared to represent me and a lawyer hadn't been found. I would have to request legal aid representation. I was called before the bench, made my request, and the judge ordered the case to be heard during the afternoon court session.

The legal aid man approached me. I had been ordered to sit off to one side, and looking at me he said, "I have sympathy for sex cases and drug cases and draw the line at violence. I dislike violence." Meanwhile, he had seated himself next to me and was scanning the wording of the charge. I explained briefly a little of my feelings of frustration, and told him I wasn't hooked, that I had been released from my last sentence not quite a month back. He asked me several questions such as, did I have a bag of junk in my possession when arrested? What had I been doing since my release? What kind of work do I do? I answered his questions directly and honestly, admitting to the possession, telling him I am a writer and am editing and assembling my writing into book form, that I expected to have the material in the hands of the publisher by fall. He interrupted me, asked me if I had a title for the book, had I ever had anything published and what it was about. I told him there was no title and that it was a collection of my notes and stories of places and people and my use of drugs, the things I'd seen and done—a kind of journal. I told him of my few published things, their titles and publishers. He wrote a great deal of this down and then said, "You know, I think you're fairly well adjusted, and you are in luck. This judge is intelligent, and one who has compassion and understanding. Also, the DA is an erudite man and likes to read. I am going to see if I can get you a suspended sentence. This judge is probably the only man you'd stand a chance with. Sit still; I'll be back. Now understand—it's a gamble." He was gone a short time. He told me he had spoken with the arresting officer who promised he would not say anything to jeopardize the chance. He also said, "You will have to make a little speech, loud and clear, a public statement about your writing, and explain that the purpose of your book is to have it act as a warning against using drugs, and that you consider yourself an example of proof, a wasted life, jail at the age of fifty, still standing in a courtroom, charged with narcotics possession." He said, "I think you can do it." I wasn't sure whether or not I could deliver what he wanted, but with crossed fingers and another silent plea for help, I'd damn sure try.

And that's it. I pleaded guilty. The judge studied my case history, all the formalities were fulfilled, and before passing sentence he asked me if I had anything to say. I made my statement, and apparently delivered the goods since the judge passed a sentence of six months—suspended—and I walked out of the courtroom.

It was an exhilarating experience, and when I left the court building and started walking the streets, my heart was glad, and I felt a touch of youth again in my blood.

QUAGMIRE

IN MAKING THE CHANGE FROM MY RECENT INCARCERATION TO MY present state of freedom, I have encountered several difficulties. The most frustrating has been the problem of clarifying my position regarding the voluntary report to the Department of Mental Hygiene. At the hearing for change of sentence, or specifically, suspension of executing my second six-month term, the request was granted with the proviso that I report to a court-designated hospital to be checked for drug addiction, the implication being (since I had already been in jail a matter of almost six months) there was little reason to believe any evidence of drug addiction exists. And it was therefore presumably only a matter of physical check-up and I would be free of further responsibility to the court. All this was couched in rather vague statements. I complied per instructions, and was interviewed at Manhattan State Hospital, only to discover I am expected to undergo a three-month period of physical and mental observation before the hospital would be willing to sign any statements regarding my either being still addicted or not. At this point, it appears I will have to enter the hospital in order to clear myself with the Law and not create further complications for those who have used their good names in my behalf.

The whole routine is ridiculous and somehow rather frightening. I am not at all sure what to expect. Also, the hospital is huge and cold and looks to be awaiting victims to swallow. It sits in a sort of concrete morass of twisting, turning ramps and overhead roadways. I have until next week to try and straighten the situation out. Meanwhile, I am uncomfortable and ill at ease.

I feel trapped and unable to escape. The hospital looms ahead of me like some ravenous monster waiting to eat me alive. I have and am given no opportunity of avoiding it unless I simply cut myself off from my whole means of remaining in touch with people I respect and consider friends.

My circumstances have me in a position where it is impossible to function without stealing. No hospital—no chance of legitimate employment. There will be a bench warrant issued by the courts, and the first time my name comes to the attention of the authorities and they are able to locate me, I'll be arrested. It is possible I could remain indefinitely free of capture, but I would be aware constantly of the threat of being unexpectedly investigated, and were I stopped by the police, regardless of their original intention, as soon as they checked my record, I would automatically be faced with a term in prison.

I am tempted to leave this area entirely, and if I was fifteen or twenty years younger, there would be no question about it. I would go head for new places, hitchhike, ride freights—any way at all.

I have little resistance. There are no drugs available without becoming involved in a rat race. My few sources of amphetamine are undependable, and I haven't any money to seek and try to find new connections. There is plenty around and not difficult to contact, but again, I'm too tired and indifferent to become interested, and I know the grind of supporting a habit would be more than I am capable of in the way of effort and energy. Pot is everywhere, but although I enjoy smoking it, it hardly replaces my preference (amphetamine), and also again, there is the lack of money.

I am annoyed thinking of entering the hospital on my own volition. I almost vegetate now, and after ninety days of their intensive therapy program, I should be in as negative a position as possible.

Several of my friends will and do expect me to do what they consider the sensible and ethical thing—to enter the hospital. I am sure several of those same people believe psychiatric help will be good for me and are firmly convinced it can do no harm. It happens I thoroughly disagree. I do not want any part of the program and at best think it a complete waste of my time. If I must die a lingering death, I don't want it to include personality and behavior adjustments at the hands of bureaucratic psychologists and their cohorts, the do-good, social-service, program-conscious, specialized and conscientious psychiatrists. I am far too old and settled in my ways for rehabilitation, and have no desire to join or slip into the so-called society of present standards, nor to concede for one moment that it is other than maladjusted. What rankles most is the manipulative nature of the bureaucracy and the indifference to the individual's wishes. If I take drugs, it is most certainly my business, and if it is against the law and I am caught, that becomes my loss, and I must pay in their coin. But they have no right to force me into a position where I must submit to mental probing and investigation under the guise of what is best or right for me.

When asked to have my case reviewed with a possible resentencing in view, I assuredly did not want a change in institutions or their purpose. Had I originally been recommended for a drug cure program at one of the hospitals, I would have offered but little complaint or resistance, but for the judge and courts to tie me up in a mental hygiene–type project, supposedly out of kindness and humanitarian consideration, is a bitter dose to swallow. I strongly resent anyone forcing me to accept something against my wishes—particularly where my good is involved.

I can already sense the gathering vultures.

FLORENCE

FLORENCE'S PAD——EVENING. FLORENCE JUST CAME IN. SHE IS LOOKING
well and a bit agitated, perhaps unsure, although I seldom apply insecurity as a measure of what to expect from one's behavior. She is a strangely
beautiful woman. She is and has been good to me. I am not exactly sure
what our combination is apt to produce. I have, way in back, a sense or
perhaps an awareness of guilt, believing that my behavior toward her has
been tinged with selfishness, and that I have treated her unkindly.

She and I have been violent on many occasions. In one instance, I
became dramatic, screaming at her, forcing her back into a corner, falling
over a chair, yelling, "I'll kill you——kill you——shut the fuck up, please——
please stop," half choking her, half insane wondering how in hell I'd
become involved with her in the first place. We both had habits and it
had all started with bickering and complaining about trouble getting a
hit. On other occasions, I struck her. We yelled and argued; snide remarks, sarcasm, hate, general shit.

Florence is a very open and love-giving person. She is extremely hip,
having moved thru several wild and great scenes as far back as Charlie
Parker's early years in the city. She has been in touch with the jazz scene,
digging music and musicians, active and swinging people, hustlers and
knock-around people. She likes living and has a direct way of accepting
all experience. She is neither bitter or hostile. She is a trifle reserved
when meeting people, using a fairly hard set of so-called ethical evaluations while growing accustomed to the person. Yet she is without illusion, and regardless of the manner or sudden awareness of having picked
the short end of the deal, or having become stuck with it, she takes it in
stride and continues to know the person or people, explaining their
seeming deceit or treachery rationally and with a kind of understanding.

She is cognizant of a basic truth within herself and she tries living
close to that awareness.

We lived together last year beginning about April. We met at Arnie's

pad on Houston Street. She came in during a session of amphetamines
and pot smoking among a group of manipulative people moving around
mixing solutions, painting, searching among boxes and in corners, behind hangings, passing from room to room. She wanted to cop some
horse and sounded on Arnie who in turn introduced us. She startled me
a little, and I began digging her surreptitiously, wondering how she fell
in and what she was doing getting straight. She didn't, in a sense, look
like what one might unconsciously associate with schmeck. Arnie gave
her the stuff and asked me to hit her. While we were getting the hit, we
talked briefly. She said she was anxious to get away from the scene, get
back to her place. When we had finished, she thanked me and gave me
a kind of running patter about how easily I had given her a hit, what
trouble she sometimes had, and suggested maybe I stop by her place with
Arnie. She departed and I was attracted to her and hoped perhaps I'd see
her again.

Not long afterward, Arnie and I were out walking and just sort of
knocking around the streets and, being near Sixteenth Street where she
lived, we visited her. She was living in a small but oddly comfortable
room and her actions were seemingly sure and had an air of being pro-
ductive. She was charming, and I felt she liked me. She invited us to
have dinner with her the next evening; we were planning on copping
some shit, relaxing in her place, and eating.

She has and has had for the past several years a great little companion
and pet, a sharer of woes and love, a very wise and good poodle, who
is definitely a personality, and individualized in all senses of the word—
Florence's little dog. Florence named the little dog Pooka, explaining
that a pooka is a legendary little creature of one's own imaginings, sort
of made to order, existing in Irish mythology. She and Pooka are inseparable, and much of Florence's desire to be demonstrative and affectionate
is directed toward Pooka.

The dinner was fine. Florence is a good cook, and doesn't let the
physical effort required to organize a good meal and prepare it drag her;
she can cook good things to eat. We all got high, laughing, talking,
exchanging stories and ceasing, for the moment, to be weighed down
with paranoia. We passed several hours, and Arnie finally cut out alone.
Florence talked with me about her loneliness and said she liked me and
would like overcoming, to some degree, her aloneness, in my company.
I was lonely also, and although I wasn't sure we would become or might
become close, I liked her with a feeling of respect, and enjoyed her

considerate little overtones of affection. Florence took care of me and was unselfish, sharing everything with me and materially far more giving than I. She supplied money and I copped. We shared our junk equally. The time accumulated and Pooka, Florence and I drew closer.

We decided to move and Florence and I walked the hot July streets looking for a new spot. Florence was against moving to the Lower East Side. Florence and I both didn't want to be invaded by amphets heads. I simply didn't want the responsibility of having to be constantly on the alert, perhaps protecting our possessions (or at least Florence's). Florence didn't want that kind of excitement. We confined our looking to the West Side. With the help of an ad in *The Village Voice,* we located a small but great little place on Ninth Avenue and Fourteenth Street. Sneaking most everything out of Florence's old pad to avoid paying the last week's rent, we became established after several trips carrying boxes and suitcases, odds and ends such as a plant of green leaves, dishes, pots and pans, a couple of lamps, a painting Arnie had done which he gave to me which was huge and square and filled with bright tempera tones of royal blue, yellow, green, red, amber, of happy cartoon-like figures of St. George and the dragon, the five- or seven-headed Hydra, an active little angel hanging in the sky above the scene, acting as a kind of referee or guardian type. All the figures had wings and St. George carried a yellow sword. It took the entire night to accomplish the move.

Florence had had a bank account when we first met, and after the account ran out and we were uptight for money, we would cash a phony check against the account. Later this became our only source of income and we both had long daily conferences about cashing checks—whom we could hit, whether we should write for ten or fifteen dollars, twenty or thirty-five dollars, figuring each possibility for all it could offer. It took us no time to run through the local stores where either of us were known. Florence had a wider range than I, since almost all the places knew her as a nice little lady who sometimes had to cash a check. We tried any and all leads. Our habits had increased and we were living comfortably. Florence received a weekly unemployment check that we used to pay rent, stock in groceries, and cop three or four five-dollar bags. Our connection was on the East Side, and the first thing we would do in the morning of the check delivery was to rush to the check-cashing store, get the bread, grab a taxi, and head to see our man and get straight.

Gradually, we began cashing checks with close acquaintances and friends. Florence visited people she had known for years in Long Island,

Astoria, and Brooklyn, while I began calling on people I had met on a more conventional level. I burned several good friends. This through most of the summer. At one point we lost our connection, who had decided to pack everything in, kick his habit, and get off the scene. We had been good customers, and before leaving, he arranged for us to meet a half-load connection (a half-load consisting of fifteen bags for twenty-five dollars). Between us we averaged ten bags a day and we planned on selling the rest.

We started, at this point, copping half-loads every day, finally copping as often as three or four times a day. I began getting customers and had a good business going. Still, we never managed as efficiently as required and our lives became a steady grind of scheming and conniving, shooting more junk, finding fault in each other. We became careless about our dealings with people who knew our address and they came threatening and pounding on the door demanding money, promising to cut us and get even. We were behind on rent and had to get out.

Florence got her weekly check and we sneaked out again. Clive and Erin helped us. We had acquired a little black cat we named Mister, and we had Pooka. Somehow we managed to get out with clothes and a few odds and ends. We stayed with Erin and Clive a couple of days and then found a room on Tenth Street just off the Bowery on Third Avenue.

I had been in contact with an old colored junk pusher. He was anxious to set up a business arrangement on the Lower East Side. We discussed plans and he agreed to paying a month's rent for Florence and I and himself and a little chick he was taking care of. His name was Charlie and he had been in the business a long time. He would supply the merchandise and I would handle the business.

We located a spot and we moved in. Our location was on Tenth Street near First Avenue. The pad was a sharp spot and we lived there from July—maybe August—until October. By late September I had a good business going. We lived comfortably, shot all the junk we wanted (or at least we kept our habits going steadily without too much hassle). Toward the beginning of October, Florence and I began having differences of opinion. It began with drugs, or at least I became increasingly more annoyed and spoke nastily. Florence was irritated also and became more tense. My business sense is not keen, and Florence complained of Charlie not coming through fairly. She was getting her check and buying food and copping extra bags from Charlie. She was disgusted and wanted to get out. She began using goofballs and getting completely stoned.

Much of her frustration was directed at me and I became unpleasant. Either Clive offered his place on Avenue A and Twelfth, or Florence asked him if she could stay there. She moved her things out. Then she called me to please bring over a bag and the works and please hit her because I knew how impossible it was for her to hit herself. I made the run, delivered the bag, cooked up the fix, and hit her. She had taken several Doraphen, and when the stuff hit her, she sort of zonked out. I shook her and made some kind of contact, asking if she had taken goof-balls, and she lied and said she hadn't. I couldn't get hung up with her at that point, going over and shooting her up, having her collapse, with doubt in mind about whether she'd ODed or not. She staggered over, Pooka by her side, and stood in front of the building rocking back and forth, staggering away finally to Avenue A. This all settled into a regular routine, and then one afternoon she had convulsions. It was my first experience with a physical condition where there was violent muscular contortion, a stiffening of the body, quivering rigidity, gurgling, gasping for breath, dribbling streams of saliva hanging from the lips, jerking, straining black eyes, fear and confusion. I held her. I spoke with her. I pleaded with her, tried placing a silver spoon on her tongue—something about not swallowing her own tongue. I cradled her in my arms, trying every way to calm her and to help her. I succeeded finally—partially bringing her round—and then she had another seizure, not as bad as the first, nor as long. My own nerves began calming a little bit and I could function a bit more effectively.

The days passed somehow and things remained tense and uneasy. A cat burned me on the streets. Called me requesting four or six bags, arranged where to meet me, and when I got there, there were two cats, one standing in the doorway. We passed him, and I caught a glimpse of him at about the same time the cat stuck a knife at me, coming on hard, saying, "Come on, man—give me the shit. I don't want to fuck around—give it to me." I was carrying it in my hand and sort of passed it to him, trying to pull away and keep aware of the whole scene. There was no difficulty, and as soon as they had the shit, they split. The cat in the doorway bounced out and cut past me, joining his partner, and they faded into the night as I returned to the pad. I discussed it with Charlie and he felt we had been lucky it hadn't happened sooner. It happened again about a week or a week and a half later. Another pair of cats. They also beat me for a ten-dollar bill.

One morning Charlie and I were just getting up—his chick had been gone a few weeks, and Florence was off the scene. We were alone. Charlie was making a phone call and we were preparing to get organized for the morning fix. I was sitting on the edge of my bed, just having finished lighting a cigarette, when the apartment door was wrenched open, and in walked two members of the narcotics squad. They had received a tip on Charlie and he was supposed to have sold to an agent on an earlier date. They were easygoing enough, snooping around, making wisecracks, locating our stuff in the drawer, our works—finding a bag in my wallet and arresting me for possession. We were permitted to dress. Charlie explained that we hadn't gotten straight and we would probably be getting sick and asked if they would let us cook up. They didn't let us cook up, but instead gave each of us a bag, and when we got to the station house, we snorted it. It held us together through the day.

They offered us a proposition concerning Avenue C, lining up pushers, and helping them to clean up the avenue. They said they would arrange a bail of twenty-five dollars cash for me, and I'd be on the streets that night. I agreed and was released and told to appear in court the following Wednesday..

As soon as I left the building I headed for a place to cop. I copped and went up to the pad. I felt it would be wise to split. Many of my customers were still ringing the phone, some had copped other places and hadn't waited. I had no other connection than Charlie, and he handled the bread and source of supply. I stayed two and a half days, uneasy and unable to get anything practical going. Florence had told me I could stay with her and I packed my cases, deposited them and myself with Florence. We talked of my kicking—I could use her technique. Taper off with goofballs. She would go and see her doctor, have him make out a prescription for fifty Doraphen. I don't know if I believed I could kick my habit, but at least I could cut down. I felt beat and defeated and agreed to her suggestion. We got everything in order, copped one more bag of heroin, did it up, downed two or three Doraphen, and I remember nothing more until I awakened in the emergency ward at Bellevue. I was bewildered and knew nothing of how I had gotten there. They told me my wife was also in the hospital and that we had set fire to the mattress and probably would have died of smoke poisoning. The police had brought us in an ambulance.

I stayed in the hospital a week. Florence and I had a short visit. She had been examined, and they wished to take X rays. She was an ill woman, probably in need of surgery. We kept indirectly in touch by way of attendants coming down from her floor, delivering packs of cigarettes. Meanwhile, the day of trial arrived and passed without my hearing from the police. I felt sure they had been notified, and my arresting detectives would be there to pick me up. The next day I was released.

Erin came up and picked me up and took me over to her place. Erin had some amphets which she kindly gave me. I did a lot of writing, sleeping, walking, and staying straight with amphets. I had lost my horse habit, but was weak and beat.

Something happened with me concerning Florence and hospitals. When she called to ask why I hadn't visited and to tell me of her pending operation, I was unable to respond and I accused her of dramatics and hurt her feelings, until toward the end of our conversation she said, "Fuck you, Huncke," and after a short outburst of anger and hurt feelings, she hung up.

Time passed and Erin and Clive wanted the privacy of their apartment. Thru circumstances, I ended up living with Noah and Paul on Third Street. Christmas came, New Year's—and then one day about eleven o'clock in the morning (I was alone—Noah and Paul were gone) there was a knock on the door. I asked who was there; a strange man's voice replied, "Do you know this woman? She says she lives here." I opened the door to find Florence swaying in front of me.

I looked at the man, and I said, "I don't know her" (and shut the door in her face). All was quiet for a few minutes while I stood beside the door, my mind a whirlwind of thought, shame, rationalization, sadness, and anger at Florence, who was obviously goofed up on barbiturates. She knocked again and I opened the door, rushed at her, shaking her and telling her to stay out of my life, I couldn't take her in, I had no real business being there myself. She argued with me. She fell, losing her glasses. She sat on the top step refusing to leave, and I hit her, hissing at her to leave the building, away from me. She cowered on the step, holding her arms and hands up around her head in protection, and said, "I'm going." Then she looked at me and said, "You fool—you fool." I went into the pad and shut the door. Several neighbors had stepped out to see what had happened, and they helped get her under way.

I thought of it all day and my mind remained conscious of it for a long time.

Events occurred—changes—another jail term for me and then back on the scene in June. I heard from friends that Florence was around and looking well. We encountered each other on the street. She was the same Florence I first met—bright-eyed and forgiving and lonely.

She invited me to visit and stay with her. She tries to make things comfortable. She has bounced back up on her feet. She wishes to share with me.

I sincerely love Florence. Somehow I behave with Florence as I never have with anyone else.

I am relaxed and comfortable. Pooka is looking great and chasing her ball, is petted, wagging her tail, generally adjusts to the scene. She is affectionate, playful, a little bit naughty now and then, but a little imp-ish beauty.

Florence is sleeping. She arranged everything for me before lying down so that when I am ready for sleep, all I'll find necessary to do is undress and fall into bed.

I'm here, but it is really Florence's pad. It is bright and neat and fresh and white. It gives off a kind of sparkle, and I am afraid my presence alone will serve to dim the light.

MÉNAGE À TROIS

THERE ARE CERTAIN PEOPLE THAT, WHEN THROWN INTO DIRECT CON-
tact with each other for any length of time, make the atmosphere and
surroundings immediately around them become charged with an element of danger and evil. Forces exist sometimes threatening only one of
the group or perchance everyone. When there are only three people
involved, and one of the three is a woman, it is usually she who is destined to suffer, to be, if necessary, the sacrifice required to appease the
Furies.

Two men and a woman. One man considerably older than the
other—tired and weary to die—who sits brooding, withdrawn and confused and is no longer capable of actively maintaining his independence
as to the manner of paying his way. He's dependent almost entirely on
the contributions of the other two for his food, the place he shares with
them in which they live, and the doses of narcotics they give him, saved
from their own, which are as important to each as the air they breathe.

The young man is hooked and uses large quantities of heroin. He
shoots up as frequently as possible throughout the day and he schemes
and connives constantly, sparing no one in order to keep his supply
going. He has lived on the streets almost all his life and he knows all the
tricks. He will steal from those he lives with as quickly as he will from
strangers. Anyone he has met or who has taken him to their home is fair
game and he has no friend he will not take from, although there are
several he holds to be close and prefers to take from. He seldom tells the
truth and bears love toward no one. He is always lonely and is filled with
resentment toward everyone. No one escapes his anger for long. He can
change suddenly—from the affable companion to the menacing
enemy—because of a reply he doesn't quite grasp the meaning of, and
is immediately convinced he has been taken advantage of and he must
have revenge. He has many people on his list of those he will someday
cut or knock the shit out of the next time he meets them. Most of his

threats are meaningless and never become fact. He is certainly more than able to fulfill his threats and once or twice has hurt his victims rather badly. He is anxious for the older man to be removed from the scene as this would enable him to take over the entire front section of the apartment. The apartment is really too small for three people and it would be better if only he and the woman were to share the place. Of course in the beginning it hadn't seemed too bad since he hadn't realized how beat the other guy was, and even then he hadn't suspected that the guy had lost his heart and simply couldn't make it. He remembered when he had been all right, had made it every day and kept up a twenty-five- to thirty-dollar-a-day habit going strong.

WHITEY

I FIRST SAW WHITEY SITTING IN HIS ROOM IN THE HOSPITAL ON THE EDGE of his bed. We were both in the section of the hospital reserved for drug addicts who are taking a cure—or kicking their habits, if you prefer. Several floors have been set aside for drug-addicted patients participating in what is referred to as a methadone withdrawal program, which doesn't necessarily bring about a permanent cure but certainly helps the patient cut down his habit, regain strength, and affords a period of rest invariably needed. As the cure progresses, one is transferred from one floor to another in a sort of rotation progression.

I had just been transferred to the sixth floor, and been assigned a bed in a large room toward the end of the corridor leading to the gym and recreation room. A chance acquaintance from the third floor who had been transferred with me was walking alongside of me, and as we passed a room along the way, he interrupted our conversation to call to a friend he spied lying on one of the beds. "Wait up, Huncke, I want to speak to this good cat from the Bronx." We both entered the room and walked over toward the bed his friend occupied. As we approached, we were introduced all around and, wearing a smile which spread clear across his face with eyes full of a look of amusement, there sat Whitey.

At the time, I didn't pay too much attention to him, although I had certainly observed the smile and felt a good openness about him. We didn't stay very long and went on about the business of locating our beds and making them up and settling in. My bed was located in a corner and I was fortunate in that there existed a certain feeling of privacy although the room was large and, in a sense, wide open. From my bed I could observe the entire room comfortably.

Pat, a very beautiful young cat, had entered the hospital in order to cut down on his habit and fulfill a promise to his parole officer, who had told him if he would take a cure, perhaps he could be reinstated; otherwise it would be necessary to return him to jail. He took an immediate liking to me, and while we lined up for evening snacks he had mentioned that perhaps his girl would come by with some hash and pot. He explained there was a way open for lowering a line from one of the windows. I hadn't paid close attention and later, when he called me aside to help, I was excited by the whole incident. Pat's girl came and we quickly lowered a line made of torn strips of sheet, weighted on one end with a Ping-Pong paddle, out of the window. Fortunately there wasn't a hitch in the operation, and drawing the line in, we were delighted to find a good-sized package of pot and four chunks of hash. Two fellows had stood guard and there had been no difficulty. Still, there is no way to keep everyone from discovering some kind of action was taking place, and several of the more alert younger cats were hanging, trying to find out what had come in.

Pat quickly made two packages from the lot—one of which he quickly handed me under cover and told me to hold it. The other he handed to another of his friends, telling him to roll some joints.

That night everyone, or nearly everyone, on that floor turned on. We had all taken our sleeping medication and then drifted off into groups of three or four, out of the way of attendants and nurses, and had smoked.

The result was one of the most incredible experiences I've ever had smoking pot. I walked around simply entranced by the scene of an entire floor of patients in a hospital—supposedly ill and run down—all laughing and talking and emanating an awareness of rapport and good feeling. It was great.

We were strolling around together talking. I was struck by the beauty and great openness of most of the people. Perhaps it was an unusual group of people simply come together under circumstance, but it was a remarkable gathering. All around me was an aura of sharpness and open friendliness. We passed or stopped and spoke with one after another of alert and aware young men. I felt alive and warm and friendly. My only discomfort was that of not being able to say some wise and knowing thing so that all of us could continue to rise above the emptiness and meaninglessness of the world we are surrounded by, and my guilt became intensified when I was addressed directly and asked a question I was unable to answer honestly without fear of destroying perhaps self-belief or hope and yet help eliminate falseness and guilt, looking directly into clear-cut and still trusting eyes. All any of those beautiful young men desired was peace and joy and the right to live in a healthy world.

We had passed Whitey's room several times, and as we started past again, Whitey walked up and joined us. He has good-looking features and a certain quiet dignity of manner, heartening to encounter. As we continued talking and more or less taking stock of each other, I found myself relaxing in his presence, and soon I was aware of a feeling of underlying goodness and was drawn to him like a magnet. Instinctively, I felt as though I had found a friend and my whole being seemed suffused in a deep feeling of trust.

We all three exchanged names and I said to him, "Would you like to smoke a joint?"

"Hey, man—are you kidding?"

"No, man, come on—let's cut down toward the showers at the other end and light up."

Pat, the third member of our threesome, decided not to join us.

Whitey and I smoked together, and it was like a bargain was signed and sealed, so that from then on we were no longer alone and we were each looking out for the other and what was good for one of us became good for the other.

Soon, I met many of his friends—mostly young Spanish-American cats. We continued getting high and turning on as many as we could.

One of the most interesting happenings of each day's routine is the final time of medication when everyone lines up for their cup of sleeping medication. I'm not exactly sure what it's made up of, but this I do know: few can take it without getting strangely high—some stagger off to their beds; others sit around talking, trying to enjoy the last few minutes before hitting bed, in touch with one another, communicating and exchanging dreams and ideas openly and with a certain uninhibitedness induced through the sleeping draught.

The first night of our acquaintance with each other, Whitey and I took our sleeping medication; then, taking a walk away from the central crowd of people, smoked a joint and the last of the hash together and decided to sit and talk on my bed. My corner had become a sort of meeting and gathering spot for some of the more swinging and active people on the scene. Several cats were singing softly in Spanish, and a few were in a group next to my corner talking and laughing.

From one of the windows, one could see directly into the apartment building on the opposite side. It was soon discovered that one of the chicks or women occupying an apartment directly within our range of vision was either completely aware of being observed or simply negligent about drawing her shades on the windows down, and each night at least five or six cats were lined up taking in a scene of a woman alone in her room undressing and preparing for her night's rest. She was an extremely good-looking woman of about twenty-eight or twenty-nine years of age whose body was an obvious delight to her, and she seemingly enjoyed running her hands down herself, sort of massaging her hips, her buttocks, and her legs. I imagine there was a mirror to one side of her room because frequently she would, before removing her last piece of clothing (usually pink panties), stand looking at herself, half fondling her breasts, occasionally bending slightly forward for closer inspection so that her posterior loomed out largely, offering a beautiful view of her lower extremities. She was a trifle on the heavy side, and well rounded. At last she would disappear into the bathroom, supposedly for the last-minute details of her nightly ritual, and when returning to view would be wearing a nightgown. This happened almost every night of the week and was certainly one of the happenings of each day's routine most popular with many of the cats who watched her nightly display and kept up a running account of each of her attributes, knowing her down to a large brown mole just below her left buttock.

Whitey lay across one end of my bed while I lay across the other. We had watched the disrobing scene and Whitey was making very amusing and entertaining remarks about her more prominent features. Gradually he grew drowsy—once apropos of nothing, he interrupted himself and looked at me and said, "Wow, man—I feel beautiful." Finally he drifted off to sleep. I lay awake a long time, observing him occasionally in the shadowy night light, glad of his presence, and comfortable in the closeness of his human contact.

Our boys in the next bed had dug up some hard-boiled eggs left from the morning breakfast tray and offered me one, which I accepted and ate. One of the cats said, "Dig man—Whitey is out cold." Finally almost everyone had settled down for the night. Two fellows on the other side of the room were still talking in undertones to each other, chain smoking, and I watched the red glow of their cigarettes cut strange arabesques in the darkness. One of our friends from the next room cut over to me, asking me for a last-minute cigarette, and sat talking for a minute or two about junk and habit, people and places, at last departing for his own room. I, too, fell into a light sleep, awakening about three-thirty in the morning to discover Whitey still asleep, hardly having changed position. His presence was cheering, and it was with some reluctance I shook him awake. As he awakened, he seemed amused not to find himself in his own bed. His face lit up in a big smile. He kind of mumbled sleepily about going to his own bed, finally getting up, and as he departed he said, "Good night, bro—good dreams."

Our smoke was gone and the next day we made plans for replenishing the supply. Our boy Pat who had made the first deal was still with us, and he decided to pick up once more. Once again, all went well and the next two days most of our crowd—and several cats who were mutual friends although removed from the scene slightly—stayed fairly straight.

Whitey and I had become good friends, and both of us had finally reached the end of our methadone program. Both of us were becoming restless and bored. We had laughed about all the things we found funny and amusing in the immediate surroundings. This time when the smoke ran out, our boy Pat had reached the end of what he could stand and decided to sign out. I talked like the proverbial Dutch uncle to him about staying for a medical discharge but to no avail, and that afternoon we watched him split.

After he left, Whitey looked at me and said, "It would be great to cut out. Do you think you would go straight to the cooker, man?" Then we both laughed as we realized the humor of the question, and I answered him saying, "What do you think? How about yourself?" He answered me saying, "Could be—and then again, maybe not."

That day I called Bob, a friend of mine who smokes pot continually, and asked him to bring some, explaining the procedure—the whole idea he found somewhat intriguing. He told me to call him later, and he'd let me know. I discussed with Whitey exactly what I felt I should tell Bob and mentioned Clive's name—filling him in to some extent on both their present set-ups and their origins. Whitey asked if they were close friends and suggested if they were, perhaps Clive would be willing to accompany Bob and lend moral support. Later when I spoke to Clive, I asked him to call Bob and, if willing to do so, tell him he would help make the delivery. He was most willing, or at least sounded willing over the phone, and later when I called Bob and told him Clive would join him, he became excited over the prospect of the whole adventure and we made final arrangements before hanging up. I immediately sought out Whitey, who had gone to the gym and was hitting the punching bag when I reached him, and explained in detail what had transpired conversationally. Whitey seemed pleased, and we spoke briefly about making an effort to keep everything secret and turn on only our personal friends.

That night, once again both of us attained a beautiful degree of communicative contact and the hours rushed by.

The next morning, I awoke feeling depressed and lying in bed, my eyes closed, I felt the limitations of my immediate surroundings and became involved with thoughts of the street, of what the future might produce, gradually becoming depressed at the idea of once again having to live alone and assume responsibility for my actions.

The depression became more intense and a cloud of despair seemed to hover above me. Finally no longer able to accept the sadness, I arose and sought out Whitey, who also seemed preoccupied and, as I joined him, said, "Man—let's split, sign out." For a moment I was startled—I had been thinking exactly the same thing. I hesitated a few moments and then, looking at Whitey, asked him if he had taken into consideration the ramifications and what signing out would mean in the way of an immediate change.

We sat talking, half selling each other the idea. Finally Whitey raised his head, looked at me a moment and said, "Fuck it, man—let's go and sign out." He began to move toward the counselor's office. A mutual friend, Tony, had been asking us every five minutes if we had made up our minds to leave and what were we waiting for—why not get going; after all, we had bread—if he had just five dollars he'd split fast and go directly to the cooker and get straight. Let things happen as they might— at least he'd turned on. He was a pleasant young cat of Spanish-American parentage and he and Whitey had sat frequently talking in Spanish; occasionally when I had been with them, one or the other would interpret for me, and next to Whitey I had learned to like him best of the innumerable cats on the scene.

At the moment he was laughing and describing in vivid detail what his next moves would be following his turning-on—how his old lady would be right there waiting for him to get straight and then make love—and it was in the process of his telling how he would hold her tenderly, pressing his whole body tightly against hers, allowing his hands to rove from the back of her neck down over her shoulders on down the center of her back, when Whitey interrupted him, looking at me saying, "Let's go, bro. You and me. We don't need any more cure or anything the hospital can offer. You say you got fifteen or twenty dollars and that's enough to get us feeling righteous and to buy a screwdriver. Man—I cracked cribs when I was ten for the first time, and baby, I'm good. Just before Christmas, my old lady and I made plenty of bread, and if you want to work with me, you've got it made."

I listened to him, almost entranced watching his face and thinking about all he was saying and remembering the time when someone had made almost the same proposition and how great it had turned out and how down I had been then and it had worked out like my being reborn and if this time could possibly be as great and silently thanking God, lucky stars, and Fate for again providing me with a friend who, from all I'd been able to discover, liked me and was willing to accept an everyday association with me, become my partner, and thereby give me a real reason for wanting to continue living.

Exactly as in the previous relationship, upon our first becoming acquainted, and without provocation, Whitey did what Johnnie had done: he had convinced me of his sincerity and then, looking me directly in the eye, had said, "Man—I like you and want to be your friend," and my heart had responded and I had felt as though I had suddenly touched the source of a new supply of energy. Yet even then I hadn't thought much about future developments, and now Whitey had just told me his wish was to be my friend, to share our daily existence together—just be together—let what might come, come and to hell with everything else. It was difficult for me to accept at first and then in a flash all doubt was gone, and from then on my entire purpose in everything I thought and did was for the two of us, and all that meant anything at all to me was that I had a friend I could love and trust and that I no longer felt lonely.

Without further discussion, we signed out. The morning was extremely cold but when we stepped out onto the street, both of us were so full of good feeling, we were barely aware of the icy wind which was blowing in a constant rush thru the city, and as we walked along the street, on the outer side of the parked automobiles in the street, with traffic rushing by, searching for a taxi, sometimes walking backward, laughing, exclaiming to each other and the surroundings at large about fresh air, the sun, how great just to be walking, cursing because an empty cab failed to appear, laughing about how Clive and Bob had looked down below, as seen from the window overlooking Second Avenue— observing the activity on the street and the long line of knotted strips of sheet dangling six stories down from the front of the hospital, and the two of them—Bob hiding in the telephone booth, and Clive taking the opportunity of reaching for the line and attaching the pot or dropping it into the two-thirds finished leather bag—Whitey had been making it, having gotten materials from the occupational therapy worker—and suggesting it be used for the end of the line, both weighing it down and to make it easy for the man below—and at last we caught a cab after two and a half blocks and asked to be driven to Eighth Street between B and C.

I could not think of anything in a practical sense beyond the plans of the moment. I felt good. My steps were light, and I moved easily and not like a man of fifty-one years. I felt ageless—neither young nor old. I felt sharp and as though my appearance were interesting and that I still retained what was referred to when I was younger as sex appeal. I looked at people and smiled and looked at Whitey, watched him, and it seemed he also felt good and rather happy. We talked and rode along or simply dreamed aloud to each other of what was going to be. Of making a few stings, of getting bread together, of Whitey contacting his man and connecting for weight in heroin, and of pushing. Whitey had spoken of his old lady being uptight in jail, of her owing the state time—seven years—and her having popped out just before he had entered the hospital and her trying to beat her present charge and then maybe she would be reinstated and she would not have to go back and serve the seven years or any part of them, and now he and I were making plans to include her—having a pad large enough for all three of us. Whitey had told me a couple of times that he was sure we would like each other. He had also mentioned his sons. He had two and they were living with his mother. He had called them every day while in the hospital.

Finally we reached Eighth Street and I tried to cop. The man was out and there was a note on his door saying he would be back the next day. I was embarrassed because I had assured Whitey there would be no problem about making a connection. From there we headed to another spot where we were again disappointed. I was beginning to feel stupid and annoyed. I wasn't absolutely sure I'd be able to find anyone else and it embarrassed me to ask Whitey to cut around the cold streets with me while I tried to locate someone else. Thinking to get him in out of the cold and have him wait for me, I stopped by Bob's pad and rang the bell. Bob wasn't home or refused to answer the bell and I had to continue dragging Whitey with me. He kept assuring me it didn't matter but I could see him shivering and I felt disgusted at the turn our luck was taking. At any rate, we did run into someone who knew his way around, and after about an hour and a half of knocking on doors, walking, asking people, and covering a large section of the neighborhood, we scored.

I couldn't think of where we could get off. My works were stashed at Erin and Clive's pad and I had called them on the phone and they didn't answer. I tried Bob's place again and he was home and answered his door this time. I asked him if he had works and he said, "Yes, but they are up at Debbie's. I did a little schmeck with Debbie and Alex the other night and left them up there." I introduced Whitey with much enthusiasm and Bob was very pleasant and appeared to take an instant liking to Whitey. He suggested we try Debbie's to see if she was home and go up there and use the works if she didn't mind. I called her and she invited us to visit her. Finally we got off.

It wasn't the greatest shit we'd ever had but it got us straight.

Again, my old friends liked Whitey. Debbie and Alex were delighted with him. About then, we got in touch with Erin and Clive and they told us to drop by. On the way over, I tried sounding on Whitey about the people he had been meeting with me in order to try and discover his reactions to these new kinds of people for him. I was sure he had known few unconventional people and that most of his friends and acquaintances had fit neat and conventional patterns, even though many of them were out of the ordinary because of being hustlers, junkies, and neighborhood hipsters. The people he was meeting with me were a varied lot, the majority intellectuals and bohemians. He had mentioned meeting a beatnik, and since I detest the expression and don't understand it, I assured him there isn't such a creature but that there are a great many people who lead unusual lives in the everyday sense but that they are usually swingers and beautiful. He had liked everyone he'd met and fit into the scene perfectly. Erin and Clive were charming and Whitey opened to both of them.

Clive was annoyed with me and my irresponsibility. He thought the very least I should have done was stay for the three-week cure and not blown welfare. I had been on welfare when I entered the hospital, and if I had stayed for a medical release, welfare would have continued aiding me. My signing out ahead automatically canceled out my case. I had taken all that into consideration, but somehow I didn't care. I had decided not to let it influence my behavior one way or another in the beginning when I'd entered the hospital long before even knowing Whitey existed, and after our plans began developing, it didn't matter to me in the least. Once, hung up and disgusted, I had thought it would be better to go back to stealing than sticking around for welfare. I simply didn't want, nor do I now want, to be on welfare.

Erin didn't seem to mind or worry at the time as much as Clive, and she and Whitey and I got along splendidly. Whitey immediately liked Erin and Erin liked Whitey.

And so it went. Whitey and I cracked a crib over in the Village, and almost hit a blank. We were both disappointed, but it didn't bother us. There were a couple of people who were kind and they sent and gave me money and we lived and managed very well.

We rented a room for several days, and when we did so we were both confident it would only be a matter of time until we hit a good sting.

Meanwhile, we scored two and three times a day for stuff and once or twice we went to bed stoned. When Whitey was feeling very good and he wanted to communicate with me, he'd say, "Oh, man—I feel good—I feel beautiful," and his face would be wreathed in a huge encompassing smile.

Everything remained at an even tenor with us, and once or twice when the going was rough, I asked him if he wouldn't rather be home and he answered, "No, man—I like it here with you. We're friends, man. This is it from now on. We're together." I told him, "You're the first cat in a long, long time ever wanted to hang out with me. It's been a long time since I've had a partner. Baby—we've just got to make it— one good sting—just once, and from there on, it will be boss."

The first weekend rolled around and with it came the winter storms. Saturday hung us up in the morning, but the evening was great and we got high on everything in the book. But Sunday was a real drag—cold and miserable—and began with both of us getting sick, and no prospects of getting any money; nonetheless, we did manage to get straight and went to bed on one bag apiece, with a morning fix for the next day.

The next day we tried again to get out and organized early in order to try our luck over in Hoboken. We never did get to Hoboken that day but we did get smashed on drugs. We smoked some excellent hashish, swallowed about four Seconal apiece and shot up three or four bags of horse.

That evening I was fortunate, and got my hands on enough money to handle the evening comfortably and leave us enough to operate without difficulty the following morning. That day and the days following proved to be fruitless. It seemed no matter what we set our efforts to, we were doomed to failure. Whitey didn't complain but anyone could tell he was disappointed and his patience was running out. I asked him several times if he was disappointed and each time he reassured me.

That evening, not having a place to go, we fell by Gail's pad, where we were made welcome. Gail seemingly could accept the situation with her usual off-the-record manner and also rather liked Whitey, which made me feel very good, as it did Whitey. Gail was more than anxious about where people were sleeping. She was charming and invited us to stay until we could get swinging.

We talked it over, but held out, hoping we would get straightened out soon and then invite her to stay with us. Whitey was rather smitten by her and I neither discouraged nor encouraged him, figuring that if they were going to make it together, it would happen and all my suggestions at the time would fall short.

And so the week went—somehow—some way, without any real setbacks or real progressions, and although each day produced its particular pleasure, we were nonetheless concerned with getting started and all our efforts were directed toward making money and getting ourselves set up.

We were pleased with each other, and Whitey gave no indication he was other than satisfied with our arrangements. We could still laugh wholeheartedly, and although we admitted our failures, we still believed it would work out.

Friday arrived and this was to be the day we were sure to make at least a small sting and be set up for the weekend. It didn't work out that way, and although we got by per stuff, the evening found us outside Gail's door, asking if she would mind our making it at her pad a few days. She was very nice about the plan and we moved in.

Whitey and I spent the early evening with Gail, meeting some old friends who came by—Jake, Joel, and Janine—beautiful Janine I hadn't seen in almost four years. She had been living and traveling in Europe and her lover had just died and she had come back home. She was even more beautiful than when she left, and I was excited and happy seeing her.

When she was ready to leave, Jake and Whitey offered to escort her to her destination. Whitey turned to me just before departing, saying, "I'll be back soon—five or ten minutes. I'm going to call the old man and lay some kind of a bullshit story on him for money." As he was talking, the thought flashed across my mind that he would never come back and I said to him, "Be careful, man—if you call your old man, that's it. Back you'll go to Brooklyn."

He kind of laughed and said, "Don't be crazy—I'll be right back." And he swung out the door.

That was the last I saw of Whitey. He never came back and as far as I know never will.

AGAIN, THE HOSPITAL

ONCE AGAIN IN THE PROCESS OF ENTERING THE HOSPITAL, PRAYERFULLY hoping nothing goes amiss and that today winds up my efforts and that by nightfall I'll be a registered patient. I am in all probability as desperately in need of medical care as I have ever been—physically run down and exhausted, my nerves frayed, my whole being tense and anxiety ridden and my body covered with sores and patches of flesh germ infested and ugly—particularly my face which appears misshapen and twisted due to large splotches of infected skin, irritated from rubbing and squeezing because there were areas where (quite possibly due to a vitamin deficiency) intense itching developed and it became seemingly impossible to refrain from scratching and rubbing, especially when upon close inspection in front of a mirror I discovered tiny black mites or specks infesting the sections of tingling and raw flesh, and the slightest degree of pressure caused them to pop out to the surface. Also there was—or at least seemed to be—just below the surface a sort of network of channels containing black blood, unsightly and filthy appearing, and it became a conviction in my mind that these channels were the breeding areas of the black creatures and that it was necessary to merely break the outer layer of skin in order to rid myself of their unwelcome presence.

This condition of the skin is not new to me, and even though in the past the results have been similar, I don't believe I have ever experienced anything to equal present conditions. Not only are the spots red and raw in appearance as well as swollen, but where the skin has broken, there are ragged lines of fluted and ruffled dry and dead grayish-white skin.

I have gone many hours without sleep and it is reasonable to believe that these sections are not only infected, but contain torn and injured nerve ends as well.

The ordeal of having to face people while walking along the street is almost beyond endurance and, accompanied by the awareness that it is self-inflicted, is so humiliating—at this point, I can only wish for death, or that by some miracle or other I'll become invisible and pass through the crowds of people unnoticed.

Today is the third day I've spent trying to get into the hospital, and if I don't make it in today, I can't even guess what I'll do to get by until tomorrow. My habit continues to make the usual demands and I've run out of people who are in a position to help me or are willing to do so. Allen claims to have run out of money and Panna has reached the end of her patience and there is no one else I can think of.

JOSEPH MARTINEZ

JOSEPH MARTINEZ IS A TWENTY-FOUR-YEAR-OLD MAN FROM BROOK-
lyn who was born in Puerto Rico. He is a drug addict and a thief. He
is proud and full of vitality and a sensitive and fully wide awake young
man. Recently while in the hospital, we met and became good friends.
We first saw each other in the waiting room of the hospital on the morning of our admittance. We looked at each other and flirted a little with
our eyes, but we didn't speak to each other or become acquainted until
later when we went upstairs and had settled down to the daily routine
of our withdrawal program. We were waiting in line to pick up our last
methadone shot for the first day. I had been in line ahead of him, and
after stepping up to the nurses' station and taking my shot (I use the
word shot very loosely since what I mean is that I drank a small glass of
methadone—supposedly 15 milligrams), I turned away and looked directly into his eyes. He was three men behind me in the line, and, still
looking at each other, I began easing past the men saying, "How are you
doing? Do you feel bad?" He answered, "What room are you in? I'll
stop by as soon as I've copped and we can rap until time for sleeping
medication."

I told him my room number and said, "Boss baby—I'll expect you.
I'm doing OK but it sure would be great to hit the cooker about now."

We both laughed and I continued on to my room where I stretched
out on my bed and waited for him to show. My mind was full of curiosity
and speculation. I had just started comparing him in my thoughts to
Whitey when he came into the room with a big smile on his face and
holding a couple of candy bars in his hand. He walked up and sat down
on the edge of the bed; offering one of the candy bars to me, he said,
"You dig candy when you kick? I do, man—I can do up some candy
when I kick. You look better already. Man, when I saw you downstairs,
you looked wasted. What's that rash on your face? You take *bombitas*?

My name is Joe—in Spanish it's pronounced José—my full name is Joseph Martinez."

I liked him. There was something at once physical and of the essence of living and of energy and soul. His eyes were full of light and expression—communicating constantly—and I imagined I could detect a glimmer of love and I opened up to him a little, and soon we were beginning to know one another and he began telling me stories of his life—of his first love—and he told it to me with feeling and sensitivity.

Supposedly she was ten when he first made an approach toward her and he was fourteen. He spoke to her in tones of tenderness and always with a certain awareness of her physical being. It was almost the classical romantic love story of the shy and poor Puerto Rican mountain boy in the city alone and on the defensive—part of the scene yet sure to prove his worth—when he would eventually fall by in his convertible, draped in a fine suit and wearing a neat sharp tie with one of those English collars (the very latest style) and a boss hat, the brim snapped down in front, sort of tilted a bit over one eye. Really looking good, with a pocket full of money, and then her parents won't object to him anymore or interfere with their seeing each other, and her putting down the man her family forced her into marrying, and of course she respects her husband but her heart is for Joey. He said, "Me, Joey Martinez—I'd show everybody, Huncke—everybody would see how sharp I am and not bad. I'd even go to her church, although I've had a chance to see that it's full of shit—also hypocritical—and I don't believe in their kind of God, if I believe in any. Anyway, her priest sold out to her old man because he kicks in steadily to the pot (fives, tens) and attends the church functions. Naturally he could pat me on the back and tell me he understood, and he'd speak with her father it would be wiser to send his daughter back home to the island, to Puerto Rico, for a while. There were some wild scenes and one, Huncke, where I called them all punk motherfuckers and I kept myself uptight to keep from smashing something over their heads, a chair—even the priest who kept trying to calm me, not even letting me talk. And her punk father pulled her away from me, telling her I was a no-good junky, a hoodlum, hanging around corners, probably out sticking people up and taking their money and using it to buy filthy dope to shoot into my arm, nodding out full of the stuff, and I'd always be no good and should be in jail. We had talked about my quitting for good, and I had almost made her the promise I'd stop if we could only go on seeing each other and her family wouldn't interfere, and I'd gone to this church affair just to speak to her mother and father and ask them to let us see each other and I'd get a job and maybe he could help me, and all hell broke loose when they had seen me walk through the door. It hurt me so much all I wanted to do was kill somebody. And I don't like to hurt people. I don't like fights and baby, I can fight. Finally a cop came in who knows me and he calmed me down, and he took me out with him and bought me a few shots at the bar, talking to me and telling me he saw things my way and they were all full of crap, but I should remember nothing was worth going through all that kind of thing in the church, and maybe I should wait and maybe after I had lost my crazy feelings I should try to see her again and then talk to her people.

"I fucked everybody—I left him and went and saw some friend who turned me on and gave me sixty bags on consignment and I became a dealer and made a lot of money."

I had listened intently and had watched him—his movements, the hand gestures, the lifting of the head, the fierce expression in the eye when he had spoken of some point where he had gotten the upper hand or when he had evolved some scheme, and his slightly boastful tone when he had been clever or someone had pulled a cutey. I had known all along, even though he was telling me a tragic experience and recognized all the fine points, he never failed to retain his sense of humor. I was pretty sure while he was enlightening me about himself that he was still very aware of me and that not a word or gesture of mine had gone unnoticed.

We became fairly steady companions and made a sort of comrade-like love scene—full of a sort of promise of becoming even more intense in the future. Frankly, I was attracted by the idea but wasn't at all sure I wanted things to take that turn between us. Joey wasn't Whitey. He had much the same interest, but he wasn't as full of guile as Whitey, and would be hurt easier than Whitey simply because he was already aware of loneliness in a manner Whitey had never been and therefore was more honest about his feelings.

He made me happy with his charm and brightness and I only wished I could do some beautiful thing for him.

Instead, I signed out, leaving him to remain for the medical discharge in order to meet the demand of his parole officer and fulfill the required behavior pattern; also he would receive welfare assistance. He didn't want me to split and I had to be unkind, but under the circumstances I had very little choice in the matter.

He asked me to meet him the morning of his release, and I thought of doing so but unfortunately was unable to keep the appointment.

He would sometimes brag and point out his good looks, his form, his coloring, and his great smile.

One thing he did tell me made him rather special. He had been speaking at length of his neighborhood, his junk habits, and he told of a couple of his capers and of the money and how he'd spend it and also how he felt he was thought of in his neighborhood. He had been very open—showing no embarrassment at some of the revelations he at the same time thought needed qualifying—and we were strolling down the corridor toward the nurses' station for the final medication of that day, and he suddenly began telling me of a dream and what message the dream had given him, and looking at me he said, "Nothing bad will ever happen to me because someone looks over me and takes care of me." I asked who he thought it was and he answered, "My guardian angel."

FANTASY

I ASKED ELISE IF SHE STILL HAD HER NOTEBOOKS AND IF SHE MANAGED carefully. She said, "My lord—I think it is time." They both grew intense, and when the car in front moves forward, we also turn up another deserted country road—where I meet you—and we will continue as if this was the day of our last resort. . . . You are now and for many. Most girls were staying all night and would be glad for a wild winter storm.

Tony put all he thought she could stand in the screw twist and nearly drowned everyone—I asked for my mixing bottle back and no one would as much as lift his hand to give it to me. I told you I would not be saved if all this fanfare dies down hard.

PART THREE | GUILTY OF EVERYTHING

EDITOR'S NOTE

GUILTY OF EVERYTHING CHRONICLES HUNCKE'S LIFE FROM EARLY
teenage years until roughly 1968. The manuscript went through many
changes and editors until it was finally published in 1990 by the now-
defunct Paragon House. Unlike *Huncke's Journal* and *The Evening Sun
Turned Crimson*, which were taken from Huncke's notebooks, *Guilty of
Everything* as published in 1990 was an edited series of interviews, padded
with passages from earlier stories to fill gaps in chronology. The manuscript, according to some reports, had existed in a variety of forms since
the late sixties. Taken as a whole, *Guilty of Everything* sheds light on the
circumstances surrounding the times Huncke's stories were written. The
following excerpts utilize elements of Paragon House's version and earlier drafts, and feature several "outtakes" that have never been published before.

EXCERPTS FROM *GUILTY OF EVERYTHING*

RIGHT FROM THE VERY BEGINNING I WAS PREPARED FOR SURPRISE, ready to have everything swept up from underneath me. As soon as I was old enough to manage even a little bit, I ran away. That was when I was twelve. My mother and father were by then divorced. My brother, Robert, was four years younger than me, and of course my father showered all of his affection on him. I could understand that. He felt that I had been gathered in by his mother-in-law, whom he loathed, and by this screaming wife he'd married. So naturally he began to think he could correct some of the mistakes he had made with me by handling my brother in a more sensible way. So Bob ended up with a great deal of respect for him.

When I was very small, I couldn't do anything that didn't get on my father's nerves. If I was playing with a toy, or if I was trying to make something, he would get so irritated watching me. I suppose he couldn't help it: suddenly he would snatch the toy out of my hands and say, "No, it's got to be done this way."

As I say, I first ran away at twelve, and I was having the time of my life. I was being picked up by all kinds of strange people. I learned one or two things that kind of amused me. I had my first blowjob, I think, when I was about a hundred miles outside Chicago. When that happened, the guy got scared, because he realized that I was very young. He shoved a ten-dollar bill in my hand, stepped on the gas, and took off—leaving me in some little town. Here I was with a whole ten-dollar bill.

I'd started out with a dime. I rode the Chicago surface lines as far as they would take me out of the city, almost to South Chicago, which eventually becomes Gary, Indiana. You could ride streetcars or trolleys that far. It was just fantastic. I felt so free and light; all my shackles were suddenly dropped. I didn't want to see anybody I knew ever again. It had never occurred to me that anyone might miss me. And if they did, I thought, they'd soon get over it.

Of course, I neglected myself pretty badly. My hair got long—today it wouldn't be long, but it was unkempt. My shirt had gotten dirty and rumpled, and I guess I must have looked strange, standing there on the highway thumbing a ride. I never told anybody that I was running away. I had picked up a road map at a filling station, and had decided to say I was going to the next big city. "Well, I live in such-and-such a place." Once or twice I got into a little difficulty because people began asking me questions I couldn't answer, but nobody pushed it.

I don't know what they thought. They probably assumed I was simply fantasizing. I was fairly well-spoken for a twelve-year-old kid, and I could size people up well enough. I didn't always know what was going on, or what people's designs were, but I could tell when they bore me malice. If I ever felt afraid, I certainly don't remember.

I wasn't doing drugs at that point. I'd done a little drinking, but that was the popular thing to do at school. They used to sell these tiny flasks. They'd have a big basket of them on the drugstore counter. This was during Prohibition. Kids thought it was great fun to have one of these flasks, and they'd go home and fill it up with some of their old man's whiskey or gin. They'd come out with it in their back pocket. Nobody ever really got drunk, though one or two got sick. We all pretended we were far more drunk than we actually were. Silly stuff like that. I was ready to graduate from the eighth grade at that time. You didn't go to junior high. You went directly from eighth grade into high school, and you had four years of high school and finished. You were supposed to prepare yourself for college.

I finally made it into Geneva in New York. Geneva is a neat and proper little town, between Albany and Buffalo. I had wanted to go back and see what Greenfield, the town of my birth, looked like. I'd hitched a ride out of Detroit and the guy was going up toward Albany, if I remember correctly. I had a vague idea that I would like to get up into Massachusetts and then come down the east coast to New York. New York City was my ultimate destination, because I wanted to board a ship somehow, from there, and sail across the ocean, go around the world.

One thing always stands out in my memory very clearly. Outside of Geneva they grow onions, and I had never smelled an onion field before. It was honestly the most refreshing thing I had ever smelled. I thought, God, the world is really such a beautiful place. That was when I first realized there was something beyond all our petty personal quarrels and arguments. My God, the scent of the onions growing was just marvelous.

So I was in an exceptionally good mood when I hit Geneva, and I walked right on through. I never tried to pick up a ride in town. If I had to walk clear through the town, I'd wait until I got to the other end before I'd start in hitchhiking. When I got to what I thought were the outskirts of town, I started to hitch.

Eventually somebody in town had seen me and reported me to the police. These towns, they know everybody. It was obvious that I certainly didn't belong in Geneva. All of a sudden, zoom, here comes the motorcycle cop alongside me. "Where do you think you're going?" He started in questioning me. I got very cocky. I wasn't going to tell him anything. He said, "Tell me where you're from and where you're going."

I said, "I'm going to New York."

"Well, what are you going to do in New York?"

"That's where I live."

And he named a couple of places in New York and I had no idea where they were. He said, "I think you're lying to me. We'd better take you back to the station." He put me on the back of the motorcycle, told me to hold on, and we arrived at the station house.

I remember being shocked that the fire department, police department, and city hall were all in one building. That was the first thing that really knocked me out. The police captain was a heavyset man sitting behind a desk.

"Where do you live?"

I said, "New York."

"Yeah, well, we don't think you live in New York." I can't remember the conversation exactly but it got so bad that finally the motorcycle cop that had picked me up went over and whispered into the captain's ear.

The next thing you know the big cop was saying, "You know, maybe you're not a boy at all." Oh man, I had never had anyone question my sex before. This was the ultimate, I thought. "Maybe you're a girl. Why don't you get up and walk across the room?" I got up, and my face must have turned red as a beet. Of course, I was so self-conscious, I don't know whether I walked like a man or the biggest faggot that ever came down the pike, but I did walk across that office. He said, "All right, now walk back." So I walked back. He said, "I don't know. Maybe there's someone looking for you someplace. Maybe you're a girl in boy's clothes." I was so mad I pulled my pants open and said, "Look, there's a cock. I'm a boy." That cracked those guys up. The motorcycle cop couldn't look at me he was laughing so much. "Oh yeah, well, you think you're pretty tough."

I called them cops. The first thing he said to me—"We are police officers." I said, "You're cops to me." Oh boy. He said, "Jim, this is a hardened case we got here. Better lock him up." They took me downstairs and put me in a cell. Now by this time I was really upset. It was my first time in a prison cell. I looked around. They didn't have anything but an old spring mattress in there, a toilet bowl, and the typical little round plug-in washbasin.

I lay down and I started to cry. I was all alone, and I cried—more out of frustration than anything else. All of a sudden the motorcycle cop appears, down the stairs. He said, "Look, we didn't want to be mean to you. Why don't you give us your name and this will all be over with?"

I said, "All right, my name is Herbert Huncke. I live at such-and-such an address in Chicago. You can get in touch with my folks there."

So he said, "Do you need anything? Are you hungry?"

I said, "I'm not hungry, but I sure could use a couple of cigarettes." So the dude gave me a couple of cigarettes and he left.

Out of sheer exhaustion I lay down and went to sleep. The next morning the cop came down to get me. He said, "Your father's here. He's a very nice man." Of course, my dad could put it on. You would have thought he was the greatest dad you'd ever met. He was always a fine-looking man. He took good care of himself, and he dressed well. Fine clothes, star sapphire, the whole bit. He came to get me and he'd been talking to them.

I said, "Well, I can't see him like this. At least let me wash." I guess there were tear streaks down my face. They let me get back into the washroom, and I washed my face and hands and came out. I didn't know what to expect. You'd have thought that I was his long-lost loving son. "What did you do this for, Herb? Don't we try to give you everything?

Don't you have a good home? Your mother is nearly crazy." Of course, he didn't tell them that he and she were separated, or divorced. "Your mother hasn't slept a wink since you left the house."

See, what happened was this: my mother had supposedly reached the point where she couldn't control me anymore, so she rang him up and told him that I was incorrigible, I was this, that, and the other thing, and he said, "Send him down to me." So she gave me one dime, that's all, no money besides that one dime to get downtown to see my father. Of course I never showed up. They never thought I'd have the nerve to split the way I did.

He went through the whole routine of laying a couple of hundred bucks on the cops. We got a hotel room, and he took me to the city emporium and bought me a clean outfit. We got a double berth going back, an upper and lower berth in the same compartment. Going back through the sand dunes he awakened me at the crack of dawn. He said, "I'd like you to see the sunrise over the sand dunes."

When he finally brought me back to Chicago I'd already gotten a taste of the outside world, and I knew they couldn't trap me much longer in any one place. This was during the Depression, and I would have washed dishes, anything to keep away from the family. But I couldn't really get free until I was fifteen.

It was around then that I first got high. I'd learned about pot but had never smoked it. I was coming home from somewhere and I stopped off for a bite to eat. It was around eleven o'clock in the evening, and even in those days I didn't like to walk the streets late at night. Bad business.

I'd taken a cab and the driver tipped me off to it. He turned around and looked at me. "You look like a pretty wise kid. Did you ever smoke marijuana?" I said, "No, but I've heard about it." He said, "Be my guest," and he laid a joint on me. I put it in my pocket and sort of forgot about it.

We were hanging around the so-called Village in Chicago, Rush Street and Chicago Avenue. There were several places where you could sit all night and drink coffee: the days of the cafeterias. You could write a whole book on them, because people settled the problems of the world in cafeterias. They discussed everything, and there was nothing they missed, from birth control to balling to the cosmos to what have you.

About two months later we ran into some people who knew how to smoke, and Jesus, the first time I turned on, I couldn't stop laughing. I felt like a damned fool—like somebody had pasted a smile on my face and I couldn't take it off. Everything I looked at seemed hilarious. I really enjoyed it.

But my interest was beginning to develop in H, in horse. I was a natural for it. As a kid I was thrilled by a book called *The Little White Hag*. It dealt with smugglers and Chinese junks and opium dens in Shanghai, posh layouts with cushions on the floor and naked or half-naked women and men lying about. It was called lying on the hip. You sat in a big circle, and there was a gigantic bowl of fruit; velvet and satin curtains, soft lights and soft music, dancing girls, the works. I don't know where I got this book from, and I know I wasn't supposed to be reading it, but it fascinated me. Of course, it ended up that everybody went to hell, but so be it. It sounded like a pretty interesting way to go to hell to me. I had made up my mind that if I ever had a chance, I'd try it. I was that way about everything.

My buddy Johnny was using quite a bit, so he'd say, "Why don't you let me put a little in the cooker for you?" Naturally, I said yes, and I thoroughly enjoyed it. I had to be hit the first time. The idea of sticking a needle into my arm terrified me. I never snorted, and to this day I couldn't. The taste is so foul when you snort it. I think if everyone started out by snorting, you'd only have about half the addiction problem.

Johnny was a friend of mine from the time I was nine years old. He and his sister Donna, and I all went to school together in Chicago. They lived in a building almost down on the lakeshore, just one building away from the beach. It was an upper-middle-class neighborhood, which was ridiculous, because most of the people were in debt. When the Depression came it was incredible: entire buildings emptied out. People couldn't pay the rents.

My father immediately put my friends Johnny and Donna out of his scope of understanding simply because they were Catholic. "All right, fair enough, but God, they're Catholics." The only thing worse than a Catholic was a Jew, he thought, being a Jew himself. My father was a German Jew who hated Jews. That was very prevalent among German Jews, oddly enough. My father went out of his way to prove his Aryan background. He became a member of the Bund movement. He had grown up in Chicago in a German neighborhood, and there was a famous restaurant called the Red Star, near the old Plaza Hotel. It was one of the boundary lines of the old Gold Coast. This restaurant catered to big German families when they'd come in on Sundays. The waiters with their big bellies would say, "*Ja,* Mr. Huncke." My father loved that sort of thing.

Johnny and I were into all sorts of things together, though he was in deeper than I was. He was more active, partly because by this time he had moved into a hotel, downtown, where stuff was being pushed. I'd call Johnny and say I'm coming downtown, and then the two of us would run around. Whatever he got into, I got into. We hung out around a huge hotel, right in back of the Drake. One whole floor was a brothel of the most expensive call girls—beauties, all of them. They were not allowed to appear cheap in any manner, shape, or form. Their clothes were picked out for them, and their rooms were decorated to suit their personalities. The hotel manager got as much as $150 and $200 a night for these chicks. He knew what he was doing. Another floor in the hotel was given over to gambling. When the Depression struck and the covers began to be pulled off, he finally jumped out the window and committed suicide. Around this time Johnny and I met Elsie John, the hermaphrodite.

I want to tell you about my first OD. Donna had developed a crush on a girl named Esther. She was supported by a guy who was co-owner of the biggest nightclub in Chicago. He was an old Greek. I doubt if there was any sex involved. He liked the idea of having this young girl, and he kept her in a fairly nice apartment in the Near North Side. When he wasn't on the scene, Donna and Johnny and myself and others whose names I can't even recall now would party there for days on end. Either she would have junk, pot, or both. On this particular occasion, we had taken off all our clothes and were just generally balling. I don't know who was balling whom or what, but we were sitting around naked. During the course of the night someone came in with a bottle of moonshine.

Of course, I had to play the whole hog. I was already knocked absolutely unconscious on pot and heroin, but was still functioning. As the story goes—this was all read back to me later—the last I recall I was taking a drink. They tell me that suddenly I fell on the floor and began gasping for breath, and they didn't know what to do. People just didn't OD in those days, and if they did, it was in another section of town. It had nothing to do with us.

At any rate, there was a doctor who lived in the building nearby and John got his clothes on first and left me with the girls. The rest of the people cleared out, so there were Esther, Donna, Johnny, and myself. Johnny ran out and got the doctor and he injected morphine and strychnine into the nipples of my chest to keep my heart beating. Meanwhile, of course, he'd notified the police, and the girls had proceeded to dress me. Well, at that time, to add a touch of levity to the whole thing, girls had just started wearing little briefs, like Jockey shorts, and they had put a pair of these briefs on me and a pair of pants.

I was rushed to the hospital, and when I came to I was lying on a table in the emergency room. I came out of a complete state of oblivion. It was very strange. I felt oppressed. I was fighting. I caused them a great deal of trouble. Suddenly I became aware of the doctor telling me he had just saved my life. All I could think of was "Oh shit. Big deal. Why the fuck didn't you people leave me alone?"

Then nurses rushed in with black coffee and orange juice, which I would immediately regurgitate. I kept trying to sit up, and they pushed me back down. Gradually I became aware of the people standing around me. I spotted two huge detectives, and then my father.

One of the detectives said, "Well, what happened to you? Were you using drugs?" I had enough sense to say, "No. Nothing to do with drugs. What are you talking about?" This whole bit. "Well, what happened?" I said, "Well, I was drinking. I must have had something to drink that didn't agree with me." They didn't push the issue.

By this time I was sitting up. I was so shaky, and wobbling around. When I put my legs over the side of the table to stand up, the pants dropped all the way to the floor, and of course, I was wearing these dainty little briefs. My poor father. He said, "Jesus Christ! What next?" I'll always remember that.

It was just the end as far as he was concerned. My father was so thoroughly disgusted at me that he didn't even want to talk to me. He took me in the car up to my mother's apartment and said, "Take him off my hands. You do whatever you want with him. I'm through. I've had my fill. He's beyond me."

Not long after that Johnny was making deliveries. He got involved in a group of dykes and whores, a whole scene that I didn't know much about. He was dead two days before I found out anything about it. There was a hotel in Chicago on the outskirts of the tenderloin where he had taken a good amount of stuff with him to deliver to this whore. When he approached the door, she wouldn't let him in. She was tricking or something; I don't know the details.

At any rate, they stupidly made this transaction standing in the hallway. He just began to hand the package to her when they pinned him. Turned out they were Treasury men, and they ordered him to stop. He was a young kid and didn't know the score. He started to run. To make a long story short, he didn't make it. They shot him.

That took me off the hook pretty fast. I went to my mother and laid my cards on the table. I said, "Look, you know Johnny and I have been friends since elementary school"—we were still in our early teens. Then I said, "I'm a dope fiend." Nice thing to tell one's mother. She was a bit shocked. But I was strung out.

When I missed my first fix I was beginning to feel incredibly bad. At first I thought I was just plain sick, that I had a stomachache and a headache. I thought I was coming down with a case of pneumonia or influenza. There was a little chick living in a hotel in the Near North Side who found me wandering around the streets. She said to me, "Wait, you look in pretty bad shape. You look like you need a fix." It hit me— "Well, of course, *that's* what's the matter with me." She was kind enough to take me up to her pad, saying, "I haven't got much, but I'll give you enough to take the rough edges off. Then you'd better get busy and get yourself some money. If you get enough and haven't got any place to cop, come on back and I'll cop for you."

Now that I was able to talk straight I went back to my mother. "Look, I've been using drugs all along with Johnny and Donna. I don't think I have too bad a habit, but I have a habit." She said, "Well, what can we do about it? Do I take you to a hospital?" A hospital didn't sound like the right answer to me, so I said, "No, no hospital. I'll tell you what. I think if I can get about two and a half days' supply, and I come home here with you, I'll stay in the bedroom, and you can measure out the amounts. We'll work out a schedule. I think I can kick."

It worked. It didn't work too well, but it worked. She was absolutely aghast the first time she saw me hit my vein. She thought I didn't know what I was doing. She said, "My God, you've drawn blood there." I felt sorry for her.

———

Through the whole period of the thirties after '34, for six years I didn't do anything but float around the country. If I've hit New Orleans once, I've hit it four or five times. Same with California. A favorite of mine was Route 66, because I could make it straight across the country, as a rule.

In my travels, sometimes it would be hard to find junk, sometimes not. I'd find it in strange places. I hit Galveston, and lo and behold, I ran into H just like that—in Texas, of all places. I'd passed through Houston and almost been busted for standing on the corner. You just never know. In New Orleans, of course, it was easy. New Orleans has always been a junk city. There's a little town called Algiers immediately across the river from New Orleans. The junk would get to Algiers, and it acted as a distribution center for narcotics that extended from Algiers to Memphis, from Memphis to Chicago, Chicago to New York, to California, to St. Louis. And there were a lot of little places I'd stop off at. East St. Louis, for example, was a half-assed gangster town.

I'd heard of East St. Louis before, but I had a call one day from a guy I knew. He said, "Hey, man, get on a bus and get down here. Things are going crazy down here." And they were. I got down there and I met this dude who thought he was a second Al Capone. He had a white felt hat pulled down over one eye. The next thing you know, we're driving down the street like we own it. We stop off in a barbershop and he orders shoeshines, haircuts, shaves, a brushup for all three of us, and he wants it pronto. "Yes, sir." Such service you never saw.

He had been ordered by somebody to smash someplace. I don't remember what the story was, but the next thing you know, we're driving hell-bent for election down the street and right up on the sidewalk. He slows down long enough to pitch a brick through a plate-glass window. You could hear it for blocks.

We hadn't gone two blocks and the cops pulled up. As the cops were dragging us in, this Al Capone type's nudging me and handing a gun to me, asking me to stash it down behind the seat, so that's what I did. The guy was clean, I was clean, and they really wanted this other guy. They said, "Hey, take a walk. We want him," and boy, I went back to Chicago as fast as my legs would take me. That was a little too exciting for me.

When I started out on the road, I had gone straight to California because it seemed like everyone on the road was heading for California. On my way back, I got a lift in Needles, going up to Las Vegas, Nevada. When we got to Las Vegas, that was as far as the ride was going. Las Vegas in those days wasn't anything like it is now. It was just a two-by-four town then. In fact, everybody went to Reno because Reno was the center of activity out that way. Vegas was a spot on the map, and I found I could not get out easily when I was dropped off. I didn't want to stay there overnight so I kept thumbing and thumbing, but nobody picked me up.

While I'm standing there on the side of the road wondering what to do about getting out of this town, this dude walks up to me and says, "Man, you'll never get out of here like that. What you've got to do is catch a freight train."

I'd heard about freight trains and I wanted to try riding the boxcars, which sounded romantic and adventuresome. "Well, how do I go about it?" He said, "Look, they make up trains right over there. You stick with me." So finally, sure enough, here was a train. "They're making a train that's going directly east," he told me. "You can probably get right into Chicago on it." I did want to make it back to Chicago, so I decided to hop this train. We waited 'til they linked up the various cars and gave the highball, and then we caught it on the fly.

I got onto that train and everything was fine. At last it pulled into some little town along the way. We were riding on top of the boxcar, and now we got down off the train. We did not want to ride into the freight yard, so we killed some time stretching our legs. The train was about to pull out again, but this time, instead of going up on top of the boxcar, we discovered that one of the boxcars was open and decided on riding inside the car, which is the favored way of traveling.

We pulled out and we're clickety-click, clickety-clack, riding along, a beautiful night. The moon was out. All of a sudden I heard someone say, "Hey, Jack, there's somebody got on this last stop." I hadn't considered there'd probably be any number of people on the train with me. This wild dude comes shuffling over and looks down at me. He says, "Hi, kid. Where you going?"

"I'm going home," I say. "Chicago."

"Chicago?" he says, "that's the Windy City, right? What's that you got there?"

I said, "That's a cigar box."

"Cigar box?" What you got in it?"

"Socks," I tell him.

"Socks?"

"My razor."

"Razor?" He says, "What kind of goddamned situation is that? Traveling around the country with a cigar box? Get rid of the goddamned thing."

I'll always remember that, because he just didn't see the point of it. A cigar box—he thought I was off my rocker completely, and he chuckled about it. As soon as I could, I got off that boxcar.

I did ride all the way into Chicago on the freight. Of course, I hadn't realized that by riding on top of a freight train you could get filthy dirty. Man, the soot was ingrained in my skin. I had to ride in on top because whenever they highball into Chicago the boxcars are usually loaded, and you can't find an empty one anywhere along the line. I looked and looked until this kid said to me, "Come on, let's get up on top. What the hell." When I got off, though, I was a sight.

I hung around Chicago for a while, but it wasn't any time before I finally left it for good. No one in the family was speaking to me, and I had decided that Chicago was a big hick town.

When I walked out of Chicago, I said, "I'm never coming back." And I never have. It was all this midwestern conservative stupidity that I had learned to really loathe, that narrow-minded bigoted attitude of not recognizing that there's a huge universe all around us. They're so smug in their little world, Chicagoans particularly. I thought, Well, I'll get out. So after sobering up a little, I threw a few pieces of clothing into a little overnight case that had belonged to my grandmother, and thought, New York, here I come.

I'd hit New York a couple of times on my trips around the country, and I loved it immediately. It was the first place I'd found where I felt secure, oddly enough. I didn't feel as though I stood out from the crowd like a sore thumb. I felt as though I blended in, in some way, and that people were not always staring at me. I could walk down the street and hold my head up without having to look away.

Then I began to meet people who were very hip, so to speak, and I soon learned a little bit about the more sensitive aspects of life.

[Huncke permanently settled in New York City in 1939.]

When I first arrived in New York I was stone broke, and like every other young kid who hits the city broke, I went directly to Forty-second Street. I hadn't known anything about Times Square except the name, but nevertheless there I went. In no time I became hip to the hustling routine, getting by fairly easily, meeting all kinds of people and having experiences I had never suspected possible. I soon became acquainted with many of the regular habitués—Russian Blackie, whom I joined with as part of the crowd that hung around the cafeterias, Bickford's, Chase's, Hector's, the Automat; Detroit Redhead, whom I'd known well as a popular Times Square prostitute in the forties and who eventually married—becoming, last I heard, the typical suburban matron, active in the PTA; and typical young cats who hustled the street for a living.

I was quick to catch on. I was always quick in picking up on the scenes, and I took to Forty-second Street. I was a natural for it. It was exciting. I didn't see all the tinsel and tawdriness about it then, and it took me quite a while to finally detect the horror of the surroundings. But the Pokerino with its neon flashing, the little passageways from one street to another that were off the record, guys sitting around talking about the clip they'd made—all of this was completely new to me, and I was captivated by it.

I had led something of an open life in Chicago, but it was comparatively protected. I had never really been out scuffling on my own. No matter how bad things were in Chicago, if I couldn't get it from my father I could bum it from my mother. But in New York I didn't know anybody. I was strictly on my own for the first time.

At this time there were a lot of drugstores in New York that were doing illegal business. They were selling hypodermic needles under the counter, Benzedrine pills. The first place I hit was on Eighth Avenue, between Forty-sixth and Forty-seventh, cold turkey. I didn't know anything about it except that it was near Forty-second Street. I had already cruised a couple of times, so I figured if push came to shove this would be a good headquarters. As it turned out, it was.

Around the area at that time were a few rooming houses on West Forty-third Street. There was even a place just off Seventh Avenue right across from the old Paramount Theater, where one could rent studio rooms. They were cheap enough, and one could live halfway comfortably, so after the first couple of scores I'd made I found myself a place to stay. I soon discovered that my clothes just didn't go with the New York scene at all. I had to get a couple of pairs of slacks that at least fit properly and one or two items that bespoke New York and not a hick from the hinterlands.

One night, about three o'clock in the morning, I was stoned out of my mind on goofballs. A guy I'd seen around the neighborhood, and who had been pointed out to me as a pretty tough customer, came over, sat down, and said, "Hey, I've seen you around. My name is Roy; I'd like to get to know you." I said, "My name's Herb, Herbert Huncke. Most people call me Huncke. Give me a little skin." We went through that bit. He said, "Listen, I'm going out and I'm going to make a little money. Would you like to come along?" I said, "Sure, I'm almost tapioca. Let's go."

Roy was going on his second year as a Forty-second Street hustler. He did some stealing on the side, and he'd take me along, showing me how to break into automobiles or to steal items like suitcases, topcoats, suits. One night we got caught, and each of us ended up serving time on Rikers Island.

The two of us staggered out of a bar and headed over to the East Side, hoping to make a score. We passed a car that was packed with luggage. We fucked around with the vents, trying to get in, because neither of us had a tool. Later I learned to crack a vent with no trouble at all, but this was a new thing to me on this occasion.

We ran up into Bryant Park and pulled this sign that said STAY OFF THE GRASS out of the ground and walloped one of those windows with it. Glass in every direction. "All right," he said, "let's go, get everything you can."

He's going through all this stuff and meanwhile I'm doing everything but having a heart attack. I'm so out of it that I'm not sure exactly what is happening, but I know something is not right. We settle for a portable radio and some socks. We shove socks into our pockets, dump everything else, and leave the car with a broken window.

Nobody has paid the slightest bit of attention to us, or if they have, they've gone right about their business. Here we are now, arm in arm, staggering down Fifth Avenue. Somehow we get over to Thirty-fourth and Lexington, and right in front of a building with a doorman we spot another car. Both of us had to be crazy. We've been carting around this goddamn two-by-four piece—we've knocked off the sign part. We walk up and let loose and bust that car open.

I'm climbing in the car and throwing things out, when all of a sudden somebody grabs my shoulder. I'm dragged out and thrown down on the sidewalk. I look up and here's a cop. "You rotten little bastard, what do you think you're doing?" Meanwhile my pal is putting up a fight, swinging at cops. They almost break his arm trying to quiet him down. He's calling them everything he can get his tongue to. Of course, then, I think the least I can do is "Why don't you guys leave us alone? You're nothing but a cop anyway." Whammo! "Officer to you," he says. So officer it is.

Meanwhile I look up and everybody and his brother is hanging out the window. The doorman is strutting around like King Tut. He put in the report and kept an eye on us to make sure we didn't get away. Until then, everything had gone so smoothly that it was like we had a license. The next thing we know we're over in the precinct, and I'm beginning to sober up and I'm thinking, Jesus, I'm going to jail. We've destroyed two cars; we've stolen merchandise. Nothing shorter than five years, surely. It never occurred to me that there were such things as misdemeanors and felonies. I didn't know any of that yet.

Now we were downtown in the old Tombs. It looked like an old fortress with towers in each corner. They'd used that awful red stone brick. There were two buildings. One was the annex for the drug addicts and that was where we ended up. They had taken it for granted that we were drug addicts because we were both falling all over ourselves, though this guy did turn out to be an ex-junky and I had a few needle marks on my arms.

After going back and forth to court and talking to legal aid, they'd got me down to a six-month bit for accessory. My partner got a year because he had a long record, not only for stealing but for pimping, too. He was a choice character all the way around. We were separated.

I was so green that when I went to jail, I thought, This is one place where everybody will be together. We'll all have one thing in common—we're all in jail, we all want to get out. It never occurred to me that there'd be cliques and classifications.

In those days Hart's Island was being used as a prison for city cases. Rikers Island had just been finished. It had been the old garbage dump before they began building Rikers. Guys were scared to go out in the yard at Rikers because there were rats running around. It was kind of funny when you look back on it. They'd just gotten over a big scandal on Welfare Island, and they just were not going to have another. Rikers was going to be run as it should be run. Everybody was going to toe the mark—the prisoners, the guards, the principal keeper, the warden, the whole thing.

Hart's Island is, of course, potter's field. Out at the very end of the island they have a section where they bury the dead. In those days all the so-called drug addicts were sent up there because they had this theory about the fresh air. Also, they needed people to bury the dead. If you were lucky, you were assigned to be dormitory clerk. And they used to have a tailor's shop, so you could work there; or you got on the paint gang. But if you were a fuck-up you made the cemetery gang, and were known as a "ghoul." Those guys were tough customers. They used to come back with rings off the fingers. The blood would still be dripping from the boxes.

You went to Rikers Island first, the reception prison. Then, twice a week, they sent the stiffs up the river on a boat to Hart's, and along with the stiffs they sent a load of prisoners.

I thought I had reached the end of the line. I couldn't begin to understand half of what was happening to me. The first shot out of the barrel was that I was locked in a dormitory with 52 men on one side, 52 on the other, and one guard for every 104 men. There were four dormitories, one on top of another, with a cement yard below. The mess hall was a short distance away, and in the winter they used to tie a rope you could hold on to to get to the mess hall.

They gave me a bed in a dormitory. I was a pretty cute kid, and when I came down the aisle people were looking. I could feel what was going on. I was scared. I didn't know what I was going to do because I had already heard of one case. A kid had been given what was known as a blanket job. Seven big black guys got him down at the end of the dormitory, threw a blanket over his head, and each had a crack at him. The experience was so awful for him that he went completely off his rocker. His name was Joe, and he was never the same again. Joe was a musician's musician, and nobody could play a piano like Joe. He had soul, and he was a beautiful guy, inside and out. All that inner beauty emanated from him. He was thin. He had gold curls and innocent blue eyes, soft skin. He didn't know anything about fighting. He didn't know anything except music. That had been his life. That's what he loved.

Now I'm in the dormitory, and I'd heard about this. Our beds were far apart, with a locker here for me, and a locker on the other side for the next guy. For about three days nobody bothered me, and I made a few friends. I can play cards pretty well, so one night one of the guys asks me, "You play cards?" "Yeah." He said, "We need a fourth for bridge." So that was the first crowd I got into. No hanky-panky. It was straight, guys that just wanted to be friendly. But the guy that slept next to me was another story. I have always had a theory that people who constantly see homosexuality in others are invariably afraid of it in themselves. Nobody ever walked into that dormitory the whole time I was there that this one guy next to me didn't call "broad," unless it was some old man. Well, he had me pegged for a broad.

One morning about three o'clock somebody reaches over. I'm sound asleep. I wake up and there's this "Shh. Hey, hey." He lifts his blanket and he's lying there with a hard-on. He says to me, "C'mon, give me a blowjob." I say, "Man, are you crazy? You've got the wrong guy." Jesus, I'm thinking, what am I going to do? They used to give us heavy shoes with thick soles, and the only thing I could think of was these fucking shoes. I couldn't hit him with my fist, and I'm not supposed to holler "Guard!" because that makes me a rat, so I say, "Hey, man, just leave me alone." I reach down. "If you don't leave me alone I don't know what I'll do, but I'll do something." He says, "You can't do a fucking thing. All right, if you won't blow me, give me a hand job." I tell him, "I'm not going to give you fuck-all."

I picked up my shoe and clobbered him across the top of the head. I cut the whole side of his head, and he started to bleed. He said, "You motherfucker, I'll get you for this." I put the shoe down. I didn't give a fuck what happened. If there was going to be any ratting it was up to him. What he told the guard I don't know, but they let him go. He never bothered me again, except verbally. Every time he'd see me he'd say, "You're gonna get it before you leave the fucking island, I'm telling you."

This sounds corny, and I hate to use the expression, but when it comes to whether a guy is black or white, it never made much difference to me. If a guy treats me right he's a friend of mine, if he'll accept my friendship. It took me a long time to understand that just because I was white and I offered my friendship to a black guy, he didn't have to like me. Why should he like me? No big deal. But I had several black guys in the joint that had treated me straight. One of them said, "Huncke, don't you ever worry. Nobody's going to bother you. You declared yourself that night." The word had gone around. Two guys across the dorm had seen the action. If he had started in after me, what would I have done? I'd have been licked, except that there'd be no fuck. We'd have just rolled around and both ended up in the hole.

So that was how I established myself as far as the joint was concerned. Later on, when I did other bits, it was surprising. There were guys that talked about me. I knew that. I got so that it didn't bother me. If they were talking about me, they were leaving somebody else alone. A bunch of guys together, let me tell you, women don't hold a candle to them. They sit and gossip and tear each other apart. I'd be ashamed to do it. I used to look at these so-called regular guys and there they'd be: "You see that one over there? Well, I heard that one takes it in the ass. This one over there, he was knocking old ladies down and stealing their purses. Don't have anything to do with him."

When I came out of my first experience in prison, I was a whole new dude. Prison, even a short bit like six months, takes something out of you. You don't have the same enthusiasm. You no longer believe in people quite the same way.

I had three dreams as a kid: acting, dancing, and writing. If I've held on to anything of so-called value in my concepts of life anywhere along the line, it was that I've always respected creative people—people who wrote, painted, played music, or what have you—because this was something that I secretly dreamed about, thoughts that I carried deep inside of me no matter what was happening.

For a long time I tired to justify my actions and my behavior. Of course, it got to the place where I couldn't do that anymore. I have done things that do not hew to the line by any means, and I can see where a person, if one was going to pass any kind of judgment, might certainly object to my behavior.

As any young person does, I had dreams about the future, and what would happen in my life. I had excused my escapades into these more or less questionable environs by telling myself, I'm gathering material for a book. It was very funny. I would speak of it occasionally at that time, until one night I heard someone make the statement "Oh, I'm gathering material for the book." This person was so obnoxious—his whole presentation of himself and his personality—that from that point on I made up my mind never to repeat those words.

I finally decided that I couldn't write. The way I was living, well, there wasn't any time to—although I would make occasional attempts to write in a notebook. But a lot of that stuff was lost. I don't know if it even matters any, because it wasn't until I was about thirty years old that I felt I was able to evaluate sensitivity, responsiveness, or perceptions at all correctly. Prior to that, I'd been fairly callow. I say with no pride that my only interest in people when I was in my teens was in how I could use them.

I reached the conclusion that if I couldn't write myself, I would encourage others that I would meet that could write. I found that no matter what kind of life I was living, invariably there would be two or three of that nature who would either seek me out or I'd somehow be able to get to know them.

I would try and recall the things that had hung me up and prevented me from doing some of the creative things that I wanted to do. I could see when people were unhappy because they felt they were wasting their time on things that didn't matter, on trivialities. It didn't matter one way or another in the final summing-up from the standpoint of whether it was right or wrong. Nobody deliberately sets out to be wrong. There may be some that do, perhaps, but basically people are shooting to do whatever they think is the best thing they can do. They play it by ear.

When I'd meet this type of person who was ebullient with the desire to write or to see the world, it was exciting for me. I wanted someone else to accomplish this since I felt I could not. I was pleased that they would allow me to be a part of their circle. My life changed some because I chose to be friends with this type of creative person, although I certainly didn't stop misbehaving or befriending other types of people. I continued to live on the streets and steal.

[Phil White was an early companion of Huncke's who eventually committed suicide in jail. He appears as Sailor in Burroughs's Naked Lunch.*]*

When Phil and I came back from the sea voyage, one of the first things that happened was we met Bill Burroughs. We had been gone five months, didn't make any money, and of course did not kick our habits as planned. When we hit New York we went directly to the apartment, and that evening when Bob—who was working as a soda jerk in a drugstore near Columbia—came back from work he said, "Jesus, good to see you. I've got a guy lined up, gonna be down tonight. I want you to tell me what you think of him. He approached me the other day. He's been coming into the drugstore quite regularly, and he's been talking about capers of one sort or another. He just told me he has a sawed-off shotgun and some morphine Syrettes that he wants to get rid of."

We'd been using morphine Syrettes for I don't know how long. It sounded good to us.

Bob had this wild dream of becoming a mobster of a sort, and I must say he had the potential, except that underneath all of his swagger and bravado, he was really a very gentle guy. He would much prefer lying up in bed with some chick making love to doing anything else. But when he wasn't doing that he was scheming ways to make money.

Sure enough, who appeared at the door that evening but Burroughs. I took one look at him and said, "Jesus Christ, get him out of here, man. This guy is heat." He was standing there stiffly, with a chesterfield overcoat on, his snap-brim hat sitting just so on the top of his head, wearing glasses, and obviously well groomed. Certainly his appearance was not indicative of anything suggesting nefarious activity.

Bob said, "No, this guy's all right. I've been rapping to him, man, take it easy, just take it easy." Phil was also interested in talking to him. "Man, if he's got any morphine, we can do some business with him. Maybe we can get a little taste out of him." So Bill came on in.

Burroughs sat down at one of the tables in the kitchen and I sat opposite him, kind of looking him over. Phil was also sitting at the table, and Bob was in the other room rolling up some joints. He was going to turn everybody on to some pot. Now Bill hadn't taken off his overcoat. I said to him, "Listen, man, why don't you take off your coat?" He hesitated, then finally got up and removed his coat. He wore a conservative gray suit, tie and collar, the whole bit.

I still didn't feel comfortable with him. He obviously didn't know any of the underworld language. He appeared to me like a fish out of water, and I was sure he was FBI and that Bob had made a mistake in bringing him down. Finally Bob got around to mentioning the sawed-off shotgun. I said, "Well, where did you get it?" Bill went on to explain that a young fellow he had known for some time had picked it up—in fact, he had broken into a drugstore, and he'd come across this shotgun, and the morphine Syrettes. He had several gross of them.

Phil was delighted. Bill didn't bring the gun with him, but he did have a pocketful of these Syrettes. He pulled out several and threw them out on the table. Phil anchored into him right away. He knew how to talk to Bill, and I sat back and watched. Finally Phil said, "Come on, Huncke, let's you and I shoot up. You don't mind, do you, Bill?" We were calling him Bill by this time. "No, not at all," he says. "I've been thinking about this. You know, I'd like to try that myself. I've always sort of had an interest in that kind of thing." I gave Burroughs his first shot.

Phil and I walked into the bedroom and cooked up enough for the three of us. Bill was fascinated by the whole process. He came into the bedroom and by this time his suit jacket was off, and he was watching us. I shot up right away, and right after I shot up Phil did the same. "Now look," I said to Bill, "there's enough in the cooker for you to shoot up." So Bill said, "Well, what do you think? How do you go about this?" He was very hygienic about the whole thing. He thought it would first be a good idea to rub a little alcohol on the arm. He also thought it a good idea to clean off the spike before he ran the risk of injecting morphine in his system. In those days hepatitis hadn't become quite as popular as it's since become. We managed to dig up some alcohol and dipped the spike in. I drew up what I figured would be a fix he could handle.

Morphine, incidentally, can be pretty frightening the first time you shoot it up mainline, because it gives a terrific pins-and-needles sensation. You can literally feel the drug traveling through your system, until it finally hits right in the back of the neck. You get a flushed feeling, like a heat wave, and if you're not prepared for it, it can shake you. Whenever

I have been in the presence of people using drugs for the first time, I have always made it a point to try and describe what the sensations might be, so the person is somewhat prepared for it. It's so completely different from anything else that one might have ever felt or reacted to that if you haven't an idea of what to expect, it's apt to throw you for a loop. So, not knowing Bill or how stoic he might be, I felt it was wise to describe a little of what I knew morphine would do to him.

We tied him up with a very effective tourniquet. He rubbed a little alcohol on, then turned his head the other way. I got the needle in and drew up a little blood. I said, "Loosen the tourniquet." He loosened it, peering down at his arm, and began to feel the sensation as I shot the morphine into him. All of a sudden he said, "Well—that's quite a sensation." He kind of looked around and said, "Well, that's very interesting." He gave the impression of being scientific-minded about everything. As I explained before, his appearance was indicative of a reserved sort of conservatism. He hadn't given me any indication of where his interests lay, but he was so methodical about everything that I felt his approach came from a purely scientific standpoint. As I discovered later, it was. He became a drug addict principally as a result of research.

The first time I met Kerouac was on a day not long after I had first met Bill. I was hanging out in Washington Square Park when Bill and Jack walked by. Bill introduced me, and then told me he'd picked up something in the way of a narcotic and asked me if I knew anything about it. I can't recall what the drug was but I had not heard of it. I didn't think it was something I wanted to fool with, simply because I did not know what it was.

I remember thinking Jack was green, but he was taking everything in and making little comments to Bill—mostly about the scene in general. His eyes were flashing around. Kerouac was a typical clean-cut American type. He looked to me like the Arrow-collar man. They always had these clean-cut young progressive American businessmen in their ads with the hair cut neatly and a twinkle in the eye. That was Jack.

Bill invited us up to his room over on Waverly where we decided this drug was something that should be shot intramuscularly. We did shoot it that way, and nothing happened. Bill tried to talk Kerouac into shooting up, but Jack said no, he would pass on it, though he was obviously curious about it. At that time Jack would smoke a little pot, but he was leery of the needle.

We went back outside and then we split up. They wanted to go and get coffee but I had a habit and I knew I was wasting time with them, because I'd already sounded them down for money. Neither had any bread on them so I went on about my business alone.

It was through Burroughs, also, that I met Ginsberg—a man who's had a very big influence on my life. Allen, not quite twenty years old, wasn't sure what he was to become. From a practical standpoint he had decided that it would be best to become a history teacher, since he was specializing in history at Columbia. Meanwhile, he was attending a poetry course under Lionel Trilling.

At the time, too, I met Allen's brother, who was studying law and is now a lawyer. It surprised me to meet this rather conservative young man who was Allen's brother. He certainly didn't fit into the picture that Allen had surrounded himself with then. Allen's interests were far more flamboyant. He had naturally sought out the outstanding people at Columbia at that particular time. Most of them were literary, or interested in psychiatry or journalism or things of this sort.

Bill was interested in hypnotism, and had tried to hypnotize Allen on several occasions. Whether he was successful or not, I don't know. Bill was interested in many things. He was one of the first weight lifters I ever met, and it was funny because he wasn't at all a weight-lifting type. To see him in his room with these huge barbells struck me as incongruous. It just didn't fit his personality. At any rate, he introduced me to all of these people that congregated at Joan Adams's apartment.

Eventually, Bill did bring me up to Joan's apartment, around the time that he himself was to move in. She had rented a rambling apartment up near Columbia on 115th Street. It had three bedrooms and a gigantic bathroom with a huge tub. It was old fashioned and had been built about 1915, just when that area was beginning to be developed. It was right in back of Barnard, and it cost about seventy-five dollars a month. She kept the kitchen and the dining and living rooms for herself, and she rented out the three bedrooms to students from the university. When she met Bill she was immediately attracted to him, and she saved her prize room for him. It was a beautiful room, gigantic, in which he had his books and a bed and a desk—all to himself. Just beyond that was a bathroom, and beyond that was Hal Chase's room.

The clique that was sort of congregating there also consisted of several Oscar Wilde types who were very effete and very witty, with terrific bite—almost vitriolic in their sarcasm. The could carry on some extremely witty conversations. I didn't much care for them, partly because I was intimidated. I couldn't always understand them, and it used to make me feel humiliated because I obviously did not know what they were talking about.

Joan particularly fascinated me. I had never met a girl quite like Joan, and to this day I remember her as one of the most interesting people I have ever known. She was an attractive woman—beautiful both physically and inwardly. She was dark—her hair was what I called mahogany-colored—not as much red in it as mahogany, but a very rich brown. And her skin was a nice cream, with a faint color which was natural to her. She used to wear a blouse—like a peasant's blouse, sort of flopped down off the shoulder, with a drawstring—and she looked so beautiful, so natural. Joan was a quiet woman. She was an observer, but invariably her remarks never failed to start action of some kind. And she took to the underworld types like a natural too. In no time I became very much smitten with her in a strange sort of way.

[In 1946, Dr. Alfred Kinsey was in New York City gathering data for his groundbreaking study of the sexual behaviors of Americans.]

One afternoon when I was sitting in Chase's cafeteria I was approached by a young girl who asked if she could join me. She was carrying several books in her arms and was obviously a student. "There's someone who wants to meet you," she told me.

I said, "Yes, who?"

"A Professor Kinsey."

I had never heard of him and she went on to say, "Well, he's a professor at Indiana University and he's doing research on sex. He is requesting people to talk about their sex lives, and to be as honest about it as possible."

My immediate reaction was that there was some very strange character in the offing who was too shy to approach people himself, someone who probably had some very weird sex kick and was using this girl to pander for him. But I sounded her down.

She must have known what the score was insofar as sex, but I didn't know that. I didn't want to shock her, but at the same time I wanted to find out exactly what the story was, so I questioned her rather closely about this man. I asked her why he hadn't approached me himself, and she said, "He felt it would be better if someone else spoke with you. He has seen you around, and he thought you might be very interesting to talk to. I'll tell you what I'll do. I'll give you his name and number." At that time he was staying in a very nice East Side hotel. "You can call him and discuss the situation with him."

I had nothing else to do, and I said, "Well, I might as well find out what this is all about."

I called Kinsey and he said, "Oh, yes, I'd like to speak with you very much."

"What exactly is it you're interested in?" I asked him.

"All I want you to do," he said to me, "is tell me about your sex life, what experiences you've had, what your interests are, whether you've masturbated and how often, whether you've had any homosexual experiences."

"That all you want?" I said.

"That's all I want."

"Well, I think it's only fair to tell you," I went on, "and I don't want to be crude—but I do need money."

He said, "I'd certainly be willing to give you some money. Would ten dollars be all right?"

"It certainly would."

We went through a funny exchange. Kinsey wanted me to come up to his place, and I said, "No, I'd rather not do that. I'd rather meet you somewhere first." I did not trust him yet. There was just something about the whole thing that sounded very offbeat to me. I arranged to have him meet me at a bar. "I'll meet you at the bar, but I don't drink," he said. "But I'll buy a drink."

"All right, fair enough."

"I'll know you when I see you," he told me, "so you sit down and order yourself a drink and I'll be there in a while." We were to meet at a popular bar on the square, though not the Angler.

I didn't have enough money to buy myself a drink, and I sort of kicked around in front of the place until I saw a cab pull up and a man get out. Kinsey had a very interesting appearance, strictly professorial. His hair was cut very short, slightly gray. He had a round face that was pleasant appearing, and he was dressed in a suit—obviously a conservative man, I thought.

He walked up to me and said, "I'm Kinsey, you're Herbert Huncke. Let's go in. You'd like to have a drink."

I said, "Yes, I'd like to talk to you a few moments before we go to your hotel." He again gave me much the same story the girl had, and he assured me that the only thing he was interested in was the discussion, though he did say he wanted to measure the size of the penis. He showed me a card which had a phallus drawn on it. He said he'd like to know the length of it when erect and when soft. Naturally, I was wondering when he was going to get to the point. It was all so strange, and I still did not quite believe him, but I thought, Well, hell, I might just as well go along with him and see what it's all about.

As it turned out, it was a very delightful experience. As I started rapping to Kinsey about my sex life, I sort of unburdened myself of many things that I'd long been keeping to myself. For example, I'd always masturbated, all the way up until I kind of lost interest in sex altogether around the age of fifty. When I told others of my confessions to Kinsey they all said I was off my rocker, but I must say I was thankful by that time to get it out of my system. Sex had always played a prominent role in my life. I earned my living from sex at one time and have met all kinds of people, and heard of and had experiences with some very strange fetishes.

I told Kinsey most of these things. In *Huncke's Journal* I describe an interesting experience I had as a young boy, and I spoke to him about this. It tells of a young fellow, about twenty years old, who, after telling me dirty stories and arousing me with pornographic pictures, suggested we go up into a building together. We did, and he suddenly startled me by dropping his pants. There he was with an erection. This thing looked gigantic to me, being eight or nine years old, because it just happened that it was dead in front of my face. I drew back but at the same time I say in all honesty that I was somehow interested. I felt no fear.

He said he wanted to feel me. I was embarrassed. Here was my tiny hunk of flesh and then this gigantic thing standing in front of me. It didn't seem right somehow. Anyway, he did try and convince me that it would be a good idea if I'd allow him to put it up my rectum. I certainly drew the line at that, because I knew it'd be very painful. I assured him I wasn't about to cooperate, and he didn't press the issue. He proceeded to masturbate furiously and then he ejaculated. That was my first experience with anyone other than children my own age. This was the first thing I thought of when I began to masturbate. It would excite me. Instead of following the normal course and being pleased by visions of a little girl, I was attracted to this big phallus—a cock. It was quite an experience. I had never told anyone about it until I told Kinsey. It was this sort of thing that I unburdened myself of to this man.

As I continued to speak to him, he became so adept at his questioning and his approach that there was no embarrassment on my part, and I found myself relaxing. The one thing I could not supply him with was a size to my penis. He finally gave me a card and asked me to fill it out and send it to him later on, which, incidentally, I never did.

Kinsey turned out to be a very intriguing man, a man that I learned to respect and whom I began to see quite a bit of. We met for interviews several times, but I also began to see him outside of his office. He only remained in New York on that first visit. I believe there was some difficulty about the grants that would enable him to continue his research. He had to return to the university; but he did come back, this time with a companion. He was a nice young man, someone who had studied with Kinsey and that Kinsey had taken on as an assistant in his *Kinsey Reports*.

I believe I was one of the first in New York to be interviewed by Kinsey, and certainly one of the first from Times Square. Kinsey had apparently seen me around the square and was fairly sure I'd have information to give, if he could get it from me. He had walked up and down Forty-second Street, and he realized there was action of some sort going on there. Of course, he didn't know too much about the underworld aspect of it, but it was still pretty obvious. One walked by doorways and saw young men in tight pants with their whole profile on display. And there were the many flagrant queens that used to fly up and down the street, not to mention the more sinister types that could be noticed if one paid attention, and they can still be seen to this day.

Kinsey gave me money for the interviews. I wouldn't have accepted anything from him if I hadn't needed it very badly at the time. He told me, "Now, if there's anyone else you know that you think might be interested in being interviewed, by all means send them up. I'll tell you what. For every person you send up from Forty-second Street, I'll give you two dollars. I know you can use the money."

"Yes, I can."

It was nice to know that when I was uptight I could get two dollars. All I'd have to do is waylay somebody I knew and say, "Hey, man, want to make a couple bucks?"

"What do I have to do?"

"Well, all you have to do is just sit down and tell this man all there is to tell about your sex life. There's no hanky-panky involved. The man is doing research on sex." Of course, there was no problem. I sent a number of people I knew up to meet with Kinsey. I think I pretty much made his Times Square study. There were others, of course, whom he'd met through me that kind of took over for me. It got to be quite competitive for a while there, what with all the running about for interviewees.

In fact, I introduced Burroughs to Kinsey over at the Angler Bar. Bill, of course, is a very knowledgeable individual. He's been all over the world, and as a young man he had studied medicine in Vienna. The two of them talked the same language. When Kinsey came back to the city the second time, he spent more time out and we'd all meet at the Angler. Joan would come around, and Ginsberg, and though I'm not sure, each of them interviewed with Kinsey as well. It was at these long discussions when we all sat around talking with Kinsey that I came to see that Bill is an extraordinary person.

On the other hand, Bill sometimes irritated me. First of all, he gave me a rather hard description in *Junky*. He wrote how he looked around and somebody introduced him to this strange-looking person whose name was Herman, who was scrawny-necked and looked emaciated. Bill had gotten himself a place down on Henry Street for about thirty or forty dollars a month. It was about two blocks from where my place had been. He threw down a couple of beds and a mattress into it, and once in a while he let me live in it. He made a nasty crack in *Junky* that annoyed me: "Of course, it never occurred to him to pay the rent." Since then he may have learned, because I understand there have been financial reverses in his life, although he's living very comfortably now by his own work and effort. At that time he had a trust fund he could draw from, so he had no conception of what it meant to be strictly on your own, scuffling to get by. He could very well say that it never occurred to me to pay the rent. It damn sure didn't. And I was hoping he'd never bring the subject up. I was certainly grateful for the place because, my God, I'd spent many a night out in the cold wandering the streets.

Around Christmas 1946, Burroughs said he was driving to Texas. A friend of his had interested him in citrus farming. The guy was the son of a millionaire, apparently, a playboy who had nothing to do but fly around Texas in high-powered sports cars. Finally, he rammed one into a tree and killed himself.

His father had sent him down to Texas, and of course he had nothing more to do than just sit back and collect. These people live on elaborate farms or plantations, in big, comfortable houses, and they have people working citrus fruits or tomatoes. It's a very good business. This sounded good to Bill, but Joan did not like that particular element. They went down anyway, and while they were looking around for land they found this incredibly beautiful little cabin back from New Waverly—about fifty miles from Houston. It's East Texas—Brazos River territory. Bill decided that this would be a good place to experiment with growing pot, and maybe to try his hand at growing Oriental poppies and see if he could produce a little opium.

I remained in New York for the New Year, and fucked around some back on Forty-second Street. It felt like home. I'd see Ginsberg occasionally, who had returned from one of his trips to sea and was back at school at Columbia. It was during this time that he introduced me to his mother, to whom he wrote *Kaddish*. She was insane. They could not permit her to stay outside and thought it best to keep her in an institution. At the time I thought her a somewhat rational though very sad woman. There was something very uncomfortable about meeting her, but Allen took it well, as he does most things.

He received a letter from Joan and Bill which said they'd like to have me come visit them in Texas. I had absolutely no idea what part of the state I'd be going to. They'd sent Allen some money and instructions to get Huncke on a bus headed for Houston, where Bill would meet him and pick him up.

I had a powerful habit at the time, and of course I immediately started to fool around. This little bit of money I received was spent on my connection. I figured Bill would probably like a little taste of something. He had hinted in his letter that it'd be nice if I would bring something along.

When Burroughs settled in Texas, he'd cased every town for miles around for paregoric, a mixture with a tincture of laudanum sold over the counter. He had recently succeeded in getting a paregoric habit. He would chill it overnight, skim the surface off, burn the alcohol out of it, end up with a fairly clean texture of opium mixture, and shoot it mainline. It gives a nice lift, but he didn't really like that. He was very anxious to get his hands on something closer to the real thing—preferably morphine.

I left for Texas in midwinter. Ginsberg put me on the bus. I still had a little stuff for shooting-up purposes. I tried to string it out but it was long gone by the time we hit the Gulf of Mexico, Gulfport, Mobile, and that territory. I was ready to find myself something else.

I didn't have bad withdrawal at the time, though I did suffer through some changes. When I got into Houston and met Bill, he had some paregoric and that helped me through it. Also, he had some Pantopon which a friend of ours, Bill Garver, would grind up and send down to Burroughs through the mail. Bill Garver was a tall, gaunt man with long, dangling arms and a very elegant way of speaking whom I'd met in jail and had introduced to Burroughs. Bill would send Garver a money order and Garver would score, save a little for himself, and send a good supply of the stuff down to us in Texas.

As we were driving back from the bus station in Houston we passed a drugstore, and I said, "Bill, I think that drugstore could be made." He kind of laughed and said, "OK, sometime when you're back in Houston you might try it." I don't know how I knew the place could be made. It was an instinctive thing. I knew that Bill, who was driving around to drugstores all around New Waverly looking for paregoric for himself and Benzedrine for Joan, was becoming a little paranoid, thought he was attracting too much attention, and as a matter of fact he was. I thought I could help them out on that end. It wasn't long before I was back in town, because I needed to score some pot seeds.

Supposedly, I was to have brought seeds down with me from New York. Vickie had saved half a mason jar full of pot seeds. I didn't know anything about it. Bill was terribly disappointed that I didn't have them. Finally, one day I said, "Look, since we're so close to the Mexican border, why don't you let me have some money and I'll go down to Mexico? In all probability I can score. At least I can score some pot, and if it hasn't been cleaned, we can get out seeds that way." So Bill, thinking it a good idea, gave me two hundred dollars and got me to Houston, en route to Mexico.

When I got into Houston, instead of making arrangements right away to go to Mexico, I decided to try here first. There was a shoeshine stand I'd cased about a half block from a hotel I'd checked into. Apparently, during World War II, this particular hotel had catered to seamen coming in and out of Houston. It was a typical southern hotel, tropical in atmosphere, furnished with wicker furniture, two-bladed fans revolving slowly in the ceiling. It looked out over Houston's Chinatown, which consisted of about three buildings with pagodalike trimmings and a small area where the Chinese congregated and had their headquarters. The hotel had a very lax air about who came through the lobby and who didn't. There was nothing really shabby about it, but at the same time it wasn't quite genteel either. It was clean, and the maids were very accommodating. There were nice black girls that were still affected by their southern background. They did everything to make one comfortable that they possibly could, and I'm sure that they would have been even more accommodating had anyone pressured them.

Right around the corner of the hotel, where the shoeshine stand was, was the Black Belt. There were two or three beauty parlors and that sort of thing where the blacks gathered. They had a routine going with the shoeshine rag. I fell up to the stand and started rapping with one of the fellows. He said, "You sure don't sound like you come from around here."

"I don't," I told him. "I come from New York."

"Oh, the big city, the Big Apple. Man, I've always wanted to go to New York."

We got to talking. I said, "Listen, you don't know where I could maybe turn on to some smoke, do you?" Actually, I probably said grass, or tea. He was reluctant about owning up to the fact that he did know, but finally he broke down and told me. I said, "What I really want are some seeds. I'm visiting some friends here in Texas. We've got a big spot and we want to plant some grass. If I could get just a jar, it's worth twenty dollars to me." Twenty dollars at that time was of course big money, and I could see his eyes light up. He said, "Well, man, I just might be able to do you some good. Listen, I can't knock off here until a little later in the day, but if you want to we'll meet later. I have a taxicab and we'll drive out to a couple of spots I know. I'll turn you on to a decent joint, and you can decide whether you want some or not. When they clean up, I can tell them to save the seeds. Sure, I can get you twenty dollars' worth of seeds."

We did meet, and we drove out to a couple of honky-tonks. He didn't let me go in with him, but he came up with some grass to smoke and some seeds.

But I still hadn't contacted the drugstore, and Joan had made me promise that I would see what I could do about getting Benzedrine inhalers, which I'd started using with her. Lo and behold, it turned out that this very drugstore I'd first spotted was the main place for connecting. I used to buy inhalers by the gross. The guy gave me a regular wholesale price for them, and he offered me anything in the way of barbiturates that I wanted. It began when I walked in and began a conversation with this one guy and said to him, "I don't suppose that if I wanted a dozen of these Benzedrine inhalers you'd let me have them, would you?" He said, "Maybe something can be arranged," and that was how the whole operation built up. They were very accommodating, and later on, I asked him if he knew a doctor in town that I could go and see to get morphine prescriptions. He thought for a moment, then said, "Well, I know two doctors. You might try them." I never did, though. I got to thinking and thought it just as well not to get hooked. It'd have been a hassle.

I became a steady customer of his from that point on. I'd make that trip in from the cabin at least every two or three weeks for a fresh supply of inhalers. Sometimes I'd pick up a few downs to go along with it. Also, we were in dry country down in Texas, and Bill wanted his drinks in the evenings. I would pick up liquor in town too, and take it all back out to our place.

Bill and Joan's cabin was completely out of the way. Our nearest neighbor was at least a mile and a half away through some pinewoods. Although there were people living throughout the area, there were none that we were close to at all. We had, I believe, around ninety-three acres all to ourselves. It began at the top of a small hill and carried down into the bayou. It was fantastic. Once I rode a horse all through the territory. There were little paths through the pinewoods and down along the edge of the bayou, with a place to cross. It was really incredible.

In the summer there was a mass of all kinds of flowers, and everything was so lush and beautiful. And there were a lot of cedar trees draped in

Spanish moss, hibiscus bushes, big coral-colored blossoms. Little chameleons all during the summer when they'd mate, with their little throats bubbled up rose-colored. Armadillos were all over the place. Once, Bill shot an armadillo on his property. I'm ashamed to say I suggested it. Afterward I buried it and said prayers over it.

Bill was very interested in guns, and he'd purchased a .22 target pistol and a holster to carry it in. It was an attractive gun, and he'd stand out in back of his cabin and aim at the barn. The sound would echo throughout the area. One day when we went to a place not far from the cabin to buy supplies, the people there said to us, "Oh, you must be the fellows that live over near such-and-such a place in the pinewoods. We thought there were a couple of gangsters over there, there was so much gunfire." They were obviously curious about what was going on.

Bill and Joan's son, Billy Jr., was born while we were there. Joan had become pregnant during the time I was in jail, just before Bill had been pinched. I gather that they were making it together, although honestly I have never been able to figure out that whole scene between them. To my knowledge there was no physical contact to speak of. I know, for example, there wasn't any while I was in Texas—and yet she was pregnant, and we all believed it to be Bill's child.

One morning about two A.M. she calmly knocked on Bill's door—he had his own room—and said, "Bill, I think it's time." He said, "All right, just a few minutes." He got his clothes on. Naturally I got up to see what was going on, and she said, "I'm going to have my baby." They hadn't made any arrangements at all. There was a hospital a short distance from New Waverly and I guess Bill found someone to direct him to the hospital. Sure enough he was back the following morning and said, "Joan's had her baby. It's a boy." She returned the following day.

What has always astounded me about Burroughs was his complete indifference to other people's comfort, and especially toward Joan. I could not understand that relationship. I believe he did respect her, as she was very intelligent and could match him wit for wit. But as far as love—in the accepted sense of the word—I'm sure he had little or no deep affection for her. She was interesting to him in some way, that was all. He did not like to be annoyed by her too much, though she demanded he give her a little attention each night. Just before we'd all go to sleep she would spend maybe an hour with him in his room, and they'd talk. She'd leave and go into the front of the cabin, which she used as her room. It was a strange household, all the way round. At the same time, after we finished fixing the place up and straightening everything out, it was quite a nice scene.

Once, however, Bill and I had an incredible argument. We were both zonked and things had been building up in one way or another and, now that the barriers were down, so to speak, I proceeded to tell him off. I can't recall the details, but I know I was insulting. Joan told me that I made statements that were utterly ridiculous. God knows I tried to help the two of them. I tried to keep the place clean; I helped build a fence and a dining room table. Bill just did not know what it was he wanted to do.

One day Allen showed up at the cabin along with his new love, Neal Cassady. I had met Neal briefly back in New York and had heard stories about him, but it wasn't until Texas that I got to know him.

We were pressed for sleeping quarters and, because I knew there was some sort of a relationship between Allen and Neal—though I was never quite sure what—it occurred to me that they'd prefer the privacy of a room. I had this idea to give up my room to them; anyway, I did not mind sleeping in the screened-in porch where I would lie at night listening to the night sounds. I tried to fashion some sort of bed for the two of them from a couple of sideboards and an old Army cot. The only place I had to work was dead in front of the cabin, so everyone saw me making this fucking bed, and there were a lot of meanings read into my efforts that were simply not true. Here I thought I had a good, practical idea—another place to sleep. It appeared as though I was trying to make things comfortable for these two lovers.

Allen was still a typical student, so unsure of himself, and here was Neal, the confident cocksman if ever there was one. His success as a lover, I've always felt, was actually the warmth of his body. He generated such a terrific warmth that one couldn't lie next to him without feeling the energy coming from him. Allen and Neal were not as close as Allen hoped they'd become. During their Texas trip there was a lot of emotional confusion.

Neal accompanied me on a couple of my trips to Houston. One

weekend I was supposed to come right back with Neal but we were having such a good time I did not feel like returning just yet. When we did return I was greeted with hostility. I thought that somehow or another they were unjustified in their attitude so I did not pay any attention to the matter.

So many good things happened in Texas. I used to enjoy staying up nights high on Benzedrine just talking with Joan—but the end was near. I was completely in the dark as to Bill's eventual intentions. When he decided to leave it was like a bolt out of the blue. I think when Bill first came to Texas he had some idea that he'd find his way into a wealthy crowd; but Joan did not want any of that, as I've mentioned. Joan was not interested in keeping her nails painted red, and in all the socializing and sitting around. That wasn't her shtick at all. She simply wanted to get back to nature.

We were there from January to October of 1947. There was never any discussion with me about their plans to leave. Bill announced that the routine was over and that everybody was going back to New York. I know he didn't want to face the winter down there, and I think he was just fed up with the whole situation. That was my impression. He didn't like being so completely removed from everything. Also, he wanted to see what we could do with the pot he'd grown, see if we could make any money on it.

Joan went back to the city by train and Neal Cassady, who was still around (Allen had left earlier), drove Bill and me back. By this time Burroughs had purchased a Jeep and Cassady, who loved to drive, was delighted to take us back to New York. Bill was concerned because the whole back of the Jeep was packed with mason jars full of the pot he'd grown. (It turned out to be bad stuff.) We drove nearly straight through without stopping.

During the trip we got to talking. Now Neal was a hard guy to get to know intimately because he lived very much within himself, as gung-ho as he was. I can't recall how the conversation got around to the subject of sex, but invariably when you were with Cassady it got around to sex somehow. He told me he was terrified of becoming a queen or homosexual. Apparently he worried a great deal about homosexual pro-clivities in his makeup. I told him that I thought it foolish to allow it to get to the place where that bothered him so much it affected his attitude to life in general. Actually he was a gentle man.

When we reached New York, Bill asked me where I wanted to go. "You better drop me off at Vickie's," I said. It was the only place I could think of to go. Joan, the baby, and Julie were waiting for Bill at Grand Central Station with a big, old-fashioned trunk. She'd packed everything. Bill hadn't wanted to take much of anything, besides his guns, which he stashed behind some clothing. That was practically the last I saw of Joan.

They found a house out near the oceanfront around Brighton Beach in Brooklyn and disappeared from the New York scene altogether, except for their contact with Ginsberg, Kerouac, and a few others. I was very definitely cut off at that point from almost any association with them. The following year Bill and Joan and the kids went down to Mexico to live; and shortly after that the unfortunate incident occurred— when Bill accidentally shot Joan. I was in prison when that whole thing came down. In fact, the FBI came to visit me. They had some photostat copies of letters I had written to Bill and Allen, or they had written to me. They called me in and started reading these letters to me, like I had something to do with it, I suppose. It was a bad scene all round.

I guess the final time I saw Neal was when he was driving the bus for Ken Kesey and his so-called Pranksters, sometime in the mid-sixties. His kick was speed, but he was interested in all kinds of stimulants. But he, of course, maintained a great deal of drive and energy and interest on his own. By this time his looks had coarsened some as a result of his bit in San Quentin at the end of the fifties. This happens to many prisoners. They go into jail looking one way and, although they're the same people when they come out, their facade has changed somehow. They develop a certain roughness, a certain crudity.

Cassady still had his devil-may-care attitude for the most part, and he could still drive. I'd *always* felt comfortable with him at the wheel. He pulled up in New York in Kesey's bus after driving clear across the country. It was painted in psychedelic colors, and he parked it in front of the building where they were staying on Park Avenue. They had tape re-corders and cameras and, oh God, the beautiful girls. Every cat had a chick, and there were probably around ten couples. I know Neal, though, could never find a chick to settle with.

[Little Jack Melody and Vickie Russell, who was known on the street as Detroit Redhead, formed a thieves' ring along with Huncke that operated out of Allen Ginsberg's apartment.]

When Jackie came back on the scene he took Vickie with him out to his family's house on Long Island.

The two of them began to visit me at Allen's place. Vickie had met Allen before. In fact, she had been involved for a short while with Kerouac while I was down in Texas. They knew of my operations with Johnnie and I had let it be known that I would like to get into action again if possible. As a rule I didn't like to go out with Jackie, but one afternoon I did go. He wanted to take the house of a detective he'd had some friction with. It was about five o'clock on a Wednesday or Thursday, and we took the swag back to Allen's apartment.

This was the same day that Kerouac had gotten a contract for his first book, *The Town and the City*. He came around that evening and we did some drinking and smoking and we were going to try and cop some stuff. I had some cash in my pocket. Things were jumping and Jack invited us over to John Clellon Holmes's place for a party they were throwing for him in honor of the book contract. Holmes was writing a book later to be called *Go*. We went over there—Jackie, Vickie, and myself—and stayed for a while. It was one of the first times I'd met Holmes, certainly the first time we talked at any length. I found him interesting and always cordial. Whenever I met up with him he was always considerate of me.

The three of us left the party together, and Jackie and Vickie were in the midst of a family quarrel. They were snapping at each other and were beginning to get on my nerves. Jackie had gotten himself a car, though he didn't have a license, and the car was stolen by some associates of his—they wanted to cut back out to Long Island. I said, "Look, you two guys go on. I'm staying in New York." They dropped me off and instead of going home I went downtown and fucked around. I got smashed and ended up at the Clinton Hotel for some reason or another.

At any rate the next morning I cut back to the pad and nobody was there. This was unusual and I knew somehow there was something wrong. I went into the apartment because I wanted to get straight. I had a stash of stuff there and I settled down and cooked up. I had just gotten myself organized when the door bursts open and there's Vickie with her hair standing on end. Allen was behind her, without his glasses, being led by the hand into the room by Vickie. He looked dazed.

Vickie had tears in her eyes, and said, "Man, Jackie's been busted." I said, "Oh, no. What happened?" She laid down this story about how they were going over to see a new fence out in Long Island. They'd stopped by the apartment and Allen suggested they first drive him up to Columbia. It was a beautiful spring morning, and then they asked Allen if he wanted to come along for the ride. Jackie got onto the Island, and because he and Vickie were doing one of their conversational bits, he made a wrong turn on the expressway. Just then a cruiser spotted them.

Instead of pulling over, Jackie made a U-turn over the center island and stepped on the gas. The cops came hauling after them. When he tried to make another turn he hit a stone stanchion, and boom! There's the scene. He gets out and goes one way and Vickie grabs Allen and they go another. Apparently Allen left all his books and notebooks in the car and it was through them that they eventually connected with the address to this apartment.

Now Vickie and Allen were standing there telling me this and my first thought is, I'm not going to leave all this swag. I didn't have any cash and I knew I could take this stuff to a hock shop. I told them, "Look, let's get a few things together and get the fuck out of here." I wanted to get started but they were sort of milling about. I wanted to leave things in order a little bit and get my wits together, so I began to sweep the floor. I hadn't any more than started when there was a rapping at the door. I said, "Here they are."

Next thing we're all in a car together and we're being driven out to Long Island. I end up in a precinct house without really knowing what the score is. They haven't booked me yet. I'm beginning to think that maybe I can walk out of this when somebody comes up to me and says, "Oh, you're Huncke. We've got a screamer on you." They had a warrant for my arrest. They booked me then. And they booked Vickie and Allen too. We all went to the Long Island detention prison. Later on Vickie was separated and was taken to the old Women's House of Detention in Greenwich Village.

My imprisonment ties in with Johnnie, my old partner in burglarizing. When I got busted, they hadn't known I was involved because I hadn't

GUILTY OF EVERYTHING | 266

been at the scene of the accident. When they found the apartment they didn't know whether I was involved with these people or not. They had to go figure it, of course, but they didn't know what the score was. The screamers started coming in on me around four o'clcok in the morning. I was wanted in New York for cracking a doctor's pad in Flushing and taking a .32. I was really heartbroken, because the only way they could have possibly found out about that was through Johnnie.

I was credited with fifty-two burglaries, but that was only a small portion. Johnnie and I must have broken into at least a hundred places.

Ginsberg's brother, the lawyer, arrived and Allen got out fairly quickly. I remember looking up and seeing him standing at the bars peering around with a woebegone expression. It was his first time he'd come so close to anything of this nature. He was saying Jewish prayers. I felt so sorry for him. He got out of jail but he ended up at Columbia Psychiatric Institute for treatment. That's where he met Carl Solomon and that whole bit. It was a turning point for him.

Jackie and I both laid up in that detention prison for most of the summer. Fortunately, his people came and kept in touch with him, and thereby somebody kept in touch with me. But I was tapped right out. I didn't have a thing. When we were separated I went one way and he went another, and I was on my own after that.

I ended up doing a bit. Somebody had to do it. When the parole board began their investigation they got in touch with my father. I had begged them not to. "Please, whatever you do, don't bother my people," I asked them, "because they have nothing to do with me. I have nothing to do with them. They won't want to hear anything about it, and they won't be of any assistance one way or another. So please do me a favor and don't get in touch with them." "Oh, we wouldn't think of it." Immediately they did get in touch. My father sent a letter back, on his own stationery— H. S. Huncke & Co.—and I was so ashamed I hung my head.

It started out by saying he had done everything a father could do. The parole board told me that from what they could judge, my father was a fine man, obviously respected, and a hard worker who had established himself in show business in Chicago. They were just like him. A five-man parole board based their case on the letter. "We can't help but feel that we have to agree with your father's summation of your character.

He states that you have always been a weak sister, and apparently this is what you are." I didn't say anything. I simply stood there and let them say what they wanted to. I knew I wasn't going to get out, had known it from the jump. I knew I was a bad parole risk—no real roots, and couldn't depend on the family for a thing. I had to depend on myself always; nobody else was going to help me.

What can I say about prison? This was my first extended bit, my first time at Sing Sing. I knew I'd be going there and I was very curious about this place. I knew, though, I was getting into something entirely different from what I'd ever been in before.

When I got to Sing Sing I tried to take things in stride. I was still very shy about the whole thing. What else can one do? It was difficult for me to adjust. I had no money and the first thing that you do to establish any prestige at all is to go to commissary. If you can't go to commissary, automatically you're uptight, because there are certain things you are going to need. I knew I either had to depend on people I might know or do some kind of scuffle.

I was fortunate. I met a couple of cats that I'd known from Rikers Island. They were glad to see me. Needless to say the feeling was mutual. While I was waiting to be oriented we got together some. Sing Sing is generally a kind of relay prison. They have these tables in the recreation halls instead of courts, and they have long strips of gas plates where you can cook. That's a big item in Sing Sing—you cook meals. There's always a pot of coffee on, and this is your recreation.

I was waiting for my case to be filed in Albany. I was to be established with a number and a file. In my case, where there were no relatives or such, there was no problem of my being sent to one of the upstate prisons. This time I was sent to Greenhaven State. It's not a very good prison; I preferred Dannemora much better. I was sent there on my next bit.

I did my time in Greenhaven, over three years, and I came out in '53 owing a year. In order to get out early I had to get a job. I was grateful to Jackie's brother-in-law for offering me a job in a dye factory.

I started out working, and I was in touch with people who had money. Now the drug scene by this time was flourishing. The pushers had come back out onto the scene again after nearly disappearing at the end of the forties. There was a new attitude among the drug addicts now; it all seemed to be much more wide open.

This coincided with the bebop scene, which followed swing. Bebop jazz clubs were getting to be the big thing, and when it was discovered that a lot of the jazz musicians were using, gradually the drug scene began to erupt all over again.

A couple of hot places began to operate. This one I recall most vividly was the Royal Roost, up on Fifty-second Street. All of the jazz greats at the time played there. The doorman at the Roost was a big connection. You had to go down to the john to shoot, where the guy that ran the men's room would then duke you whatever the doorman had written on a note. You'd pay upstairs and then go downstairs to get the shit.

The funny thing was that the drug scene was no longer confined to just any one neighborhood. It started to happen in all neighborhoods, much more so than previously when you'd cop, say, in Harlem. More and more people, different types, began to use—not only heroin and morphine but amphetamine too. When I came back to the scene after my second bit, in '59, it was even more obvious. It was the younger generation becoming more involved, a batch of new junkies were making their move, and the old-timers—guys that dated back to the days of Welfare Island—were leaving.

I was assigned a parole officer—a black man, and one of the nicest guys I've ever met—who was very reasonable. In the first few months there'd been a tight attitude toward each other, but we gradually opened up and eventually I came to consider the man a friend. When I got out, I had to sign a lot of statements in order to stay on parole. I said to my PO, "Look, I've signed all these—sixteen things you're not supposed to do while out on parole. I'm not supposed to do this, I'm not supposed to do that. Look, I know many people. I can't ask everybody I run into if they've got a police record, or if they're using junk, or things like that."

"I understand that," he said. "Just use your head and stay out of trouble. Get yourself a job, and keep it. That's one thing. Make your reports, that's the second thing. I want to see you once a week without fail." I never missed. I saw him once a week until toward the end, when I went down again—I'd been so stoned that I'd have been ashamed to go down there and lie to him.

Eventually he knew that I was using again. He never said much about it. He really was a conscientious guy. I think if I'd been in any serious trouble—of course I did get into serious trouble—but where his help might've made some difference, I believe he would have helped me out.

The dye factory was situated out on Long Island, in Queens, just the other side of Long Island City. All the women in the family dyed ribbons and nylon threads and things of that sort. It was a small outfit and was kind of interesting in its way. They shipped their material to the garment center in Manhattan, and they used it for trim and the like on dresses. They did a pretty good business.

While I was working I met up with Bob again, and we started knocking around together. He was using goofballs, doing a lot of drinking and, because he was very much a ladies' man, always prowling for chicks. I became partially involved with the Times Square scene again but not in as beat a way as before, not as much on my ass. I could function better now, and I was working and in touch with people who had money.

Things had been happening to Allen following his being picked up with me. For one thing they had insisted he continue to see a psychiatrist regularly. He still wasn't quite Allen the poet yet. When Bob and I went up to see him, we had trouble getting into the building. Finally, we were directed to the top of the building, the garret apartment.

It turned out he was now living with Gregory Corso. Corso wasn't Gregory the poet yet either, but somehow or another they had hooked up and managed to find this place down on Fifteenth Street. The first thing Allen said when he saw me was "Oh no, I'm not prepared for you at all. My psychiatrist has told me that I can have nothing to do with you." This came as such a shock to me that I simply could not believe it. "Well, of all the fucked-up situations." I couldn't think of anything to say. I turned to Bob and said, "Come on, let's go."

Incidentally, this was the first time I met Gregory Corso. Gregory and I have never been good friends. I do admire him as a poet but we haven't really associated with each other all that much. Gregory's always sure that I'm going to try and take him off or something. This is probably because he left me sick on one occasion and he knew he had it coming to him. Once, I did just that—deliberately. I figured I might as well have the fun of it, and it came at a time when I needed the money anyway. We were both using and this time I was straight and Gregory was sick. He couldn't score, and I told him I knew of a guy over in the old Broadway Central Hotel down on Broadway at Bond Street with stuff, and if he'd give me the money I'd cop for him. He was reluctant, naturally, but he was so sick he couldn't say much about it. He came along with me, and when we got to the hotel I told him to stay put and I'd go up to score. He looked at me like I was going to take him off, so I reassured him by telling him the room number and the guy's name and so on. Then he gave me the bread. Naturally, when I went inside, I split from another door. He had it coming, though he still might not think so.

[In 1954, Huncke was arrested for burglarizing a doctor's apartment. He served five years, remaining incarcerated until 1959.]

Coming out after that second bit was like heaven. I got into New York City in the evening and I wanted to kiss the streets. Everyone was rushing around; no one knew where I was from. I could only think, It's great to be back! I checked into a YMCA, and one of the first things I did was find myself a job at a glass-importing company on Fifth Avenue.

I had been given charge of the warehouse. As far as positions were concerned it didn't mean anything, but it turned out to be a good job because I was able to make a lot of money on the side. On every case of glassware—Italian crystal, West German candy dishes, cut glass from Copenhagen—they'd allow a certain amount of breakage. All I had to do as I opened my cases was pull packages out, restack them, check them—and sometimes I'd end up with, say, five or six dozen Capri cocktail glasses. This particular style of cocktail glass sold for about $100 to $115 a dozen. I'd gladly let it go for $40 per.

My outlet consisted of all my truck drivers, girls that worked in the sweatshops where they made flowers and ribbons and whatnot, and workers from the factory district around Fifth Avenue. By word of mouth I was moving them so fast that I had a hard time keeping up with it. I was making almost as much as the boss, but he didn't give a damn. His day started at eleven o'clock in the morning when he'd come in, look the place over, pull a chair up to the desk, push a button, and a small bar would wheel open and there'd be scotch, bourbon, whatever—

and he'd fix himself a drink. He'd be shaking so he could hardly look at you and say, "How's everything at the warehouse this morning?"

He made his money. He drove a Lincoln Continental, and his wife used to come in dressed to the nines—straight out of Lord & Taylor, Peck & Peck, Bergdorf Goodman. She was a stunning-looking woman and had him licked before he started. He was damn near his seventies. This woman was his kick—that and his liquor. Otherwise it was my play, so it was a wonderful job for me.

The first paycheck I received, I got myself together and I went and tried to locate Allen. While I was away, Allen had become "Allen Ginsberg." I had read an article in *Life* magazine on the "Beats" and about Allen. There had been a shot, I believe, of Allen reading at the Gaslight, a café in the Village. So I decided to look for him over there one night.

It was my first experience with a coffeehouse and that sort of thing. I had deliberately avoided Greenwich Village in the past, principally because a lot of my grief in Chicago had occurred in the so-called Village section of the city. I was fed up with a certain type of Bohemian. Fine, I like creative people, but I had come to the conclusion that they weren't necessarily always found in the Village.

When I entered the Gaslight I wasn't familiar with its procedures. There were a few people in the place and it was kind of smoky. I sat at a table and a chick in a black leotard and black turtleneck, with heavily shadowed eyes, came over and asked what I wanted. I was told they had nothing to drunk in the way of liquor. It would be either coffee, cappuccino, or the like. "I'll have a cappuccino," I said, "and when you serve it, I'd like to ask you a question." She put in the order and I could see her buzzing with the guy behind the espresso machine. They looked at me. Obviously, I thought, I appeared like the law to them. I was dressed in a suit and tie, and my hair was cut short. I did not fit into the scene at all, and felt it instantly. I thought I could overcome some of these disadvantages and was sure that as soon as I asked for Allen everything would be all right.

When the waitress returned with the cappuccino I said, "Listen, I'm very anxious to get in touch with Allen Ginsberg."

She looked at me. "Are you?"

"Yes. Could you tell me where I might find him?"

"I really don't know," she told me.

"Well, can you give me any idea of who might know?"

"No, I couldn't. What do you want to see him for?"

I said I was a very old friend of his and that I'd like to see him. "I've been away for quite some time and this is the first time I've been in New York for several years. I read in one of the magazines that he'd been giving readings here."

She asked my name. I told her Mr. Herbert Huncke, and she said, "I don't know where he lives, but sometimes some of his friends come by, and if you wait a while maybe somebody'll come in." I thanked her and she went back to rapping with some other people.

They kept looking my way and finally one of the characters came toward me. He was wearing dungarees and a chain around his neck, and he had a beard and an interesting face. "Who are you?" he asked me.

"I'm Herb Huncke."

"Oh," he replied, "I've heard your name. You're a friend of Allen Ginsberg's. My name's Ray Bremser. And that's my wife over there, Bonnie." He turned around and called to this beautiful young chick in spotted dungarees and an old sloppy sweatshirt and pea jacket. Ray kind of gestured at me. "Bonnie, this is Herb Huncke."

"Oh, we've heard Allen speak of you," she said. It turned out that Ray was a poet and a friend of Ginsberg's. I asked him where I could find Allen. "All right, we'll take you over to where he lives."

"If you'd do that I'd be very much indebted."

"Can you afford a cab?" he asked me. I said sure, and we caught one upstairs.

In the cab, Ray and Bonnie were rapping away, and Ray produced a joint. "You want to turn on? We hear you've been away." I told him I was in the joint. He said, "So was I. I've just been out a short while. What do you do? Do you do anything?"

I said, "What do you mean?"

"Do you write, do you paint?"

I said, "I really don't know. I do a little writing, that's about all."

We were heading over to the East Side. "Allen will sure be glad to see you."

In those days the Lower East Side was known only as a ghetto where the poor Jewish immigrants had been forced to live. Of late, though, it seemed that people from the West Village were finding that the rents were considerably cheaper on the East Side and some were moving into the neighborhood. Eventually they established among themselves what has since become the East Village.

Allen had found an apartment on East Second Street. We pulled up in front of this old tenement and I paid the driver. Ray and Bonnie were still chattering away as we entered the building. Ray knocked on a door on the second or third floor and a handsome young guy opened the door whom I hadn't seen before. This was Peter Orlovsky. He said, "Oh, hi, Ray. How are you?" There was an exchange of greetings. Ray asked if Allen was around. Peter said he was, and meanwhile he was looking at me. Ray asked him, "Peter, do you know who this is? This is Huncke."

"Oh, you're Huncke," and he cases me up and down.

Just then who comes sliding around the corner but Allen himself. He had a growth of beard and he certainly looked different than the young man I remembered. He had aged some, his hair was longer, and of course he had gained a reputation as a poet. It showed in his self-confidence and poise, something that was lacking when he was younger. He was now something more than the starry-eyed Allen I recalled from when I first met him.

"Hi, Herbie, " he said. He still calls me Herbie, which I have always disliked. I believe he does it intentionally.

"I've been hearing some great things about you," I said to him.

"Nah, it's nothing. I decided I'm a poet." And he went on, "This is Peter. This is the light of my life." Peter was busy making coffee and asked if I wanted some.

Ray pulled out another joint and we sat around and turned on. It was very pleasant. Allen asked what I was doing, and I told him I was working and living over at the YMCA. He said, "Man, you can get an apartment right here in this building for about thirty dollars a month, maybe thirty-five." He had five nice rooms. The woman who ran the building thought Allen was just the end. She owned several buildings, apparently, and Allen said he'd do what he could to inquire about apartments in the building.

I thought to myself that it would be nice to have an apartment where I knew somebody and where things were happening. So we sat there asking each other questions and I spoke of my experiences in jail.

On the floor above Allen's there lived an interesting girl named Elise Cowen who, it seemed, had developed a great crush on Allen. She was a rather strange girl, a Barnard graduate it turned out. Allen had already acquired followers, or disciples, that would invariably run up to him when he walked down the street. It was quite amazing how rapidly he'd come into his own. Soon afterward, I was accompanying him to all the coffeehouses.

*[The Seven Arts Club was where Huncke gave his first public reading, and
also where he met the poet Janine Pommy Vega, who would become a
dear lifelong friend. In Huncke's Journal, Vega appears in "The Magician," "Beware of Fallen Angels," and "Faery Tale."]*

Another place where we used to gather was up on Ninth Avenue between Forty-second and Forty-third streets, of all places, and it was called
the Seven Arts Club. A Polish friend of Allen's ran the place, and he
began letting poets read there on Allen's suggestion.

It was in the Seven Arts that I first met Janine Pommy. She was young,
barely over the fifteen limit, with piquant features and extremely long
hair piled up into a funny knot on the top of her head. Absolutely beautiful. She was acting as a waitress in black leotards and turtleneck. How
can I describe her? She wasn't at all an urchin; neither was she the gamine
type—but there was something very aesthetic about her, I must say. She
was thin and willowy, beautifully colored skin, big eyes. She was near-
sighted and she was always peering around, trying to see things. She was
fascinating to watch and she and I got along splendidly from the jump,
the first night I went up there. I was completely smitten with her.

Before making it to the Seven Arts regularly, I had taken an apartment
in Allen's building, moving in from the YMCA. It was the apartment
directly above Elise's, and as soon as I moved in people started falling
by, just a constant flow of people in and out. It was a communelike
affair, except that everyone had their own cell.

Gradually, with the help of friends, I was beginning to open up. After
all, I'd been away for a long time and had been cut off from the world.
Though I was interested in this new scene I wasn't overly impressed by
any of it. It didn't sweep me off my feet by any means, but it was nice
to simply have friends again, nice to be around those I could relax with.

At the same time, it *was* interesting to see that the people I had believed in at the beginning were actually doing some of the things that
I'd wanted them to do—and that I'd wanted to do myself. It was good
to see Allen was writing and accomplishing something. I didn't know
anything about Peter at first except that it was obvious to me that he had
talent of some sort, the qualities for self-expression. I think Peter is probably what one would call a natural poet, if there is such a thing. His
whole life is poetic in a way.

Also on the scene, and whom I should mention, was a guy by the
name of Irving Rosenthal. He was soon to become a very good writer

and editor in his own right. I believe he was one of Bill Burroughs's first editors.

This is what I had stepped into when I came out of prison, and everything was running along smoothly for a while. But, of course, it wasn't any time until I'd found some heroin and was shooting up again.

Because I was making good money at my job, I'd reconciled myself to both working and maintaining a habit. I had discovered that if I handled my drugs carefully, during the course of the day I could work effectively without any trouble and get through the workday—nobody the wiser—saving my relaxation for the evening. Usually I'd take a nice heavy fix after I had a bite to eat and then sit around and dream. I was doing very well with a connection that came right to where I was living on Second Street.

That's the way I was situated when the panic came. One day the phone rang and my man told me, "Huncke, I can't cop anywhere. There's a panic on."

"What do you mean?" I'd never heard of a panic before.

"The streets are dry. There's just nothing. I might be able to get you a little something later on in the night. There are a couple of people I know, but you'll have to sit tight."

It dried up that fast. In the morning I'd seen him and everything was fine. He'd started me off for the day, just like every morning. First thing he'd stop by and wake me up. That was my get-up in the morning. I'd hear a knock on the door. "Who is it?"

"It's Joe."

I'd let him in and we would sit there and have coffee and pastry and he'd cook up for me while I brushed my teeth and piddled about, making myself presentable for the day. He was a prince. He'd have my shot all ready, tie me up, and I'd just sit there and play and he'd say, "Baby, it's good this morning."

"Yeah, man, everything's fine," I'd answer.

So to have all that joy suddenly cut kind of scared me. I didn't want to believe it. I thought, well, all right, maybe a shipment was slow in coming in or something like that. So I decided to spend some money, and told Joe, "Look, all I can get hold of in cash right now is two hundred dollars. Take that. If you know the guy, lay it on him and get what he's got. This looks like a tie-up of some kind. We might as well get out from under." And he set out.

Four o'clock in the morning I get a telephone call from him. "Huncke, I can't get you anything. And not only that, all I got left is twenty dollars out of the two hundred." I trusted him so I knew he wasn't lying. I said, "Come on over. I'll get you some more money." I managed to get hold of a hundred dollars more and I gave it to Joe, and he did score. He scored what would ordinarily be a five-dollar bag that had cost him forty bucks. He got it for me and it got me to work the next day. This was what I was concerned with most—keep me in work.

I didn't want to blow it. I'd been sick all night and this score did knock the sickness off, but that's all it did. I didn't feel good, so I said, "Man, I'll go get some more money." Meanwhile in the papers, PANIC ON DRUG ADDICTS. NOBODY ABLE TO BUY.

I got a hundred dollars and I went up to Harlem myself. The street corners were literally teeming with sick addicts in the copping neighborhoods. I couldn't believe it. There were guys making money hand over fist selling dummies. Two would come rushing out on the street: "I got something here, man." And guys were fighting to get up there and hand them their money, snatching a bag of shit. A dude cleaned up near a thousand dollars in a one-block radius. He had two henchmen, and by the time he got down to the end of the block and the customers were wise that it was nothing, they'd start coming after him. But they were ready; the guys had a car. They all jumped in and sped away. It was murder.

There was absolutely nothing I could do. At last I got wind of a doctor who used to have his offices nearby. I went into his office and he said, "Get out, get out. You're the one-hundredth guy who's come in here today. I cannot do anything for you."

"Look," I said, "I'm working, man. I've got to get something to keep me going. This is my job, my life. Won't you write for even three grains of morphine? That would at least get me through the night until I can get something." I was persistent and I refused to budge. I talked incessantly and didn't give him a chance to say anything. He'd start to say "No," I'd say "But," and finally he wrote a script for five grains of morphine for me.

I was running short on money, too. I had been taken at least three times for something like twenty, thirty, and forty dollars on different occasions, hoping against hope each time I copped that I'd finally succeed in getting the real thing. No such luck. I started to make drugstores for the cashing of scripts. They wouldn't cash even the one legitimate one I had. I ended up in this pharmaceutical outfit up on Third Avenue. The clerk said to me, "If this is legit, I'll cash it for you, but if it isn't, you're not going to get out of that door. You'll go to jail. Now, before you give this to me, I want to know."

"It's legitimate," I said. "Please, you can call the doctor. I don't care. I'll take you to the doctor. I'll have the doctor call you. Whatever. I need that, I'm sick." Finally he filled the script for five grains. I went home, put in a grain and a half, and it didn't touch me. I know it was morphine, I could tell, and I had to do the whole five grains just to get my sickness off. I was in bad shape.

Anyhow, three or four days of this went by, and it was just long enough for me to blow the job. My boss says, "Huncke, I like you, but look at your shipping room. What's going on with you? What's your problem?" I can't say, "Well, Mr. Smith, I'm a junky. I know you can understand a little because you're a juicehead." To make a long story short, I had to quit my job. Now I'm back on the streets in my old role of hustling and scuffling. Just about then the panic is over. Stuff is back on the streets but five-dollar bags have gone up to eight dollars; ten-dollar bags are now fifteen.

This went on for another four months. One morning the streets are bare again. Not a drop to be found anywhere; and this went on for the next three years—off and on, off and on.

I think the panic was caused by the politicians. How else could it have come about? There's no other way to account for it. Their story was that they had just grabbed a million dollars' worth of heroin out of a Portuguese guy's attaché case. But, Jesus, on the west coast there's two million dollars' worth being shipped in by who knows how many diplomats in their attaché cases. So you know it has to be coming in, and they must be building a supply. I say this as though I was in the know. I honestly don't know for sure, but this very thing has been told to me many times by people whose opinions I value.

Meanwhile, of course, the whole charade was playing hell with me, and with all junkies. The junkies were now sick 75 percent of the time. They had always been able to maintain something of a front, but many were now running around in rags, and more and more people were being stuck up. Crimes were becoming more violent. More gang wars were being organized.

I was right back where I had started, out on the streets, scuffling away and beginning the whole rat race over again. My case was only one in thousands. Guys like me would come out of jail and it was essential that they get work. Of course, one doesn't have to start using again, but when you're in jail it's just a long time between fixes, that's all. I've heard junky after junky say that.

Before Allen had left for Chile, I spent a lot of time going up to the Seven Arts with Peter and Allen. My relationship, in turn, had developed with Janine so that I was seeing quite a bit of her as well. Finally I gave her a key to my place, and frequently when I'd come home at night she'd be there. Our setup was congenial and rather tight, and she became part of the growing crowd.

Ginsberg and Orlovsky were the stars of the show, so to speak, the main attraction. On Friday, Saturday, and Sunday nights the Seven Arts Club would be packed with people listening to Allen read, or maybe some other poet that Allen had invited to read. I recall once when the poets Philip Whalen and Michael McClure came through the city and they both read at the Seven Arts. And all this was free and easy then, there was no monetary concern.

It was at this time that I wrote the story of Elsie John and, on Allen's suggestion, I read it aloud at the club. It was accepted very well. It was my first time reading in front of an audience. I was a little shaky but the fact that it was received so favorably pleased me, and I gained some self-confidence because of it.

There were so many interesting people that were part of the clique cutting in and out of that place that I can't name them all. Ray and Bonnie Bremser would join us, and sometimes they would read; LeRoi Jones at the time would frequently read there, as well as in other places. All in all it was a lot of fun. The guy who ran the place was a jazz buff and he'd always be playing jazz on his hi-fi. After the club officially closed up there'd be a small group of us left and we'd sit around smoking pot and listening to sounds—Billie Holiday, Charlie Parker, he had recordings of all the greats.

———

When Allen returned from Chile he approached me with an idea. He'd recently attended a psychiatrists' convention in Washington, and while he was there he'd met a doctor who was in charge of the psychiatric division of Jacobi hospital in the Bronx, which was a very progressive public hospital. He told Allen that if he knew of anybody in the drug area that was in need of rest, or that wanted to get in off the streets, he, a Dr. Hornig, could arrange a situation whereby the party could be admitted to Jacobi.

Allen had told the doctor something about me, and now he was suggesting that if I'd spend some time in the hospital I'd do better—or at least get a different slant on things. When he first suggested the idea I didn't react too favorably, but now, I thought, it might be an excellent solution. What did I have to lose? My habit wasn't so bad that with a little effort on my part I couldn't kick it. It was just a matter of getting away from stuff and keeping away from the neighborhoods that I'd cop in—sort of gritting my teeth and coming out of it.

I'd been told, when I went up to Jacobi, that they could not accept drug cases at all. They were not prepared to accept addicts, they'd told me. I had to say I was depressed and had thought of suicide to become a likely prospect for admission. And since Dr. Hornig recommended me, the weight he carried finally got me admitted. I spent roughly eight weeks in Jacobi hospital in their mental ward.

When you were first admitted to the mental ward you were taken to their closed ward. If you weren't literally raving mad, then they transferred you to an open ward. I spent one day in the closed ward and I must say it was certainly an interesting experience. There were people running up and down the corridors screaming. One man was absolutely off his rocker. He'd shit on himself and then become very abusive to the nurses, or anyone, when they got too close to him. He struck one of the nurses and they had to put him into a padded cell. And there was this woman who, as the story went, had been a prostitute. She would run up and down the corridor screaming at the top of her lungs, bloodcurdling things. I was glad to get out of that ward, to say the least.

The setup was entirely different in the open wards. I met several interesting people there including an old gray-haired Chinese woman; no one knew why she'd been placed there. And another woman, who was Scottish and had snow-white hair and was very charming, was receiving shock treatments for some reason or other. I never did find out the nature of her case.

There were also about five young people on the ward, kids they'd accepted through the courts. They were incredible, so bright and energetic. Some of them were pretty full of hell and they would torment the older patients. The supervisor was kept on her toes at all times just trying to keep these kids down. They were the focal point of my interest. They made the place sparkle with life. And they took a shine to me, they liked me. I could put my cigarettes down and be sure they wouldn't be touched—but there were others that did not receive that much consideration.

While I was in, they gave a couple of dances. I got along with the nurses so splendidly that I was expected to attend. The nurses and I had a marvelous time. And we used to sit up at night and play whist and talk. It got to be fun in a way. I was glad to leave but I did get a lot of rest and regular meals, and I went through my withdrawal with no trouble whatsoever.

In the two months I was there, I didn't do much in the way of therapy. In fact, I don't know whether you'd even call it therapy or not. I would have a weekly consultation with a psychiatrist but it was little more than a bullshit session.

A couple of my friends had brought me some gauge when they came to visit. There was this long corridor with an open area that they'd let patients out into when the weather was nice. I used to go out there and turn on, then come back into the hospital. You know how removed you can become from the immediate reality, so to speak, and sort of observe it from a distance. It was all very strange to me. How did I end up here?

When I came out of Jacobi I was faced once more with this business of getting myself organized. Janine, naturally, had been regular in her visits and Elise had been up two or three times, as well as Allen. When Elise heard I was being released she said, "You come right on back to my place. You're welcome to stay with me."

[Circa 1961, on Avenue C on Manhattan's Lower East Side, the Scottish writer Alexander Trocchi hosted his "Methedrine University," where many an amphetamine user and artist congregated, including the painter Bill Heine. Heine would become a central figure in Huncke's Journal, *appearing in stories such as "The Magician," "Beware of Fallen Angels," and "Faery Tale."]*

The very first thing Elise told me when I arrived back on the scene was that there was a warlock in the vicinity. I had known very little about witches, warlocks, and these things, and have never actually questioned whether or not they exist. I have a whole slew of superstitions of my own but I've never associated them with anything like "magic." Apparently this "warlock"—Bill Heine was his name—was a very powerful personality. He had swept both Janine and Elise off their feet.

Most important, as far as Elise was concerned, was that Bill was using amphetamine. And they thought that amphetamine would be a much better thing for me to use than heroin. Elise was very anti the heavier drugs, and she believed that amphetamine might help solve my junk problem. I said, "I'd certainly like to give it a try." I'd heard a great deal about it. Both Elise and Janine spoke of it, and even Allen and Peter, when I stopped in on them, were commenting on it. Allen said something to the effect that I might find that I'd like it. "Instead of getting back onto the streets with a heroin habit, why don't you try a little amphetamine? It's not a bad drug."

I had used Benzedrine in the past, but they were talking about shooting amphetamine. I had never shot it before. In fact, I didn't know that it could be taken intravenously.

They were all very anxious for me to meet Bill, but the next person I heard about was the writer Alexander Trocchi, who was supposedly running some kind of college-of-the-streets type of thing on the Lower East Side. Because Trocchi was an experienced and first-rate writer, it was natural that he'd come in contact with Ginsberg. Between the two of them they were helping create something of a new scene in the Lower East Side.

Apparently Bill was spending a great deal of time with Trocchi. One night when I was visiting Allen he suggested that we go over to see Trocchi, and so we started out. We got as far as Avenue C, and as we turned the corner there was Trocchi coming our way. And who was with him but Bill. I frankly did not like Bill at all on first sight. I thought he was a very intriguing-looking person, though, what with his brown felt hat and beaded band, worn Indian style, and his shoulder bag made of leather and fur and fairly packed with books, and his flute. Every now and then, while others were talking, he would put the flute to his lips and blast a little tune.

We talked there on the street for a few minutes, and Trocchi wasn't just then planning on being home. That cut off the business of going up to his place, so we turned and went back to Allen's with Bill in tow. First we stopped into Elise's apartment, and Janine was there. As soon as she saw Bill it was obvious to me that a certain spark existed between the two. Although later in a fit of anger Bill referred to her as a provincial chick that didn't know her ass from a hole in the ground, at the time he was pretty taken with Janine. I guess he'd immediately made up his mind that she would be his old lady.

At the time, though, Peter and Janine were in the midst of a fairly romantic affair. Peter would play Wagner's *Tristan und Isolde* and they'd make violent love and so on. Wherever he was, she was, and she followed him down the streets. They were a beautiful pair, but Janine was now facing a funny situation. At this time Allen and Peter were getting ready to leave for India and she knew that it was only a matter of time before Peter would be gone for an extended period. I suppose she was just that much of a little girl in her attitude and believed that Peter was going to change his mind and stay in New York with her. She really believed that. Of course, Pete had no intention of changing his mind at all.

She hadn't realized that when Peter left she was going to be alone, and she did not want to think about him leaving. It was a strange day when he did leave. Allen and he had their bags packed and I could tell that Janine was uptight, but she refused to break down and cry. And not only Janine but Elise too was upset, because she had been secretly nurturing a crush for Allen. So here the two of them left me in the center of all this drama.

In the meantime Janine had gotten to know Bill and she responded favorably when he set his sights upon her. He had given her a shot of amphetamine and they hit it off. The first few times you use this drug it seems almost miraculous. It gives you incredible energy. You can go for hours and hours without getting tired. You can work at any task, no matter how unpleasant, do it, get it over with, and do a good job of it because you have all of this feeling of energy and elation.

Bill had already gained admittance to Elise's establishment and thought nothing of knocking on her door at eleven o'clock and trooping in with five or six different people. A bass player, a drummer, say, a singer, a poet or two. Or perhaps a young girl who had shaved her head almost bald—enough to startle anyone in those days. The first thing Bill would do after bursting in was to whip out his paints and paint the Jewish good-luck symbol on the door. He then immediately began pulling things out of various pockets and pocketbooks while one guy was tuning up his bass and another was stroking his guitar.

Once there was a chick in the crowd who, upon entering, had found a table about half the size of a desk and turned it over. She'd brushed everything off the top of it, set it in a corner, and began to pull out a number of things from her bag, eventually surrounding herself with a homemade altar of a sort.

The shades would be pulled down and the next thing you knew there was a bottle of cobalt blue loaded with liquid amphetamine. Everyone immediately tied up. There was no fuss about who took off first—just let me get off, that was all. We all shot up and you could *feel* the vibrations in the room begin to change.

The portable RCA record player would be turned on to the sounds of Yardbird Parker, Nina Simone, Billie. I always expected the police at the door at any moment, but they never came. This would go on all night.

The day Janine said good-bye to Peter and went for a walk to wipe away her tears, she came back to a scene like this and Bill was waiting for her. He had set up his Buddha with rocks of varying kinds, urns full of incense wafting a lavender smoke into the air, music vibrating. She was pulled right in, needless to say.

This was the beginning of the whole Lower East Side scene. This kind of thing went on constantly. It was incredible. Supposing I suddenly knocked on your door and I'm standing there with about seven people. We all march in, shut the door, and you are trying to play host and discover at last that it doesn't mean a thing. "Hey, man, who are you? Mike? Nice knowing you, Mike. There's a corner. What do you do, paint? There's plenty of paints. Do you blow? Fine, man, there's a session going down." I'd never witnessed anything like it. I'd never seen a group of people just walk in on somebody and literally take the place over.

Now the payoff is that when it came time for everyone to leave, nobody was about to move. This chick here had found her little niche. She'd curled up and gone to sleep, and refused to be bothered. "Come on, man, you'd better go." "Please, leave me alone. I'm tired and I haven't had any sleep."

Bill always managed to build some kind of reclining area for himself in which he'd thrown pillows and cushions. He'd be there with a couple of chicks beside him talking away and they'd be listening. That man could talk. Though at one point he stopped talking. His tongue was cut out, not literally, but something happened to him and he just dried up. But in his prime he could command a discussion. He'd hold the floor and he wouldn't leave either. Elise, whose place it was much of the time, was by then so exhausted that she could not hold her eyes open any longer and she'd snuggle up where she was and fall asleep.

And—self-appointed guardian of the establishment—I'd put my feet up on the table, get myself as comfortable as I possibly could, take a hefty fix of amphetamine, and proceed to write for the rest of the night. Much of what I wrote then is still around, fortunately. Some of the best things I wrote I did under amphetamine, though some of the stuff is a bit lost, even to me.

Let me tell you about this amphetamine. It's not as habit forming as the opiates. You can kick amphetamine in a matter of days. But the thing is that you are lethargic, completely wasted. Your weight is down, you have no interest in anything, and all you want to do is lay up and sleep because your body has been put through a terrific amount of strain. I've heard people say they've gone as much as nine or ten days without sleep. I've never done that myself, though I have gone three, four, or as many as five days with no sleep. But I did rest some. I finally worked out a little system for myself. If I couldn't sleep I would simply force myself to lie down for a while and try to relax as much as possible, with the idea that I was at least giving my body a rest, if nothing else. And since your appetite is cut down to nil, you don't want to eat. I would make myself eat a little something, such as ice cream. Ice cream was always a big item with me; no matter what I was doing I could eat that. I'd always see to it that I got something into my system to work with.

When amphetamine was first brought into the scene on a large scale, it was very inexpensive. When I first started to use, you could go into a drugstore and with a little bullshit you could buy an ounce of it for eight or ten dollars. So nobody thought anything at all of putting an ounce of it on the table for people to use as they wanted. When the druggists became aware of the fact that they had something going for them, they began to jack up the price a bit.

And when speed was first making the scene the cops didn't know anything about it. They figured it was some kind of pill or something. As a result, when junkies got picked up they would cop a plea behind "Oh, man, all I'm using is a little amphetamine."

It never occurred to anyone that all of a sudden there was going to be a shortage of it, since it was so easily available. The shortage came about, of course, because people discovered they could make money selling the stuff—just like the junk scene. Suddenly, instead of being able to buy an ounce for ten, fifteen, or twenty dollars, it was up to fifty and then a hundred dollars. When it reached that price, the guys who were using regularly naturally didn't have the money. A lot of them became thieves and muggers, though in the beginning they weren't at all.

A lot of users had some kind of psychiatric quirk or idiosyncrasy or frustrations of a sort, and they believed amphetamine could do something for them. Many were sexually frustrated and used it because they considered it a sexual stimulus. And it is, contrary to the effect it gives you in the very beginning. The first reaction is that it kind of kills the sex drive—but later on it works just exactly the opposite. Sex, of course, is to a large extent mental, so that suddenly, when you are comfortable with the drug, you believe it is something of an aphrodisiac. You can get really crazy behind it. It can be a marvelous kick but, as I said, it's a terrific strain. For example, you can go for hours with an erection and not ejaculate until you've worn yourself to a frazzle. Of course, the girls think it's the end—but these are the kinds of routines you go through when you let your hair down.

On the strength of the relationship between Janine and Bill our whole circle of friends began to change. It was a pretty horrendous affair in many respects because it changed Janine from a very innocent and beautiful young girl into a—well, still beautiful, but also a more worldly and cynical woman. I suppose, though, it's to her benefit, because today she is a very wise woman and there aren't many that can put anything over on her.

Now that Allen and Peter were gone they weren't the focal point any longer. When they left for India there were still three weeks left on their rent, so I moved into their place for the three weeks. Naturally, the first thing Bill did was bring over several of his friends and take the place over.

When Bill first hit New York he was an innocent little drummer boy—but a good good one. How he originally got involved in the Village scene I don't know. All of a sudden, it seemed, he blossomed into a leader. He had been very close to Trocchi, and when Trocchi left, Bill took his place. Trocchi had to leave because his place was raided one night by the cops and because of various legal problems; he decided the best thing to do for the time being was to split the scene rather than come to the attention of the cops.

Bill came with several strange and powerful personalities in tow. I say powerful because they emanated a certain amount of energy that you could almost feel when in their presence. Very dynamic people.

Bill, incidentally, was one of the most creative persons I've ever known. He could take a white sheet, fold it in such a way that it was the size and shape of a skull, wrap yards of silk thread around it to keep it together, and then inject it with a huge hypodermic needle filled with paint. He would draw various colors up into the needle and jab it into the sheet again and again. He'd work on it for about an hour and then snip the threads and open up the sheet until it fell apart like a chrysalis with the most exquisite colorings you've ever seen. He made the most beautiful hangings, and every time he left a pad invariably there'd be one of these hangings left on the wall of the place. It was all so fantastic, actually, what with all the ritual that went into it.

When Bill unloaded his shoulder bag he'd pull out more from his store of tricks. He had a brass Buddha, all kinds of precious and semiprecious stones—amethyst, topaz, carnelian—and he'd fashion an altar for himself. It got to be a nightly ritual with him. In fact, it got so he didn't even take it down after he settled in.

At one point I tried to get him to show his work in a gallery, but the gallery people weren't willing to take the risk, saying that the only way the hangings could be appreciated properly would be to have them stretched and exhibited in such a way that light would be able to shine through them. They did not have the facilities to accommodate him. He did have beautiful stuff, no question about that. In fact, he was probably the first to invent tie-dye. When I first met him, no one had ever heard of tie-dye. It's amazing how popular it's become since then.

Bill had something about him too that attracted a certain type of person to him. For example, there was this young chick named Rita who happened on the scene for a short time. She'd wear long black dresses and black boots. She knew a great deal about stones and wood, things that I'm sure she must have studied at one time. She also wrote some very good poetry. And there were times, as well, when she'd become completely inarticulate. You know, I don't know what finally became of her. She may be dead, although I ran into someone not too long ago that told me she'd been in the hospital. I'd rather that she be dead, I think, than end in a hospital, because she was such a free individual. She loved her freedom. She was the kind of person that would run down the street and laugh simply because she was running, or who would put on a dance performance on a corner for the joy of it.

There were many others in Bill's orbit, some that I did not cotton to. I found a few just a little too treacherous for me. When we left Allen's, and had sort of wrecked the place, Bill, Janine, and myself moved in with Elise once more. Eventually, we found a place of our own on East Sixth Street.

It was a fine layout. We had the floor clear through. It had apparently been a warehouse at one time, and the people that owned the building had converted the first-floor section into a storage place, with an office in front, and rented out the other two floors. The place was protected by the police, oddly enough. It was funny because, God knows, some of the scenes that went down there—if the police had had any inkling of what was going on, we'd have all ended up doing some kind of time. But we were never bothered, not once in the whole time we were there.

We decorated the place with hangings and paintings, and it got so that we were having amphetamine jam sessions up there at all hours of the night. I soon discovered that the father of the family that rented the floor above ours had been sentenced to a five-year bit and they were perfectly satisfied in their quiet. I don't believe it would've mattered to them if we'd torn the place down. We had things pretty much our own way there, and it turned out to be a fantastic spot.

Allen had left a few pieces of furniture behind, so we moved them

over to this new place. It was in the apartment that Janine and Bill began
the intensity of their relationship. It began to function in a way that
everyone who came into our place was aware of the tension that was
being built up. I tried to stick around because I was worried about Janine.
I could not figure Bill out, to be honest, and I did not know what he
had in mind. After all, Janine was something of a child.

One night she came to me crying, saying, "I don't want to be Bill's
old lady." She was furious with the idea that Bill had been referring to
her as his old lady. And there were other scenes like when Bill would
come running out of his room cursing and damning everything, with a
hypodermic needle pointed at his eye. I don't know what it had been
about, but Janine was weeping and hysterical, and Bill was shouting,
"What do you want me to do? Put my eye out with this thing?" The
whole dramatic bit. I'd have to sit back and watch this and hope like hell
nothing serious would come of it.

From that point on, our scene became even more outrageous. There'd
usually be ten or twelve people in the place at a time and the record
player would be going full blast with Charlie Parker, of course, or with
some incredibly fine Afghanistan teahouse records. Also, a friend of Allen's had made some beautiful recordings of the kef festivals in Morocco
where everyone pitches in and sings, beats on drums, blows whistles.
Ravi Shankar was becoming popular about then in America, and we had
too some fantastic Indian records. So there was music going day and
night, and a continual stream of people. Some were painting, some were
building things or making things—just a lot of action and movement.

Alex Trocchi moved into the apartment. At that time there was still
a case pending against him which would finally force him into sneaking
out of the city again, across the Canadian border, and eventually into
leaving for England from Canada. When he was living with us, though,
he and Bill would do some remarkable things together with wood and
knives. I can remember Trocchi with this knife that must have been a
regulation hunter's knife. He had acquired at least two- or three-inch-
long tracks on his arms as an addict, and he'd allow them to scab over.
He had a habit of standing with one of these knives underneath a bright
lightbulb, picking the scabs off with the point of the knife.

The scene continued on all that summer and into fall, and then it went kaput. Too many notorious people came into the place. There were scenes, there were fights, there were people running out into the streets. Then it got so bad that some got to burning each other. A guy would come up with thirty or forty dollars to cop an ounce of A with and someone else would go south with it. Also, too many junkies came into the scene.

So things fell apart and it was partially due to Janine too. I finally convinced her that she had better get out of there. I didn't want to see her doing a lot of the things that I knew would occur if she'd kept on. I didn't want to see her on the streets hustling.

Bill had set guard over her for so long that it was nearly impossible to get to her. I couldn't even talk with her without seeming to interfere. One night I waited until Bill was asleep and I got hold of Janine and said to her, "Look, you've got to get out of here."

"I just can't walk out without telling him," she said.

"That's the only way you're going to get out," I said. "You've had your share of grief. Now you've got to split. I want you to get out of here, go home for a little while, think things over, and, if you want to come back, why all right, come on back. But meanwhile you've got to split now." After arguing with her and being afraid Bill was going to wake any minute and find me, I got her outside and said, "Now, I'm going to get you on the bus for Jersey to see your people."

Bill went absolutely insane, threatening to kill people. He tore up and down the streets looking for her. It was unbelievable the way he ran through the stairways of old tenement buildings in the neighborhood, hoping to somehow locate her.

[After the loss of the Sixth Street apartment, Huncke moved to Avenue C with the poet John Wieners.]

I was flat broke again. I hadn't been able to score anything, and was sick besides. I had given up as far as stealing was concerned, given up breaking into cars. As a matter of fact, I wasn't doing much of anything that was illegal, other than use drugs—just petty stuff, like clipping somebody for a ten-dollar bill or giving someone a tale of woe. Yet I have to admit I *was* up against it.

I was staying with poet John Wieners on Avenue C, and one night we were both so sick I decided that someone had to go out and get something. So I started out cruising the streets, one after another. I'd made it all the way to Fifty-ninth Street on foot and hadn't found a thing. The streets were bare. In disgust I started back down Fifth Avenue. I didn't have carfare home. I got to Twenty-eighth Street, and between Fifth and Madison there are two or three nice hotels, second-rate commercial affairs. I had on several occasions prior to then cracked a couple of cars on this street, and they'd been successful enterprises. I'd always kept this area sort of in reserve when I'd felt desperate.

I cut down this street. I was cold, tired, disgusted. There was a station wagon pulled up near the entrance to one of the hotels. As I passed it I glanced in and sitting on the front seat were two moneybags. I said to myself, My God, what is this? I checked around, stopping in my tracks. I went back, gave the door a little twist, and pulled it open. I reached in and snatched one of those bags, got it open a bit, glancing around all the while. I couldn't believe anyone could be so stupid. This thing was packed with money, and I didn't know what I should do.

What I ended up doing was grabbing hold of that bag and hauling ass down the street. There was a boardwalk around this new office building going up at Madison and Twenty-eighth, so I walked over there and stepped inside. I set the moneybag down and thought, Well, what the hell, I might as well go back and get the other bag.

When I returned to the car, I decided at first to let it stay because it was just too heavy for me. I thought, God, walking down the street with two moneybags will be more than anyone can handle. If they stop me, I'm really stuck. But then I saw an attaché case and grabbed that, dumping the money in it. There were a couple of bottles of whiskey inside, too.

My conclusion about the circumstances was that these people were with a whiskey company and they had run some sort of contest or something. They were from Canada because the money was in Canadian currency. What were they doing in New York? I'd seen two or three of those cardboard advertising cutouts so I guessed they were in town for some sort of special occasion. I was so skeptical of it all, though, that I wasn't even sure it was the real thing. How could it be? Nevertheless, I took it.

The following morning I went to a bank with a couple of the bills and told them I'd like to exchange them. They gave me ninety-two cents on the dollar. Fantastic. But I didn't know exactly how I should exchange all of the money because I figured the theft would be in the papers. I looked for some mention of it that day but there was none.

What I did was take about two hundred dollars' worth of bills in at a time, and I hit several different places where they changed money.

Then I moved into a hotel on Washington Square and stayed there for quite a while. It was an odd period of time for me. Janine was in a bad way and I was worried about her. I had sort of rescued her and I brought her up to the room. She just laid up for two or three days until she began to feel better. I got some food and fruit into her because she was terribly run down, both mentally and physically.

There was also a fellow at the time who'd sort of attached himself to me because I had given him a little money and straightened him out. His name was Joel and he was very gay and very strange. He looked something like Harpo Marx with his big bushy hair, large nose, and strange features.

I said, "Joel, why don't the three of us—you, me, and Janine—go up to Canada? We'll take this money with us and spend it, and nobody's going to be the wiser." And that's what we did. We cashed in enough to get bus tickets.

I wanted to be as inconspicuous as possible, though of course I could've chosen better traveling companions. Joel, who had an incredible sense of humor, had brought along a large suitcase into which he had packed *Naked Lunch*, and many other avant-garde books and underground publications—the type that had already created a little disturbance here and there.

Well, they refused us entry into the country. Janine looked to them like an underage girl. They wanted to know exactly who we were and what we intended to do in Canada. I suppose we were three wild-looking people. And we hadn't thought to provide ourselves with some money to cover traveling expenses.

"How long are you going to be in Canada?"

"I don't know, several weeks," I replied.

"And what are you going to do for money?" I couldn't very well tell them I was sitting on an attaché case filled with a couple thousand dollars.

Finally they said, "We're very sorry. We can't let you all in." I said that I would stand good for the other two, but then they saw all these weird books in Joel's bag. They found *Naked Lunch* and had a fit. He told them that he was here to spread the good word. So that was the end of that.

I didn't want to go right back to New York, so I said, "Look, we'll try to find someplace to stay." We ended up in a small town dead on the border of the States and Canada, a beautiful place called Elizabethville. I spoke to a taxi driver and he took us to an inn. It was a nice place, a house that had been built, according to the proprietor, sometime shortly after Washington had traveled through these parts. The inn had been handed down through the family since then. I guess they catered mostly to hunting parties and people of that sort.

I put Janine in a room by herself, and she slept for two days. She had been on amphetamine and was by this time exhausted. Joel and I were using, and I had brought plenty of stuff with me. If they'd searched me, we'd have been in trouble for sure.

We laid up in the inn for about five days. They didn't know where we'd come from, and we were very quiet about it. We took long walks, and prowled about the countryside admiring the big pine trees and fields and the whole bit. In three or four days Janine had the color back in her cheeks, and she looked just beautiful. We got to eating, and the lady of the house could cook. Oh God—big thick steaks, baked potatoes, homemade apple pies. It turned out very well.

But now I wanted to get back to the city. I got on a train just as the customs agents were getting off. They'd ridden down from Montreal, getting off at Elizabethville, and I simply caught the train there and came back into New York. I had some money left and I checked into a hotel myself, and got a room for Joel and Janine so they would have a place when they returned. I called them long distance and told them everything was fine, come on back. When they did, things went along fairly smoothly for a while until the money was gone.

That money did not last very long, though—about a month is all. I'd given about two or three hundred dollars to John Wieners, and I don't know how much I spent on the three of us. What I wanted to do, incidentally, was to go to Spain, but the Iberian lines were so expensive that I thought, Well, shit, it'll cost me a thousand dollars before I'm through buying a ticket.

One morning I woke up and found that Joel had helped himself to a good part of the cash and had taken it on the lam. He left me a note: "Really, you have enough." He was so shy about apologizing for it when I ran into him again.

———

During this time it was suddenly announced that the great Mr. William Burroughs was back in town. This is late '64–'65. *Naked Lunch* had finally been published in the States and it created an unbelievable stir. People would run up to Allen on the street and talk to him about Burroughs and his book. There was a whole cult established before Burroughs even put his nose into the scene. Many people did not know that he'd written a book before called *Junky*. But even so, it was a generally accepted fact that Burroughs was the outstanding writer of his time, and when word got out that he was back in the city everybody was anxious to meet him. I was sort of anxious to see Bill myself. Allen would tell me, "Well, I heard from Bill and such-and-such is happening."

Of course I'd read *Naked Lunch* immediately. I enjoyed the book and even peeked into it later from time to time, but I found his satire a little too biting, a little too cold. I think he has an incredible style—there's no getting around that. As a writer he is a master, and he had certainly ripped the covers off present social standards. But there is that coldness—he's forgotten the human element somehow, it seems to me.

Anyway, all the young writers and artists were waiting to see him. It was finally arranged for him to come to this place where everyone was reading, and when the night rolled around the place was jammed. People were lined up out on the street. Of course, he took his sweet time about getting there. There was a loudspeaker so they could announce him, and he arrived in his dignified, reserved way. Everyone was gaping. It was all quite amusing.

Not long afterward, a woman named Panna Grady decided to give a party for him. Allen and Peter had met Panna in San Francisco not long before. She was a Hungarian countess and, in fact, one of the most gracious women I have ever met in my life. There was no affectation—just naturally genteel. She was a real lady in the truest sense of the word. She'd made a terrific impression upon me and I didn't realize until later on that she had a title. Of course, there were many comments to the effect that a woman that had been raised with her advantages would naturally have charm and grace. It was partially due to that, but there was an inner quality to her I truly believe was part of her, regardless.

Later she told me how she had met Allen and Peter. She had given a party and the two poets were invited. She'd stepped out into her garden during the evening and there were Allen and Peter, stark naked, dancing in the moonlight. She said it gave her such a thrill and that it was something she'd never forgotten. On the strength of that she immediately developed an interest in both of them, though in Ginsberg she recognized his potential as a major poet. She became a patron of literature, and of the arts in general.

Panna, I believe, has had experiences of all kinds. She's had lesbian lovers and men lovers, but her weakness was Irish poets. Her ex-husband is an Irish poet, a man by the name of Grady. As I understand it, without knowing all the details, after they married he became even more of a heavy drinker. He finally became so unbearable that she had to divorce him. They'd had a child, Ella, and she too was beautiful. She was being raised with all the advantages, spoke several languages, just like her mother.

As it turned out, Panna had a crush on Burroughs. She told Allen that she would give a party to welcome him back to New York after being abroad for so long. She believed she could handle a hundred guests and asked Allen to select some of Burroughs's closer friends. Allen passed the invitation along to me, telling me she was a friend of Bill's and that she was very wealthy. She had an apartment in the Dakota building, up on Seventy-second Street, an absolutely incredible place. It was furnished very simply in antiques. When someone scratched a dining table that dated back several hundred years, I commented saying, "Oh, that's a shame." She replied, "Oh no, Herbert. You see these marks? That happened probably a hundred years ago. And these? Fifty years ago. This just happened now." I thought that was such a beautiful way of accepting it instead of fussing about it.

She had a bar with two bartenders serving drinks as rapidly as they could. There were two gigantic rooms that overlooked Central Park, and in one she'd set up the bar and the other was her music room. She'd moved all the furniture out of it and had this incredible hi-fi system going, blasting all the best music. Folks were really letting their hair down. The dining room table was piled with baked hams, bowls of fruit, everything you could imagine.

Cabs were pulling up as though it was a nightclub. I never saw anything like it. As one group of people left, another mob would arrive. She hadn't expected anything like that. I was amazed at her ability to stand at the door and, with all the charm and grace of a hostess, greet the people whom you'd think twice about before speaking to on the street. The only thing that she stipulated was that there be no press people. *Life* magazine tried to do a spread on it, but she wouldn't allow it. She wanted no notoriety, but, by God, word of mouth was enough for it to get around.

It happened that at least four hundred people came to the party, and finally Panna had to call down to the desk and tell them to turn people away.

Of course they stripped the place down. I don't know whether she lost personal things or not. Some of the women's bags were rifled, but other than that there was no stealing. LeRoi Jones arrived with several of his friends, and when he couldn't get in, he got in a very heated argument with the doorman. They ended up in a fight and he broke the man's arm. Of course, Panna handled all the expenses for that, but it was too bad because it spoiled an otherwise exciting evening.

Burroughs and I had a chance to speak briefly at the party. I said to him, "Well, Bill, you're looking well."

"I feel well," he said. "I've decided there'll be no more drugs in my life. Anybody that uses drugs is a damn fool. I won't have any more to do with narcotics."

"Your first love has always been alcohol anyway," I replied.

"I guess it has." Then he confided, "This affair is for me but I don't like this kind of thing. As soon as I possibly can, I'm gong to leave."

"You must admit, it's quite a turnout," I told him.

Panna, though, hardly got a chance to speak with Bill, as he was one of the first to leave. He'd put in his appearance; but I guess they arranged to meet for lunch or something before he left. When I got ready to leave, she stopped me and said, "I hear you're a good friend of Bill's."

"I'm not really a close friend," I told her, "though I have been associated with him on and off for some time."

Then she said, "Well, feel free to give me a call," and she gave me her phone number.

When I left, I decided that I *would* get in touch with her. I must admit that it occurred to me that she might be able to help me financially. It was so obvious that she had money and, in fact, Allen had said to me, "Herbie, perhaps Panna can be of some assistance to you." At the time I was barely existing. I'd lost my place on Attorney Street and was living with Bryden on Eleventh Street. But I wanted to get out of there and get a place of my own. It occurred to me that if I could get hold of a couple hundred dollars, I could pay the rent on an apartment and have a little something left to operate on as well. This was the plan anyway.

I make plans. I get just so far and then things get all screwed up, always, but my intentions are good. At least most of the time they've been good.

I finally called and she said, "Oh yes, I'm seeing Robin this afternoon, but why don't you come on up?" Robin was an artist friend of Burroughs's who'd done several covers for his books. Most of his stuff was abstract, and a lot of it looked like Oriental calligraphy. He was very British. I'd met him for the first time at Panna's party—she'd made a point of introducing him to me—and he said, "Oh, I've heard a great deal about you, Huncke. It's a pleasure to meet you." He'd been draped in sartorial splendor, a white suit and the whole bit: a typical Englishman in many ways but something of a soldier of fortune, who had become close friends with Burroughs while he was in Tangiers. They would travel back and forth from London to Tangiers, and I guess Robin had come through with Bill when he returned to New York.

When I arrived at Panna's, Robin was there showing her some of his pictures. She wrote out a check to him for four hundred dollars for four of them. I said very little. At last she turned to me: "Now, what can I do for you?"

"I'm in a bad situation financially," I said, "and it occurred to me that possibly you'd be willing to help me."

"Well, what can you tell me about Bill? Maybe if you can tell me something nice about Bill, I can be of some assistance to you. What sort of man is he? I hear that you lived with him in Texas with his wife, Joan."

"Yes, I did." And I told her a little bit about Texas and about our relationship there. And I said something to the effect that I'd stopped and spoken with him the night of the party, and that he didn't like big crowds of people but that he did say he thought she was a very charming lady.

"Oh," she said, "that's worth a hundred dollars," and she sat down and wrote me a hundred-dollar check just like that. "Keep in touch," she told me, and I said, "Oh, I will, of course, and thank you very much."

I had made an appointment to see Burroughs. He had invited me to dinner one night, several weeks after the episode with Panna. We went to the El Quijote, in the Chelsea Hotel, where Bill was staying at the time. The place was packed, and we had a marvelous dinner. Bill said to

me, "I suppose you could use a little money. I hear you're still using
drugs. You're a fool, an absolute fool."

"Okay, so be it," I said. "I can't help that, Bill. I still use drugs."

He gave me twenty dollars. "Maybe that'll do you some good."

Almost all the money I'd gotten from Panna I used for drugs. I did
not get a place of my own as I intended. When I'd returned with the
cash, Bryden and his lady and I had a party. So everything was cool for
a couple of days, but then—right back where we'd started from.

Allen had approached Burroughs and told Bill that I was really in need
of a place to stay, that I had been hanging out first in one spot and then
another. He suggested that Bill put up a hundred dollars for a place for
me, and Bill said he'd do it provided Allen saw to it that I got the pad.
He'd given the money to Allen, and Allen went with me to the rental
agent and took care of the situation. I found a place a block away from
where Bryden was living.

My first visitor was Bill Heine. He'd somehow discovered where I was.
He had been moving around himself from place to place, in and out of
the scene. But meanwhile there was a whole new mob of people that had
entered into it. The Lower East Side was becoming the "East Village." If
I thought for a moment I could name dozens that were new to the scene
just then—many of them painters and writers.

Bill came to see me and dumped his things down, saying, "I guess I
can work here."

"That's nice," I said in response. "It's OK with me. Just don't take
over the entire place. I want my own location." But all Bill's friends
immediately found out where he was and there were big scenes at all
hours of the day and night. Someone was always demanding to see Bill
and I was supposed to see to it that no one disturbed the master and his
work. Finally, of course, it got to be too much.

It wasn't Bill that bothered me in the place. He could do what he
wanted. He could paint the walls, paint his pictures—that didn't bother
me. All I wanted was peace, to be left alone. Of course I didn't get it,
because he had too many people coming in and out.

Finally, one of his cohorts from way back showed up. His name was
Rob, and Rob was someone I have never liked. He repulsed me, and I
did not trust him. Bill, though, had allowed him into the place and so

he would come and go. Okay, I could deal with that, as long as he didn't make a headquarters of our place.

Toward spring, when Bryden had decided to go back to San Francisco and Bill had sort of vanished into the unknown, I was somehow stuck with this guy Rob. I wasn't big enough to manhandle him and force him out. I was getting tired of the pad but I wanted the satisfaction of proving to the bastard that I was not going to tolerate him coming in and taking over.

At last, I confronted Rob. I told him, "Listen, I think you've stayed long enough. I want the place for myself now. I'm not going to stay here much longer but I need a rest and I want you to leave."

"Look, Huncke," he answered, "you get one thing straight. I never leave a pad until I'm ready, for one thing, and I never leave until it's broken up either. I've decided to break this place up. Now what are you going to do about it?"

I said to him that there wasn't much I could do, but that I was going out for a walk now and when I got back he'd better be gone. This was all just talk. I didn't have any idea of what I was going to do.

While out walking, I bumped into a guy I knew casually who was carrying a machete. He asked me if I'd like to have it. "Man, what am I going to do with a machete?" I said, but then I stopped. "Oh-oh, wait just a minute. Yeah, I would like to have it. I'm going to clean up a place. You want to come along and watch?"

We started back over to the apartment. I unlocked the door and here's Rob in the center of the place, stripped down to his trousers, swaggering around with a couple of his friends. It was like a madhouse and I was sick of it.

I happened to have a pair of boots on, and when I walked in saying, "Look, Rob, you see this?" I slapped the machete against a boot. It made a nice loud snap. "Now look, I want you out of here, and I mean I want you out right away. I wouldn't advise you to force me to use this. Now get out." I was shaking. I am not a violent person, but I had made up my mind that if he gave me any trouble I was willing to at least slap him with the broad part of that knife, and he knew it. He turned white.

One idiot that was with him was laughing, saying, "Come on, Rob, why don't you start breaking up the place?" I told him to shut up or he'd be next. Rob said, "Jesus, Huncke, oh man, let me get my clothes."

"Get them and get them fast."

Finally they left, and I was delighted. I closed the door and that was the end of Rob.

Sometimes we would see each other on the street. He finally flipped his lid. He walked around with a Bible in his hands, would come up to you and ask, "What did you say?"

"I didn't say anything."

"You didn't say anything?" Then he'd take the Bible, open it randomly, and say, "Let's see what this says," and he'd read whatever passage he opened to.

"Ah," he'd tell me, "you're the devil. I can see the devil. Get away from me." He would back away from me and keep moving down the street. Or when I passed him he'd cross to the other side of the street, point his finger at me and say, "There goes the devil." They picked him up eventually, and I suppose they put him into a hospital until he dried out.

About this time the ODs started. You'd hear of somebody, and boom! The next day he ODed. It got to be quite sordid, this ODing thing. From having been a really exciting and exhilarating scene, it had passed into a session of chaos. And it began to decay. Things were rotten, and more and more people were getting sick or dying. The pace had picked up so frantically that a lot of people just flipped completely, or simply disappeared altogether.

[Huncke appeared on The David Susskind Show *in 1968.]*

Because of an appearance I made on WBAI radio, David Susskind, the talk show personality, got wind of me. I met up with Susskind eventually and he said he'd like me to come on his show. Apparently, he was running some kind of "secret people" interviews. He was exceedingly nice to me, both he and his soon-to-be wife of the time. Of course, I was aware they were exploiting me, but I didn't mind. I knew what I was doing—and it wasn't being done in an underhanded manner at all.

During the initial interview Susskind was just as charming as he could be. All of his questions had been generally friendly and not too pointed in any one direction. He was merely seeking information. When it came to the program itself, I suddenly caught on to the fact that his questions were now taking some direction. I know he would have loved for me to say, "Junk has ruined my life. It's bad. I want to put it down—the rest of you should never have anything to do with it."

Instead, I believe I shocked about a half million people, if that many were tuned in, when I announced that I had shot up a cooker full of heroin just before the show, and on top of that I'd taken a hefty shot of amphetamine. Plus, I said, on the way to the studio I had smoked a joint. He asked me if I was telling the truth. "I absolutely am." I know I must have looked it because of my eyes. I held my own very well, though, and even surprised myself. I was far more at ease than Susskind was.

Afterward, he did help me out some by helping to get a story of mine published in *Playboy* magazine. The story was "Alvarez," and it ended up in the October 1968 issue.

Things continued to progress, fortunately. John Wieners, who had straightened himself up enough to be given a job at the University of Buffalo, had contacted Allen and me and offered us a chance to read the following spring at an arts festival that was part of the Buffalo school program. John also gave me some money for another story which he had published in something called the *Frontier Review*. This appeared before the *Playboy* thing and it was the first time I had a story published in something other than an avant-garde pamphlet or publication. I was pleased and excited.

We made quite a group when we appeared in the university. Allen had rented one of those oversized VW buses. I don't know how many miles we put on that damn thing, but he and Peter and others drove it all over and more. Panna too went along with us on that particular trip.

You should have seen us. Peter had allowed his hair to grow to his waist that winter—his very thick Russian peasant hair that he tied with a ribbon in back—and he'd put on a sharp lightweight jacket and a pair of boots and gloves. Allen had his attaché case and his guru bag with all his OM paraphernalia, and he shuffled his funny shuffle alongside Peter. I was there, of course, and Harvey Brown joined our crowd, and Panna. Of course, John Wieners was not to be left out of it. We cut across the campus with Peter taking the lead, marching ahead, looking neither left nor right, ready for action.

The students were awestruck. They appeared completely stymied.

They could not open their mouths but to say, "I can't believe it"—but they were curious.

We had a marvelous turnout for the reading. The regular literary crowd at this spring festival won't forget that, I'm sure. It turned out to be one party after another, and all the faculty members outdid themselves to entertain us. We had full run of the entire motel we stayed in.

We drove up on a Tuesday, and I wasn't scheduled to read until Friday. The truth is I hadn't really wanted to. I thought the only way they'd get me up there was to hog-tie me. I had never read before a large crowd, only small groups. And by this time I had grown somewhat weary of being put on display. Yes, I was using junk, and that meant I had to smuggle my works with me and buy enough before leaving to hold me over. Naturally, I went through it faster than I should have. By Friday when I was supposed to read, I was cold sober and getting sick. I had to fly down to New York to cop so that I would be able to read. When I came back everything was hunky-dory.

One of the professors gave us a welcoming party. His son had a rock band and they played for the guests. Somehow the name "Huncke" had circulated throughout. Apparently I was something, if not legendary. I honestly don't know what these kids expected to see, but they were sneaking up to me and asking me if I had some grass. Now I'm in one of their parents' homes. I wouldn't have given it to them if I had any. One or two were quite nervy, asking me to turn them on. I told them that it was out of the question.

This professor had that elite, backbone-of-the-country, midwestern attitude toward those who have deviated from the beaten path, regardless of *what* path had been taken. Drugs, heroin addiction—there was nothing lower, in his opinion. Now that I was in his home he believed he'd really kicked over the traces completely. When he spoke to me the first thing he said to me was "I hear you've written a book. I suppose it's about junk." I told him that it was partly. "Oh, and what else?"

"It's about people I've known, places I've been," I said. "A little about prison."

"I didn't know you'd been in prison, too." He seemed very shocked by all of this. And he wasn't the only one. You could feel the vibrations of hostility coming from them. I was like another creature to them all the way round. I ran into that off and on the whole week there.

The younger people, the students, were fantastic. I ended up giving two readings; one was scheduled on Friday, the day of the big reading. The place was packed. I read for hours, it seemed, until I was hoarse, but they didn't want me to stop. They sat and listened. It made me feel very good. People came up to me afterward and said such encouraging things to me. It revitalized me, in a manner of speaking.

I remember it as a beautiful experience and one that I'm not likely to forget. However, that type of essentially negative person that I encountered there is one I've run into more and more. There are certain people that do not know anything at all about the matter, haven't any idea, though they want to put in their two bits. It's as though I deliberately went out to become a junky, that circumstances hadn't played a part in it at all. To these people I am simply a fiend of some kind that has been let loose on the public, and that's all there is to it.

Fortunately I don't have to deal with it very much because the people I know and associate with are more liberal-minded. If you want to smoke pot, it's perfectly all right. If you don't want them to do it on your premises, that's fine too. Most people know I'm an ex-addict now, that I'm on methadone. It was not long after that Buffalo reading that I finally went on the methadone program and I'm better for that. My friends treat me as though it doesn't matter to them in the least—they're very tolerant people, I'm glad to be able to say.

PART FOUR | PREVIOUSLY UNCOLLECTED
MATERIAL

BRYANT PARK

[A rare example of Huncke adopting the third-person narrative voice, this piece is among the earliest of his known writings.]

THE AFTERNOON BEGAN CLOSING. HUGE BUILDINGS SPEWING FORTH office workers who rushed madly across streets, around corners—down subway entrances—toward late appointments and train depots—onto buses—into restaurants and stores and homes. It was late summer and the sun began disintegrating into sunset shooting saffron and pink and purple thru the sky and catching the reflection of windows like large gold spangles and sending ever fainter but longer shadows in phantom cascades of gray and delicate lavender patterns barely perceptible. Crystal-white light began gleaming whiter and the lurid reds, greens and blues of neon become bolder and more frequent as the thin pall of darkness gathered substance and the sky, losing the batik-like quality of the sunset—shone a clear turquoise blue—slightly cold and not quite stark—yet rather menacing—holding the moon in the first clearness of its appearance. Several stars shone gem-like above the great stone pilings and the air seemed permeated with the early scents of autumn—that particularly sweetish aroma of dying leaves and yellowing grass and summer decay.

Night sounds began ascension. Automobile horns, screeching brakes. Conversations dealing with pleas for dinner engagements—theaters and dates—for dancing and walking down lovers' ways. Vibrations of whispered last-minute details and suggestions of activity dependent on caution and secrecy for its realization gathered in momentum filling the atmosphere with the awareness of dark uncharted courses thru ebon glades. Footfalls becoming less strident and of slower tempo, intermingling with the hurry but gaining greater fullness as all settled into the dinner hours. New footsteps—unheard during the brightness of the day—also crept into being and greater tenseness assumed larger proportion.

The appearance of the people began shifting now, rapidly, from the deeper tones of sun-observed skins to those drenched only in moonlight and neon glare. Also the eyes of the people changed noticeably. The people of night have more searching eyes than those of the day—that is, they seem deeper and larger and less penetrable. White faces with large dark brown eyes hinting of having seen sights of wild description—or of death and tragedy—of weariness and defeat. Of cunning and treachery. Of suffering and malnutrition. Of broken minds and sore-infested souls. Of idiocy and wandering spirit and cruelty and perversion and confusion and addlement and bewilderment.

The people also began moving in more positive sexual consciousness at night. Searchers thread the course of street corners, urinals, crowded sections, theaters, and streets where the pulse beat is one of sex and great awareness of it. Sex is the great pounding and sounding and rumbling of universal transition.

Kurt moved leisurely along the stone balustrade at the back section of Bryant Park. The park is located immediately in the rear of New York's Public Library at Forty-second Street and Fifth Avenue. It is, upon first entering thru any one of several entrances from Forty-second Street, Forty-first Street, or Sixth Avenue, almost startling to sense the aura of rest and quiet which exists over the area. There are few public spots of rest which cater to larger numbers of people and certainly none located in a less-conducive-to-stillness position than Forty-second Street and Sixth Avenue, almost at the core of one of the most surging and active spots of civilization—Times Square—yet actually an awareness of silence and peace does exist and can be felt. The play of human appearance and typification with an element of local habitués is constant and has remained of a similar temper since the early days of its existence. There is a richness of historical (civically speaking) background typical of New York which, even though lacking information, one can realize or perhaps feel. Kurt felt a sense of exhilaration and an awareness of vast understanding and sympathy for his fellow creatures—as he continued his stroll, leaving the rear of the park by ascending several steps to the level of walks lined with spaced benches beneath a literal roof of shade trees which surround the outer walks completely down each side. He had descended on the Forty-first Street side with an idea of circling the park to see who might be there he knew and perhaps could get to know before reaching the rear again.

His age is about nineteen. He is five feet ten inches tall and weighs about 150 pounds. He has dark blue-black hair, neither straight or curly, with a neatly combed wave in the front. Dark brown eyes—inclined to be flirtatious in what is called a knowing manner. His features are symmetrical, a bit on the aquiline side. There is a slight scar on his left cheek just beneath his eye. He explains it happened when he jumped a moving freight train when he first left home at the age of fourteen.

He was dressed in blue denims which fit him as though he had been poured into them—displaying the contours of his buttocks and the size and shape of his penis—and which clung to him tightly almost to the knees where they filled out into bell-shaped legs. His shoes were good strong brogues of ox-blood tone and highly polished. The denims had been laundered several times and were faded in a washout blue tone, but they were spotlessly clean. He had a white shirt open three buttons down the front and with the sleeves rolled above the elbows. He walked with a light step but a bit on the swagger side. He looked healthy and clean and virile and anticipated making use of his appearance for financial gain before the night grew much older.

He continued his stroll leisurely, sensing the eyes of people. He speculated to himself about those passing him. He needed money and the need rather dispensed automatically with any forgetfulness—sudden awareness of it would come upon him and everything else was gone for the instant. He spotted several acquaintances. One person passed him—he had seen him on several occasions around the park, talking with a few of the old-timers, once with a bunch of the winos in the back. He remembered a number of times he had gotten blind drunk and knocked out cold on Nembutals, Seconals, and marijuana back at the time he had palled around with a fellow from Chicago named Polack Joe.

Looking up for a moment he caught sight of someone he wanted to see—it was Red Stone. Red pushed hay—sold weed, reefer. He could be depended upon to light up—also Red was an interesting guy all the way around. Kurt didn't feel it was necessary to have any explanation complete or pat in his mind as to why or any particular reason Red Stone stood out from the crowd. Upon first meeting Red, he had come recommended as a right guy and his acquaintances were fairly widespread and mostly in, at least, selective groups. Also, Red was a junky. Kurt was sure someone had assured him he and Red should know each other, since they would at least have junk in common.

There is something magnetic about attractions. Something beyond any conscious acuteness affects the relationship between two parts instantaneously upon recognition of one another. The contact is cosmically created. The two complete an urge.

Red greeted Kurt with a wide smile and said, "Hi, man—what do you know? I just saw the Russian on Forty-second Street near the Times Bar. We just lit up, man. Real gone stuff. My man just picked up from some spic. It's from Mexico. Real golden leaf. Mellowed in the sun. Come on, man—out on back around the park with me, and we'll light up."

Kurt fell in line with Red and they moved directly toward a row of benches at the back of the park. Red lit a stick of the weed and passed it to Kurt. Kurt took several deep pulls of air and smoke—holding each breath before releasing—and then passed it back. They passed it between them until the cigarette was completely gone. A small cloud of the aromatic hung just above them, floating gently up into the night.

Kurt's eyes watched the darkness and the faces of people walking. He felt much better. He was no longer bored with the possibilities of the night. At least he would feel a slight elevation above the people, as though everything were a bit sharper and clearer. He became aware of much detail in the scene in front of him he would not ordinarily have noticed. Weed always gave him an added feeling of zest. He remained talking with Red, who described some girl he had met and what a hustler she could be if she would listen to a little reason.

1946

A FIX

I HAVE BEEN ASKED MANY TIMES, AS IS ALWAYS ASKED USERS OF narcotics, what a fix does to me—how it makes me feel. I suppose each user gives a different answer or his own way of avoiding making reply. It is impossible to tell someone else exactly how a fix reacts since the individual is the one affected and what applies to him will hardly apply to another, and particularly with narcotics, which create new perspectives identifiable only by the perspective of the individual user. I say this only believing it is true and with no assurance.

I want a fix because it helps me believe in life again, enabling me at the same time to accept it calmly and with peace. It completely eases my sickness and even makes me well while I have it. I do not particularly want solitude nor many people around me—not any people near if they happen to disapprove or lack understanding—yet I am not unhappy if either situation occurs. I am not aware of loneliness—it ceases to exist—if I am alone. On the other hand, if the case be people—I am aware of them and am certainly more responsive to their redeeming characteristics, and I sure seem better to them.

Perhaps what I like best in a fix is that it becomes possible to forget tension and anxiety—not necessarily blotting it out but instead helping me feel whole enough to look at their causes in a true light and not get tossed by new ones. It takes away concern of trivialities and there is no need to be harassed by anxiety. A fix helps me to create a state of well-being and takes me away from all false things which have resulted from my contacts in daily life and shows me a new concept of reality, one I can relax in without having to either cheat or steal—because the need no longer exists.

I do not see great fantastically beautiful gardens nor great misty vales of some enchanted land. All I am aware of is quite definitely part of the same reality you see and feel, but I think I see it more honestly than you because when I am fixed no part of me is sick and I am quite able to overlook all we account unimportant or important if necessary, and above all if the fix was just right—I don't mind being alive.

1948

A LETTER TO DAD

March 23, 1949

Dear Dad:

How many times have I thought of writing to you? And how many times have I told myself, "You can't write to your father—not now—perhaps someday if you straighten out—amount to something—at least have money—or some show of not being a failure—then you can contact him—your people—even perhaps arrange to see him." Several times—I've created pictures in my mind of calling you on the phone from one of the better hotels in Chicago and of inviting you up to the room for a drink and then taking you to dinner—always the old Red Star Inn—and of trying to give you the impression I've actually succeeded in some undertaking of which I need not be ashamed. Other situations too in which I don't appear as I am—a wastrel, a thief, a bum, a chiseler—a petty small-time character not even good in amounting to nothing. Certainly no one you want to be associated with in any respect. Oddly—I've always felt the least I can do is remain obscure—out of your life completely. I bring only disgrace and shame.

Why suddenly I want to tell you these things I can't quite understand myself. It has nothing to do with some vague notion of reform or of a desire particularly to change my ways. I'm too completely beat for that. Nor am I seeking aid from you—although, speaking quite honestly, in speculating with myself as to why I'm writing to you within the few mintues of the actual writing, the thought has flashed thru my mind—are you really trying to tap some new source for money or assistance? Truly that is not the case. There is nothing premeditated about this moment—nothing at all. Frankly, I wanted to write. I have just returned from a walk. It is one of the first spring evenings of the year and upon entering the place I'm living I felt an urge to try and justify being alive and free to feel trees and shrubs and the clear bright night and all the other poetic musings which spring into play at moments like this. The idea flashed thru of write to your dad. All of which reads disgustingly corny and rather like something from a third-rate melodrama. But it is as close as I am able to come to honesty.

As I began, I said to myself—sort of what you do to write—what do you find you are capable of saying? Try and speak plainly and direct. Say whatever comes into your mind to say. Also—the thought that perhaps you might want to hear from me and that—no matter how miserable a specimen I am—you in your heart feel some love for me. Then, too— I would like to hear of Bob and Marguerite.

I am not exactly a sentimentalist and I've knocked around enough to hardly accept the old stories of—she is your mother—he is your father— therefore blow your top—cry and weep. All quite touching but alas— I'm afraid pretty much hooey. The world—or should I say life—isn't exactly like that—not anymore, at any rate—nor do I think we are losing a great deal in letting it pass. People are people—simply, and can be regarded and valued only on their worth as individuals and (all this is my opinion—of course) not just because they happen to be parents.

Can you believe or understand me when I say I've regarded always— both you and Marguerite—as rather amazing and certainly interesting personalities. In all honesty—I've thought of you always in terms of dad or father, while with Marguerite it has always been Marguerite first and mother last. I think I was always closer to Marguerite than to you, and primarily because I always was and still am somewhat in awe of you, I never quite succeeded in fathoming your personality as clearly as I could Marguerite's. Perhaps it was due to your finding it necessary to play the role of the disciplinarian more frequently than Marguerite. In fact, I can hardly recall—except when I was very young—ever being seriously chas- tised by her—although I certainly can remember scolding, and ranting and tears and general frustrations to no end. But it remained with you to put down the rules and laws and regulations (and they were far from unreasonable) which brought hell and high water if disobeyed. Then, too—Marguerite and I lived rather intensely several years, in which our relationship was of necessity—more in the nature of an older woman and young man forced thru circumstances to share each other's existence on the basis of friendship rather than mother and son.

With you it was quite different. You remained the parent always. As a young boy—I was quite frightened of you. I felt your punishments were sometimes unjust—and, incidentally, I still regard some instances in the same light; but what I realize now and could not understand then is—you governed yourself according to what you sincerely felt to be right—always. For that I respect you. When I became a young man—I no longer feared you. The predominant reaction was one of dislike. I thought you were cruel and unkind—deliberately. Now I realize that was not so—oh, of course, I don't doubt that occasionally you permitted yourself a bit of sadistic indulgence—knowingly—you must have—but altogether you were simply sticking to the rules as you felt they should be. In fact you conducted yourself in the manner which you in your heart considered to be for the welfare and in behalf of myself.

None of what I am attempting to say is in the nature of criticism. I want you to know the controlling factor in my thoughts of you and Marguerite is one of love and to a great extent admiration. I am really proud of you. I think you are a great man. I wish I might be half as fine as you. I always remember you as a positive person—keen and intelligent. Admired and respected as a man among your associates, looked up to by some and always with an air of good breeding and dignity.

I can also remember rather sitting back in your desk chair, with your hands smoothing the back of your head—speaking in weary and beat tones of being licked and weighted down with responsibilities, wanting to get away from it all, worried over money and family problems. I am sure had I been in your place—I would have chucked the whole idea and cut out for distant ports—but then I would never be the one to get into a similar position in the first place.

And so it all goes—and at long last I've written a letter to you—not waiting until I'm worthy of doing so but just doing it anyway. Who knows—to sound real trite—but what if this is the last opportunity I'll ever have—and somehow I want you to know—all these years I've loved you and thought of you as father.

—HERBERT HUNCKE

ALONE

I HAVE NEVER FELT SO COMPLETELY ALONE—REMOVED FROM EVEN A sense of human relationship. I cannot understand what has happened to me. I have felt loneliness before but certainly not quite as I do now. It is as though understanding has suddenly been taken from me. I cannot even begin to comprehend much of what races constantly thru my mind. I begin to think and feel it, and instantly it is as though I am in a trap in which although I believe there must be an escape—it remains elusive. Each time I feel I am about to free myself, an overpowering realization of it being the impossible I seek floods thru me. I no longer know how to speak with others—perhaps not speak but rather transmit. Also it seems pointless—nor am I trying to convey that therefore I think everything is pointless—but instead that one cannot hope to reach everybody or even the special few and should save energy with which to induct one's being when the exceptional establishes contact. I say this because it is one of the instances in which I think perhaps I can be released—only to feel jointly that actually there is never any contact. This I have felt for many years—believing it and not quite believing it—wondering if perhaps it is at all and yet also trying to believe that there is more—because I think there should be more. Now I no longer feel there should be more—I have been deluding myself with a false value. Still, this aloneness is frightening and everywhere I look there is a blackness. Maybe I feel it particularly because I am the sort of person I have been—one who allows others to assume my responsibilities—a sort of leech—a parasite. Perhaps this awareness of fear or frustration is my first real conscious knowing of death. Perhaps I will continue as a sort of zombie, unnourished and devoid of all feeling—an example of humiliation and disgrace—which is what I am rather confident is what is meant to be implied when I am classified as a parasite. Frankly, the term and the implication don't bother me but rather that I am supposed to feel ashamed—and although I am undoubtedly parasitical in many respects—I feel fairly sure I am also a great many other things and should not be relegated to so narrow a term. And it is quite true that the prospect of having no one to lean on must undoubtedly affect my present emotional stress. It is unpleasant to discover there isn't anyone who is anxious to see you, to want you near, to feel that you can think and that you are a true personality and that you have contributed your share and that you do exist fully—constantly—and with your whole being. But what is even more unpleasant is to discover that there is almost no one you desire understanding—that is greater and fuller understanding—from, and that although you are in contact with several people you are responsive to—you are not disappointed it stops there.

There is so much confusion and tension and everyone is rather sick. One senses it in the atmosphere. One sees all around only frustration and emptiness. Everything seems false and already decayed—rotten—ready to collapse. There is no longer purpose of action. Instead, people are becoming mechanical—like machines which have been released at high speed and slightly out of control. And there is a suggestion in their appearance of something like a fungus, gray and devouring, which in time will become self-destructive in that it will drain completely that upon which its existence depends. It seems rather a pallor which even the sun doesn't quite succeed in disposing of because it is nurtured on the brain cells from inside.

I believe that this is a period of transition in which the ego is beginning to stir from its encasement and confines and shed the flesh. I think it has been developing slowly since the beginning and reached a barrier which only now can it absorb. I think we have—or as we have generally thought ourselves to be—ceased to matter—and no one will be unrecognizable as we see him now. In my opinion the closer we get to the core, the closer we are to the sense of the ego. It is sort of like trying to look down into the center of one's self. I do not believe that we have any real control over what we do and are, other than that which is the basic force within us moves only toward that which is its destination and purpose. This is the way the world is and it will change only in that manner in which life is its way. All that exists serves a purpose even if it is for only an instant. I believe even that which we might call accidental—the result of festering—eruption—explosion—rumblings—groanings—comets— all we term elemental upheaval—has its bearing and is part of a conditioning process.

The ego—or awareness of "I"—must at last be set completely free.

Then can man hope to grow and expand and cease to exist only as a physical being—frustrated and driven only by chemical and biological seethings. I believe that once not only the elements, but true consciousness of the ego becomes united, man will become truly civilized or happy or whatever it is that he will name. Actually—it won't be necessary to have a name for it because all feeling will be in harmony.

1948

LOVE

Everywhere I look I see love—pouring from eyes—emanating from skin—shining halo-like over heads—and I receive all this love—full charge and I glow and am clean.

And this morning I saw a surrey going up Eighth Avenue and it was filled with young angelic boys in bright green—red—blue—lemon-colored shirts and they were laughing and singing and there was an aura of light all around them and it was moving slowly and one boy would jump in and out—and sometimes run up ahead and walk beside the horse—and strut and kind of shout in bebop to his companions or just up into the air—and people were watching and smiling and there was a whole cloud of love.

1959

COSANYL

[Cosanyl is a morphine-derived cough syrup.]

HOW THEY ALL MUST KNOW ME—UP AND DOWN 17TH ST. "PARDON ME— I would like a bottle of Cosanyl." I know every drugstore below 17th St. all the way down to 320 B'way where I make my weekly reports. Bottles of Cosanyl from Chinatown—the Bowery—3rd Ave.—2nd Ave.—Ave. A-B-C—uptown—all over the city they have heard my request—over a year of it—Cosanyl—Cosanyl—Cosanyl.

No wonder I'm having such a bitch of a time kicking: 5-6-7-8 bottles of the shit in one day.

It was amusing for a while as I had a regular route—from one spot to the next—like an automaton—always repeating the same statement—"A bottle of Cosanyl—please." It was strange, occasionally I would run into a sort of holier-than-thou type—who would peer down their nose and say, "Sorry, we don't carry the stuff." Or "We don't handle that," said very curtly and haughtily. But I found several willing to handle my daily needs—and finally one who would sell me as high as 3 or even 4 bottles at a time—so that one day before leaving the district I had picked up about maybe 10 "bottles." The guy means well—figures he might as well get the money—since I'm going to spend it for the shit anyway. Guess he buys blackmarket—or so he said. He told me it's going to be really hard to get soon—one reason I'm trying to kick—there are other reasons as well—but that is certainly one of the main ones. Perhaps it's me—but so far—I've had a rough time. All the usual withdrawal symptoms—plus a couple of new ones—I had never experienced before. Foolishly—or maybe wisely—the first night I loaded myself on Tuanol— that is the first night I cut myself off completely from Cosanyl. I got home to the room and downed something like 5 or 6 Tuanols. Actually I recall very little of what happened. I began coming out of a state of complete oblivion about two days later. During the time I had fallen down—scraping both knees until bloody—the side of my forehead all black and blue. There are and were tiny little nicks or sores all over my body—where I had bruised myself in one fashion or other. All this was taking place, appropriately enough, while one of the worst storms of the city's history was raging outside. I vaguely recall—peering out the window on several occasions—wondering about the pelting rain. I haven't cut myself off completely from Cosanyl as yet—but I am down to 1 or 2 bottles every 24 hours. I have had this habit almost a year—and perhaps longer—no, just about a year. Of course in the beginning it wasn't quite so bad but I kept increasing it till it was costing far more than I can afford. Physically it doesn't seem to have done much harm—or at least noticeably. There is naturally a high sugar stuff content which may have helped to bring on diabetes or even anemia—if so I don't know it yet. I have kept my weight up—perhaps even gaining a few pounds. My skin seems clear enough—and my mental senses seem fairly alert—although I have noticed slight lapses of memory. I had presumed originally that the narcotic form I was using was a mild codeine—instead I have discovered—it is a sort of concentrated morphine derivative. Whatever—it does the work most effectively. Part of my kicking of a narcotic habit—there is what I'll call a sort of overlay of mental anguish. By overlay I mean—a condition one is aware of hanging so to speak just over one's head, so one is constantly awaiting some sudden collapse of mental control—a sort of psychological threat. It is felt from time to time—in little ways—a sudden overwhelming self-pity—or maybe a touch of almost manic-depressiveness. With me it has always been a great sweeping feeling of aloneness—as though everyone in the world has deserted me and I am left alone. This is usually accompanied by acute melancholia—so that I break out in body-wracking sobs—leaving me limp and almost inert—unable to move. I begin invariably thinking of someone I have loved—and from that point it follows a sort of natural course. I think of all emotional disturbances—the one caused by loneliness is the most shattering. To suddenly realize with one's entire being—one is alone—is pretty shocking. Yet—we are all alone—and I suppose there are parts of our body which have always always been alone, have never known responsiveness. I think our hands—and faces—probably the arms—chest—legs—thighs most frequently have known contact—but there are areas inside which have always remained alone—recognizing their aloneness—probably never really needing an outside stimulus. At any rate—when one's whole being has nothing beyond the self—it can be tragic or at least seem tragic.

Fall 1960

WHEN I DIE

WHEN I DIE—I WOULD MY SEED BE BLOWN TO SOME INACCESSIBLE MOUN-tain crag—and there become a sturdy bush or tree—to cling there tenu-ously thru wind—rain—storm—and seasons—living in my aerie—visited only by an occasional venturesome mountain beast or perhaps cast shade upon a visiting snake or hold the weightlessness of a high-flying bird. That is my prayer. I love the earth and would spend the next few centu-ries there above the tumult of the cities and away from people.

I am afraid God won't grant that wish—since I have been of such weak stuff here. Why trust my roots to a wind-swept mountain—I'd undoubtedly lack the stamina to push down deep enough to really hold—and the first good wind would pull me loose—and I would end up bleached and dead behind some boulder in some gully far below.

Fall 1960

EASTER

["Easter" stands out as a prime example of automatic writing, and a
multilayered description of daily life on Avenue C while Huncke was living
with poet Janine Pommy Vega and artist Bill Heine—times also
described in "The Magician" and "Beware of Fallen Angels."]

EASTER SUNDAY MORNING—EARLY—NOT QUITE DAYLIGHT—A LARGE
moon rides the sky since early yesterday evening—first a soft glowing
spot of white cloud—later—clouds gray moving—breaking into lace-
like patterns—the moon—silver and moonlight—into the hours after
midnight—the sky clear—stars—the moon resplendent—the entire expanse of the world—aware of the world—aware of the moon—shining
at one point thru fire escape—into our rear window—a shaft of shadow-
crossed moonlight—gone now—the moon directly over Ave. C—rows
of sparkling red stoplights—reflected in metal plates at several street
crossings—dampness—last of the rain—a few Puerto Rican cats on the
street going home—perhaps—some ambling in the morning—prowling
a bit. Coming from Irving's—having joy—Rigby—Ed Marshall—Irving—the radio with good sounds of jazz—much pot—laughter—people reaching tenderly—delicately in the atmosphere—perception and
self-awareness—reticence—shyness—self-denial—one cat making himself heard—Rigby—young—twenty-five—with a bit—about revolution—Cuba—Castro—also—a hang-up about his wife—drinks and turns
on—not liking contemplation exactly—has a record—Louisiana police—grave desecration—human bones found under his bed. Is beautiful
physically—body attractive—graceful masculinity—occasionally gauche.
Ed Marshall a great poet—poetically natural—a touch of Irish charm—
fine—smoking pot—full of good for everyone—the lonely man—his
awareness part of the universe—sensitive—responsive to rushing
winds—lofty mountain peaks—tamarack—yellow and white pine—the
tips swaying and swishing—on the stillest day—not a breeze below
lighted with green sunlight—white sunlight thru branches in spots—cold

shadows—rocks—carpets of browned pine needles—small berry bushes—cold stream water—winding along—the banks—fern and water plants—small blue—white—yellow flowers—moss and rocks—now in the prayer room—a live iguana—people—good rich earthy pot—having climbed this Manhattan mountain—honeycombed with squared caves— steps marble—worn down from the many who have gone up and down—who do now—and will—alerted to sounds of the flowing blood—the throbbing breast—the pulsations—this the city of the pack— halted—separated from the wilderness by layers of steel—cement— brick—no longer the same—new breeds—keen to the call—no longer recognizing the instinct—not knowing—frustrated—inwardly aquiver— shutting the doors—even then chained—snapping at intrusions of their own strain—hating—sisters—brothers—mothers—fathers—whole strange things going—frayed exposed nerve ends—charged electric contact with subways—careening below the surface level electrical webs holding in the weaving threads—impulses from the outward pull—gas fumes— smoke—black and curling into the air upwardly—soot—ash—carbon particles sifting down—thin layers coating the surface of the area— whirling ripples of wind—scattering dust—bits of paper—newspapers— the strong sea air blending and heavy with city odors—spending only a short period in the beauty of a rare—man—whose immediate presence carries the full flavor of the single jewel—perfect in the inner quality of the one—alone—priceless. This man of Persian exquisiteness—serving cups of tea from Formosa—made in red clay and ceramic-lined teapot— in constant touch with creative drive—mostly among—poets—writers— dancers—painters—in an aura of the god spectrum gentle yellows— blues—iridescent rays strong warm red hues imperceptible—perceived in mellow reflective candle glow—later—at the moment of a kind gesture toward the human plight—nurtured energy—tended—revitalized— developed into a blooming flower of individualized beauty. From the heart—flows the universal contact—directly toward all. A wise good man. Ed going on to new searching. Irving—Rigby—on to Ave. C and the moon overhead. Two o'clock then—change—to purchase candles— cigarettes—under my arm—a paper bag of slices of cheese—a taste of Swiss—a small cut of cream cheese—a cut of cheddar—two bananas— one onion—slices of dark bread—at this point unsure of locating a store open—cutting into the opposite side of the avenue in the direction of bright light—nearing the scene—aware of a policeman his back to me— talking with a young Puerto Rican busy—fitting plywood squares over a door frame the glass panel smashed out—lying in chunks on the side-walk—most of the rubble disposed of—a cellar door flung back—another man—older—serious expression of responsibility—from his eyes and furrowed forehead—dejection hanging from his bowed head and sloping shoulders—he held two more squares of plywood—he placed up against the door—for measurement—the policeman—advising him—the side to nail pieces on—answering me as I came up—inquiring "about what happened"—saying—"the door was smashed—these fellows came all the way from Brooklyn—I had to call them." I asked if they had candles and cigarettes—if they would make a sale to me. There was an exchange of glances—among the three—the youngest—asking—"What kind cigarettes you want?" Moving into the store—back of the counter—the policeman hesitated a few moments then walked in after him. I followed on in—talking of candles—fishing the change from my pocket—counting—ordering another package of cigarettes—candles—three for a nickel—the policeman at this point—taking over the completion of the sale—knowing the stock better than the young man—selecting a dozen and a half candles—a pack of cupcakes—counting the dimes—nickels and pennies—explaining about the candles—no electricity till first of the week. Bid all good night walked out to moon-drenched street—crossed at angle toward home—around next corner—and upstairs to Janine—Laf—Bill—greeting me with questions about food and candles. Tired—talking a while—I had neither been heard correctly or understood—and the sound of my voice grating on my ears—the pad great—rich looking—Bill's art filling the place with beauty. A shot of methedrine—a stick of pot—bed switching for Janine—who decided to rearrange her room—this notebook—a red ink pen—my Easter joy—the sun coming up. And now to sleep.

1961

HART'S ISLAND: LETTERS FROM PRISON,
FEBRUARY—JUNE 1964

[In 1964 Huncke was arrested for possession of narcotics and sentenced to one year in New York's Hart's Island, though he would be released after six months. The following excerpts are from letters written during his incarceration to friends Clive and Erin Matson (whose drawings would be included in Huncke's Journal) *and Noah, with whom he had fallen in love.]*

February 19, 1964 (letter unsent)

Noah,

Skimming thru the news today the movie review on the Jonas Mekas film [*Guns of the Trees*] and particularly noted Ginsberg's name. Received an exceptionally moving letter from Paul. Words flow from his pen creating passages of sheer beauty. He is a great person and gains strength and stature seemingly before one's eyes. How fortunate I am knowing both of you. His woven of fine-spun threads of gleaming silver and gold. Yours of hard cobalt—glorious reds—umber and angry yellows. It is strange each induces the same hypnotic trance—while reaching deep into the heart's core—searching out the same truths—declaring the same convictions—exposing repeatedly the wonder of the organic basic qualities of the mystery of the soul. Trying to reach each of you from here—in this old building of three floors—constructed in a sort of H form—each floor a huge dormitory housing many, many men of all ages—but mostly old—the misfits and maladjusted—the derelicts and lost—the tired and hungry—on this beautiful little island—where seagulls also make their home—and the wind sometimes sweeps them in their flight toward the sea while their screeching becomes the sound of keening women—rather like peering toward a winter sun seen faintly thru a veil of pale gray clouds. Also it is difficult retaining an impersonal (the very idea of anyone at any time even pretending to be impersonal is, of course, ridiculous) attitude. Nevertheless it behooves me—at this point—to pay lip service—so to speak—to the commanding forces. I can only hope you understand. I had a very impressive dream recently in which I saw you standing at the prow of a ship. You sailed past me. I called to you—asking your destination—and you smiled at me but did not answer. I looked away for a moment—feeling very sad and lonely—and I thought I will not show my concern—so I quickly looked back and you were surrounded by many people and you had changed some way—so that I had difficulty recognizing you. All of a sudden—I know you were happy and I was glad.

Huncke

March 16, 1964

Noah—it seems our positions have become similar in a rather vague sense. I also find it difficult writing letters these days—particularly to you. Of course my reasons are perfectly obvious. I am in jail. My present environment presents a limited scope. I have no news. . . . Your letter was both a pleasant surprise and somewhat disturbing. As much as you may dislike living at home—I can't help but feel it is in all probability for the better, at least until you feel you have developed some degree of self-reliance and can no longer stand the restrictions. From what you said in your letter it does sound as though they are making an effort to extend themselves. Remember—it doesn't lie entirely to them. You also must make concessions. In fact—since basically yours is the most tolerant attitude—in the final analysis—you must carry the heavier part of the load. Hell, Noah, I can't talk to you—it seems—without coming on like a dimwitted-advice-dishing-out old fool. It is utterly impossible for me to say any of the things I know in my heart should be said—if there is any hope of retaining your friendship. You—the one person I must desire to speak truthfully to—are the one I am the most evasive with. Why? Of one thing I am sure—it is certainly not because of the Allen G. and Peter O. type thing. . . . It is something much more than that. Anyway, try and bear with me. I can't honestly say I consider Monroe and Bill Heine the best company you might choose. Actually—I'm envious—and only feel thusly because I'm not there with you—although envy isn't the only reason. Frankly I'd worry less were I on the scene because—in my opinion—you are pretty vulnerable—when all is said and done—and I'd feel better if I were there to run interference—so to speak. Boy—if I deliberately set out to make you reject me—I couldn't do much better. Regards to Diane. Be as good to her as you can, Noah—she needs love. For that matter—don't we all? Incidentally, with enough of the right chemical substance, the idea of traveling . . . sounds like a great idea. I don't care how raunchy the note—or short—send it anyway.

Huncke

P.S. This is the first of two letters composed to you—saying essentially the same things. Maybe I'll send the other tomorrow.

H.

March 16, 1964

Noah—Damn my present situation. I am stymied—unable to unleash my words—say things to you—I want to say—in the way I desire saying them. [At] this point I can't even reply to your letter in full scope—but must curtail my speech in a manner not to offend. As a friend this cuts me deeply—nor lessens my sense of shame at my failure to speak openly—straightforwardly and from the heart. Still I will depend to some extent upon your ability to understand my circumventions of the truth in such a way the truth will be what you deduce. To begin with—and at the risk of your rejection (I won't even bother enumerating the reasons)—I am not exactly pleased to learn of your association with the Harry Monroe and Bill Heine crew—irrespective of chicks with piercing blue eyes—or escape from the parental pressures I know to be distasteful and without question stupid. As a matter of fact—should any harm of drastic nature befall you—through or because of your contact with that particular group—especially Heine—you may be sure I will ask for an accounting. I know Heine well and grant he is interesting and an accomplished artist but I also know he respects neither himself nor anyone other than those capable of cruelty and deceit. Wow—how like a worried father I sound—one trying to come on sensibly—man to man—and all that crap. And I don't mean that at all.

March 27, 1964

Erin . . . Spring approaching hesitantly but surely—one day warm and balmy and the next windy and chill. This is a beautiful little island whose roots reach deep toward the core of the earth. It juts forward toward the ocean and is the favorite haunt of seagulls whose shadows play across the surface while they glide in sweeping arcs up on the ceaseless March winds. The buildings are all red brick mellowed with age. There are many trees—some old—gnarled with age—and others still comparatively young but already strong and twisted from the angry blustering sea winds of winter. . . .

I'll let you in on a little secret—one I would share with no one else—at least from the present. I no longer feel quite so defeated and that living has become a drag. I actually look forward to the future. In fact—occasionally—I become afraid I am tempting the Fates by speaking of it. I love you—

Huncke

April 29, 1964

Noah—God forbid me ever becoming an ordeal. Promise me should our relationship ever reach the point you continue our association out of pity or because you believe I might suffer not seeing you or hearing from you—it would be far kinder to simply say—you are no longer interested in continuing the friendship. I say this not because I necessarily feel this might come about—although, of course, it might—but rather because I want assurance from you I can unqualifiedly believe in you as a friend.

May 16, 1964

Erin—Clive—

. . . If this has reached you it is because I've succeeded in making use of the prison underground mailing system I was recently put in contact with. It is rather an expensive way of sending letters—collateral—cigarettes—two packs per letter . . . but if all goes well—I'll attempt using it from time to time. This place in some respects is considerably more lax than the majority of similar institutions. Thusly the possibility of the underground mail route. In prison vernacular—sending mail in such a manner is called "flying a kite."

. . . You know—just being free to say anything I please in a letter gives me a kind of thrill and all sorts of silly things are going around through my mind. Like—I love Clive—I love Noah—I love Paul. Be it ever so innocent—one simply never says—love—in connection with a member of one's own sex. Homosexuality, you know—and although these places run rife with it—the petty little clerks, jerks and agents that keep the whole fucked-up bureaucratic nightmare operating frown upon such things.

This has nothing to do with my love life. He is just not my type, but I did meet a very interesting cat who since his departure has been corresponding with me. One of those way-out, intellectual types—Columbia—Social Psychiatrics—New York University—psychology and languages—etc.—literary aspirations and a snob—terribly, terribly frustrated but sort of sad and oddly beautiful underneath. Thinks I'm unique.

That's all.

H.

May 19, 1964

Erin—dear Erin—I am attempting to write this while an amusing typical Lower East Side (Hollywood-style) Italian semi-hood—actually a gambler by profession—numbers writer and race bookie—whose conversation dwells on such subjects as masturbation—boy ass—girl ass—the respective sizes of pricks, cocks and pussy in all shapes—is reading the horoscope from "The Stars and You" by Consuela in the *Daily News* almost in the manner of a child who has but recently learned to read—interlacing the sentences with asides—such as "Listen to this fucking shit—who the hell is Consuela?—some fucking faggot—what a whole lot of shit this is. Consuela sucks and anybody who believes this crap is crazy." Somehow it is very funny and again—as I frequently do—I wish I had a tape recorder. He is in jail because he failed to pay off one of the local police sergeants in his neighborhood on time. He rather likes me and one of his complements is—"Huncke—you may never win a race, but you're still my horse."

. . . Noah hasn't written recently—so your information about him was apropos—and welcome. Of course, you are well aware of how much I am concerned with him. He is one of the most strangely beautiful people I have ever known. Clive is amazingly perceptive in associating him and Elise together. Noah is remarkably like the male counterpart of Elise even in appearance but less vulnerable and certainly less suicidal in potential. As dark and brooding as Noah is, he respects living much too vigorously to take his own life and I predict we will hear much and from him in the future. Frankly I worried about him for a while . . . but from his last letter I gathered he was staying close to the home front and was seemingly taking things pretty much in stride. I am pleased he is making it—clean—these days. He suffers greatly coming down off anything he takes and I think it is wiser he remain free of most stimulants. Regardless—I love the guy—and if we never meet again—he occupies a special spot in my heart.

. . . Oh yes—there is a doctor here—a psychiatrist—an inmate—serving time for nonsupport . . . who is probably full of shit but who has promised to keep in touch with me when he leaves—or at least give me an address where I can reach him after I'm released— . . . to get me all the amphetamine I want. I am not at all convinced I can depend on him, but it sure sounds great. Who can tell—maybe with enough amphets I might even write a book.

. . . This will be the last letter I'll mail—this route—for a while. Too expensive.

One thing—next we meet—I'll have some fresh stories for you.

>Love to you—
>>Love to Clive—
>>>Tell Noah to write—
>>>>Regards to all.
>>>>>Special hello—Ed Marshall

P.S. . . . Can just see Ed Marshall these days. Tell him I said behave—or I'll manifest before him when he least expects it.

>>>>>>H.

>>>>>May 28, 1964

Erin,

You don't burden me with your woes. Your letters are always a source of pleasure to me even on the few occasions in the past when you scolded me. There are a very precious few, including yourself, who can do no wrong . . . and although their unhappiness brings me pain, it is the pain of loving and being unable to bring peace to the loved one. Many times in my daydreaming I have wished for great wisdom in order that I might at any required instant say, "Do this and all will be well." I suppose there is nothing unusual in such a wish and I only mention it in passing. . . . What of my own complaints and the many personal problems I lay at the feet of my friends? You know, I detest clichés and recently I have noticed a tendency on my part to use them constantly, both in conversation and in letter writing. Sometimes I awaken in the night—reach over and light a cigarette—then lie thinking of the past mostly, but of the future as well, and once in a while I am filled with a deep wonder about the whole business of living and loving and dying and I become sad. Then again—I carry on long inner conversations with maybe you or Clive or Eila or

Allen or Janine or Roberta or Noah or once in a rare while with someone entirely of my imagination or—and this I enjoy the most—with myself.

May 29, 1964

To Erin Matson

. . . There were several inmates playing "ghost," a word game you are probably familiar with, and since the lights were turned out—except for the night-lights—just sufficient enough to read or write by with a bit of strain—and all was supposed to be quiet for the night—the game was being played sotto voce which is far more disturbing than loud sound, and besides, the players kept asking me questions. It was as all such pastimes are in jail—both annoying and highly amusing—annoying usually because one is invariably expected to either participate or monitor in a sense—regardless of personal interest—and amusing invariably because of the various strangely unrelated concepts—per rules—and related ideas involved. Here it is particularly difficult to remain free of such involvement primarily because we live in dormitories—huge barracks-like rooms providing little opportunity for privacy. I am dormitory clerk and—although it bugs me sometimes—it is unquestionably one of the best jobs as it removes me to a degree from complete regimentation, permitting me opportunity to exercise—to an extent—my personality in a sort of public-relations-type behavior. It can be and often is fun. Modestly I add I am considered one of the best clerks on the island and frequently my fellow inmates josh me by saying, "Dorm Three—that's Huncke's dorm." You should just hear me carry on—bellowing out orders—answering questions—helping fill out interview slips—for Social Service—Chaplain interviews—and general information pertaining to personal problems concerning dates of release and supposed errors in sentencing—plus helping wording of personal letters—answering questions of every nature—almost frighteningly indicative of complete submissiveness to conformity and indoctrination to a system entirely devoid of individual considerations—filling out forms required for the bureaucratic gullet on each new arrival and departure—entering the name and number in the receiving and discharge ledger—making out a file card—including name and number—date of arrival—disposition of the charge—amount of time to be served here—where assigned—bed location and work detail and where received from—the Tombs—City Prison

Bronx or Brooklyn—New Queens—Old Queens. Probably the most satisfying aspect for me is my close contact with the people in authority and the opportunity to observe them up close and the constant undercurrent of the knowledge that at all times it is necessary I maintain almost perfect balance between my relationship with them—aware that the slightest error in judgment—mostly sensed and only slightly rationalized—will cause me trouble—and at the same time remaining in the good graces of my own people—the inmates. But enough of all this bullshit.

Again it was necessary for me to stop writing. I am picking this up late in the afternoon—after four o'clock change of the guards. This period more or less winds up the day's activities with only the evening hours for observing the almost ritualistic business of watching television—playing cards—washing clothes—sox—pants—shirts—underwear—if so inclined—or maybe talking or reading—writing letters—making one's bed sans mattress—incidentally or simply lying back in a state of semiconsciousness. Every day exactly the same with only slight variations on Saturday and Sunday—such as not going out to work—preparing for a visit if one is lucky enough to rate a visitor—spending two hours in the yard with such recreational pastimes as baseball—horseshoe pitching—lifting weights—Foosball—Ping-Pong—available if one desires to participate, and of course on Sunday there are religious services—Catholic, Protestant, and Christian Science. Week in and week out.

I can't seem to get away from these goddamned details. Fuck it—they simply aren't worth the effort and anyway everyone knows the score—jail is jail no matter what diversions are offered and the very idea is rotten.

I wrote Noah last week asking him to get in touch with you and Clive about seeing Mr. Zuchor the lawyer who represented me in court—a prime fool if there ever was one. . . . I have been told there might be an error involved in having the two cases sentenced consecutively since both cover—in a sense—narcotics. Two six-month sentences on narcotics charges running consecutively should be served at Rikers and not at Hart's. . . . My sentence is excessive, and if brought to the attention of the court there is a possible chance of it being changed. Clive is very efficient at handling matters of detail and if perhaps he has—or can squeeze in—the time he will at least investigate the matter for me. If so it must be done before June 20—at which time my second six-month begins.

Noah still hasn't written. In my letter to him prior the last I told him

I would prefer not hearing from him if his only reason for writing me was out of pity or in a sense of obligation. His letters are amazingly revealing. He certainly has touched a spot in my heart and I find it difficult remaining calm and sensible concerning him. No fool like an old fool, baby. Hell—he is a beautiful cat and I love him—and if that makes it homosexual, well, I'm a stoned homo. And off the record, I can't imagine a sex bit with him, so where in the name of God does that place me? I worry about him—so if you have any information when you next write—pass it on.

Allen finally wrote. A short, typical Allen letter—shorn of flamboyant speech—practical and kindly. I liked the old Allen best. His wild outbursts and long rambling dissertations on cosmic consciousness—trans-human awareness—and his very human concern for Allen and Peter—good old Bill Burroughs—Huncke—Lucien and Kerouac. He mentioned talking with Kerouac on the phone. Said he sounds terrifying. Would guess he refers to Jack's drinking. . . . Also he tells me that Irving's book [Irving Rosenthal's *Sheeper*] is probably to be handled by Grove. [Irving] is waiting for Eila to finish typing my stuff and then will begin editing and assembling. As much as I respect him, I am just a bit frightened of his heavy hand. We shall see. He assures me the publishing will be no problem but I am a long way from convinced. Paul made a very wise comment in one of his letters. He suggests everything be published posthumously and fuck reputation and all that jazz. Might be a good idea.

June 1964

Erin—This is one of those days I am familiar with—when deep inside I am aware of seething inarticulateness. I feel possessed. I want to say anything—and nothing comes through. I am frustrated and despondent. I need someone to put their arms around me and unexpectedly tell me they love me. I am weary of watching those I love—cautiously—carefully—analyzing each move—making sure of their motives—always questioning—always unsure, never secure in the belief their love is from the heart, free of ulterior motivation—hating what I see in myself. And this has always been so with me. . . . Words are so damned inadequate. Oh—for a better means of communication. Telepathy is the answer. If it were possible—what a bombardment you would receive.

DIDI

THE TICKING OF THE CLOCK I FOUND YESTERDAY STOPPED AND I WOUND it and now it gives out the life beat of the hours.

For an instant I almost felt the need to begin in another place in this notebook but—after a flash reflection—continued with this which is already started.

The weekend was incredible with many people falling on the scene I hadn't been in touch with. It was a weekend of all kinds of drugs from ordinary pot through barbiturates, amphetamines, heroin, cocaine, and LSD. The general tenor of last Friday, Saturday, and Sunday was good and several people spoke of it as the time of Leo's ascendancy and coming alive. I know several people born of that sign and one in particular— Didi.

Didi the beautiful one—sensitive and fleet—who believes her nature with shaded eyelids and languid cat-green eyes that see everything. She is small and can assume any role assigned her. Her hair washblond color when we first met—through my boy—dear John Wieners—and the three of us walked in the fresh gentle morning winds bathed in the pale light and Didi and John and sometimes I sang songs of the past. Roughly six years have passed since then.

Didi has never permitted me too deep a glance into her—so very vulnerable a being—which knows too well loneliness and need of love— but whose strength sends it ever seeking even though invariably it drops defenses at a moment's notice and Didi is again a lover and a woman of fortitude and cunning—sharp and keen—strong and enduring full of wit and good spirit yet the eternal female—ever ready to fulfill whatever obligation is required to complete the unit of two—the male and the female—man and woman.

She feels deeply and probes deeper still for her answer and—although her mind is alive and healthy—her heart is large and dominates the mind and has made her one of the not only beautiful women of her era but one of the few honest women—or men for that matter—I've known or know of.

She will always be as long as I live (and I would make of that a very positive thing—were it within my power) and—if my fates are generous with me—my heart's last beat will stop the quicker and with cleaner severance from the life force for the fine and good love and friendship of Didi.

1960s

KATMANDU VALLEY

[In the early seventies, Huncke and photographer Louis Cartwright traveled to Katmandu, where this poem was written.]

Reflected in the street lamps—streets of
    blood—
While angels remain fixed—mixed
    in concrete.
Children's tears flow thru gutters.
A thousand roaring pistons—a
    dirge for keening women.
The moon bathes the scene with
    luminous green white light
    and a comet trails fiery
    splendor.

TED BERRIGAN

[Ted Berrigan (1934–1983) was a leading figure of the second generation of the New York School poets. During the sixties and seventies, Berrigan was a charismatic focal point of the thriving poetry scene of New York's Lower East Side in and around the Poetry Project at St. Marks Church. He was the author of many books. Penguin published Berrigan's Selected Poems *in 1994.]*

THIS AFTERNOON, TRYING TO ORGANIZE THOUGHTS ABOUT TED—A MAN I didn't get to know as well personally as I would like to have. A respecter of his peers and extremely well liked by his friends, he had known the Lower East Side for many years and the terrain for many miles into the body of New York City. Friends everywhere. He was soft spoken— wise with his observations—humorous—full of wit. His sensitivity was constantly alert—keen. His eyes were bright and twinkling—deep brown and a bit sad. One could sense basic goodness—integrity—pride—and a sort of awareness of loneliness.

Unquestionably, one knew he was warm and deeply conscious of love for mankind, for the world, and everything in the universe. Within his immediate range he revealed once to me a great, almost overwhelming concern for his sons—and whether or not he was worthy of their love.

He was a kind, tender man and I will miss the experience of meeting him on the street by chance—talking with him—feeling the warmth of his being.

November 15, 1983

BOXCAR BERTHA

[This book review ran in the January–February 1989 issue of American Book Review. *It is the only review Huncke is known to have written.]*

Boxcar Bertha: An Autobiography
As told to Ben L. Reitman, with an introduction by Kathy Acker
New York City: Amok Press, 1988

There are times when I say to myself, where has the color gone, the flavor, the character I used to come in contact with so often in my life? Perhaps I'm to blame, I'm older now; but I somehow believe those days of the free spirit, so to speak, are behind us.

A new book I've come across, called *Boxcar Bertha*, is an autobiography of a woman hobo from the thirties, and it brings back to life that spirit, the adventure and the eccentricities of what I feel is an American heritage we've lost somewhere along our way.

I can honestly say that I wish I had met Bertha on one of my own rail rides. I would very, very much like to've known her. She seems a charming, forthright young woman, one who could take care of herself in all situations. Riding the rails was not an easy business.

My own first experience with rail riding occurred near, of all places, Las Vegas, Nevada. I'd hitched a ride with a crazy man if there ever was one just south of there and I was sorry to learn that his destination was Las Vegas, because I rather enjoyed that ride (and, in fact, preferred hitching rides to hopping rails). When he left me off, I ran into another guy along the highway who asked me where I was going. I told him to California, where a lot of us were headed in those days. He replied that by God, I should jump the next freight train out of town if I wanted to get there fast. Well, I thought it was worth a try, though not without the risk of danger. Following his instructions as close to the letter as possible, I got my first thrill of riding then, but oddly enough did not end up in California at all! I made it to Chicago instead, my home at that time. I returned, though, with the knowledge that I could leave town anytime I wanted with whomever I wanted, and the illusion that I was free to come and go as I pleased has never left me.

The closest I came to anybody like Boxcar Bertha was on a run outside Louisiana. We considered ourselves lucky to get aboard a train with a woman in the crowd. I could and did talk with her and learn from her. My first thought was then that she was something of a whore. But I soon learned otherwise; she had high moral standards, and chose her men accordingly. This only comes, I recognized, from many experiences riding and trying to make a living all about the country. I myself felt that I did not yet experience quite as much.

This Boxcar Bertha commanded the respect of all the bums and yeggs and reds and grifters of the road. And her book is really a wonderfully revealing and evocative period piece. The knowledge is here, the bravado and the understanding, the compassion. I recall I often thought to myself, where was I to go, what was I to do? Bertha made traveling the road an option of livelihood in itself. As did Ben Reitman, who I recall as well was a real champ at this game.

Lastly, I'd like to say here that I've had young people mention to me over and over again how relatively unscathed by my many experiences I am, commenting upon my so-called intrepid spirit and the like. Well, I say time and again that they would certainly do, and could only do, what I did, which is—believe it or not—play it primarily by ear. How can one plan most things, least of all a life on the road? *Boxcar Bertha* illustrates the unexpected leaps one takes when traveling from place to place with no sure destination in mind.

INTRODUCTION TO *PIPE DREAMS* BY MARTY MATZ

[Pipe Dreams is a collection by San Francisco poet Marty Matz, who was a longtime friend of Huncke's.]

MARTIN MATZ IS IN MY FEELING ONE OF THE MOST POSITIVE AND eloquent poets it is my privilege to be in touch with. How fine and beautiful are the opium-drenched lines in his *Pipe Dreams*, exquisitely presented in manner: delicate, mysterious and wondrous. He succeeds in developing an awareness of the strength and awesome beauty, the hidden power and intricate structure in the heart of a stone; the intangible mystique beheld in the flight of a hummingbird, the wing of a dragonfly or exotic butterfly kissing and drawing the sweet nectar from each flower. His demanding retentive memory in order—the essence complete and alive of that instant in time—fuses into revelation, of all which there is to see: the surface, the depth, a vibrancy we can instinctively recognize; the perfection of the moment. Thus he has lived, and knows the great power of what I refer to as Spirit—a word I believe, quite honestly, very often fails to consider the rush of life, or all that we find somewhat difficult to accept or handle.

There exist certain people of strange, mysterious bent who see the palest of colors of each day—who look beyond the heavy gray rolling clouds periodically illuminated by revealed areas of light, patterned with mist and wisps of gently fringed pearly smoke like bits of swirling cloud fragments. The eyes see what is not there, not necessarily due: agitation and undirected time—thought moving steadily through the inner being, alerting our senses to the charm and almost imperceptible awareness of the inspiring beauty, the outpouring of an energy pulsing within the scene unfolding before one unexpectedly. Mr. Matz can successfully blend the strange and fascinating dream-level reality with the mundane daily experience most perfectly, weaving perfect magic.

All of this only a fleeting moment, now indelibly marked most vividly within the pictured memory of that moment. The poem becomes the memory we will instinctively know—and, unequivocally, always remember.

It seems to me I spend a great deal of time racking my brain while attempting something in the way of verbal or written description in order to speak of a friend—a poet, a prose writer, a painter, a musician— anyone who is alive, I suppose, is what it comes to—if I am to be understood. Regardless, I attempt this introduction with a sincere desire to speak of a man I admire not only as a man to be respected as a friend, but as an unusually fine poet as well.

When I think of his poetry I think particularly of his words . . . or should I say his choice of words, words that he has rolled around in his thoughts, perhaps tasting their sounds in his head, his mouth. His lines are strong yet tinged with a touch of pathos. His world of color and ancient life, caught in the web of deep wisdom and deep knowledge and response to mystique, makes dreams unfold before him. There is a "force" at work within the whole of his poetry, very nearly in every one of the poems I've read. But it is most definitely true of the poems in this volume. This can be sensed most clearly when Mr. Matz reads his poems aloud—there is felt an exotic richness, as well as an almost world-weary sultriness and throbbing in the voice as he reads his *Pipe Dreams*.

And he draws support for the solidity of his statements from the earth, the soil—all of nature; trees, rocks, and gems—upheaval and restless winds—strange dream-producing flowers. His is an awareness of the endless mystery we are all so much a part of. Of such stuff are we allowed to fill out the shape of our lives, no matter our aim—or better, our hopes. Nor does it matter what dreams and memories compose the substance of our future. The moment is all. Marty Matz has lived the moment, and his poetry speaks of it wonderfully.

Summer 1989

AN ORAL HISTORY OF BENZEDRINE USE IN THE U.S.A.

GO BACK TO THE 1930S—THOUGH IT MUST HAVE BEEN DISCOVERED SOME-
where in the twenties. I'm almost sure—start from, say '32, undercover
before '33, I know that—Benzedrine was then only known by a few:
nurses and doctors, students in universities where they'd come in
contact with science types and medical people, and a few oddballs
like myself. I grew up in Chicago—so say at the University of
Chicago, someone would say, "Man, I have to cram for an exam
and I'm exhausted"—and someone would know someone who was
a nurse with knowledge of this new thing called Benzedrine—"Hey,
why don't you get a few bennies" (right away it was "bennies")—I'm
guessing it started to spread like that, students in the know. I learned a
lot about amphetamine through them.

Soon I learned that a lot of people who weren't of the underworld
were piddling around with the stuff—one experience I had was the summer when I took a job as an elevator boy at the Illinois Athletic Club
on Michigan Avenue in Chicago. A guy stepped into the elevator one
night and asked me to buy him a bottle of pills—I think two dozen, 10
mg, for about eighty-nine cents. This guy was considered a great athlete,
and upper crust—I guess he figured I was only going to be there for a short
time, and that I wasn't likely going to squeal. Me, I could do a bottle of
twenty to twenty-five in a period of about three days. It was a stimulating
thing, as you know, and you could go for long periods doing things you
liked without feeling exhausted. I liked to talk; it was a perfect talking
drug. One used to stay up all night and end up at the jazz joints after
hours. Life fascinated me no end. To end up over into the Black Belt
in the South Side of Chicago—there wasn't anything that knocked me
out more.

Everyone's complaint about it though, at the beginning, was that it
killed the sex drive—so many stopped using after a short while. But OK!

Perseverance corrected that assumption! See, in those days, people were uptight about sex, so psychologically, you know, once bennie kicked in . . . well, it teases you a little. Sure—it kind of encouraged the freakish aspect—so you had to let go, and when you got going you could go for hours and hours. We found that it *helped* the sex drive! So that's how basic sexual discoveries began to come about—letting go in bed, and then afterward being less embarrassed to talk about it—they just followed their inclinations!

Benzedrine gets to the mind, too—I don't like to separate the mental from the physical, and while I was jumping around I'd start thinking about things I'd never thought of before. Although it gave you all this energy, as I say, it didn't make you angry. One would simply pass out the stuff—no one needed to make a buck off of it—one wasn't inclined to steal or anything like that—that wasn't the idea at all. You need a bennie? Here, I have ten, here's three or four—we weren't so paranoid in those days. . . . And I'd travel around with it, too—town to town, popping. I'd leave Chicago and I could still buy without any problem—this was about the mid-thirties. Of course I kept myself well groomed at all times, and while people didn't look down on the drug so much yet, it always helps to have a good appearance. Once, I ran into Toledo and I had a problem getting some. It was obviously getting more popular, and some drugstores were picking up on that. I had to buy caffeine tablets at that time, and suffered from it—I got ill and could not talk well.

If you start to feel trouble, of course you want to know what the trouble is, right? It still wasn't illegal, but it had come to the attention of many people because, I think, workers in the industrial areas and truck drivers were buying it more and more to keep alert on their jobs. I remember in the road stops—in the rest room stalls—seeing "George the Bennie King Was Here," or things like that.

It was when they got hip to the pills, and they became difficult to get, that Smith Kline & French—who had a priority claim as Benzedrine manufacturers in the U.S., to the best of my knowledge (they were located in Pennsylvania, if I recall)—well, they switched over to these nasal inhalers. These quickly became a big item in drug counters. It was put into a small metal container—later plastic—stuffed with some kind of gauze and rolled very tightly with not only Benzedrine, but oil of lettuce and menthol and God knows what else. The problem was you not only got hooked on amphets but on this other shit too! We used to share the inhalers, sitting in a cafeteria with a cup of hot coffee—by the time you got up and walked out, you'd be a new man! They were very delightful, just euphoric. The world was beautiful.

They didn't last for very long on the streets—they knew they had a problem almost immediately. Anslinger, who'd already ruined the pot scene, got on the ass of Benzedrine and got carried away with this new thing—oh, we got something else to take care of now! Don't you know there were a lot of payoffs down the line in the process. The cops—who still didn't know what the fuck amphetamine was on into the fifties—didn't mind because, after all, what was an inhaler when it came down to it?

By 1939–1940, when I hit Times Square, bennies were illegal, but there were those of us who still managed. Over on Eighth Avenue there were a couple of drugstores tucked away that street people like myself—who hadn't tipped our mitts—used to get by.

THANKSGIVING, 1991: HARRY SMITH

[Harry Smith was a groundbreaking filmmaker, painter, archivist, magician, alchemist, occult specialist, folklorist, and ethnomusicologist.]

MANY PEOPLE TELEPHONED—WISHED ME AN ENJOYABLE DAY. I WAS pleased people were thinking of and about me—it is good being thought of, regardless how, although the nearer the thought to love—the closer— an awareness of happiness is apt to exist.

I have never been a close friend of Harry Smith. Our paths have crossed many times and I knew the majority of my friends spoke well of him—concerning his mind or perhaps I should say—his ability to be creative with his interests—film, film animation, and experimental projects (which I know nothing about). He was also a knowledgeable and learned philosopher and mathematician. I really knew little of him. Today everyone who phoned—or almost everyone—mentioned he died—either late in the day—yesterday—or perchance—early in the morning.

He was respected, admired and liked by many, many people—all over the world. It embarrasses me, I can't list his accomplishments—one, two, three—on down the line—so to speak.

As I said—we met off and on—here and there—since early so-called Lower East Side hippy days. We had mutual friends and many similar habits, thusly he became popular among various groups of people. Allen Ginsberg knew and liked Harry. Allen helped him in many ways as have Raymond Foye and Panna Grady—people at the Chelsea Hotel—Stanley Bard, Linda Twigg, Paola Igliori, Vali Meyer and others throughout New York, the entire country and—in all probability—the world.

To speak honestly—I didn't respond comfortably to his personality. His appearance made me feel skeptical of his trustworthiness.

How dare I make any comment that should indicate how petty I am?

About ten or ten-thirty A.M. my phone rang. My caller was Allen Ginsberg—who immediately offered me a belated but heartfelt greeting—pertaining to the Thanksgiving wish for enjoyment for the seasonal period—so to speak—as well as to tell me of Harry Smith's death.

We chatted mostly comparing our information about Harry as we knew him individually. I did ask Allen about Harry's age—mentioning I had been told—by several people—he was in his early eighties but that quite a few other people thought him younger—somewhere in his late sixties. Allen said at some point he had seen Harry's birth certificate and was almost sure sixty-eight was closer to factual. Although that was closer to what I felt was correct I was a bit surprised—since in my opinion, at least, Harry looked nearer to eighty, if not older. Allen agreed with me—qualifying his reason for thinking so by telling me Harry had abused his system by consuming vast amounts of strange and little-understood drugs and—although he wasn't specific—I got the impression Harry had been a somewhat heavy drinker. Apparently, Harry had been internally bleeding from some disorder and coughing up blood for nearly a year or maybe longer. The sum total of the information implying Harry had been in deplorable physical condition a long time. To judge by the obviously decayed and rotten condition of his teeth, one can easily accept such diagnosis. Why Harry adamantly refused to permit anything to be done toward correcting whatever problem existed concerning his mouth is presumably anyone's guess.

Allen, in passing, did speak of the possibility of Harry having been a member of some group, influenced perhaps by the teaching or belief of Aleister Crowley.

Before closing our conversation, we both agreed Harry was strange and exceedingly fascinating.

I sincerely feel annoyed as well as a bit sad I don't know more about him. Even though I have always been aware of him as a rare and unusual man, I was never enthusiastic about becoming closely involved with him. I suppose it wouldn't be particularly difficult to analyze just why I stayed more or less clear of him. Perhaps I feared his seeing me too clearly, seeing my vulnerability and the weakness in what I believe my personality consists of—so to speak.

I am trying to end all these words—I'll try to give my impression of his appearance, since inside I feel his appearance had much to do with why I didn't try to get closer to him as a human being.

If my memory stands me in good stead, I met Harry the first time in Allen and Peter's apartment on Second Street about January of the year 1960. In an attempt to indicate, the reason why I refer to the apartment as Allen and Peter's is because in fact they did rent the apartment in name and also because I think it bore a sort of reputation as a focal point for the very early days of the Lower East Side, a creative gathering place, for writers, poets, visual artists, musicians and, in a sense, new-type thinkers of all kinds, trying to break free of the rigidity of the so-called social behavior and thinking of so-called normality. I merely offer a generalization of the lifestyle beginning, at least, to seem freer of taboos that no longer seemed necessarily right or applicable in every instance, allowing for a greater display of individuality. All of which deserved a fuller accounting than I offer here. It, putting it mildly, vibrated (all this, in my opinion) with much activity and heavy conversation, not to pass up the constant coming and going of people of every description.

And so it came about, I think, one evening I, who was spending much of my time at the apartment, met Harry Smith.

He was noticeably small of stature, with sharply defined, small facial features. A small sharp nose, which came almost to a point. His eyes, I think, were gray or green and twinkled sometimes and became piercing on other occasions, behind small, plain, perhaps metal-framed glasses that fit in the center of his nose, held in place with thin metal bands which extended to his rather faun-shaped little ears, projecting a trifle obviously from both sides of his small face that ended below his mouth, thin and somewhat colorless, with his sharp, pointed chin. I seem to recall his hair as being a little curly or wavy, with a somewhat high forehead, light brown in color and neither sparse or very abundant. The neck was thin, centered between narrow fragile-appearing shoulders with thin arms, ending with small hands. He wasn't what could be referred to as tiny, yet he was short and small, giving off an attitude I thought of as resembling a little fox, although not as appealing as a fox might appear.

In all probability I am entirely out of line, offering any comments concerning the man. Still, speaking honestly, I never really was comfortable with him nor felt inclined to develop his acquaintance or friendship. On the other hand—continuing this list of clichés—I did not wish him despair or pain, and certainly not death.

So be it.

POEM

Comments—vague
threats, broken noses,
lumps—observations
something about to go down
10, 20 years
already passed
16, 15, seldom younger
exceptions in reformatories
hellholes without doubt

Fear permeates the walls
steals down the corridors
fills each cell

Whisperings, giggles
cruel laughter
plots and plotting
vows of loyalty—sudden changes—
one side to other

Odd moments pertaining to sadness
and jails
penitentiaries
prisons
workhouses
breeding their brand of
sentiment
on and on . . .

1994

THE NEEDLE

THERE ARE INNUMERABLE WAYS OF WOOING. ON ONE'S KNEES WHILE gazing fondly into the eyes of the one being wooed, and then words—so I am told—are effective. Not to mention the ever handy kiss, or stroking, touching tenderly, and, of course, inspired endearments; but nothing surpasses the wicked needle. How titillating that first tiny prick. Both slightly painful, although not quite, as the eye watches and then quickly looks away, only to once again become aware of the tiny point pressed against the outer casing of the waiting vein, one instant in rejecting and then hopefully anticipating the moment of penetration and recognizing the sensation felt as that little point has entered the flowing blood already seen through the glass of the first syringe, beginning a pressured course sending it back to rejoin the original stream diluted with a wondrous new sensation—once known, never forgotten. Continue then this strange communication. I've known the needle well and wondered at the occasional gentle touch—both shy and determined—once or twice cruelly—yet always inwardly charming. Strange still at this late period, knowing the arrival of the death entity. The end already started. Reaching neither timidly or eagerly. Offering the last of rapid heartbeat. In fullness, never suspected as part of the finishing experience, nor imagine contemplation as possible. Wishing deeply it be known and accepted. Thusly the perfect bringing together of our involving magnetism, richly charred with the old and the new.

1994

A STORY BY HERBERT HUNCKE FOR TURK

[Turk and his dog Gingin are well known to residents of the Chelsea Hotel.
Gingin can often be spotted in the lobby.]

DAY BEFORE YESTERDAY—WHATEVER THE DAY WAS—ABOUT TWO
o'clock, I was hanging my coat in the closet when I thought I heard an
unusual sound at my door, a kind of sniffing. Certainly I am not accustomed to sniffing outside my door and I thusly—so to speak—became
aware of something vaguely familiar about the mystery. It was Turk's
baby, his friend, and pet, Gingin.

On frequent visits Turk had let him come upstairs with him. Thinking
about Turk and his pal Gingin, I opened the door to see Gingin—all a
kind of golden-hued fur—reminding one of a collie-type dog, rather
pointed nose, beautiful expressive brown eyes, a fine jaw line, good
white teeth, beige, and a very pale blond color, with the tail, long and
feathered, curved and held high, almost honey-toned. No Turk, only his
friend Gingin.

He kind of looked at me, drawing back a little and his tail wagging a
sort of breeze. I spoke to him, using his name, coaxing him to come into
the room, which he did, midst excitement, tail arched in a slight elevation. He began investigating everything, thoroughly smelling and sniffing
in every direction. Once in a while he paid attention to me but it soon
became obvious he was losing interest and began eyeing the door. Whatever he had come searching for was not in the room and he perhaps had
sensed a possibility of somewhere else.

He had brought a good feeling, or so I felt, and I had talked to him,
patted him on his back, scratched him behind his ears and made a fuss
over him. Seemingly he accepted the reception he received as his due;
now he would like to move on. I had thought perchance Turk would
come up also but it was past a logical period of time for it to have happened so I opened the door and let Gingin out.

He made something of an issue of his departure, half stopping once or twice, looking over his shoulder at me, while all the time aiming and moving forward. Of course the tail continued wagging and fanning behind him.

Gingin is an incredible, lovable dog. He was rescued from an uncertain fate from the city pound and has had an interesting life thus far and, in my opinion, will continue to be highly thought of as pets are considered. He is an exceptional example of warmth and friendliness. The dog, man's best friend, all the rest, he is quite simply Gingie, Ginger, and a few more, yet always Gingin for me.

1995

JUXTAPOSITION

*[Huncke read this story at his last reading, on January 10, 1996, at St.
Marks Poetry Project in New York City. Also reading that night was
Gregory Corso. Describing some bizarre occurrences at Huncke's basement
apartment at East Seventh Street and Avenue D in New York's East
Village, "Juxtaposition" ends with a touching remembrance of his companion
of twenty-five years, photographer Louis Cartwright, who was murdered
in 1994.]*

HEADING HOMEWARD—LATE AT NIGHT. THE LIGHT AT THE CORNER—
dark and only very few lamps lit in the dwellings along the way—helping
create shadows—somewhat sparsely spread here and there on down
toward the end of the street to the end of the block. The wind a bit
gusty—making a sense of movement just beyond range of vision. A cluster of about six or maybe seven—still occupied—old shabby buildings—
on down the way with garbage cans set out in front—surrounded by
hungry food-searching rats suddenly aware of my approaching sounds
which caused them to become alert and they began running to hide—
down basement steps—jumping off the curb and out of sight—across the
street—under automobiles and under steps—bushes—and into tall
grass—here and there—so that in a few minutes there remained only the
sound of scratching claws or an occasional squealing. It had been disturbing, leaving a somewhat scary and uneasy feeling hanging in the air,
so to speak. I was glad and more at ease with myself, finally passing on
by where a few moments ago there had been rushing scrambling rats,
who upon first being seen gave me the impression they might give up
interest in the garbage and decide to attack me.

After passing by—every now and then I would glance back to make
sure they were not coming behind me. Having passed the area I had seen
them—I already felt a bit more at ease and began walking a bit faster
toward the entrance of the house I occupied the basement apartment
of—to the gate flush with the sidewalk—where a wrought-iron gate

opened onto a pair of steps—flanked by two good-sized garbage cans—
a rather ornate porcelain doll had at some time earlier been tossed haphazardly onto the top of one of the cans. As I reached the gate I began
observing the doll in detail. She was—in all probability—two or two and
a half feet in length—dressed in a dusty and full black skirt—a violent
pink-colored blouse. She wore one scuffed black shoe—peeping beneath
the bottom of her skirt. One of her eyes had been damaged and hung
down on her red-painted cheek—and the other—of faded blue—
although in place appeared a trifle misshapen and looked a bit sad. The
face gave an impression of having at some point been a bit pretty surrounded by a head of bright red hair.

How and why she had been placed—or tossed—there perplexed me,
and although I let her stay there at the time—I said to myself sometime
later I'd move her and throw her away from the front of the house.
There was a feeling of disgust which permeated my feeling about her
being there—causing me to feel uncomfortable—and filled me with a
kind of revulsion.

Later I did remove her. Carried her on through my apartment to a
somewhat large backyard, where in a far corner I had on other occasions
disposed of things. Left her there and—in a manner of speaking—stopped
thinking of her.

Several weeks passed, following the episode of the disposal of the doll.
Once or twice thoughts of her having been left in the garbage can came
to mind which were forgotten—until one evening when another doll
was left behind in the can—this time it was only a small silly-looking
little doll—maybe two inches and of entirely the same material (that is—
made of same stuff—head to toe), kind of celluloid bright colors—yellow
hair—dark blue eyes—pink cheeks—red mouth—short bright green
dress with little-girl-type legs—knees a bit dimpled and legs bare down
to white ankle-length socks and foolish-appearing one-strap little shoes.
It bore an insipid smile which gave me the impression that it found me
funny to look at—giving me the idea it might find me rather obnoxious
and would prefer my being elsewhere. Needless to say—she soon joined
her predecessor and I soon forgot her.

Most of this had taken place a short time after the summer months,
and the month of October was well under way when again I would
come home to a doll of ordinary description somewhere around the front
of the building—lying once immediately up against the door leading into
my apartment and another time an old rag-doll hanging by her neck

from a cross piece of the gate. It became obvious—to me—someone was deliberately leaving them—with some intention of drawing my attention to them for whatever reason was behind the action, and I was beginning to be, feel, disturbed. I had asked my neighbors for opinions or if perchance one of them was responsible. I had inquired of various acquaintances if they by chance knew of something that might give a slight inkling of why I was seemingly the target of someone or even a group— anxious to make me uncomfortable or at least annoyed by the onslaught of dolls.

I had been looking for an apartment diligently for many months before moving into my basement flat and felt rewarded finally locating where I was living at the time of the dolls. The place was not only large but interestingly laid out with spaciously sized rooms back to front and two small areas built to one side. The one objection had been the bathroom— a somewhat small space causing a rather cramped condition to exist between the kitchen and one of the side rooms I used as a small work room—that along with the kitchen opened up onto the backyard, which provided—due to three good-sized trees—a place of relaxation and shade to spend time in and to some extent forget the headaches of city living.

Over many years of living in the area, I developed a number of close friends and became not only a neighbor of the immediate surrounding area but a somewhat well-liked—as close as I was able to observe—and outstanding person—mostly—I believe—because no one knew exactly how I maintained my living quarters and kept myself well groomed.

The fall of the year became winter with cold, uncomfortable weather. Snow covered everything, followed by sleet, rain, leaving behind mounds of soot-covered frozen melting snow. At most of the corners throughout the section, large pools of slush—and gray dirty water—gathered where the drains continued to remain clogged by chunks of ice and a mixture of debris.

Christmas came and the New Year came and my eightieth birthday in January—shortly thereafter, my friend and close companion knocked on my door. We had known each other twenty-six years. At this point we had been apart almost two years.

When we had last seen one another, our lifestyle had, as always—it had been—hectic—as to daily activity—one day passing rather smoothly—in a sense—and the next full of the unexpected. Money usually spare and then a sudden sufficient income of plenty—bright with good times—doing as we desired—sometimes together, or on other times going off on our own—never knowing when we would meet again. Regardless the inconsistency—liking the strange attachments which always brought us back together seemingly to last to whatever end—as a matter of fact—seldom bothered with the thought.

KEROUAC

*[On October 6, 1995, Huncke read this piece at the Lowell Celebrates
Kerouac Festival, an annual event held in Kerouac's Massachusetts
hometown, dedicated to the celebration, enjoyment, and study of Jack Kerouac
and his writings. "Kerouac" was written in a rice paper notebook
bound with string that Huncke's friend, poet Zachary Wollard, had
given him.]*

TO BEGIN—

I am pleased to receive this beautiful notebook as a gift. My problem
now is guilt—marking the pages, the pleasure is extremely physical—
there is an elegance in the manner it is put together. . . . It is a very
inspiring gift, and this is like a special way of thanking young Zachary
in public for his thoughtfulness.

I can't think at the moment of a more appropriate type of paper to
use to write of Jack Kerouac—a somewhat rough, crude Tibetan rice
paper, given to me a few days ago, in notebook form. Notebooks have
always pleased me. This notebook suits Jack's personality as I saw it. Here
is a very serviceable book of unusual appearance—sturdy and distinc-
tive—made by hand and of a subtle shade of plain purple cover binding—
soft, tan pages—suggesting a touch of the Eastern or Mideastern culture—earthy in texture and handsome. And Jack—with his rich flow of
language, his eyes—filled with a look of tenderness, innocent wonder of
all they beheld but affected deep inside, beneath his conscious knowledge
of a wondrous world filled with awesome and bewildering beauty constantly stressed by the varying degrees of disintegration—much of his
belief about the strength of purity died with his spirit flooded with sadness. Purple has always seemed a trifle unhappy color.

Although I can't say I knew Kerouac as well inside, I do feel qualified
in saying I wish he had been as loyal to himself and what I think of as
his inner quality as I believe he tried being to his mother.

Meeting Jack, I was impressed to a large degree with his typically

American appearance of what had become the accepted standard of the clean-cut young men of his period—healthy and ambitious—always anxious to face the challenges of future happiness—regardless of their nature or threat. Oddly enough, I didn't become aware of his writing desire or ability until we became better acquainted, although even then, speaking honestly, I failed perceiving what a strong influence he would have on the literary history of the world.

September 24, 1995

A MOMENT

[Huncke wrote this shortly before his death.]

DRIFTING INTO A CONSCIOUSNESS—THE SURROUNDING CHAOTIC scene—both sad and in a strange way stimulating—fired energetically from a depthless source—a nameless supply of energy force. For the moment—confused—caught in an almost-frozen instant of not knowing—anything, so to speak. Names of friends—gone—their faces flash by full of smiles and farewells. *All* of which becomes vague—pointless—and (in a sense) meaningless. Not worth bothering with. Certainly—recognizable to everyone—immediately. Morning—after long hours crammed with thought and pain. My head being lost someplace of seemingly empty gray terrian. Sleep—once again beckons and I'm ready to respond. As I think of Irvyne's visit and our friendship throughout these many years, a surge of warmth permeates my thoughts as I smile—closing my eyes.

1996

EDITOR'S AFTERWORD

I MET HERBERT HUNCKE IN THE SUMMER OF 1993. I WAS WORKING AT Allen Ginsberg's office, and one day Huncke came by. He was wearing blue jeans and a denim jacket, and headed to one corner to speak with Ginsberg's secretary, presumably regarding the financial situation of what was known as the Herbert Huncke Fund. I watched him curiously: poised in a swivel chair, he rested a fist on one knee, leaving his arm to carry the slight weight of his body, gesticulating with his right hand.

I'd read Huncke's *The Evening Sun Turned Crimson* and *Guilty of Everything* while still in high school, and many other books pertaining in some fashion to the experiences he'd had. But more than the well-documented extremities of his life, Huncke's own rendition of his story resonated deeply with me. His somehow detached yet compassionate observations, rich with precise detail, moved me with their openness and abundance of subtle sympathy. Naturally I wanted to meet this man.

I took note of when he appeared to be readying himself to leave, and then headed toward the stairwell for a cigarette. It worked so that I left just before him, so in the hall we stood together. He asked where I was going. I said I was going to smoke and he was welcome to join me. "Well . . ." he said slowly, thinking it over, and then quietly, "Why not?"

In the stairwell next to a window looking out over the north side of Union Square and Seventeenth Street, I handed him a cigarette and he said, "Oh, my Marlboro man," and asked me where I was from. When I replied "Indiana," he immediately launched into a story about riding a train through the dunes near Valparaiso, Indiana, heading to Chicago, watching the sun rise pink over fine white sand.

By 1994 Huncke had moved into the Chelsea Hotel, and I began stopping by on his invitation. These visits became something of a ritual. I would call from home, check his mood, and then call from the downstairs lobby before coming up. We began an exchange of sorts. Often, though he would not ask for anything, I would bring some essentials, like bananas, a sandwich, his beloved Snapple, a little grass. We would sit in near silence and look out his window, speaking quietly about the smallest of details—the shapes of the windows on nearby buildings, the color of the sky, the women sunbathing on rooftop tar beaches. His eye for detail changed how I look at the world, and these days I'm more apt to notice a half moon over the steeple of St. Marks than a roaring ambulance braying down Second Avenue.

Walking into Huncke's room was like stepping into a universe where every detail was quantified and precise. No comparisons were allowed here. Every thing, place, or person stood or fell based on its own merit, not in relation to others. As Huncke has often said, "I just don't weigh or balance things." Once I mentioned that I was "as well adjusted as I've ever been since moving to New York." He rolled his eyes and explained that I shouldn't compare one phase of my life to another, that such compartmentalizing would inevitably create tension between "phases" and thus anxiety. Better to look at life as one picture, not groupings of separate events, places, and people. You can't compare life's phases because they're all part of the *same* life.

From my first visit he always read me whatever he'd recently written. Sometimes he gave me copies, though many of the pieces I heard in the Chelsea never resurfaced again. One lost piece I remember in particular, a poem about London with a songlike refrain: "London town, London town." He was very self-effacing about his writing, and lacked confidence in his natural ability—he was more comfortable calling himself a storyteller than a writer. He did not write with the idea of publishing a book, of becoming famous. Huncke wrote out of long-standing habit, to sort out his own confusion, and to describe in precise detail his "adventures and strange experiences."

I would not know Huncke for very long, but our friendship deepened and we moved into a comfortable routine of my coming by once or twice a week for several hours of measured conversation. Once I was out of work, completely broke and depressed. Huncke gave me sixty dollars, which bought me enough food until I found another job about two weeks later. But more important he raised my spirits, said I could sleep on his floor if worse came to worst, asking nothing in return. He never sounded me down for money, despite all the stories of his legendary parasitic behavior. It wasn't until later that I understood that Huncke did not ask for what a person could not afford to give—he knew I could afford a sandwich here and there, but that was about all.

Once his health began to deteriorate seriously, a tag team of his many friends, especially Raymond Foye, Tim Moran, and Jerry Poynton, made sure he would not be left alone. As the end approached, I came by nearly every day and sat with him by his bed, holding his hand while he drifted in and out of consciousness, his eyes occasionally opening; upon seeing me or another friend in the room, he managed a weak smile.

The night before he died in Beth Israel Hospital, he spoke to three or four friends standing by his bedside, barely a whisper: "Tomorrow we'll all get together for a *pow*-wow." He was eighty-one.

ACKNOWLEDGMENTS

THIS VOLUME WOULD NOT HAVE BEEN POSSIBLE WITHOUT THE ASSIS-tance, support, and good faith of many people to whom I owe my deepest gratitude. Jerry Poynton, executor of the estate of Herbert E. Huncke, was extremely generous with source material and provided invaluable editorial advice. His concern for and understanding of Huncke enriched this collection. Raymond Foye, besides contributing the Introduction, helped convince Huncke that such an endeavor was worthwhile and shared his intelligence at every step along the way. Bill Morgan provided expert bibliographical advice and photo research. Greg Clayton, whose knowledge of Huncke's publishing history is unrivaled, spent hours on the phone helping compile a selected bibliography. Jim McCrary of William S. Burroughs Communications facilitated the writing of the Foreword, for which I also wish to thank James Grauerholtz. The late Allen Ginsberg provided his characteristic enthusiasm and unflagging support. His office staff, Peter Hale and Bob Rosenthal, generously shared their time, knowledge, and resources. Laki Vazakas provided source material and offered encouragement throughout. Casey De Groot, editorial cavalry, coedited much of this volume. Huncke's original texts were provided by Simon Pettet. Jeremiah Newton helped locate material, and Kim Spurlock came through when needed.

I would also like to thank the editors, publishers, writers, typists, and friends who preserved Huncke's writing through the years: Erin Black, Harvey Brown, R'lene Dahlberg, Gail Deeb, Diane di Prima, Dede Doyle, Raymond Foye, Brenda Frazer, Roger Goodman, Panna Grady, Don Kennison, Arthur and Kit Knight, Eila Kokkinen, Joel Markman, Alan Marlowe, Clive Matson, Paul Metcalf, Charles and Pam Plymell, Irving Rosenthal, and David Sands.

Will Schwalbe at William Morrow and Company gave the green light, Jon Moskowitz was the perfect editor, and Bruce Giffords's copyediting was precise and sympathetic.

Herb Bronstein, David Carter, Sophia Murer, Roger and Irvyne Richards, Ali Rogers, Janine Pommy Vega, and Ellen Winner were generous with their knowledge and resources.

Nothing could have been accomplished without Michael, Marianne, and Matt Schafer. The same goes for family extended: Toby Broadie, Tom Glasel, Michael Hall, and Jason Miller.

Highest thanks to Herbert Huncke, for writing it all down and fearlessly sharing his insight for eight decades.

—BENJAMIN G. SCHAFER
New York City

APPENDIX: TWO CHAPTERS FROM *SHEEPER* BY IRVING ROSENTHAL

[No writer evoked Huncke's charm and complexities more accurately than Irving Rosenthal, whose novel Sheeper *was published by Grove Press in 1967.]*

Chapter 30:

HUNCKE

HUNCKE SAYS, "I USED TO BE THE YOUNGEST IN THE GROUP I RAN around with. Now I'm the oldest. Well that's life." But I cannot believe that Huncke's age ever mattered, or that he was ever very different from the way he is now, agelessly reminiscing about times gone by: "When I lived on the Square I used to have a friend and sidekick named Jack Melody . . ." "The only time I ever saw anybody cut bread like that was in Wales, in a town called Newport, a few miles below Cardiff . . ." "I was first turned on to opium by a half-Chinese sailor, or ex-sailor, who ran a small bar in Havana—I don't remember his name I'm ashamed to say, and I liked him a lot . . ." He must have been a secret wise old man when he was fifteen and his skin glowed like his eyes—those eternally adolescent eyes that everyone remembers as blue though they are hazel. For their cosmetic care alone Babylonian kings would have accorded him the use of drugs—opium to tighten his eyes into shrapnel and cannabis to make his pupils black roses. He must always have dropped offhand remarks that shudder through the ages, and he must have been a wise old man at fifteen when he sat at the dinner table with his family and a messenger came in with a bouquet of roses from an admirer.

I cannot believe that Huncke ever talked about sex any differently from the way he talks about it now, as something joyful but no longer indulged in, and he seldom closes a story's paragraph more poignantly than when he says, "and then we stripped and balled." How did he talk about sex when he was fifteen, as the romantic activity of a childhood then gone forever? Or did his voice and mind add fifty years to the act that had taken place the night before?

I am sure that Huncke has been the same since he was born, and to an extent Marrows bears me out, for the passages which deal with Huncke in Marrows' first book, which covers a period twenty to thirty years ago, are fair descriptions of Huncke today. And in that book Marrows has an old-timer say, in speaking of a still earlier time shrouded in myth, "Huncke was a beautiful kid when he first came to New York. The trouble is, he lost his looks."

This remark is sharp, and in fact Marrows portrayed Huncke unsympathetically. For example, Marrows wrote: "Soon I was buying his drinks and meals, and he was hitting me for 'smash' (change) at regular intervals. He did not have a habit at this time. In fact, he seldom got a habit unless someone else paid for it. . . . It would not have occurred to him to pay the rent himself. He had lived in other people's apartments all his life." And Huncke answered back gracefully in a little red notebook now in my possession: "It is true—I have lived in other people's apartments a good many times, but I have had a few of my own which were great enough for me to feel that Bill wasn't quite fair and that in summing me up so narrowly he gives clear evidence of a certain smugness which is hardly becoming to an author of such rugged realism as that found in *Adder*."

In spite of his portrait in *Adder*, Huncke has always spoken of Marrows affectionately. Think of this image, of Marrows drunk and asleep, angelic and delicate skin, of Huncke sitting on the edge of the bed to admire him, of Marrows waking and trying to make love, and Huncke all wise and coy saying, "Aw Bill, now I know you're drunk," and Huncke laughs again as he relates it, his eyes all shining with being desired.

One day I said to him, "I've been doing research on you, Huncke. Rereading Marrows." He said, "I have never been happy with his treatment of me. He makes me out a scrawny leech or parasite—and while I know I sometimes—I mean if someone has a little bread—"

"But you don't do it—ah—maliciously."

"Exactly."

The truth is that Huncke puts the touch on you only for what he thinks you can afford or are willing to give. Perhaps he asks for a little more than you can afford—as an insurance—but he always settles quickly for whatever you offer. However he makes you feel slightly guilty for not having given him what he requested, and if you are in a giving mood he extracts as much as he can. For example he may ask you for money, telling you he is out of bread, out of milk, out of coffee. You may say, "I have no money but I can give you a sandwich." He accepts that gratefully, but while he is eating he may ask, "Do you mind if I fix a sandwich for Kinky, who I want to fall in on, and who hasn't had anything to eat for days?"

Actually Huncke's moral code is very strict, and he will ask for things only of people he considers more fortunate than himself—which is nearly everyone. Whatever money he comes into he squanders at once, and so he is always down and out. And perhaps that is just as well because, as he says, whenever he comes into bread he gets busted. Sometimes he says it this way: "Just when I start collecting a decent wardrobe I am busted."

His "wardrobe"—and all other personal effects—are put together from the one or two articles he keeps for himself out of each of the suitcases he steals from parked automobiles. So he lives, when he is not in jail, surrounded by golden manicure sets, big bottles of fairy cologne to splash himself with, and silk pajamas striped like window awnings. And what can he feel when he gets out of bed in the afternoon, unrolls a pair of socks acquired the night before, and a slip of paper zigzags down to the floor—he picks it up and reads this note, writ in a woman's hand:

> I'm everywhere
> I love you
> XXX

Coming down off amphetamine, Huncke grunts and he groans. His lips swell. His nose runs. He sleeps all day, farting at intervals. And when he's not asleep he's bitching. "What? You don't have any cornflakes? Well what *do* you have? Look at how swollen my hands are. I hope that coffee isn't for me, you know I don't like glass cups. What will I tell Kinky on Sunday? He gave me a double sawbuck to score, and I lost it or blew it all, I can't even remember. And my hemorrhoids have started bleeding again, do you have a tube of Preparation H and a clean pair of shorts? At this point my life is so fucked up I can't even think. You're looking at my legs as if you never saw sores before. Well they're from scrubbing myself in the shower to get the scabies off. Scabies are microscopic animals that live on sores. Joan and I discovered them under a magnifying glass. Now don't cock your eyes like that, it's a proven fact. I wish I had a copy of the Mayan Codices, because I could show them to you. We actually identified the little beasts in the Mayan Codices, and that's why Joan originally went to Mexico, to do research on them. My fingertips are sore. What will I tell the parole officer on Monday? He

was nice as he could be, but he warned me if I didn't have a job by
Monday I would go back to jail. What will I tell 'unemployment' next
Tuesday? How am I going to explain why I didn't report last week? No
money, no clothes, not a particle of shmeeaz to help me come down
with, and you have the nerve to send away a guy who might have laid
a bag on me, I'll never forgive you for that, what will become of me?
And stop hinting that I should go back to bed in your little sneaky way,
I'll go when I'm ready. I just lie there writhing and can't fall asleep."

I do not mind giving further examples of Huncke's petulance and
little temper storms, for even if I listed them all, that man would still
stand high as cliff flames, and those eyes would not lose a wisp of their
mercury vapor. Sometimes his eyes are like grubs in his skull, cold living
beings you come to notice are pulsing slowly, and then as Huncke turns
his attention to someone who is talking, they hatch into darning-needles
hovering in front of the speaker (Huncke listens with his eyes), and they
make a whole series of sewing-machine stitches of information before
darting back home to the brainpan and inner intelligence headquarters.

One might he forced me to make him a bacon and tomato sandwich
as his price for cooperating enough to be taken in a taxi to a mental
hospital as the last resort and excuse for his failure to have reported to
his parole officer for weeks, and a bench warrant had already been issued,
and the sympathetic doctor at the hospital had warned us to be there
before eleven that night, when he, the doctor, would go off admission
duty for the week, and it was 10:35 when Huncke balked as we were
going out the front door, sat down, said he was hungry and wouldn't go
a step farther without being fed, and insisted on a bacon and tomato
sandwich because every prisoner gets to choose his last meal before being
led to execution.

Another time I innocently asked a friend of his what kind of work he
did, and Huncke exploded, accusing me of the worst prying ill manners
he had ever encountered, and he vowed he would never again bring any
of his friends over, especially a prostitute named Flory who did a little
fencing on the side, and whom he had wanted me to meet; but now he
would never think of submitting her to the kind of inquisition I prac-
ticed. "My friends are very sensitive about how they earn their living.
And I'm not going to bring her over here and put her in the center of
a whole group of intellectual people who can come on, and I know how
they come on, with their pointed questions, and there isn't another
whore in the crowd."

But time and time again I have seen him quiet little crackles of hostility in those around him with love and patience, not as a cunning way to keep the peace, but because he believes enmity to be an improper state, as much his own responsibility to redress as the wrongdoers'. And I have seen him befriend those men who are to me pariahs—who have sold out or copped out or want to stop up the life and art that come screaming from souls. He is always sorry for them and thinks there is a chance they can be reformed. Off the page and out of the book we kick the trouble he (therefore) always brings with him, and the malicious mischief he sometimes engages in. These are the dry leaves we rake off the page and burn or forget, to have a book, or live with men at all. And should I have to suffer the tragedy and disaster Huncke always brings with him, or the beautiful boys he tows like an old queen but is unable to make (and makes me curse my innards if I should so much as smile at one, that Huncke's pride should not be hurt or jealousy aroused), or boys retracing lonely steps on littered sidewalks looking for God knows what lost ring or wristwatch, or fortyish husbands in alcoholic sleep curled up outside the tenement door their wives won't open?

And although we are born with the knowledge that once we penetrate each other's fears we will arrive at the spot where the nest is feathered for all mankind, still death forces stay me from answering soul-searching letters for months. It is a disaster to be human, and for that, goaded by the little compassion I was born with, I strove for art—the only place we can win. Art lets us be the best and truest that we are, all drugs do. I always get stranded waiting for a bus on the coldest days. —As at certain moments Utaemon's tragedy—the secret personal tragedy (who knows what it is?) of that great Kabuki dancer who in a lifetime of acting has never betrayed a leg withered six inches shorter than the other by infantile paralysis—fits the tragedy of The Courtesan so absolutely as to make me ashamed of the bullshit I live in along with the other swine when I am not dreaming.

The moon gives me a hard-on. Which spoke out loud reaps a short Huncke riff. "I've jacked off in the moonlight. Many a time. I like to jack off in the moonlight, in fact I like to jack off period. By myself or with others, and I've jacked off other inmates under circumstances you wouldn't believe possible, like across two feet of concrete between cell doors."

If there were a Saviour, Huncke would preach Holy Gospel, and if dead souls could speak, he would fall into trances. Well there are drugs, that I know, and he turneth us on. "You're sure you don't want a taste?" he says, drawing the junk up into his dropper. "You're sure now? It's good shit. I can leave you a drop in the spoon. Well, you can have the cotton if you change your mind."

I crooked my index finger covered with rings and said, "Huncke, you would turn your own mother on."

"Would turn her on," he said, "I did turn her on." He quickly added, "Only to pot. She didn't like it too much, made me rub her side, under the arm. She was afraid her heart would stop beating. She was hip in many ways. Used to chaperone me on dates with my boyfriends."

No one knows anything in this world as well as Huncke knows the anatomy of his arm veins. But this time his luck was bad. First he tried a tiny vein in his upper arm without success, and muttered, "I'll get you some day you little bastard." Then he tried a tough, rubbery vein in his lower arm one, two, three, four times, but the vein kept eluding the needle, by slipping to one side of it or the other, once the skin had been punctured. "That one is a roller," Huncke explained; "but even so I don't usually have to probe this much." Then he came clean: "Guess I'm showing off a little . . . aw shucks." Either he is always pointing to junk, or else I cannot see through it to what he is pointing.

Huncke is no sooner out of jail, than he is hooked again and turns to theft. He is apprehended in a matter of months. Never was a criminal more petty and unsuccessful. And then he is always trying to draw his friends into witnessing his pathetic courtroom appearances, into raising bail for him, into writing him letters to keep up his morale. Why bother with him at all?

Because he is a Beauty Trap and the finest storyteller my spirit has ever lifted to. He always says he relates just what he remembers, but he picks and clips unconsciously, transposes and condenses on each retelling, till his stories conform wholly to the beautiful configuration of his mind. His tales light up with compassion the most blighted and bizarre personalities, and he can portray these unfortunates with such flash and splendor that they turn into creatures of gorgon beauty before your eyes, or their beauty, pathos, and horror may jar unresolved in your mind for several days afterwards, finally condensing into beauty pure and clear, but with that slight jangle or derangement to it, that fixes it forever.

In telling a story he becomes a spirit risen high above his mortal

body—risen high and drifting even higher in the empty space. He talks
through his flesh below like a ventriloquist. It may be Huncke's voice
box which says "I," but it is that high astral body who holds our ear,
and who owns every fault and sin of the man below relevant to the
complete truthful telling of the tale, without the slightest shame or
dodge. Ah and those small incidental confessions the spirit calls no special
attention to in passing are like incandescent shrines of light falling on the
wretch's head below. Huncke beams, shriven, while the narrating spirit
pushes on, unaware of the magic it has wrought.

Chapter 56:

HUNCKE'S BILL INDIA

THE PERSON TO BLAME FOR INTRODUCING ME TO BILL INDIA IN THE first place was Huncke, who staggered into my apartment one day with a hanging of Bill India's over his arm. He stood there like an Arab merchant while I let my eyes be drawn through green and blue eons of time and primeval steam to where a Magic Circle glints and wheels through the air. A green light from the cloth bathes Huncke's face. His pupils are dilated. He is more lost in the cloth than I am. He whispers, "Man, it's hypodermic!" With a tremor of gratitude, a golden aleph leaps from that Circle onto his forehead.

Huncke was one of the three men who signed the pact of silence I have broken. Let him speak now with me, which he can hardly object to, since his notebooks are in my possession. Imagine that he has just fixed himself, that he is prone on a low divan, his legs crossed, his head propped up on one elbow, that he is writing, and that he stops every now and then to take a long, easy drag on a marijuana cigarette. He is a small man with a carefully trimmed beard. You should be very still, because if he hears you and looks up from writing, you stand a chance of getting lost in those amethyst eyes:

Alone—one candle burning in a tall tapering wrought iron holder— a white paraffin candle—Wagner on the phonograph—an overture and Venusberg Music—Tannhauser—writing—with red ink—my favorite color ink—occasionaly pausing—glancing from one strange, intriguing scene to another—squares of stained materials—cottons—linens—heavy paper—thin paper—oiled after hand movements—flute blowing—pot— a shot—Charlie Parker—'Hot House'—color applied with light swinging gestures—rubbing a thumb through the wet green or blue—red— violet—ink—Mercurochrome—gentian violet—iodine—patterns becoming visible—universal Gods—Temples—wayside resting places— caverns and caves—animals from another planet—steaming jungles— monkeys—baboons—huge monolithic beasts—intense glowing green— brilliant persian blue—writhing black—shadows—the face of a lion— tiger—part of the head of an elephant—an eye—eyes. I have seen all this and much more—in one large, square hanging—now folded—or perhaps—upon consideration—is spread out near Trocchi—great—also there are bottles bound and wrapped—bright Turkish red silk threads—black—blue—white—squares of soft kid—goatskin—hides and leather thongs—pieces of brass—fountain pens—paint brushes—bits of metal—trinkets—buttons—a large piece of fur—small pelts—many of short fur—mink brown—it is frequently used to fold round books—held secure with quarter inch wide thongs of rawhide. The reverse side tanned with dyes—symbols worked in black ink—splashes of silver—long thin wavering streaks—winding—across the surface—a smoke-like quality—on another fur piece—circular—a star-like geometric pattern—the skins cut into triangles—stained thoroughly with blues and mahogany red—into tones of deep red brown—symbols of silver paint—each triangle edged in silver.

All this in front of me—created and made by Bill—whose whole existence—at this point—is a great outpouring of energy—his whole chemical being—activated—tingling—tensed—alert—while each moment his consciousness searches the scene—scanning the area—picking up something—a clay idol—a knife—pencils—pens—paper—beads—stones—gems—wire—thread—glue—bleach—material—cloth—wood—bone—shell—everything suggesting a new object—a new reality—a thing springing from his fingers—hands—arms—whole body—the ever constant linking together—methedrine—pot—heroin—tranquilizers occasionally—an ever present auditory responsiveness—intonations— · talking—voice sounds—set the nerves to vibrating—he looks for danger—usually has been scheming—he is immediately defensive. He becomes irritated easily—is fretful—dogmatic—somehow unaware of how to accept the moment in peace—rather—he grabs each instant—making a challenge of everything—relaxing seldom—never for long—then in restlessness—disturbed slumber—mutterings—once in a while in a chair—lolled back—eyes closed—now and then fluttering lids—deep breathing—interrupted with an hissing sigh—cry-like sounds—a sort of moan—rolling the head with the rest of the torso slowly in swaying motion.

Picking up the flute he stands up—carefully adjusts the mouth to his—blows once—twice—followed by a series of sharp quick flute notes—takes a few steps—meanwhile rippling his fingers over the air holes. Again stops and begins blowing—along with the record of Charlie Parker—Bud Powell—preferably—with any music—or without music—

wandering back and forth—never looking directly toward one—yet seeing every detail—of one's surface conduct—catching hints of what has happened inside one's self. He doesn't spend much time investigating the causes—accepting his own responses as correct—not necessarily completely aware—yet sure of the meaning—without all the details— glossing over the omittance—rather superiorly—sure he has at some point passed through the same experience—nothing can be new—even allowing for personality differences—.

His magic absorbs his spirit—black magic—white magic—Gods and Demons. He practices magic—creating. He reads about the formulas— he knows the forces to command—he calls upon the planets—the moon—the animals—the spirits of wood—metal—stone—earth—of all things—watching for signs—letter combinations—numerical values— good omens—bad omens. Hearing him blow the day into radiance—the sunlight out of the morning sky—walking the lower east side streets— the flute sweet—clear and haunting. The shepherd greeting the first faint rays of light washing away the dark—giving thanks—to the world— mountains—rivers—streams—the flowers—the trees—the rocks—to all nature—.

This extract from a notebook of Huncke's is dated less than a week before the outbreak of hostilities. There is another, later sketch of Bill India, not so idyllic, to which is appended an elaborately drawn hex sign. Huncke had decided to fight fire with fire and was actually boning up on magic at the library, but his studies were interrupted by an arrest for grand larceny and possession of burglary tools.

Bill India so subverted beauty that for months after the war we found anything beautiful suspect. We were plunged into a frantic aesthetic paranoia, and avoided all baubles and art galleries scrupulously. And the secret pleasure with which each of us had contemplated the subject of magic vanished. That mysterious reservoir from which we Jews are allowed an occasional sip, and from which we artists draw the water to moisten our colors, dried up. Bill India burned the magic out of magic. Even the word sounds flat and dry.

BOOKS BY HERBERT EDWIN HUNCKE

Elsie John & Joey Martinez. New York: Pequod Press, 1979.
The Evening Sun Turned Crimson. Cherry Valley, N.Y.: Cherry Valley Editions, 1980.
Guilty of Everything. New York: Hanuman Books, 1987.
Guilty of Everything: The Autobiography of Herbert Huncke. New York: Paragon House, 1990.
Huncke's Journal. New York: The Poets Press, 1965.

ANTHOLOGIES AND COLLECTIONS CONTAINING WORK BY HERBERT EDWIN HUNCKE

Charters, Ann, ed. *The Portable Beat Reader.* New York: Viking, 1992.
Firestone, Ross, ed. *Getting Busted: Personal Experiences of Arrest, Trial, and Prison.* New York: Arena Books, 1973.
Hollander, Kurt, ed. *Low Rent: A Decade of Prose and Photographs from "The Portable Lower East Side."* New York: Grove Press, 1994.
Matz, Martin. *Pipe Dreams.* San Francisco (privately published), 1989.
Moore, Alan, and J. G. Gosciak, eds. *A Day in the Life: Tales from the Lower East Side.* New York: Contact Two Publications, 1990.
Morgan, Bill, and Bob Rosenthal, eds. *Best Minds: A Tribute to Allen Ginsberg.* New York: Lospecchio, 1986.
Poynton, Jerome, and Benjamin Schafer, eds. *Herbert E. Huncke, 1915–1996.* New York: The Estate of Herbert E. Huncke, 1996.
Strausbaugh, John, and Donald Blaise, eds. *The Drug User: Documents, 1840–1960.* New York: Blast Books, 1991.

WORKS CONTAINING PORTRAITS OF OR CHARACTERS BASED ON HERBERT EDWIN HUNCKE

Burroughs, William S. *Junky.* New York: Ace, 1953.
———. *The Letters of William S. Burroughs.* New York: Viking, 1993.
Cassady, Neal. *The First Third.* San Francisco: City Lights, 1971, 1981 (expanded).
Dahlberg, Edward. *The Confessions of Edward Dalhberg.* New York: George Braziller, 1971.

Ginsberg, Allen. *Collected Poems, 1947–1980*. New York: Harper & Row, 1984.
———. *Howl and Other Poems*. San Francisco: City Lights, 1956.
———. *Selected Poems, 1947–1995*. New York: HarperCollins, 1996.
Holmes, John Clellon. *Go*. New York: Scribner's, 1952.
Kerouac, Jack. *Book of Dreams*. San Francisco: City Lights, 1961.
———. *Desolation Angels*. New York: Coward-McCann, 1965.
———. *Heaven and Other Poems*. San Francisco: Grey Fox Press, 1977.
———. *On the Road*. New York: Viking, 1957.
———. *The Portable Jack Kerouac*. Viking, 1995.
———. *Selected Letters, 1940–1956*. New York: Viking, 1995.
———. *The Town and the City*. New York: Harcourt Brace, 1950.
———. *Visions of Cody*. New York: McGraw-Hill Book Company, 1972.
Meyer, Stewart. *The Lotus Crew*. New York: Serpent's Tail, 1996.
Plymell, Charles. *The Last of the Moccasins*. Albuquerque: Mother Road Publications, 1995.
Rosenthal, Irving. *Sheeper*. New York: Grove Press, 1967.
Wieners, John. *Cultural Affairs in Boston: Poetry & Prose, 1956–1985*. Santa Rosa, Calif.: Black Sparrow Press, 1988.

BIOGRAPHICAL SOURCES

Charters, Ann, ed. *Dictionary of Literary Biography*. Vol. 16. *The Beats: Literary Bohemians in Postwar America, Part 1*. Detroit: Gale Research, 1983.
Watson, Steven. *The Birth of the Beat Generation: Visionaries, Rebels, and Hipsters, 1944–1960*. New York: Pantheon, 1995.

FURTHER REFERENCES & READING

Charters, Ann. *Beats and Company*. Garden City, N.Y.: Doubleday, 1986.
———. *Kerouac*. New York: St. Martin's Press, 1987.
Clark, Tom. *Jack Kerouac*. New York: Harcourt Brace Jovanovich, 1984.
Gifford, Barry, and Lawrence Lee. *Jack's Book: An Oral Biography of Jack Kerouac*. New York: St. Martin's Press, 1978.
Ginsberg, Allen. *Allen Ginsberg: Photographs*. Santa Fe: Twelvetrees Press, 1991.
———. *Journals, Early Fifties–Early Sixties*. New York: Grove Press, 1977.
———. *Journals, Mid-fifties, 1954–1958*. New York: HarperCollins, 1995.
———. *Snapshot Poetics*. San Francisco: Chronicle Books, 1993.
Ginsberg, Allen, and Neal Cassady. *As Ever: The Collected Correspondence of Allen Ginsberg and Neal Cassady*. Berkeley, Calif.: Creative Arts Book Company, 1977.
Igliori, Paola. *American Magus: Harry Smith*. New York: Inanout Press, 1996.
Johnson, Joyce. *Minor Characters*. New York: Houghton Mifflin, 1983.
Knight, Arthur and Kit. *The Beat Vision*. New York: Marlowe & Company, 1994.
———. *Kerouac and the Beats*. New York: Marlowe & Company, 1994.

Knight, Brenda. *Women of the Beat Generation: The Writers, Artists and Muses at the Heart of a Revolution*. Berkeley, Calif.: Conari Press, 1996.

Kramer, Jane. *Allen Ginsberg in America*. New York: Random House, 1969.

McDarrah, Fred and Gloria. *The Beat Generation: Glory Days in Greenwich Village*. New York: Simon & Schuster, 1996.

McNally, Dennis. *Desolate Angel: A Biography of Jack Kerouac*. New York: Random House, 1979.

Miles, Barry. *Ginsberg: A Biography*. New York: Simon & Schuster, 1989.

———. *William Burroughs: El Hombre Invisible*. New York: Hyperion, 1993.

Morgan, Ted. *Literary Outlaw: The Life and Times of William S. Burroughs*. New York: Henry Holt, 1988.

Nicosia, Gerald. *Memory Babe: A Critical Biography of Jack Kerouac*. Berkeley, Calif.: University of California Press, 1983.

Phipps, Lisa, ed. *Beat Culture & the New America, 1950–1965*. New York: Abbeville Press, 1996.

Saroyan, Aram. *Genesis Angels: The Saga of Lew Welch and the Beat Generation*. New York: William Morrow & Company, 1979.

Schneider, Charles, ed. *Cad: A Handbook for Heels*. Los Angeles: Feral House, 1992.

Schumacher, Michael. *Dharma Lion: A Critical Biography of Allen Ginsberg*. New York: St. Martin's Press, 1992.

Tytell, John. *Naked Angels: The Lives and Literature of the Beat Generation*. New York: McGraw-Hill, 1976.